C0-ATI-085

Management Fraud: Detection and Deterrence

Robert K. Elliott, CPA
PARTNER   Peat, Marwick, Mitchell & Co.

John J. Willingham, Ph.D., CPA
PARTNER   Peat, Marwick, Mitchell & Co.

Management Fraud:
Detection and Deterrence

a petrocelli book
new york / princeton

Copyright © 1980 Petrocelli Books, Inc.
All rights reserved.
Printed in the United States

1 2 3 4 5 6 7 8 9 10

Designed by Joan Greenfield

Library of Congress Cataloging in Publication Data

Elliott, Robert K
    Management fraud.

    Includes index.
    1. Commercial crimes—United States—Addresses,
essays, lectures.   2. White collar crimes—United
States—Addresses, essays, lectures.   3. Fraud—United
States—Addresses, essays, lectures.   I. Willingham,
John J., joint author.   II. Title.
HV6769.E43   364.1′63   79–26796
ISBN 0–89433–135–3

LIBRARY
ALMA COLLEGE
ALMA, MICHIGAN

814294

Contents

Preface

Corporate impropriety and management fraud—which for purposes of this book means the deliberate, material misstatement of financial statements by top management—have been staple copy for journalists in recent years. The public is clearly distressed by white-collar crime in the business world, and the SEC and members of Congress have expressed deep concern over the state of the system of corporate accountability. Various institutions and groups—including the accounting profession and the business community—have taken steps to improve the system or to develop proposals for its improvement. The SEC, for instance, undertook its program for voluntary disclosure of improper payments and held hearings on corporate governance. Congress passed the Foreign Corrupt Practices Act of 1977, which outlawed certain bribes to foreign officials. Many businesses have adopted codes of conduct and have been emphatic in support of them. The auditing profession has been doing the preparatory work necessary to be able to provide comprehensive reviews of internal accounting controls. The role of boards of directors has been evolving toward the assumption of greater responsibility for corporate behavior. In 1978 the American Assembly, a nonpartisan educational forum, devoted its fifty-fourth meeting to "Corporate Governance in America."

This list of activities to promote corporate integrity is just a sample. A comprehensive list would no doubt show an impressive response by concerned Americans to the threat unethical and illegal conduct poses to American business. Nevertheless, the response to the problem will be wanting unless it includes additional steps by the auditing profession and the business community to enhance their effectiveness in detecting and deterring management fraud.

Management frauds are of primary importance in the family of business improprieties because to a large extent the health of the capital markets rests on confidence that financial statements are not fraudulent. Thus, the detection and prevention of fraudulent financial statements goes to the heart of the functioning of the economy. By taking additional steps to improve their detection and deterrence of management fraud, the auditing profession and the business community can provide assurance to the public as to the effectiveness of the system of corporate accountability and, at the same time, provide a constructive answer to critics who have charged that both have been indecisive in responding to the problem of management fraud. This book is intended to assist the auditing profession and the business community in responding to the problem.

Although this book gathers and presents many ideas on detecting and deterring management fraud, they are not presented as an instant cure-all. Rather than a quick-fix to the problem of management fraud, they represent an alternative to the knee-jerk prescription "more"—more auditing, more controls, more disclosure—in short, more of the same. The marketplace metes out penalties for indiscriminate attempts to solve social problems. Too many controls on business can sap its vitality, lower productivity, and depress innovation. Such penalties are paid by the economy as a whole, by consumers and job-seekers as well as by business enterprises. Additional or alternative controls and other possible deterrents to fraud must be evaluated carefully before being adopted. Society will not gain unless the costs and benefits of adopted proposals represent a desirable trade-off.

Cost-benefit considerations are equally relevant to proposals to change the auditor's approach to fraud detection. Simply increasing the amount of auditing of the current type would not solve the management fraud problem. Audits are not expressly designed to uncover management frauds. They are primarily designed to obtain evidence for opinions about the fairness of financial statements prepared by honest individuals. Therefore, although a major increase in audit procedures of the current type might on occasion reveal a management fraud that would otherwise go undetected, the increase would not provide assurance that management fraud is eradicated. Moreover, the increase would not yield benefits consistently or in the aggregate greater than the added cost of the procedures. Significant increases in auditors' detection and deterrence of management fraud that are justified by cost-benefit relationships must come from technological improvements in the audit process—cheaper and more effective audit procedures aimed at management fraud.

The market for auditing services is, to some extent, distorted by government and self-regulatory activities, but the amount, type, and distribution of audit services are still, we believe, to a large extent determined by market forces. Further, we believe the buyers in the marketplace for audit services are well informed. If these two beliefs are reasonably correct, the market for audit services should be in equilibrium, and more of the same services would be suboptimal (i.e., they would cost more than they would be worth). Aside from artificial modifications of the audit cost-benefit relationships (such as materially increasing the financial penalties to auditors who fail to discover fraud), the key method to reduce management fraud through auditing while still maintaining an optimal cost-benefit relationship is to develop less costly and more effective procedures to detect and deter management fraud. One purpose of this book is to expedite the search for these improved methods.

In reading a book on rocks, one may get the impression that the whole world consists of nothing but rocks. Similarly, in reading this book on management fraud, one may get the impression that it is typical of American business. Nothing could be further from the truth. American business is typically conducted in an ethical, legal manner, and reported in financial statements that are materially correct. Moreover, American business has a vested interest in reducing management frauds because they lower confidence in corporate America.

The Origin of this Book

The development of this book can be traced to a program of auditing research begun by Peat, Marwick, Mitchell & Co. in the late 1960s, including both in-house research and funded projects by outside experts. As part of this program, PMM&Co. undertook in 1973 a comprehensive study of the audit function and the present and prospective audit environment in the United States. The study was completed in 1975 and identified a broad range of research projects that could improve audit effectiveness and prepare the auditing profession to adjust its role to the evolving audit environment.

The study, which was published in 1976 under the title *Research Opportunities in Auditing,* identified trends in our society that might affect the auditor's role. Among these trends was the likelihood of increased pressures for auditors to take on additional responsibilities for detecting management fraud. As a result of these findings, the Firm funded two research projects on the subject.

Since the publication of *Research Opportunities in Auditing,* the trend identified in 1975 has accelerated. In response to these developments, PMM&Co. decided to expand its efforts to study methods of detecting and deterring management fraud. Too little is known about management fraud, how it is perpetrated, and how it may be detected and deterred, whether by auditors or by other parties. A fresh approach was needed, an approach that brought together different points of view, areas of expertise, and varieties of experience. Acting on this conviction, PMM&Co. commissioned a group of papers by experts from many of the relevant disciplines and held a multidisciplinary symposium to discuss the papers and the issue in June 1978. This book includes results of PMM&Co.'s research, the commissioned papers, and many of the ideas discussed at the symposium.

Many possible innovations that might be effective in detecting or deterring management fraud are mentioned in this book. They are presented solely for the reader's consideration and because they represent possible areas for further research, and do not represent prescriptions advocated either by the authors or Peat, Marwick, Mitchell & Co.

Organization

The book is divided into two parts. Part I explores the management fraud problem in depth, and has benefited greatly from the ideas discussed at the symposium. The first chapter defines the management fraud issue and discusses why the subject is of vital interest to auditors. The second chapter explores the auditor's present responsibilities for detecting management fraud and possible extensions of those responsibilities.

In the third chapter, present audit techniques and institutional arrangements are examined to identify opportunities to improve their effectiveness against management fraud. In the fourth chapter, the emphasis is on possible new audit methods—some of which are likely to be controversial. They are presented not as proposals for immediate action, but as ideas worth discussing.

The fifth chapter focuses on designing an internal control system that effectively covers top management—a group that can commonly override systems of internal control as they have traditionally been conceived. The computer gives the management fraud perpetrator a new and powerful tool to expedite and even conceal the fraud. Chapter 6 explores these possibilities and what might be done to combat them.

As already noted, auditors are not the only group concerned with reducing management fraud. Chapter 7 discusses the role played by other concerned groups: lawyers, employees of the company that engages in management fraud, the SEC, the courts, and Congress.

The research questions identified in the first seven chapters are summarized in chapter 8.

Part II of the book presents the commissioned papers plus two others: chapter 14 was prepared by an attendee at the symposium to explain and illustrate the relevance of social psychology to understanding and combatting management fraud, and chapter 17 presents the preliminary findings of one of the management fraud research projects funded by PMM&Co.

Two points should be understood about the papers collected in Part II. They are presented in a deliberate sequence, and they do not in all cases use the same definition of management fraud that is used in Part I.

The sequence of papers begins with Myron Uretsky's call for interdisciplinary studies on management fraud (chapter 9); it sets the context in which the following papers, from different disciplines, should be viewed. Uretsky believes new methods to detect and deter management fraud can best be arrived at by a concerted effort to apply various academic disciplines, particularly the behavioral sciences. The deeper our understanding of the behavior of individuals and companies that have perpetrated management fraud, the more likely that effective tools for detection and deterrence can be developed.

Jerry Turner's paper, chapter 10, is also relevant to the subsequent papers and to research on fraud in general. He classifies acts of fraud and, in effect, warns that research on fraud can be a Tower of Babel if those who study the subject do not define their terms with care and make clear distinctions among the types of fraud. The classification scheme he develops demonstrates what can be done to define useful categories.

The papers by David Saunders, Donald Cressey, Jack Katz, and Martin Greller (chapters 11 through 14) are a related set. They approach management fraud from the vantage point of the behavioral sciences. They also illustrate a basic difference in such approaches. One can focus on perpetrators as individuals or on perpetrators as members of groups or organizations. Saunders, for instance, focuses primarily on individuals, arguing that it is feasible to analyze the psychology of perpetrators to identify "individual differences" between perpetrators and other people.

A major portion of Cressey's paper is based on his studies of the behavior of individual embezzlers. However, Cressey is also interested in the relationship between the institutional environment, particularly the moral messages transmitted by language, and the behavior of individuals. His paper employs both types of analysis, the study of characteristics of perpetrators and the study of how institutional environments affect perpetrators.

Unlike Saunders and Cressey, Katz and Greller concentrate almost exclusively on explaining individual and group behavior in terms of group settings and interactions within groups. Katz analyzes the social psychology of cover-up, how organizational relationships and ideology are used to construct cover-ups of social deviancy, such as management fraud. His premise is that the social arrangements of cover-ups are useful in understanding management fraud even though management frauds are not in all instances attended by broad, collective cover-up activity. He also explains ways to organize work to reduce the likelihood of cover-up.

Greller applies basic concepts of social psychology to management fraud, not only to illuminate aspects of management fraud, but also to demonstrate the relevance of social psychology to research on management fraud. In addition, he argues that behavioral research supports the effectiveness of control systems based on rewards (positive systems) as opposed to punishments (negative systems) and that those interested in controls to curtail the incidence of management fraud should therefore consider adapting elements of positive systems.

At some point in the progress of behavioral research on management fraud it may become clear that greater resources should be devoted either to the study of perpetrators as individuals or to the study of perpetrators as members of groups and institutions. But for now at least both approaches appear useful. It may turn out, as we learn more about management fraud, that the two approaches make equal contributions to our understanding of the problem.

Donn Parker's paper (chapter 15) stands in contrast to those using behavioral analysis. He argues that the advance of computer technology can present new difficulties for those responsible to detect and deter business fraud. He shows how computers may be involved in various types of frauds previously performed manually.

The paper by James Sorensen and Thomas Sorensen (chapter 16) and that by the Albrecht, Romney, Cherrington, Roe, and Payne team (chapter 17) have been paired because both devote considerable attention to the "red flag" approach to fraud detection, the approach based on situational indicators of possible fraud. The Sorensens develop a system for measuring the effectiveness of red flags and argue that behavioral models may enhance the productivity of the red flags now in use. Albrecht et al. identify red flags mentioned in the vast literature on fraud they reviewed. The review was a major part of their research effort, and its product, the 35-page bibliography, is placed appropriately at the end of their paper.

As noted above, a few of the papers use a definition of management fraud (or fraud) different from the definition in Part I. For example, Cressey, Parker, Katz, and Albrecht et al. use broader definitions, not restricted by the criterion that financial statements be used as the instrument for the fraud. Readers should be forewarned about this but not troubled. The papers are germane because they provide in each case perspectives necessary to understanding management fraud.

For instance, Katz's analysis of cover-up sheds light on detecting and deterring management fraud in all situations when collective cover-up is a feature of the fraud. Cressey's broad perspective on the role of morality in deterring criminal behavior applies to management fraud as well as to other corporate crime.

And the research by Albrecht et al. is useful partly because, by including all types of fraud, it sets the stage for an important step in future research on management fraud: determining the relationship between management fraud as defined in Part I and other types of business fraud and illegality. Do they share common causes? Can they be deterred by similar means? Answers to such questions would considerably enhance our understanding of management fraud and how to improve methods of detection and deterrence.

Acknowledgments

As mentioned above, many of the ideas in Part I originated at the management fraud symposium sponsored by PMM&Co. in June 1978. In addition to practitioners and researchers in accounting, the symposium was attended by financial executives, internal auditors, members of government, and academics in the fields of sociology, criminology, psychology, and computer technology. In all, there were 50 participants.

On behalf of PMM&Co. we wish to thank each of the persons who attended the symposium and contributed to its success. The attendees and their affiliations (for identification purposes only) were: W. Steve Albrecht (Brigham Young University), Brandt Allen (University of Virginia), Elizabeth Altman (Harvard University), Michael J. Barrett (University of Minnesota), Patrick Burke (Revlon), Douglas R. Carmichael (American Institute of Certified Public Accountants), Philip Chenok (Main Lafrentz & Co.), John B. Chesson (Senate Subcommittee on Governmental Efficiency and the District of Columbia), Donald Cressey (University of California—Santa Barbara), Charles H. Davison (Peat, Marwick, Mitchell & Co.), Dennis Draper (University of Southern California), Victor M. Earle, III (Peat, Marwick, Mitchell & Co.), Herbert Edelhertz (Battelle Human Affairs Research Center), Stephen Eyre (Citicorp), Gilbert Geis (University of California—Irvine), Clifford E. Graese (Peat, Marwick, Mitchell & Co.), Martin Greller (New York University), James J. Grifferty (Peat, Marwick, Mitchell & Co.), Winford Guin (American Telephone & Telegraph Company), Stephen D. Harlan, Jr. (Peat, Marwick, Mitchell & Co.), Joseph Henehan (Federal Bureau of Investigation), Ernest Hicks (Arthur Young & Co.), Jack Katz (Yale Law School).

Also, James Loebbecke (Touche Ross & Co.), Michael Maccoby (Harvard Project on Technology, Work and Character), Walter Marx (Xerox Corporation), Theodore J. Mock (University of Southern California), S. Thomas Moser (Peat, Marwick, Mitchell & Co.), James Nelligan (House Subcommittee on Oversight and Investigations), John O'Mara (Computer Security Institute), Donn B. Parker (SRI International), Henry A. Quinn (Peat, Marwick, Mitchell & Co.), Steven Raikin (House Subcommittee on Crime), George H. Rittersbach (Peat, Marwick, Mitchell & Co.), Marshall Romney (Brigham Young University), David Saunders (Mathtech), Manfred Seiden (Laventhal & Horwath), Joseph Sickon (U.S. Commerce Department), James Sorensen (University of Denver), Kenneth Stringer (Deloitte Haskins & Sells), Harold Stugart (United States General Accounting Office), C. Robert Tully (Celanese Corporation), Jerry L. Turner (Peat, Marwick, Mitchell & Co.), Myron Uretsky (New York University), Charles Vaughan (General Electric Company), Stanton Wheeler (Yale Law School), Jeremy Wiesen (New York University), and Donald Ziegler (Price Waterhouse & Co.).

We are grateful to the American Institute of Certified Public Accountants for permission to publish two key chapters from the report of the Commission on Auditors' Responsibilities—those on fraud and illegal acts.

We acknowledge the invaluable contributions of Professor Myron Uretsky of New York University, who assisted in identifying both the relevant disciplines and the experts in those disciplines, and Susan Sporer, Research Assistant at PMM&Co., who rechecked all the references, read voluminous proofs, and attended to numerous production details.

But we would like to acknowledge most of all the great contribution of Dr. Peter D. Jacobson of PMM&Co. to this book. He was involved in all phases of its preparation. To him belongs much of the credit for this book, and we are deeply indebted.

Robert K. Elliott
John J. Willingham
New York, New York

Part I

The Problem and
Possible Solutions

1

The Management Fraud
Problem

This book is addressed to all those who have an active interest in reducing the incidence of management fraud. Management fraud reflects adversely on the business community and the auditing profession out of all proportion to its apparent frequency. For this reason alone, both have a strong interest in measures to reduce it. However, publicly expressed concerns over the system of corporate accountability indicate a much broader interest, and other groups—such as attorneys, researchers, and members of government—can play important roles in improving the detection and deterrence of management fraud.

This book assumes and in places specifically argues that management fraud should be reduced. But it does not follow that management fraud should be deterred by any means or at any price. Society may be unwilling to devote the resources necessary to eradicate it, and deciding what level of management fraud is tolerable is a matter of assessing the relative costs and benefits of measures of detection and deterrence. To some extent, this is a philosophical question. One cannot put a dollar value on the desire for a more ethical society, but that desire would count in any realistic assessment of whether to adopt a costly measure to deter management fraud. Similarly, some measures to detect and deter management fraud may impinge on individual liberties, bringing another ethical consideration to bear.

Unfortunately, many of these decisions lie too far in the future. They await research on the causes, typology, and patterns of management fraud and on what new measures of detection and deterrence are feasible and effective. One of the major purposes of this book is to identify fruitful lines of research. The second is to present a comprehensive survey of what is now known about management fraud. The third is to present for the consideration of interested parties proposals to reduce management fraud together with the basic arguments for and against them.

Defining Management Fraud

It is impossible to understand the problem of management fraud without a clear definition of the term. Sharp distinctions among the types of business fraud are essential because all types of fraud cannot be detected and deterred by the same methods. Similarly, the responsibilities of different parties for detecting and deterring fraud need not be identical for all types of fraud. This section defines the term management fraud for purposes of the discussions in subsequent chapters and differentiates the definition from other categories of business fraud.

Generally speaking, fraud is an intentional act designed to deceive or mislead another party. The law distinguishes two types of fraud that cause injury: actual fraud and constructive fraud. If someone causes harm to another party because that party relied on an intentionally misrepresented material fact, the event is called actual fraud. Constructive fraud differs in one basic respect: the act is unconnected to any selfish or evil design.[1] In other words, constructive fraud is not deliberate.

Business frauds can be distinguished by classes of perpetrators, by classes of victims, and by the means of perpetration. For example, business frauds perpetrated by top management can be distinguished from frauds perpetrated by lower level employees. Business frauds that injure the investing public can be distinguished from those that injure companies, and both can in turn be distinguished from frauds that injure consumers of products and services. Finally, computer frauds illustrate a category of business fraud denoted by the means of perpetration.

The subject of this book, management fraud, is deliberate fraud committed by management that injures investors and creditors through materially misleading financial statements. This definition uses each of the types of distinctions mentioned in the previous paragraph. The class of perpetrators is management; the class of victims is investors and creditors; and the instrument of perpetration is financial statements.

The most blurred of the three distinctions is the class of perpetrators, management. It is no longer possible to define management by white collars, and the term manager can refer to individuals at various levels in corporate

[1]*Black's Law Dictionary,* rev. 4th ed. (St. Paul, Minn.: West Publishing, 1968), p. 789.

organizations. For purposes of the definition of management fraud, management refers to those who are high enough in the organization to have the power to override ordinary, day-to-day internal accounting controls or who are not bound by such internal accounting controls.

Internal accounting controls are the plan of organization, the procedures, and the records designed to safeguard assets and maintain the reliability of financial data. When a manager causes an employee to disregard an internal control procedure—for example, to record financial data that have not come

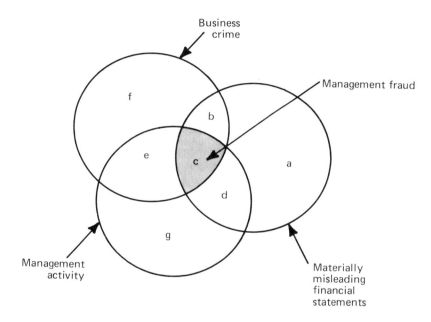

FIGURE 1.   [*a*, materially misleading financial statements caused by random error. *b*, materially misleading financial statements caused by employee defalcations (embezzlement). *c*, management fraud. *d*, materially misleading financial statements caused by errors in applying accounting principles. *e*, other business crime committed by management (e.g., consumer fraud, price-fixing, and product safety violations that do not result in misleading financial statements). *f*, business crime not committed by management and not resulting in misleading financial statements (e.g., employee pilferage and employee defalcations that are insignificant to the financial statements). *g*, other management activity, including maintaining internal accounting controls and preparing fairly presented financial statements.]

through established channels—the manager is overriding the controls.

The definition above excludes constructive frauds that might be perpetrated by management by use of the financial statements and injure investors and creditors. Constructive fraud may result when a person lacks an adequate basis to believe in the truthfulness of representations made. It may occur, for example, where management employs individuals incompetent in accounting skills who prepare materially erroneous financial statements. If management, without knowledge that the financial statements are in error, used them to induce someone to buy stock in the company, a constructive fraud may have been committed, even though there was no intent to defraud, because management lacked an adequate basis to believe the statements to be correct. Although constructive fraud may be deemed reprehensible, we are not concerned with it in this book. In the absence of fraudulent intent, there is no concealment, and current auditing methods are ordinarily sufficiently effective in detecting errors that might result in constructive frauds. Therefore, the term management fraud as used in this book connotes only intentional fraud.

Figure 1 differentiates management fraud, as we have defined it, from other types of business crime and management activity. The shaded area representing management fraud is only a part of the larger category business crime. It is also only a part of the unrepresented category termed white-collar crime, which would include economic crimes by private professionals, such as unnecessary surgery by physicians, tax frauds by individuals, and economic crimes by government officials and personnel.

Misleading financial statements resulting from management fraud are distinguished from other types of misleading financial statements because there are other ways in which financial statements can become misleading to investors and creditors. For instance, random error, *a* in Figure 1, which refers to errors in collecting, recording, and processing data, can cause financial statements to be misleading. It is unintentional human error, and even companies with good systems of internal control are subject to such lapses. Because management is responsible for maintaining internal accounting controls, management decisions on how strong internal controls should be would affect the number and the dollar amount of the random errors that occur. Nevertheless, the commission of the errors cannot be considered part of management activity.

Employee defalcations, *b,* can also cause financial statements to be misleading. For instance, an employee may ship merchandise to a fictitious customer in order to recover it for subsequent sale and personal gain. Or an employee might pocket company cash by preparing false disbursement vouchers. Employee defalcations, which generally are immaterial in amount, need not result in misleading financial statements. Those that do not would be in the larger category of other business crimes represented by area *f.*

The diagram illustrates that management activity can encompass business fraud that is not management fraud as we have defined it. Such frauds include various types of consumer fraud—for example, the sale of fake securities or of products that cannot perform as promised and the issuance of worthless, misleading warranties. Financial penalties for such frauds or the likelihood that such penalties are to be imposed (contingent liabilities) could affect the financial statements, but the frauds themselves are not management frauds as defined above.

Area *d* of the diagram represents errors by management in applying accounting principles that result in misleading financial statements. For instance, obsolete inventory, which should be written off, might erroneously be included in the valuation of inventory fit for sale. Inventory fit for sale might erroneously be carried at cost when its market value is below cost. Research and development costs may be erroneously capitalized in a fixed asset account instead of expensed. The cost of a productive asset might be depreciated over an estimated useful life that greatly exceeds the appropriate depreciable period. The distinction between such errors and acts of management fraud lies in the intent to deceive. If management intentionally misapplies accounting methods to produce misleading results, the event is management fraud.

There are other ways to commit management fraud. Two of the more common ploys are fictitious transactions and transactions without substance. Fictitious transactions include assets and revenue invented by management. In the Equity Funding fraud fictitious assets and revenues gave the company the appearance of astonishing growth though in fact it never earned more than a nominal profit in its whole life.[2]

Transactions without substance may have the legal trappings of other transactions, but they result in no economic change that deserves accounting recognition. For instance, the sale of a property conditional on the seller's guarantee that the buyer suffer no loss from operating the property may lack substance because the seller has not transferred the risk of loss to the buyer, an essential element of a completed sale. In such circumstances, no revenue should be recognized.

In perpetrating management fraud, management may arrange transactions without substance with related parties, parties that do not represent a wholly independent economic interest in the transaction because of their relationship to the other transacting party. The related party may be controlled by the perpetrators or in collusion with them, but, in any case, the transacting parties do not stand in the so-called arm's length relationship typical of the open marketplace. Related-party transactions contrived by management to make income appear as if it had been earned when it had not

[2]SEC Accounting Series Release No. 196, Sept. 1, 1976.

been earned were a central feature in the U.S. Financial case.[3] In the National Student Marketing case, the financial statements for the year ended August 31, 1969 reflected revenue from a "sale" of a subsidiary to employees of the parent company despite various side agreements by which National Student Marketing retained all the risks of ownership.[4]

Management fraud may be committed for or against the interests of a company. In the cases cited so far the misrepresentations made the companies appear to be in better economic health than they were and, for this reason, were in the ostensible interest of the company. There are, however, examples of financial statement misrepresentations that are against the immediate interests of the company. In the SCA Services case, for instance, the Securities and Exchange Commission has alleged that the former president of the company treated as normal business transactions events that were material misappropriations of company assets. This individual, who was also 90% owner of Carlton Hotel Corporation, which was in debt, caused $1.6 million to be advanced to Carlton Hotel and hidden in the financial statements as a currently collectible receivable. The funds to satisfy the receivable were supplied to Carlton indirectly by SCA through fraudulent land sales. Land acquired by colluding parties was resold to SCA at greatly inflated prices with much of the proceeds going to Carlton and the perpetrator.[5] In cases such as this, fraudulent financial statements injure investors and creditors by hiding the fact that company assets are being siphoned off by the perpetrators.

The Auditor's Interest in Management Fraud

Auditors provide assurance that financial statements are sufficiently reliable for use in economic decision-making by third parties. The assurance is given in a report which is the result of the auditor's examination of the evidence underlying the data in the financial statements. The auditor is therefore vitally interested in all events that create materially misleading financial statements—management fraud and employee defalcations as well as random error and errors in applying accounting principles.

Auditing procedures are less effective in detecting management fraud than in detecting the other three sources of misleading financial statements. This is not surprising considering the techniques used to perpetrate management fraud—overridden internal controls, collusion, forgery, contrived transactions without substance, and fictitious and unrecorded transactions. Nevertheless, the public appears eager to have auditors improve their detection and deterrence of management fraud. The Cohen Commission, an independent

[3]SEC Accounting Series Release No. 153, Feb. 25, 1974.
[4]SEC Accounting Series Release No. 173, July 2, 1975.
[5]SEC Accounting Series Release No. 255, Sept. 22, 1978.

body set up by the American Institute of Certified Public Accountants to study auditors' responsibilities, reported, "All segments of the public—including the most knowledgeable users of financial statements—appear to consider the detection of fraud as a necessary and important objective of an audit."[6]

In these circumstances, management frauds discovered subsequent to auditors' reports can damage the usefulness of the audit function. The primary justification for auditing lies in the fact that readers of financial statements need assurance that the statements can be relied upon for economic decision-making. If the statements are materially misleading, investors can be led to allocate their capital to unproductive, perhaps failing, enterprises, thereby suffering personal financial loss and committing resources that otherwise might assist more efficient companies. This process slows economic growth, just as reliable financial statements, by assisting in the efficient allocation of capital, contribute to economic growth.

The auditing profession's contribution to the process of efficient capital allocation is based on the credibility its reports lend to financial statements, but the reports cannot lend credibility to financial statements unless auditors themselves have credibility with those who read the reports. If management frauds damage the credibility of auditors, they damage the usefulness of the audit function. This is neither in the profession's nor the public's interest. For this reason, the profession must take steps to reduce the gap between the public's desire for auditors to detect management frauds with greater frequency and the auditor's effectiveness in detecting them.

Clearly, the gap would be reduced if more effective techniques to detect management fraud were developed. It might also be reduced if the public had a more realistic understanding of the nature and limitations of the audit process. The Cohen Commission found that, "Users are unaware of the limitations of the audit function."[7] Some users may be unfamiliar with the fact that the auditor tests only a sample of the hundreds of thousands of transactions executed by a large company. They may not be aware that the size of such samples is determined largely by the auditor's evaluation of the internal accounting controls relevant to the data being examined. They may underestimate how difficult it is to detect a cleverly designed, carefully executed management fraud, or be unaware of the roles of management, boards of directors, audit committees, and law enforcement agencies in detecting and deterring management fraud.

Certainly, the more realistic the public's understanding of the audit process and its relationship to the detection of management fraud, the more

---

[6]The Commission on Auditors' Responsibilities, *Report, Conclusions, and Recommendations* (New York, 1978), p. 2. The Commission was named the Cohen Commission after its chairman, the late Manuel F. Cohen.

[7]*Report,* p. 71.

realistic will be its desires for auditors to improve their effectiveness in fraud detection. Nevertheless, the primary purpose of this book is not to clarify for the public the auditor's role in detecting management fraud, but to improve the detection and deterrence of management fraud and to stimulate research that will lead to even more effective techniques for detecting and deterring it.

A research effort that leads to improved detection and deterrence of management fraud can be justified apart from its effect on the audit function. Besides being morally desirable, improved detection and deterrence would benefit the business community by enhancing public confidence in the conduct of corporate affairs. Moreover, the plain fact is that too little is known about management fraud. We do not know its dimensions in dollars or frequency of occurrence or the types of people who are perpetrators or potential perpetrators. We do not know how effective present auditing techniques are in detecting management fraud, nor do we know the degree to which auditing is now a deterrent to management fraud. It is not at this time certain how the social demand for action to reduce management fraud correlates with measures of the social need for such action. In short, research on management fraud is in its infancy, and a sensible first step appears to be to explore new possibilities for fruitful research and to take stock of what we now know about the subject.

2

Auditors' Responsibilities
for Fraud Detection

I n order to judge the effectiveness of auditors' performance in detecting
and deterring management fraud, one must assess their responsibilities
for detecting it. Their responsibilities are the benchmarks for judging their
performance. One must also consider these responsibilities in planning how
to improve auditors' detection of management fraud. The social demand for
improved detection may be met by working within the framework of responsibilities currently defined or by changing it.

Professional Responsibilities

Auditors are today professionally responsible for detecting management
misrepresentations that would result in materially misleading financial statements if they would be detected by the application of generally accepted
auditing standards.[1] This obligation is rooted in the auditing profession's
standards for performing audits. The obligation is also rooted in the accounting standards recognized by the profession (generally accepted accounting
principles). This is because the auditor's aim in applying auditing procedures
is to obtain sufficient evidence for an opinion on the fairness of the presenta-

[1]American Institute of Certified Public Accountants (hereafter AICPA) Statement on Auditing Standards (hereafter SAS) No. 16, "The Independent Auditor's Responsibility for the
Detection of Errors or Irregularities" (New York, 1977), pars. 5, 11–13.

tion of the financial statements, and generally accepted accounting principles are the framework for auditors' opinions on the fairness of the presentation of the financial statements.[2] Therefore, if the auditor performs a diligent audit (exercising due care and applying the procedures called for by professional auditing standards) and evaluates the financial statements according to their conformity to generally accepted accounting principles, the professional responsibility to detect fraud is fulfilled.

Professional standards explicitly require that the auditor extend the audit procedures if the examination indicates that material fraud may have occurred. The sequence of procedures is as follows. First, the auditor is to discuss the matter with a level of management at least one level above those involved. If after the discussion, there is still reason to believe there may be a material fraud, the auditor must determine that the board of directors or audit committee is aware of the circumstances, and then attempt to obtain sufficient evidence to confirm the presence or absence of the fraud. If the auditor cannot determine whether unconfirmed, but suspected, fraud would be material to the financial statements, the auditor's report must be qualified or a disclaimer of opinion issued. Either report would disclose the fact that evidence of an unconfirmed fraud had been discovered.[3]

A diligently performed audit is no guarantee against undetected management fraud. Professional literature makes clear that auditing procedures, appropriately applied, cannot be expected to detect management fraud in all cases.[4] This caveat reflects the fact that audits are necessarily performed on a sampling basis. Selective testing of transactions is necessary if the cost of auditing is to bear some reasonable relationship to its expected benefits. The caveat also reflects the fact that forgery, collusion, and unrecorded transactions can be remarkably effective tools for fraud, especially when there is no reason to suspect that they are being employed. In addition, no profession can guarantee that its procedures will always succeed, whether it is medicine, law, or auditing. However, even with the caveat, the obligation is a heavy one, as Statement on Auditing Standards No. 16 makes clear: "An independent auditor's standard report implicitly indicates his belief that the financial statements taken as a whole are not materially misstated as a result of errors or irregularities [fraud]."[5]

[2]SAS No. 5, "The Meaning of 'Present Fairly in Conformity with Generally Accepted Accounting Principles' in the Independent Auditor's Report" (New York, 1975), par. 3.
[3]SAS No. 16, pars. 5, 14.
[4]SAS No. 16, pars. 11–13.
[5]SAS No. 16, par. 5.

Legal Responsibilities

The auditor's legal liability to third parties for failures to detect materially misleading financial statements derives from the common law and the securities acts.[6] To the degree that these sources render auditors legally liable for failing to detect a fraud that would be detected by the application of professional auditing standards, auditors' legal responsibilities for fraud detection and their professional obligations for fraud detection are the same. This equivalency was affirmed in the frequently cited holding in *Escott v. BarChris Construction Corporation* (1968): "Accountants should not be held to a standard higher than that recognized in their profession."[7]

Despite *BarChris,* an auditor's professional responsibility in cases of fraud need not coincide with a court's interpretation of the auditor's legal responsibility to detect it. For instance, in the *Simon* case (Continental Vending) auditors were convicted of mail fraud and violations of the Securities Exchange Act of 1934 because certain significant transactions were not more fully disclosed in the financial statements, even though there was expert testimony that the additional disclosure was not required under generally accepted accounting principles. In cases not involving auditors courts have also found that compliance with generally accepted accounting principles does not preclude a material misrepresentation. This occurred in the case of *Speed v. Transamerica Corporation* (1951), an action involving an offer by majority shareholders to buy out the minority interest. Although the adequacy of generally accepted accounting principles was not a major issue in the case, the court found that the majority shareholders had violated Section 10, Rule 10b-5, of the 1934 Act by failing to disclose that the current value of inventory was significantly higher than historical cost, which was reported in the financial statements in accordance with those principles.

From *Simon, Speed,* and other similar cases Professor T. J. Fiflis concluded in 1975, "It is now apparently well-established that financial statements must

[6]Auditors are liable under common law for failure to exercise due care (ordinary negligence) in fulfilling their contractual relationships with clients. They also may be held liable under common law to third parties for ordinary negligence if the parties' reliance on the audited financial statements was reasonably foreseeable. The principal statutory provisions on auditors' liability are Section 11 of the Securities Act (1933) and Section 10(b) of the Securities Exchange Act (1934) and Rule 10b-5 thereunder. Section 11 imposes civil liability for negligence in connection with registration statements and prospectuses that are misleading because of misstatements or omissions of material facts. Section 10(b) and Rule 10b-5 impose civil liability in connection with the purchase or sale of securities for material omissions and misstatements. Documents issued in compliance with the continuous reporting requirements of the SEC (annual reports on Form 10K) are the primary vehicles for such misrepresentations. The Supreme Court ruled in 1976 that auditors are liable under Section 10(b) only upon showing of intentional or willful conduct designed to deceive or defraud investors. *(Ernst & Ernst v. Hochfelder)* For a full treatment of these questions, see Denzil Y. Causey, Jr., *Duties and Liabilities of the CPA* (Austin, Texas, 1976).

[7]Causey, p. 365. The action was brought under Section 11 of the 1933 Act.

in most cases not give a misleading impression to a layman as determined by a lay jury even if the statements comply with GAAP [generally accepted accounting principles]."[8] This standard is sometimes referred to as the "fairness doctrine," a somewhat misleading term because the question is whether financial statements should be considered fair in the eyes of a prudent layperson or fair in their conformity to generally accepted accounting principles.

Simon was a criminal prosecution, and the issue was not whether the auditor had learned sufficient information about a fraud by applying auditing procedures with due diligence. The issue was whether the auditors had acted fraudulently in expressing their opinion on the financial statements in the absence of disclosures of information they knew. However, it has been argued that *Simon* has implications for both civil and criminal liability. "The reason," Paul L. Radoff explained in a background paper for the Cohen Commission, ". . . is that in virtually every case—civil or criminal, at common law or under the Securities Acts—in which independent auditors are named as defendants, a threshold question is whether financial statements for which an auditor's opinion has been issued are false or misleading."[9]

There is a difference of opinion about the consistency and regularity with which courts have held that accountants are free from liability under the securities laws if they have complied with generally accepted auditing standards and insisted that their clients adhere to generally accepted accounting principles.[10] Nevertheless, there have been over the years a number of cases demonstrating that the courts may apply the "fairness doctrine." The "fairness doctrine" can affect the auditor's legal responsibility for fraud detection by defining fradulent financial statements in ways that depart from professional standards.

The stringent standards of professional diligence applied by courts in fraud cases have provided an additional incentive for the auditing profession to improve its capabilities for detecting management fraud. The increasing volume of such litigation has also been an incentive. The increase is largely explained by the expansion of auditors' liability to third parties, which emerged over the last generation, and by the increased use of class action suits, which emerged during the 1960s. The expanding volume of litigation is not in itself evidence of an extension of auditors' legal responsibilities for fraud detection. It is evidence of how often and to whom they are liable rather than what actions they are liable for. However, this volume of litigation, together with courts' willingness to depart from professional standards as the test of accountants' liability, has focused additional attention on the

---

[8]T.J. Fiflis, "Current Problems of Accountants' Responsibilities to Third Parties," *Vanderbilt Law Review* (January 1975): 67–80.

[9]Paul L. Radoff, *Court Decisions on Auditors' Liability: The Role of GAAP and GAAS,* Public File, Commission on Auditors' Responsibilities, AICPA Library, p. 9.

[10]For a contrast to Fiflis and Radoff, see Victor M. Earle, III, "The Fairness Myth," *Vanderbilt Law Review* (January 1975): 147–63.

nature of auditors' professional responsibilities to detect fraud and whether they should be expanded.

Should Auditors' Responsibilities for Fraud Detection Be Expanded?

There are two basic issues underlying the question of the appropriate extent of auditors' responsibilities for fraud detection. First, how should the profession respond to the fact that some courts have interpreted the auditor's legal responsibility to detect fraud more broadly than the responsibility dictated by professional standards? Second, should the auditor be professionally responsible to detect frauds or other illegalities *immaterial* to the financial statements?

Responding to the "Fairness Doctrine."   The imposition by some courts of the "fairness doctrine" has been difficult and troubling for the auditing profession. It has been argued, for instance, that the "fairness doctrine" is itself unfair. Other professions—medicine, for example—are judged liable for negligence only when their conduct breaches the standards recognized by practitioners.[11]

It has also been argued that the "fairness doctrine" can undermine the stature and meaning of auditors' opinions on financial statements. Victor M. Earle has written, "Without the assurance that accountants are consistently applying those principles that find general acceptance within the accounting profession, the accountant's opinion will mean nothing to a shareholder, investor, or creditor, unless by some magic he can personally observe the particular 'fairness' bias of the individual accountant who performed the audit."[12] If this were indeed the case, the social utility of the audit function would suffer.

The development of new professional standards can reduce differences between the standard of fraud detection imposed by the courts and professional obligations. This prospect rests on the history of both the "fairness doctrine" and professional standard-setting efforts. The "fairness doctrine" as applied by the courts has emphasized that compliance with GAAP does not preclude a materially misleading presentation because additional disclosure may be needed. This is different from arguing that the prescriptions in GAAP create misleading presentations.[13] It suggests that additional prescrip-

[11]For an example of this argument, see Kenneth I. Solomon, Charles Chazen, and Barry S. Augerbraun, "Who Judges the Auditor, and How?" *Journal of Accountancy* (August 1976): 67–74.

[12]Earle, pp. 162–63.

[13]According to Radoff, p. 31, "No cases have dealt squarely with the question expressly reserved by Judge Friendly in *Simon:* whether financial statements are necessarily rendered not false or misleading to the extent that they are consistent with formally established GAAP."

tions can establish greater conformity between compliance with GAAP and compliance with the "fairness doctrine."

Former SEC Commissioner A. A. Sommer, Jr. recognized this in 1972, seeing the profession's urgency to define accounting principles and objectives as in part a response to the evolving legal environment.[14] In some instances, standard-setting activity has been influenced by litigation. For example, related-party transactions and real-estate transactions played a key role in the litigation over misleading financial statements in the 1960s. Two AICPA Industry Accounting Guides subsequently tightened practices in real estate accounting,[15] and Statement on Auditing Standards No. 6 mandated fuller disclosure of related-party transactions.[16] The criteria for pooling-of-interest accounting, a central issue in the Westec case, were tightened by Accounting Principles Board Opinion No. 16, which was issued in 1970.[17]

The connection between the litigation and subsequent standard setting is clear from the sequence of problems in fraud cases and subsequent standard-setting efforts. In the future, at least for auditing standards, such a connection will be more direct because a formal mechanism for translating the lessons of fraud cases into new standards has recently been developed. In 1978 the AICPA set up a Standing Subcommittee on Methods of Perpetration and Detection of Fraud. The subcommittee is not only charged to study and publish analyses of methods of perpetrating and detecting fraud, but also to study and publish analyses of alleged audit failures indicating a need for new or revised auditing standards. Currently the subcommittee is gathering background data on recent fraud cases.

Responsibilities for Detecting Immaterial Frauds and Other Illegalities

The auditor's responsibility for detecting frauds or other illegalities immaterial to the financial statements has been debated in recent years primarily because of the revelations of corporate bribes, kickbacks, and other improper payments. The issue is relevant to management fraud for two reasons. First, it can be argued that such acts are properly considered material to the financial statements. Second, it can be argued that the added responsibility

---

[14]A. A. Sommer, Jr., "What Are the Courts Saying to Auditors?" (May 1972), reprinted in *Perspectives in Auditing,* D. R. Carmichael and John J. Willingham, compilers, 2nd ed. (New York: McGraw-Hill, 1975), pp. 160–61.

[15]*Accounting for Profit Recognition on Sales of Real Estate* and *Accounting for Retail Land Sales,* both published in 1973.

[16]Published in 1975.

[17]Henry R. Jaenicke's *The Effect of Litigation on Independent Auditors* (New York, 1977), originally a background paper prepared for the Cohen Commission, lists 9 auditing pronouncements that can be traced to litigation, p. 79. For details of the Westec case, see SEC Accounting Series Release No. 248, May 31, 1978.

would enhance the detection and deterrence of management fraud.

The first argument is based on an extension of the traditional concept of materiality. For auditing purposes, material financial items have traditionally been judged by their dollar amount. They include items of a dollar amount that could influence an economic decision of a reader of financial statements attempting to assess a company's earning prospects. An employee's embezzlement of cash that is miniscule in proportion to financial statement amounts would not be expected to affect a reader's judgment of the company's prospects. It would be fraud, but the auditor would not be professionally responsible to detect it because it would not be considered material.

Some people hold that information about various aspects of management's moral conduct can influence investors' decisions. By this reasoning, bribes, kickbacks, other improper payments in relatively small amounts, and abuses of perquisites can be considered material items. Such events may also be considered pertinent to an investor's evaluation of management's ability to fulfill its stewardship responsibilities. The investor, for example, might downgrade management's ability on the grounds that it permitted or was responsible for the improper or illegal use of shareholders' assets, failed to prevent embezzlement of those assets by company personnel, or subjected the company to the risk that the disclosure of improprieties would result in damaging retribution, such as the expropriation of foreign assets or injury to the company's business reputation. These arguments may be used to support the position that financial statements are misleading to investors if they do not disclose improper and illegal activities.

Paul A. Griffin's study of the effect of disclosures of sensitive foreign payments does not lend much support to this position. He analyzed the effect on common share prices of such disclosures by 74 companies between April 1975 and May 1976. The behavior of their share prices was examined in conjunction with those of a control sample of companies of "equivalent relative risk, asset size and industrial composition."[18]

Griffin found that although transaction volume and variability of price changes were greater for firms that disclosed sensitive payments than for those that did not, the disclosing firms experienced only a small, temporary decline in the value of their common shares. Within two to three weeks share prices reverted to "normal" levels. In addition, transaction volume and price variability were both affected by the dollar amount of the payments disclosed, and the earlier in the study period the disclosure was made, the greater was its impact. Griffin concluded that the effect of the disclosures on the values of the corporations "does not appear entirely commensurate" with the de-

[18]Griffin's study is chapter 22 of the *Report of the Advisory Committee on Corporate Disclosure to the Securities and Exchange Commission.* U.S. Government Printing Office (Washington, D.C., 1977), pp. 694–743.

gree of concern shown by legislators and regulatory agencies, but he distinguished his findings on economic considerations from the social implications of the improper payments question.[19]

Extending auditors' responsibilities to the detection of frauds and other illegalities immaterial to the financial statements can also be argued by its contribution to the detection and deterrence of management fraud. The arguments are as follows. First, immaterial fraud may be a component of a material fraud which would go undetected if the lesser fraud is not uncovered. Second, immaterial fraud may be the initiation of a material fraud, "testing the waters" before proceeding to the major undertaking. If so, detection of the immaterial fraud would prevent the material fraud from occurring. Third, immaterial fraud may provide evidence that management's integrity should be viewed with additional skepticism, resulting in more intense scrutiny by the auditor and, in turn, increased discoveries of material frauds. Finally, expanded detection would constitute a deterrent to all frauds, including material frauds.

If auditors were made responsible for detecting immaterial frauds and other illegalities, it would have a major impact on the cost of auditing. In absolute financial terms more money might be spent on additional detection than would otherwise be lost through immaterial frauds. An article in the *Wall Street Journal* illustrates the point. It reported that the Port Authority of New York and New Jersey spent $395,000 to have expense accounts audited for irregularities and as a result was reimbursed $10,824 by those whose irregularities were discovered. The audit was confined to the expense account irregularities and was conducted with the full cooperation of the authority.[20] If auditors were responsible for conducting searches for all types of irregularities during annual audits of the financial statements, perhaps without full cooperation from the client, audit costs would mount considerably. The dollar value of the deterrent effect of such audits would be difficult to estimate, and it might be possible to approximate that deterrent effect by searches that are less frequent than annual audits of the financial statements. This raises the question of whether it would be possible and fruitful to make periodic searches for immaterial illegalities more infrequent than audits of financial statements, or whether some triggering mechanism could be developed that indicates that a search should be performed.

The effect on the audit process of extending auditors' obligations to include searches for immaterial illegalities is now unknown. It appears likely, however, that the additional obligation could change the nature of the auditor's role and, as a consequence, change the auditor-client relationship.

[19]Ibid., pp. 733–34.
[20]*Wall Street Journal,* June 1, 1978.

The auditor's role would include a function akin to law enforcement. In fact, in order to fulfill the responsibility, the auditor might need subpoena power and the power to question under oath, both signs that the new responsibility would be linked to law enforcement. In addition, unless it could be shown that the new responsibility is primarily necessary to fulfill the auditor's traditional role, attesting to the fairness of financial statements for economic decision-making, the assumption of responsibilities would have to be justified on other grounds, most likely on the grounds of its ethical desirability. This rationale would signal a change in the auditor's role, and it would affect the way client managements view auditors.

The effect of the new role on the auditor-client relationship could very well be to inhibit management from cooperating in the audit process. This would necessitate additional and perhaps different audit procedures to provide sufficient evidence for opinions on the financial statements. It would add greatly to the cost of auditing.

The cost of external auditors' investigations for immaterial frauds and other illegalities would also have to be weighed against the cost of detecting and deterring the illegalities by other means. Strengthening internal accounting controls, including the internal audit function, may be a more cost-effective technique. In addition, this approach is consistent with the view that management is responsible for such matters in their role as stewards of corporate assets.

If auditors' obligations to identify and pursue immaterial frauds and other illegalities were equal to their obligations to identify and pursue frauds that would result in materially misleading financial statements, they would be unprepared. Auditors are experienced in evaluating whether financial items would result in materially misleading financial statements, but they do not have the legal training to make definitive determinations about whether violations of laws have occurred.

Part of the problem is the hazy distinction between illegal and questionable activities. Illegality is determined by the courts, which apply the law under stringent rules of admissible evidence and procedures to protect the innocent. Thus, even when the auditor believes certain evidence indicates commission of an illegality, the evidence can be no more than the basis for an allegation which may or may not be judged by courts to be true. Thus, prior to any court action the auditor must distinguish between a so-called illegal act and a questionable act on the basis of his or her relative certainty about whether an illegality has taken place. Auditors responsible for detecting illegal acts would probably encounter evidence of questionable acts far more frequently than evidence of illegal acts. An obligation to detect immaterial illegalities would therefore have to be framed in a way that distinguished clearly between illegal and questionable activities—a difficult distinction to make.

Obligations to Disclose Discovered Illegal Acts

Prospective fines, penalties, or damages resulting from illegal acts may have a material effect on the fairness of financial statements. Auditors are therefore required to inquire about clients' compliance with laws and regulations and to evaluate whether the effects of identified illegal acts material to the financial statements are appropriately accounted for and disclosed. If they are not, the auditor must express either a qualified or an adverse opinion on the financial statements because of the departure from generally accepted accounting principles. The qualification or adverse report would disclose the illegal act.[21]

Auditors' reports would also disclose information on illegal acts in two other circumstances. In the event that the auditor is unable to pursue evidence of an illegal act potentially material to the financial statements, the accountants' report must reflect the limitation on the scope of the examination. Finally, the report may be qualified because an illegal act's effects on the financial statements cannot be reasonably estimated, in which case the act would be disclosed.

Disclosures of illegal acts in auditor's reports derive from the obligation to render an opinion on the financial statements, not from any obligation to inform legal authorities. However, auditors who discover patently illegal acts immaterial to the financial statements must inform personnel within the client's organization at a level of authority high enough to take remedial action. If they conclude that the company has not taken appropriate action and believe the matter serious enough to warrant withdrawing from the engagement, they are obligated to consult with legal counsel as to any further action. But Statement on Auditing Standards No. 17 says, "Deciding whether there is a need to notify parties other than personnel within the client's organization of an illegal act is the responsibility of management. Generally, the auditor is under no obligation to notify these parties."[22] Thus, if management, upon being informed of an immaterial fraud, such as an immaterial embezzlement, chooses to discharge the employee rather than press charges, the auditor would not be obligated to take the matter further.

Citizens are obligated to report felonies. Concealing a felony is itself a crime, the crime of misprision. However, as David Isbell, an attorney, argued in 1974, the courts have found that "some affirmative act of concealment" is necessary for this law to be violated. Knowledge and inaction alone do not constitute a violation. He concluded that accountants therefore do not commit the crime of misprision by passivity and silence in the knowledge of

---

[21]The professional obligations described in this and the following two paragraphs are prescribed by the AICPA's SAS No. 17, "Illegal Acts by Clients" (New York, 1977).

[22]SAS No. 17, par. 19.

illegalities immaterial to the financial statements.[23] The auditor is therefore within the law in maintaining a confidential professional relationship with a client in situations where immaterial illegal acts are discovered.

The social and ethical obligation to disclose illegal acts appears in conflict with the auditor's confidential relationship with the client. The social obligation derives in part from the contribution such disclosures might make to the system of corporate accountability. This concern led the Senate Subcommittee on Reports, Accounting and Management to urge the profession to reconsider the auditor's role when illegal acts are discovered. The subcommittee's report of November 1977 stated that "illegal activities must be reported . . . to . . . the appropriate government authorities" and that "illegal acts must be disclosed."[24]

However, society also gains from confidential relationships between auditors and clients. Cooperation between auditors and clients reduces the cost and increases the efficiency of auditing, and confidentiality increases cooperation. In addition, there are alternative means to achieving the goal of disclosing illegal acts immaterial to the financial statements. The whole issue could be treated separately from the question of the auditor's role. For instance, companies might be obligated by law to inform government authorities of all illegal acts committed by company personnel. This course could also have its drawbacks. For example, if a company did not have the option of quietly dismissing an employee discovered to have embezzled funds, it could suffer both the loss from the embezzlement and an even greater loss from adverse publicity resulting from disclosure of criminality in the company. If the company is itself the party injured by the illegal act, should it not have the right to act on the matter according to its view of its best interest? The question of mandatory disclosure of illegalities immaterial to the financial statements is complicated and deserves further analysis.

Summary

This chapter has outlined the auditor's professional and legal responsibilities to detect management fraud and discussed the main issues related to the auditor's obligations to detect illegalities immaterial to the financial statements and to disclose discovered illegal acts. Under generally accepted auditing standards, the auditing profession has only a limited obligation to detect management fraud. However, courts may hold that auditors' legal responsibilities for fraud detection are different from their professional obligations

---

[23]David B. Isbell, "An Overview of Accountants' Duties and Liabilities Under the Federal Securities Laws and a Closer Look at Whistle-Blowing," *Ohio State Law Journal,* vol. 35 (1974): 277. Fiflis, pp. 142–43, agrees.

[24]*Improving the Accountability of Publicly Owned Corporations and Their Auditors,* U.S. Government Printing Office (Washington, D.C., 1977), p. 18.

for fraud detection. Extending auditors' obligations to include detection of immaterial frauds and other illegalities would have a major impact on the cost of auditing and could cause changes in the audit process, chiefly by altering the auditor-client relationship.

3

Enhancing the Effectiveness
of Present Audit Procedures

T here are now no tests that reveal management fraud the way litmus reveals acidity. The present basis for auditors' fraud detection is sensitivity to fraud-prone situations, to signs that management's integrity should be viewed with additional skepticism, and to the implications of evidence that is examined in the course of the audit. The point of this chapter is to explore ways to enhance the yield from this approach to fraud detection.

Professional Education

Graduate school education in accounting and auditing is today obtained primarily as part of MBA programs. There are a few universities with schools of professional accounting, but MBA programs are by far the predominant route for graduate school education in accounting. Both the Cohen Commission and the report of the Senate Subcommittee on Reports, Accounting and Management recommended the establishment of new professional schools of accounting.[1] The recommendation has been supported on the grounds that it can contribute to the development of "professional responsibility and independence," increase academic research on professional practice prob-

---

[1]The Commission on Auditors' Responsibilities, *Report, Conclusions, and Recommendations* (New York, 1978), pp. 88–90; *Improving the Accountability of Publicly Owned Corporations and their Auditors,* U.S. Government Printing Office (Washington, D.C., 1977), p. 19.

lems, attract more and better students to the auditing profession, improve the preparation of individuals entering the profession, and instill a professional identity.[2] Our interest is in how such schools might contribute to enhancing the auditor's sensitivity to signs of management fraud. The other suggested benefits, however, make the approach worthy of consideration because the cost of professional schools could not be justified solely by the need for improved fraud detection.

It is easier to specify the contribution to auditors' fraud detection that professional schools might make than the curriculum and pedagogical structure necessary to achieve it. Ideally, the contribution would be dual. Young auditors would receive training that compensated for their lack of field experience, and auditors emerging from the professional schools would have a background of a breadth that enhanced their effectiveness in fraud detection throughout their careers.

We do not now know the precise relationship between auditors' experience and their vulnerability to management misrepresentations. However, young auditors often deal with executives many years older and far more experienced in their industry. The executives may have spent their working lives with the company, whereas auditors usually spend only a fraction of their working year on a single audit. Such situations can operate to the advantage of a perpetrator of management fraud. They may, for instance, facilitate the perpetrator's effort to put the auditor under conditions of stress and pressure. The Cohen Commission found that poor judgment under such conditions was a major source of problems in the audit failures it reviewed.[3]

Professional schools could provide inexperienced auditors with the background to make such events less likely. In such schools, prospective auditors could discuss with other students and with professors the appropriate response to difficult field situations. Anticipating such problems and considering with others how to resolve them would make less likely a failure to react properly when the student becomes an auditor. Courses in professional ethics studied in the context of field situations might be an effective way to present the problems. A course in case studies of management frauds is another possibility. The setting and tone of the school could be as useful as the course work. If students develop a sense of professionalism while in school, they will discuss identified professional problems—including the problem of management fraud—informally among themselves.

One may question both the ability of professional schools to enhance auditors' fraud detection and the need to create additional professional schools to obtain such educational benefits. For example, if specific course work could prepare auditors to deal with fraud situations, it could be ob-

[2]Ibid.
[3]*Report,* p. 89.

tained by modifying accounting curricula available through current programs. Moreover, professionalism may be primarily obtainable from supervised field experience. If so, rather than additional professional schools, greater assurance may be needed that auditors' job responsibilities are at all times commensurate with their experience.

Recruiting and Promotion

If auditing firms had measures of individuals' sensitivity to evidence of potential fraud, the measures could be used to recruit and promote auditors with greater regard for their acuity in detecting fraud. Methods of measuring this ability have not yet been developed. It may be possible, however, to identify the psychological traits of individuals sensitive to situations in which others are trying to fool them. This is only one aspect of sensitivity to management fraud, but it illustrates the approach. A more encompassing measure might be developed if a population of auditors could be identified that had experience in management fraud situations. By comparing the traits of those who successfully detected management fraud with the traits of individuals who failed to detect it, the characteristics necessary for effective fraud detection might be identified. The weight such characteristics should be given in recruiting and promotion could then be addressed.

The identification of the traits of auditors successful in detecting management fraud would probably affect the profession's strategy for improving fraud detection. If the traits vary strongly according to direct experience in fraud situations, training programs using simulated fraud situations would appear promising. On the other hand, if psychological sensitivity to changes in the personal behavior of perpetrators—to nuances of speech, for example, or the failure to look one straight in the eye—emerges as a paramount trait, training to identify the other elements in fraud situations would appear less necessary.

Deliberately Varying Audit Procedures

The proposal to vary audit procedures from year to year is based on the premise that perpetrators of management fraud are aware that they must fool the auditors. They can benefit from year-to-year repetitions in auditing procedures because they can design their fraud taking such patterns into account. This possibility can be counteracted by deliberately avoiding the patterns. Each year procedures unique to the history of the audit would be introduced or procedures not recently used would be reintroduced.

This proposal carries with it an implied question on the validity of the underlying premise. What is the relationship between repeated patterns of auditing procedures and the incidence of management fraud? In addition, some balance would have to be struck between varying audit procedures in the pursuit of defined audit objectives and introducing procedures that are marginally related to defined audit objectives or are so inefficient in terms of achieving audit objectives that they can only be justified as measures to detect and deter fraud. In other words, the less the procedures are related to determining whether the financial statements are in accordance with GAAP, the harder it would be to justify them in terms of the auditor's traditional role.

Mandatory Procedures

Case studies of recent frauds may reveal that certain audit procedures are so essential in detection that they should never be omitted from an ordinary examination or never omitted under specified circumstances. The model for this proposal is the McKesson & Robbins case. The company's financial statements for the year ended December 31, 1937 reported assets in excess of $87 million, including $10 million in fictitious inventory items and $9 million in fictitious accounts receivable, fictitious sales of $18.2 million, and fictitious gross profit on those sales in the amount of $1.8 million. Crude drugs supposedly purchased for the Connecticut Division of McKesson were purportedly retained for the McKesson account in the warehouse of Canadian vendors and then sold for the McKesson account by another Canadian company, while the payments and collections were supposedly performed for McKesson by a banking firm. The Canadian vendors, sales agents, and bankers were fictitious, but invoices, advices, contracts, guarantees, and false credit reports were prepared to make the transactions with them appear authentic.[4]

As a result of the McKesson case, the auditing profession adopted mandatory auditing procedures to prevent a recurrence of similar frauds—confirmation of receivables and direct contact with inventories by observation of inventory-taking. Case studies of recent frauds, frauds committed in today's business environment, may reveal other procedures that should be mandatory to detect certain types of fraud.

"Red Flags"

Professional standards require auditors to be alert to indications that fraud may have occurred. The auditing profession calls these indications "red flags." For instance, in Statement on Auditing Standards No. 16, auditors are told that a high turnover rate in key financial positions, such as controller, or the fact a company does not correct material weaknesses in internal con-

[4]SEC Accounting Series Release No. 19, December 5, 1940.

trols that are practicable to correct may be a cause for concern that management has made material misrepresentations or overriden internal control procedures.[5] Statement No. 17 requires auditors to consider the implications of a discovered illegal act on the degree of reliance intended to be placed on management's representations.[6]

Statement No. 6, which provides guidance on procedures to identify related-party transactions, also contains red flags for management fraud. This is because deliberately failing to disclose material related-party transactions or intentionally accounting for them improperly is management fraud. It results in materially misleading financial statements. Statement No. 6 points out that related-party transactions may be indicated by borrowing or lending on an interest-free basis, selling real estate at a price that differs significantly from its appraised value, exchanging property for similar property in a nonmonetary transaction, or making loans with no scheduled terms for repayment. The Statement also directs auditors to be aware that related-party transactions may be motivated by conditions such as an overly optimistic earnings forecast, excess capacity, a declining industry characterized by a large number of business failures, or dependence on a single or relatively few products, customers, or transactions.[7]

Statements on Auditing Standards present red flags not as all-inclusive checklists but as examples of the types of situations that auditors should consider. Thus, auditors are obligated to consider other circumstances that might raise questions. Case studies and comparative studies of management frauds could add to the number of red flags commonly used by auditors and provide evidence of the effectiveness of those already in use. There are, for instance, no thorough studies indicating whether management fraud is more common in some industries than others, more common in small or in large corporations, more common in centralized or in decentralized business operations, or more common in recently formed or in long-established corporations. Such information could enhance the effectiveness of the red-flag approach.

The chapter by Albrecht, Cherrington, Payne, Roe, and Romney describes the initial results of their study of red flags (see chapter 17). It identifies 95 indicators gathered from a review of the literature on fraud. The research team plans to substantiate the effectiveness of the indicators by analyzing their presence or absence in 50 selected fraud cases. The research by Albrecht et al. does not distinguish between management fraud as we have defined it and other types of business fraud, such as embezzlements immaterial to the financial statements. Additional research would be necessary

[5]AICPA SAS No. 16, "The Independent Auditor's Responsibility for the Detection of Errors or Irregularities" (New York, 1977), par. 10.

[6]AICPA SAS No. 17, "Illegal Acts by Clients" (New York, 1977), par. 13.

[7]AICPA SAS No. 6, "Related Party Transactions" (New York, 1975), pars. 8, 11.

to determine if the red flags are as effective in indicating the possibility of management fraud as they are in indicating the possibility of other types of fraud.

Red flags do not indicate the presence of fraud. They are conditions believed to be commonly present in events of fraud, and they therefore suggest that concern may be warranted. But the same conditions may occur where there is no fraud. For instance, insufficient working capital or credit to continue operations may predispose some managements to misstate financial statements.[8] To an honest businessperson the same conditions would simply be a harsh fact of business life. The effectiveness of red flags depends on the auditor's correlation of different signals into a pattern that raises suspicions and perhaps leads to conclusions. For this reason, consideration of the effectiveness of red flags returns to the question of auditor sensitivity and ability.

The effective correlation of different signals, different evidence that comes to the auditor's attention, depends in part on communication among the members of the audit team. One aspect of this problem is how to ensure that subordinate members of the audit team bring enough of their questions to the attention of their superiors. If questions and relevant evidence are evaluated together, the total picture may raise suspicions of fraud that the individual items considered alone do not. On small audits it is less difficult to put together whole patterns of audit evidence. On very large audits, where the audit team is composed of a hundred or more persons, working in different cities and often in different countries, gathering evidence over a period of months, the problem of correlating evidence is much greater. The nature of the problem is indicated by the diagram in Figure 1, which compares the organization of audit teams for small and large audits. Even though the basic lines of authority are the same in each case, the structure becomes vastly more complex on larger audits.

The Sorensens (chapter 16) recommend applying a behavioral model to the audited company in order to maximize the yield from information such as red flags. The particular model they recommend is called "the stress-strain perspective," but the message is broader than the specific recommendation. It is that facts about a company have more meaning if they are related to a model that interprets the company's behavior internally and in terms of its interaction with its external environment. The stress-strain approach is still in its infancy. However, the purpose of the model suggests a proposition that is full of implications for research on uncovering management frauds: auditors' effectiveness in detecting fraud depends less on their obtaining new types of audit evidence than on their understanding fully the relationships of

[8]These red flags are noted in SAS No. 16, par. 9.

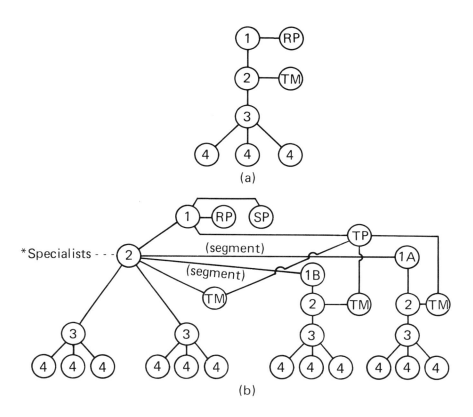

FIGURE 1.   Basic organization of audit teams. (a) Small audit. (b) Audit
of larger company with two segments geographically distinct
from main enterprise. [1, engagement partner (responsible
for audit, approves audit plan and reviews audit work, signs
report. RP, reviewing partner (reviews audit report prior to
issuance). SP, SEC reviewing partner (for audits of public
companies). 1A and 1B, segment partners. TP, tax partner.
2, manager (directly supervises engagement, performs
detailed review of audit work). 3, senior accountant (directly
responsible for planning and performance of audit work,
reviews and supervises work by assistants). 4, assistant
accountant (directly responsible for assigned field work); on
large audits there may be several hundred auditors. TM, tax
manager (reviews adequacy of tax provision).]
    *Computer, statistical, and industry specialists.

the items of evidence uncovered and the inferences that may be drawn from them.

Maintaining Auditors' Sensitivity to Management Fraud

An effective program to enhance auditors' detection of management fraud must address the question of how to prevent lapses. There are at least three threats to the auditor's alertness to signs of management fraud: the difficulty in maintaining an unrelenting vigil for a relatively infrequent event, the effect of time pressures on auditors, and potential compromises of auditors' objectivity.

The Effect of the Infrequency of Management Frauds.   Many auditors do not encounter any management frauds during their careers in public practice. In these circumstances, it is possible that one's ability to pick up suspicious signals from perpetrators can atrophy. This, of course, is one of the best justifications for the "red flag" approach, which identifies situations where additional skepticism is warranted. However, it is also part of a larger question that pervades the issue of auditors' effectiveness in detecting fraud. At what point should the auditor question or doubt management's integrity?

Mautz and Sharaf have argued effectively that the auditor must assume that there is no necessary conflict in interest between management and the auditor.[9] If auditors cannot trust management's representations, they cannot rely on the records and documents under management's control or on the statements of employees who may be under management's control. "We are left with a situation," the authors continue, "in which the auditor must first attempt to ferret out the transactions that took place, then prepare a set of records and accounts, and finally make his examination. But by the time he had performed the first two steps he would be disqualified as an auditor."[10] He would be disqualified because he would at that point be examining his own financial representations.

Mautz and Sharaf conclude that unless there is evidence to the contrary, the auditor must assume management is not involved in fraudulent activities.[11] Professional standards prescribe essentially the same stance even though they also insist that the auditor be alert to the possibility of fraud.[12]

The analysis by Mautz and Sharaf puts the problem of atrophied sensitivity to fraud in perspective. The auditor is not only unlikely to encounter management fraud, but must assume its absence in order to perform the

[9]R. K. Mautz and Hussein A. Sharaf, *The Philosophy of Auditing,* American Accounting Association (Menasha, Wisconsin, 1961), p. 45.

[10]Ibid., p. 45.

[11]Ibid.

[12]SAS No. 16, par. 10.

typical audit. In addition to red flags, what measures can provide assurance that these circumstances do not blunt the auditor's sensitivity to signs of management fraud?

Time Pressures.   The problem of time pressures on the auditor was studied extensively by the Cohen Commission. Their analysis of audit failures revealed that excessive time pressures leading to poor judgment and too great a reliance on client representations was "one of the most pervasive causes" of such failures. Among the sources of excessive time pressures, they cited tight reporting deadlines, the seasonal crush of year-end work resulting in spreading senior personnel too thin, and the concern for efficiency—often read as fulfilling time budgets—exaggerated to the point that the quality of the audit is adversely affected.[13]

There may be a fine line between providing clients, and ultimately the public, with quality services at the lowest cost, which means the fewest hours, and compromising the appropriate extent of the examination. In the end an auditor's professional judgment will determine on what side of the line his or her performance lies. Nevertheless, additional consideration of how to reduce excessive time pressures is certainly warranted, particularly because it may enhance auditors' effectiveness in fraud detection. Large transactions near the end of a reporting period have been a feature of a number of fraud cases. For this reason, Statement on Auditing Standards No. 6 requires that auditors give particular attention to large, unusual, or nonrecurring transactions recognized at or near the end of the reporting period.[14] Measures that can ensure that auditors are not at such moments subjected to excessive pressures to complete their work would probably enhance their success in fraud detection.

Earlier involvement in the financial reporting process may relieve excessive time pressures. This may be evaluated by a study of the effect of limited reviews of interim financial information on the auditor's resolution of problems. Regular quarterly reviews are a relatively recent development. Statement on Auditing Standards No. 10, which defined standards for limited quarterly reviews, was issued in 1975. We do not at this time know the degree to which interim reviews have relieved the problem of time pressures.

Objectivity.   Auditors' reports have credibility largely because auditors are understood to be independent of management's control and thus objective. If auditors are not objective or do not appear to be objective, the social utility of their product, the auditors' report, declines. For that reason, the auditing profession and the SEC have rules that proscribe certain relation-

[13]*Report,* pp. 114–21.
[14]SAS No. 6, par. 13.

ships between auditors and their clients. For instance, aside from the fee they receive for their services, auditors may not have any financial interest in clients they audit. Objectivity is so important to the profession that it is worthy of any productive research that may be undertaken. For purposes of learning how to enhance auditors' detection of fraud, however, a logical first step would be to see if compromises of objectivity have played a role in management frauds and if so, to identify the circumstances occasioning the compromises.

Two types of compromises may be hypothesized. First, an auditor may become so familiar with a client that professional skepticism wanes. In such circumstances auditors may be less likely to pick up signs of management fraud, more easily fooled and less vigilant because they are too trusting of individuals with whom they have been dealing for years. Obviously, some adjustment in skepticism is realistic if it is based on knowledge and experience that are good indicators of management's integrity. Such adjustments need not constitute abandoning the degree of professional skepticism necessary to audit effectively. The issue is whether or not such adjustments in fact lead to excessive reliance on management's representations.

The second type of compromise is intimidation by management based on their power to change auditors. Attempts at intimidation are documented. For instance, in the *Herzfeld* case the client not only threatened to withdraw its account but also to sue the auditors if a disagreement over how to account for certain transactions resulted in a failure to obtain the private placement of securities it sought.[15] As it happened the financing was obtained despite a qualified opinion, but the company subsequently went bankrupt. Data on attempts at intimidation and their rate of success in causing auditors to place excessive reliance on management representations would inform the profession whether additional safeguards are necessary.

Recent suggestions to ensure that auditors maintain their objectivity may be seen as directed toward the two types of compromises described above. For instance, it has been widely suggested that companies form audit committees independent of management with the power to recommend the auditors to be engaged and with the responsibility to serve as a line of communication between the auditors and the board. Such committees, which are now fairly common,[16] can insulate the auditors from intimidation by management. Suggestions for rotating auditing firms may be seen as directed at preventing the development of too close a relationship between the auditors and management.

---

[15]*Herzfeld v. Laventhol, Krekstein, Horwath & Horwath* [1976–1977 Transfer Binder], *CCH Federal Securities Law Reports,* p. 90,256.

[16]Audit committees are now a requirement for listing on the New York Stock Exchange, are recommended by the AICPA, and are often adopted as a consequence of settling SEC enforcement actions.

The suggestion for rotating auditing firms has been criticized because the more thoroughly auditors know their clients' operations the more likely they are to detect matters that deserve additional scrutiny. The Cohen Commission, for instance, found that the frequency of audit failures on first- or second-year audits indicated that audit risks are reduced when the auditor has a greater period of acquaintance with the client's operations.[17] Periodic rotation of auditing staff, rather than auditing firms, a policy now used by many firms, prevents unwarranted reductions in professional skepticism from excessive familiarity with clients. The SEC Practice Section of the AICPA requires member firms to rotate their partner assignments periodically. This policy retains the benefits of experience and continuity with the client.

The objection to rotating auditing firms illustrates a basic problem. If auditors' effectiveness increases with the thoroughness of their knowledge of clients' operations, curtailing the professional relationship, whether by duration of years or by other restrictions, must have its limits as a measure to prevent lapses in detecting and deterring management fraud. At some point protection against the possibility of insufficient professional skepticism would be more than offset by the loss of additional knowledge of client operations.

Research on the incidence of compromised objectivity in cases of management fraud will not be easy to perform because it would require evidence of changes in auditors' mental attitudes. The influence of economic self-interest does not weigh on the side of compromised objectivity. It is misleading to picture professional integrity doing battle against the economic self-interest represented by the audit fee. It is in auditors' economic self-interest to avoid massive financial losses which arise through litigation. The potential financial exposure for willfully participating in a fraud is much greater than the prospective loss of a fee. Litigation itself is costly and damaging to a firm's reputation. Realistic study of objectivity would explore the auditor's consciousness of the negative consequences of participating in fraud, pressures on the auditor to retain clients both from within a CPA firm and from competition in the marketplace, the influence of peer group attitudes within the auditing profession, and the weight of the auditor's self-image as a professional in good standing, which is incompatible with knowing participation in management fraud.

Summary

The proposals discussed in this chapter suggest that there are unexplored opportunities for improving the effectiveness of the auditor's current approach to detecting and deterring management fraud. Development of these proposals may lead to improvements in auditors' fraud detection. It can also

---

[17]*Report,* p. 109.

establish more clearly whether new procedures for fraud detection are necessary. Several of the proposals are linked to issues at the heart of the auditor's professional responsibility—for instance, objectivity, and the organization of audit teams most effective for evaluating evidence. Others would affect professional training, personnel practices, and the type of audit procedures applied in given situations. Thus, these proposals, if adopted, would have a significant impact on the audit process.

4

New Audit Methods
to Detect and Deter
Management Fraud

I f auditors were to adopt new procedures exclusively designed to detect fraud, it would be a major departure from their present approach. The cost of the procedures could not be justified by the benefits they provided to the audit process as a whole, but would have to be justified solely because they can detect and deter management fraud. Compare, for example, measures to reduce time pressures at year-end to the proposal discussed below to use data on corporate recidivism. Reducing time pressures can be supported because it would benefit the entire audit process, whereas the other suggestion is worthy of consideration only if it is considered necessary to detect and deter management fraud.

The major argument for exploring new methods is that some may turn out to be so effective at detecting and deterring management fraud that they are considered a necessary adjunct to auditors' present procedures. Moreover, if society wants a significant measure of additional assurance that management fraud has been detected or deterred, new approaches to detection must be explored.

Using Data on Corporate Recidivism

Information about previous illegal activities and civil litigation may be useful indicators of the probability of current or future management frauds. If so, auditors could use data on corporate recidivism the way they use red flags. In order to do so, auditors would need to have at their disposal the rank of the corporation among others in number of successful actions against the company by government authorities and private parties. The greater the relative recidivism rate, the redder the flag.

This approach is consistent with Sutherland's theory of how perpetrators learn their behavior, which is described by Cressey in chapter 12. Sutherland held that perpetrators learn their behavior from the behavioral directives they receive in their association with different institutions. It would follow that certain institutional environments inculcate types of criminal behavior more than others do and that certain corporate environments inculcate criminal behavior whereas others do not. In support of this contention Cressey cites evidence that there are patterns of corporate recidivism in restraint-of-trade cases. Offenders in some industries tended to repeat their offense more than did offenders in other industries.[1]

These findings suggest that information about past offenses may indicate the probability of current or future offenses. However, data on corporate recidivism cannot be considered a useful red flag for management fraud unless there is a demonstrable relationship between management fraud and other types of corporate illegality. It is not necessarily true that instances of price fixing, for example, indicate a greater likelihood of management fraud than a clean record on price-fixing violations. Research on the relationship between management fraud and other illegal corporate activities is a prerequisite to research on the practical questions of how data on corporate recidivism would be assembled, distributed, and updated for regular use by auditors.

Psychological Testing of Management

Identifying potential perpetrators of management fraud by psychological tests is an unexplored approach to detection. Its rudiments are as follows. In-depth psychological profiles of perpetrators would be developed. The profiles would be used to formulate tests to identify fraud-prone individuals. The tests would be designed to identify those members of client management, if any, that possessed the characteristics typical of perpetrators. Psychologists or auditors trained in psychology would administer the tests, and the audit team would then be on the alert for misrepresentations from those identified as potential perpetrators.

The feasibility of this procedure for detecting fraud depends not only on whether effective tests can be designed, but also on the willingness of the business community to accept it and auditors to use it. The business community may find the tests demeaning or an infringement on individual rights of

[1]See chapter 12.

privacy. Auditors may conclude that the approach risks unacceptable damage to their relationships with clients, suggesting doubts about integrity that dampen cooperation.

In addition, the feasibility of the approach is threatened by the fact that perpetrators and self-conscious potential perpetrators of management fraud are unlikely to give honest answers to questions designed to identify that element in their character. This would necessitate the development of a testing instrument that revealed the traits of test subjects who were trying to hide some features of their personality. Moreover, the psychological profiles of fraud perpetrators from which the tests would be developed would be based on apprehended perpetrators whose self-concepts may have altered after they were caught. This would cast doubt on the reliability of the psychological profile, which, in any case, could never reflect the traits of successful perpetrators, who had not been apprehended.

Finally, there is at this point no reason to believe that perpetrators of management fraud possess a set of personality traits that distinguish them clearly from other groups, and if they do not, the testing process would turn up an impractically large group of potential perpetrators, a group with a relatively low incidence of actual perpetration. The larger the population of potential perpetrators, the less useful the information from the tests.

The problems raised by the proposal to use psychological tests cannot be answered until research is done on the psychological makeup of perpetrators of management fraud. The research can be justified apart from the pros and cons of testing management. It could provide auditors with insight into the types of personalities that might commit management fraud. Moreover, one expert, the psychologist David Saunders, has argued that this research is feasible and should be conducted. He suggests that the study address both the differences between perpetrators (and potential perpetrators) and other people and the ways in which environmental factors, including other people, may interact to facilitate or inhibit the expression of these differences.[2]

Psychological research would also be useful if it could establish whether the characteristics of managers who perpetrate fraud through false and misleading financial statements are similar to or significantly different from the characteristics of managers who perpetrate immaterial frauds, such as immaterial embezzlements. Similarly, it would be useful to establish whether managers who perpetrate frauds at the expense of the company have a psychological makeup different from those who perpetrate frauds that ostensibly further the company's interests.

---

[2]Saunders makes this argument in chapter 11.

Questioning Employees

Law enforcement authorities pursuing alleged business crimes have found employees excellent sources of information, and this suggests that auditors could obtain useful information about possible fraud by interviewing employees. In order to pursue this approach, research would be needed on appropriate interviewing techniques and the selection of subjects for interviews. CPA firms could expand their staffs to include sociologists or psychologists who would interview the employees, or auditors could be trained to do so. The employees to be interviewed might be selected on the basis of their role in the internal control system. On the other hand, it might be more cost-effective to restrict the interviews to discharged, retiring, or departing employees because they would least fear reprisals and in some cases might be leaving because of ethical differences with the company.

There is clearly a wide range of possibilities for implementing a systematic program of inquiries to gather from employees information on possible fraud. But some gauge of the potential productivity of such a program would be needed in order to justify its development. Although law enforcement authorities have had success with this technique, it does not follow that auditors would have equal success. Employees may feel that auditors are not appropriate repositories for information they wish to volunteer about possible fraud. In addition, law enforcement agencies undertake their investigatory work under conditions quite different from those under which auditors conduct examinations of financial statements.

When law enforcement agencies undertake investigatory work, they usually have some reason to suspect a violation of the law. They may be seeking the perpetrator of an alleged crime, the circumstances of its commission, or incriminating evidence for prosecution. Their investigation begins where the auditor's would end. The auditor would be questioning employees without knowledge of a crime or an alleged crime. Except in extraordinary circumstances the procedures would be performed under the assumption that management has done nothing wrong. On the other hand, the procedures could be reserved for occasions when other evidence leads the auditor to seek additional information about possible fraud. This, of course, has the drawback that the performance of the procedures would reveal the auditor's concern and possibly result in unwarranted assertions of impropriety against the company.

A program for regular questioning of employees would have to be formulated in a way that would not generate a morally objectionable atmosphere, an atmosphere of suspicion and groundless accusations. Besides the distastefulness of such an atmosphere, it could undermine the effectiveness of the program by producing unreliable evidence.

In the end, however, the effectiveness of the proposal to interview employees depends largely on their willingness to provide what information they have about possible fraud. Jack Katz's research[3] on cover-up suggests that this sort of approach *by itself* would have limited value. He observes that individuals in organizations tend to find ways to avoid confronting the responsibility to know what can be known about impropriety within the organization and to report it. Feigned ignorance, various justifications for the averted eye, ways to protect oneself from the accusation that knowledge was available, the identification of the outsider as an adversary wittingly or unwittingly attempting to undermine the legitimate functioning of the organization—these and other devices Katz describes make cover-up understandable and imply that it is typical. To the degree that it is typical, the proposal to question employees may not yield useful information unless it is accompanied by reforms that reduce the number of cover-up systems in corporate organizations or render them ineffectual.[4]

The usefulness of interviewing employees also depends on how wide is the circle of persons who typically know about a material management fraud. We do not know, however, what proportion of such frauds are known to any considerable number of members of an organization who did not initiate them, what proportion, that is, involve the collective activity of cover-up. If research on these questions shows that management frauds are commonly known to a wide circle of nonperpetrators, it will tell us that an appropriate strategy for improving detection is to find ways to tap this source of information. It will also change the way auditors think about such frauds, as this passage by the compilers of *The Equity Funding Papers* indicates:

> The failure of any Equity Funding employee to report anything about the fraud has ominous implications for independent auditors. Traditional audit doctrine assumes that, as a practical matter, management fraud will be contained within a small circle, or fall of its own weight. . . . Obviously Equity Funding wasn't contained within a small circle. If auditors assume a broader conspiracy must topple of its own weight, their confidence is unwarranted.[5]

Equity Funding proves that this assumption is not universally true, but further research is needed to determine whether it is generally untrue.

---

[3]See chapter 13.

[4]Because such reforms apply more to the general question of how to reduce and deter management fraud than to the suggestion that auditors question employees, the reforms are discussed separately below.

[5]Lee J. Seidler, Frederick Andrews, and Marc J. Epstein, *The Equity Funding Papers* (New York: John Wiley, 1977), p. 10.

Disclosures of Material Audit Adjustments

Material audit adjustments are changes to the financial statement amounts, prior to their issuance, made because the auditor informs management that the adjustments are necessary to a fair presentation. If the auditor is satisfied that the adjusted financial statements are fairly stated in conformity with GAAP, the auditor issues an unqualified ("clean") opinion. The origin of the adjustment might be an error in processing data or a difference in judgment about the selection or application of an accounting principle.

In such cases, if management is deliberately attempting to mislead users of the financial statements, they are attempting to perpetrate management fraud. If the auditor objects and the matter is adjusted in privacy, there is no penalty for such attempts. They might, however, be deterred by disclosures of material audit adjustments in auditors' reports. Perpetrators pretending to an honest difference of opinion could no longer expect that an unpublicized adjustment is the worst they face. If they believed that disclosures of material adjustments would be embarrassing, they might be deterred from making misrepresentations to auditors because of the risk that the auditors would take exception to them and insist on adjustment and disclosure. The more flagrant the accounting misrepresentation, the worse the disclosure of the adjustment could reflect on the perpetrator.

This proposal may be criticized because the disclosures would affect equally both perpetrators and innocent parties. Errors necessitating audit adjustments and honest differences of opinion between management and auditors are routine matters on many audits. Disclosures of material adjustments may therefore injure managements that have no intention to deceive auditors or users of financial statements. Users would certainly be unwise to read into the disclosure of an audit adjustment the intent by management to defraud.

It may be argued that the embarrassment to nonperpetrators caused by disclosures of audit adjustments would be justifiable because users of the financial statements would learn of deficiencies in management's accounting. However, the disclosures would not originate solely from attempts at perpetration, on the one hand, and incompetent accounting on the other. Audit adjustments may arise even if management's accounting is generally sound and the auditors respect management's opinion. The fact that the auditor's professional judgment took precedence over management's opinion need not reflect incompetent accounting.

Because disclosures of material audit adjustments could reflect blameless behavior and because audit adjustments are so often routine matters, the public might in time give them little attention, in which case the proposal would be ineffective. Thus, as a first step in evaluating the proposal, studies would have to be undertaken projecting the public's reaction to the disclosures. If it can be anticipated that they would reflect negatively on management, a trade-off would have to be assessed. The deterrent value of the disclosures would have to be weighed against the embarrassment they would cause to nonperpetrators.

The trade-off assessment would at that point be incomplete unless it also took into account the practical problems of implementing the proposal and their consequences. Because of the necessity for disclosing the adjustments, management might oppose making many that without the prospect of disclosure they would readily accept. The materiality of the item would more often be contested and, because of the possible consequences of the disclosures, the total number of audit adjustments might drop. The result could be a diminution in the accuracy of financial statements.

Another difficulty is that it is not always possible to determine what should be considered an audit adjustment. For example, assume that during the course of an audit, but before the fiscal year has ended, an auditor discovers a possible error and discusses it with management. If management states it was aware of the item and intended to correct it, and then promptly does so, there would be no adjustment for the auditor to recommend or insist upon at the end of the audit. If the proposal to disclose material audit adjustments is pursued, should it comprehend disclosure of such items? Clearly, the proposal could raise practical difficulties.

Operational Auditing Techniques

Some argue that operational auditing techniques are more effective at detecting fraud than the procedures used in a financial audit. Unlike a financial audit, an operational audit has as its objective to determine whether an organization's goals are being achieved economically, efficiently, and effectively. To fulfill this objective operating procedures are analyzed, and it is common to question why a transaction was performed in one way rather than another. The operational auditor tries to determine whether resources are wasted in fulfilling operating goals—for instance, from uneconomical purchasing practices. Multidisciplinary audit teams typically perform operational audits. The staff of the General Accounting Office, which performs operational audits, includes attorneys, actuaries, engineers, and social scientists, and operational audits performed by CPA firms are usually the responsibility of their management consulting departments, which make extensive use of personnel trained in various disciplines.

Study of the effectiveness of operational auditing techniques in detecting fraud holds out the promise of identifying new approaches to detection that could be adapted to audits of financial statements. However, it must be determined whether operational auditing techniques would be as effective in detecting management fraud as they are in uncovering other types of fraud and illegality. The general purpose of operational auditing, to see if an organization's goals are being met, suggests its techniques may be more effective in detecting frauds perpetrated against the interests of the organization than frauds perpetrated to further those interests. Nevertheless, this is a fruitful field for research, not least because it might provide information on the contribution multidisciplinary audit teams can make to fraud detection.

Evaluating Internal Accounting Controls during Ordinary Examinations

As part of their examination of financial statements, auditors test internal accounting controls on which they intend to rely in restricting substantive audit tests. The Cohen Commission recommended expanding this practice. It proposed that the standard of professional skill and care be amended to require a study and evaluation of "internal controls that have a significant bearing on the prevention and detection of fraud." If material weaknesses are discovered, management and, where appropriate, the audit committee or full board would be informed, and audit testing would be extended as necessary. In making this recommendation, the Commission noted "that internal controls may not be effective in preventing or detecting many types of management fraud."[6]

In order to assess the feasibility of this proposal, it would be necessary to identify those controls significantly affecting the prevention and detection of fraud. The generalizations now in professional literature would probably not provide sufficient guidance. The identification would be valuable even if the proposal is never adopted. A deeper understanding of controls that contribute to the prevention and detection of fraud may lead to designing new controls, more effective in detection and deterrence.

Comprehensive Reviews of Internal Accounting Controls

There is a strong likelihood that auditors will in the not too distant future perform regular comprehensive reviews of companies' internal accounting controls and provide public reports on those reviews. The impetus for this development has come from the SEC, the Cohen Commission, the Foreign Corrupt Practices Act of 1977, and public concern for new assurances with respect to the system of corporate accountability. The Foreign Corrupt Practices Act made effective internal accounting controls a legal requirement for SEC registrants, and the SEC, in a report to Congress in July 1978, stated that

[6]The Commission on Auditors' Responsibilities, *Report, Conclusions, and Recommendations* (New York, 1978), pp. 39–40.

it is likely to require "a representation that an issuer's system of internal accounting controls is in compliance with the provisions of the Act."[7]

The auditing profession has taken steps to prepare to provide comprehensive reviews. An AICPA committee is studying the issues underlying public reporting on internal controls, and the AICPA has also set up an advisory committee to develop objective criteria for evaluating the quality of internal accounting controls. Its report was issued in April 1979.[8]

The report provides useful guidance, but does not provide definitive criteria for evaluating internal accounting controls. It concludes that the committee's work is the "first step in what should be an ongoing effort by companies, public accounting firms, academics, and professional organizations to study internal accounting control requirements."[9]

This conclusion indicates how difficult is the task of formulating uniform evaluative criteria applicable to the varied systems of internal accounting controls businesses have built up over the years. It also indicates the extent to which comprehensive reviews differ from auditors' evaluations of internal accounting controls for auditing purposes. During examination of financial statements auditors evaluate controls solely for purposes of determining the nature, extent, and timing of other audit tests. They test only those controls on which they intend to rely in order to restrict other audit tests. Comprehensive reviews will have a far wider scope because they are intended to provide the basis for an overall judgment on the quality of the control system.

Comprehensive reviews will undoubtedly affect auditors' fraud detection. The reviews will deepen and broaden auditors' knowledge of client operations and increase contacts with client personnel. In many instances the reviews will result in improvements in control procedures. These consequences can affect the incidence of management fraud and are therefore an important research area. Certainly the impact of comprehensive reviews should be assessed in order to understand whether providing them as a regular service would render additional measures to detect management fraud unnecessary. In short, no program for improving auditors' capabilities to detect management fraud can ignore the potential impact of regular comprehensive reviews of internal accounting controls.

---

[7]*Securities and Exchange Commission Report to Congress on the Accounting Profession and the Commission's Oversight Role,* U.S. Government Printing Office (Washington, D.C., 1978). p. 44. As this book was going to press, the SEC proposed rules (Release No. 34-15772, April 30, 1979) that would require management to include in annual reports a statement on internal accounting control and would also require that the statement be examined and reported on by an independent auditor.

[8]*Report of the Special Advisory Committee on Internal Accounting Control,* AICPA (New York, 1978).

[9]*Report of the Special Advisory Committee,* p. 27.

The Effect of Strengthened Controls.   Effective internal accounting controls reduce the probability of errors and irregularities. For instance, effective systems separate duties which would facilitate misappropriations if combined. Individuals with custodial responsibilities for assets do not have the responsibility for maintaining records of their existence. This prevents those with custodial responsibilities from appropriating the assets and concealing the event by altering the records. Periodic comparisons of the recorded amounts with the amounts actually in custody will reveal whether the two agree. If they do not, it may indicate that assets have been misappropriated or that the records are in error. Following up such variances can reveal employee defalcations. Comprehensive reviews of internal accounting controls should improve their effectiveness because auditors would note weaknesses and suggest improvements. These improvements would reduce the likelihood of employee frauds. The influence of any such reduction on the incidence of management fraud is a research question.

Increased Familiarity with Clients' Operations.   Because regular comprehensive reviews would deepen and broaden the auditor's knowledge of clients' businesses, the reviews could contribute to the auditor's capacity to notice unusual elements in client operations and facilitate the apprehension of red flags. Contact with client personnel would increase, making more obvious departures from customary behavior patterns during an audit. As already pointed out, the Cohen Commission found that the rate of audit failure on first- and second-year audits indicates that audit risks are reduced when auditors have a greater period of acquaintance with clients' operations. This suggests that a deeper involvement in the financial reporting process, which would occur if auditors performed regular comprehensive reviews of internal controls, might reduce audit risks, including the risk that management fraud is undetected.

Controls over Top Management.   A few members of management in every organization are generally outside the scope of ordinary, day-to-day internal accounting control systems. They can direct personnel to violate control procedures because the procedures themselves are prescribed by top management's authority. However, some companies do have controls over top management. For example, public companies have boards of directors that oversee management performance. These bodies may function in part as controls over management. If compliance with the Foreign Corrupt Practices Act is interpreted to include effective controls over top management and leads to the development of such controls, it could have a direct effect on the incidence of management fraud.[10] Moreover, auditors' comprehensive reviews of internal accounting controls might be extended to controls over top

---

[10]Top-management controls are discussed in the next chapter.

management. These developments may lead to more effective top-management controls and thereby reduce the incidence of management fraud.

The AICPA's special advisory committee on internal accounting control did not, in its April report, identify controls over top management as specific internal accounting controls. It treated the relationship of boards and managements as part of the question of the control environment. The control environment, the committee acknowledged, can have a significant impact on the effectiveness of a company's control procedures and therefore should be assessed as a preliminary to evaluating the specific controls in the system. But controls over management were not addressed specifically.[11]

The Effect of Comprehensive Reviews on Auditor's Responsibilities.

Required public reporting on comprehensive reviews could affect both the public's view of the auditor's obligation to detect fraud and the professional obligation itself. A requirement to express an opinion on the quality of a company's internal accounting controls could create erroneous impressions of the auditor's responsibility to detect fraud. The public, for instance, could assume that a "clean" opinion on the controls is a guarantee that there are no slush funds, material unrecorded transactions, or improperly recorded transactions, that auditors, by satisfying themselves as to the quality of the system of accounting controls, are satisfied that no frauds perpetrated partly through improper recordkeeping have occurred. In short, there may be an inadequate appreciation of the inherent limitations of systems of internal controls. No control system can provide more than reasonable assurance that an objective is met. For example, controls based on segregation of duties may be rendered ineffectual by collusion, sound recordkeeping practices may be subverted by forgery, and management may override the system.

Because auditors do not perform regular comprehensive reviews of internal controls, the relationship between such reviews and auditors' responsibilities for fraud detection remains to be clarified. For example, would a "clean" opinion on the design and functioning of a system of internal accounting controls provide users with any assurance that frauds concealed through improper recordkeeping are less likely to have occurred? What would be the auditor's responsibility during a review if evidence is discovered of a violation of control procedures that raises questions with respect to possible fraud? If the review is part of the audit, the auditor's responsibility would presumably be governed by Statement on Auditing Standards No. 16, "The Independent Auditor's Responsibility for the Detection of Errors or Irregularities."[12] If the comprehensive review of internal accounting controls is separate from the audit of the financial statements, would the auditor

---

[11]*Report of the Special Advisory Committee,* pp. 12–15.

[12]The Cohen Commission's recommendation does not separate the review from the audit, but binds them together in the concept of the "audit function," a concept that treats the financial statements as one of the elements of the financial reporting process being audited. *Report,* p. 60.

be obligated to pursue the evidence of potential fraud during the review or to pursue the matter when performing the audit of the financial statements? This problem may be illustrated by the situation in the *Hochfelder* case. The plaintiff alleged that the accountants should be held liable under Section 10(b) of the 1934 Act for negligently failing to discover an internal control weakness which hid a major fraud. The fraud took place in a small brokerage firm, First Securities Company of Chicago. The president of the company induced certain customers to invest funds in what were supposed to be "escrow" accounts yielding high rates of return. The funds were appropriated for his personal use. The internal control weakness that hid the scheme was the so-called mail rule. Mail addressed to the perpetrator or marked for his attention was to be opened solely by him. The correspondence included checks for the spurious escrow accounts. The whole scheme was uncovered when the perpetrator committed suicide.[13] Given these facts and supposing that the auditors were conducting regular comprehensive reviews, what would be their responsibility to detect the fraud during the review or the subsequent audit? Such questions suggest a need for research on the implications of comprehensive reviews of internal controls for auditors' responsibilities for fraud detection.

Summary

This chapter has described several approaches to fraud detection not now employed by auditors—using data on corporate recidivism, psychological tests administered to management to identify fraud-prone individuals, systematic inquiries of employees, and using operational auditing techniques. The chapter also discussed deterring management fraud by disclosures of material audit adjustments and the prospects for improved detection that may result from extending the auditor's study and evaluation of internal accounting controls. The purpose of citing these techniques has not been to recommend their use but to recommend their consideration in improving detection and deterrence.

[13]Denzil Y. Causey, Jr., *Duties and Liabilities of the CPA* (Austin, Texas: Bureau of Business Research, The University of Texas at Austin, 1976), pp. 365–66, 382–83.

5

Top-Management Controls

This chapter discusses top-management controls relevant to the detection and deterrence of management fraud, a subject that has not received much attention. Management traditionally has been considered outside the system of internal accounting controls. This view has been undergoing change, chiefly because of the ongoing reevaluation of the role of boards of directors in monitoring management. However, there has been relatively little direct focus on the role of top-management controls in preventing management fraud.[1]

Boards of Directors

Boards of directors have legal powers to govern the corporation as elected representatives of the shareholders. However, functional decision-making and the day-to-day conduct of business affairs in widely held businesses are typically delegated to management. The delegation of authority to management is so common that the American Bar Association in 1975 changed its Model Business Corporation Act to state that corporations are "managed under the direction of" boards rather than "managed by" them.

---

[1]For an exception to this statement, see Donald W. Baker, Michael J. Barrett, and Leon R. Radde, "Top Management Fraud: Something Can Be Done Now!" *The Internal Auditor* (October 1976): 25–33.

Moreover, the ABA's *Corporate Director's Guidebook* notes, "Even under statutes providing that the business and affairs shall be 'managed' by the board of directors, it is recognized that actual operation is a function of management."[2]

Although boards have historically had ample legal authority to function as a control on management, they have not always done so. In 1971, Myles L. Mace published a study demonstrating that boards' participation in guiding widely held corporations was minimal. Boards, he found, generally did not ask discerning questions, did not select the chief executive officer except in crisis situations, and did not establish basic objectives, corporate strategies, or broad policies. Directors were generally selected by the chief executive officer. Boards sometimes asked the chief executive officer to resign for unsatisfactory performance, but Mace concluded that "generally boards of directors do not do an effective job of evaluating or measuring . . . performance." The usual test was corporate profitability, and Mace remarked, "it is surprising how slow some directors are to respond to years of steadily declining profitability."[3]

Since Mace's study, a great deal of attention has been focused on boards' responsibilities, their liability, and their role in monitoring management. Boards' responsibilities and functions are in a period of evolution, and Mace's findings may not be applicable today. Effective ways for boards to act as a management control, however, are not now explicitly understood. Moreover, functioning as an accountability control can interfere with a board's other responsibilities, such as providing advice to the chief executive officer and determining broad objectives for the company. The Business Roundtable has pointed out that the board's relationship to the chief executive officer should be "challenging yet supportive and positive. It should be arm's length but not adversary."[4] There can be a fine line between these alternatives, and too aggressive a pursuit of the function as an accountability control can lead to an adversary relationship.

Several conditions are essential for boards to function consistently as effective controls over top management. First, boards must have significant outside representation, that is, a significant proportion of their members must be independent of management. Board members who are also members of management or who are financially dependent on management's decisions cannot be expected to function so consistently as a control as those who are not. It may be necessary to have the nominating committee

[2]"Corporate Director's Guidebook," *The Business Lawyer,* vol. 33, no. 3 (April 1978): p. 1603.

[3]Myles L. Mace, *Directors: Myth and Reality* (Boston: Harvard Business School, 1971), pp. 182–83.

[4]*The Role and Composition of the Board of Directors of the Large Publicly Owned Corporation,* The Business Roundtable (New York, 1978), p. 22.

composed of independent members in order to assure that nominated outsiders are independent of management in spirit as well as in their financial relationships.[5]

Many companies already have boards with majority representation by outside directors. A survey of 248 large United States companies by The Conference Board showed that as of 1976, 66% of the companies had outsider majorities. The definition of an outsider or independent director varies. The 66% figure in The Conference Board survey was derived by defining current and former employees as insiders. When former employees were considered outsiders, the percentage of boards with outsider majorities was 84%.[6]

In addition to significant outside representation, boards that are to serve as effective management controls must have access to adequate information, devote adequate time, and maintain an active, inquiring interest in corporate compliance with laws and regulations. It is not clear exactly how these generalized prerequisites should be translated into specific policies by directors, and the appropriate policies may vary from company to company. The size and complexity of company operations, for instance, undoubtedly affect the amount of information a director needs and the amount of time a director should spend on board business.[7] The best resource for making such determinations is the experience of independent directors.

This is a good argument for seminar-type training, perhaps at business schools or an institute, where new and experienced directors could exchange ideas. The seminars would provide new directors with a basis for making practical decisions about fulfilling board responsibilities, such as whether, and under what conditions, a staff is needed to serve directors, whether it is necessary to visit the sites of multilocation businesses, and what types of corporate documents should be read regularly.

At such seminars, independent directors could also discuss appropriate responses to specific situations they might encounter as board members, or may already have encountered, and the ethical issues underlying service as a director. These subjects might include what a director should do when there is reason to believe a chief executive officer is withholding information or if questionable payments come to light, how many directorships it is reasonable to hold, how one goes about formulating or evaluating a corporate code of conduct, whether independence is compromised by a deep

[5]"Significant outside representation" does not mean the board should be composed exclusively of outside directors or nearly so. Such a practice would deprive the board of membership familiar with the business and sensitive to current operating conditions.

[6]Jeremy Bacon and James K. Brown, *The Board of Directors: Perspectives and Practices in Nine Countries,* The Conference Board (New York, 1977), pp. 84–85.

[7]The Conference Board study cited above found that boards of larger companies met more often than those of smaller companies, Ibid., p. 85.

involvement in operating decisions, and the relationship between the interests of shareholders and the public. By clarifying such issues the training would prepare the directors to make a greater contribution to the attitudes pervading the enterprise and to monitor effectively the behavior of corporate management.

The appropriate amount of time a director should spend on board business is critical because it affects the way in which other responsibilities are discharged. One solution to this problem is a "professional director," an individual whose full-time job is to be a director of various publicly held corporations. Joseph W. Barr, former Secretary of the Treasury, has advocated this concept. Having at least one director who could spend additional time on board business would provide some assurance that time constraints do not damage the performance of the board. Barr requested comments on his proposal from 200 persons in industry, finance, and government; 160 responded, and their replies contained objections and concerns. The concerns included fears that the professional directors would get too deeply involved in day-to-day operations, that they would want staffs and thereby create discord in the company, and that the additional compensation might injure the directors' independence. The concept is clearly controversial, but is worthy of further analysis.[8]

Audit Committees. Audit committees are standing committees of boards of directors. They can enhance the board's capacity to act as a management control by providing it with more detailed knowledge and a fuller understanding of the financial statements and other financial information issued by the company. Effective audit committees review significant financial information, oversee the internal and external audit functions, ascertain that the company has an effective internal accounting control system, and serve as a communication link between the external auditors and the board of directors. It is usually more efficient to delegate these tasks to a smaller group than to undertake them as a full board, and boards operate under time constraints. Audit committees, therefore, often contribute to a board's effectiveness by serving as a time-saving device.

In recent years there has been growing recognition of the usefulness of audit committees composed of independent directors. In June 1978, independent audit committees became a requirement for listing on the New York Stock Exchange. The SEC and the AICPA have long stressed the desirability of independent audit committees. Joseph W. Barr's survey of attitudes toward professional directors revealed that despite objections to the concept, there was almost unanimous agreement among the 160 respondents that the

---

[8]Joseph W. Barr, "The Role of the Professional Director," *Harvard Business Review* (May–June 1976): 18–24.

audit committee was the appropriate vehicle for the work of a professional director.[9]

Independent audit committees can provide assurance that external auditors are not intimidated by implied or actual threats by managements to change auditors. If, as often is the case, the committees are responsible to recommend to the full board, and in turn the shareholders, the auditing firm to be engaged, they can insulate the auditor from such threats. This responsibility presumes that the audit committee has adequate knowledge of the performance of the external auditors as a result of actively overseeing the audit function.

The more active the audit committee is in overseeing the financial reporting process and the internal and external audit functions, the better the information flow it can provide to the full board. The oversight activity may be enhanced by a specific policy to review all audit adjustments, changes in accounting principles, and recommendations made by independent accountants for improving the company's internal accounting controls. The oversight activity may also be enhanced by personal contact with members of the staff that prepares financial data and with the internal auditors. Such contacts can make the committee more accessible to corporate personnel who wish to report information about alleged corporate impropriety because they have been thwarted at lower levels.

Audit committees may receive information about possible management fraud from independent auditors or internal auditors. The disposition of such matters may be decided by the full board. However, the audit committee may itself direct an investigation. Independent audit committees conducted a number of the special investigations into the extent of corporate improper payments which were disclosed in the past few years.[10] The SEC, in a release proposing disclosures to enhance corporate accountability, held that directing "investigations into matters within the scope of its duties" was a "customary" function of audit committees. Public commentary on the release challenged the notion that the duty was customary, and the language was dropped from the final rules on disclosures of the functions of audit committees.[11] However, the investigatory function would be a strong top-management control. Audit committees wishing to enhance their capacity to function as a top-management control might consider adopting an explicit policy on investigations.

---

[9]Ibid., p. 24.

[10]*An Examination of Questionable Payments and Practices,* Charles E. Simon and Company (Washington, D.C., 1978), Vol. 1, pp. 90–95. The study was restricted to 109 corporations.

[11]SEC Release No. 34-14970, July 18, 1978; SEC Release No. 34-15384, December 6, 1978.

Codes of Conduct.   Corporate codes of conduct may help create an atmosphere that discourages business improprieties. They can impress upon corporate personnel the commitment of senior management and the board to see that business is conducted ethically and lawfully. The codes could make explicit the types of acts prohibited by company policy and spell out procedures to follow when violations are discovered. However, the potential effect of codes on the likelihood of management misrepresentations in the financial statements is less clear. For instance, would an explicit policy, enunciated in the code, against management override of internal controls make potential perpetrators less likely to use this device to misrepresent financial data? Would it make corporate personnel ordered by management to override control procedures more likely to bring the matter to internal auditors or the audit committee? Research may provide answers to these questions.

Corporate codes are desirable for their deterrent effect on improprieties that managements and boards refuse to tolerate. They can be justified without reference to their contribution to deterring fraudulent financial statements. However, if codes have little effect on top management when it is bent on perpetrating management fraud, that finding would be important in considering the steps necessary to provide assurance that management fraud is in fact deterred.

Authorization Policies.   Boards serve as a management control when their authorization is required for the execution of a transaction. In formulating authorization policies, boards must determine the dollar amount of the transactions they wish to approve on a regular basis. The dollar threshold may vary according to the types of transactions. For instance, related-party transactions that are infrequent and nonrecurring and involve top management might receive attention even if they are smaller in dollar amount than certain fixed-asset expenditures which are not subject to review. Potentially sensitive disbursements, such as payments to foreign sales agents, may also be subject to review at a lesser dollar amount than other transactions.

Board authorization policies will vary from company to company. It is not realistic to have boards review any great volume of transactions, and it is not desirable from the point of view of corporate efficiency. However, boards that wish to increase their function as a management control may find it advisable to adopt explicit or extended authorization policies.

Officers Directly Responsible for Preparing the Financial Statements

Corporate officers who are directly responsible for the preparation of the financial statements obviously play a key role in management frauds. But that role is not sufficiently understood. For instance, it is not known what proportion are perpetrators, what proportion are conscripted into the conspiracy by pressures from superiors, and what proportion are fooled by false documentation.

Research on this question could be useful for developing additional controls to deter management fraud. For instance, if pressure from superiors is a major problem, perhaps the preparer-officer should be responsible to the audit committee. This would insulate the officer from pressures by perpetrators and could have the desirable side effect of enhancing the effectiveness of the committee. The preparer-officer's objectivity may also be enhanced by other measures. Compensation might be based primarily on producing good records and reports and have no direct connection to company performance. Stock options, for instance, and bonuses related to company performance might be prohibited.

These proposals are controversial because preparer-officers have day-to-day operating responsibilities and must work closely with other members of the management team. Establishing reporting lines that violate the hierarchy of corporate authority or compensation systems unique to certain members of the management team may interfere with the harmony of the team. The proposals, however, illustrate possibilities that research may substantiate as cost-effective, feasible recommendations. In any case, research on the role preparer-officers have played in previous management frauds could considerably enhance our understanding of the mechanics underlying management misrepresentations in financial statements.

Internal Audit Departments

Internal auditing is an appraisal function established within an organization to examine and evaluate its activities as a service to the organization. Internal auditors review and evaluate accounting, financial, and operating controls; compliance with established policies and plans; and the reliability of internal financial data. Reports on these activities enable the organization to take remedial action when deficiencies are noted or improvements recommended. In these ways the internal auditing department functions as a control.[12]

Many people see the relationship between the internal audit department and an independent audit committee as the key to internal auditors' effectiveness as a top-management control. By providing reports on their findings to the audit committee, the internal audit group increases the information flow essential to the board's function as a top-management control. Through such reports the committee can keep abreast of problems identified by internal

---

[12]The material in this paragraph is based on the *Statement of Responsibilities of the Internal Auditor,* Institute of Internal Auditors, 1971.

auditors, and, if follow-up work is done on management's remedial actions, the board can be informed of management's response to the problems. The reports would constitute a top-management control, particularly if the scope of the internal audit activities included auditing top management.

The scope of internal auditing activities depends largely on the internal auditors' independence within the organization, which is itself dependent on the individual to whom the director of the department is administratively responsible. Internal auditors, as full-time employees, can never be independent in the same sense that external auditors are independent. The Institute of Internal Auditors uses the phrase "independent of the activities they audit" to describe the desired relationship.[13] If the director of internal auditing is administratively responsible to a member of top management, he or she is not independent of that member.

Harold M. Williams, chairman of the SEC, has argued that the director of internal auditing should be responsible to an executive at a level high enough "to minimize the risk of pressure to prevent issuance of even the most critical report" and "to ensure that reports are accorded appropriate attention by those in a position to take action on . . . recommendations."[14] Williams held that the appropriate top executive is rarely the chief financial officer (usually the vice-president of finance) or the chief accounting officer (usually the controller), presumably because these officers play key roles in the financial reporting process.

One alternative is to have the director of internal auditing administratively responsible to the chairman of the audit committee. Victor Z. Brink, interim executive vice-president of the Institute of Internal Auditors and a noted scholar of internal auditing, has examined the potential consequences of this alternative. He found that the internal auditor's role would more closely approximate that of the external auditor. Internal auditors would do far less operational auditing, which might become the province of a newly created in-house audit group. Brink also foresaw possible conflicts between the work of internal auditors and the operating organization because internal auditors, to a considerable extent, would be checking on corporate management for the audit committee.[15]

The practicability of this alternative may also be questioned because the audit committee chairman may not be able to devote the time necessary to supervise the director of internal auditing. Finally, it may be argued that since management is responsible for the company's financial representations, and

---

[13]The Institute of Internal Auditors, *Standards for the Professional Practice of Internal Auditing* (Altamonte Springs, Florida, 1978), par. 100.01.

[14]Harold M. Williams, "The Emerging Responsibility of the Internal Auditor," *The Internal Auditor* (October 1978): p. 48.

[15]Victor Z. Brink, "Internal Auditing: A Historical Perspective and Future Directions," *The Internal Auditor* (December 1978): 30–31.

for deterring fraud within the company, it should have full sway over the internal accounting control systems, including the internal audit function—in other words, that management needs the internal auditing arm to fulfill its responsibilities.

The consequences of having the director of internal auditing report directly to the audit committee may be explored by empirical research because some companies have adopted the practice. The examples are primarily in banking and insurance[16] and may not be typical of companies in other industries, but the research would still be useful.

The argument over whether the director of internal auditing should be administratively responsible to the audit committee or to top management is likely to be resolved in terms of degrees of responsibility to each of these bodies, rather than exclusive responsibility to either. The Institute of Internal Auditors, in a set of standards issued in June 1978, held that internal auditors should serve both management and the board of directors. The document does not specify whether the director of internal auditing should be directly responsible to the board or to management. Rather, it states that the director should be responsible to an individual with sufficient authority to ensure broad audit coverage, adequate consideration of audit reports, and appropriate action on audit recommendations. However, the document also maintains that the director of internal auditing should have "direct communication" with the board of directors and that annual reports highlighting significant audit findings and recommendations should be sent to "management and the board." With respect to information on fraud and other improprieties, the internal auditor is told to inform "appropriate authorities within the organization."[17]

This definition of responsibilities is compatible with a direct reporting relationship to either top management or the board. It is also consistent with the current evolution of many business organizations, which now provide directors of internal auditing that are administratively responsible to management with a defined reporting relationship to the audit committee. For instance, the audit committee in its oversight capacity may be responsible to review the planned scope of internal audit work, the budgetary adequacy of the internal audit function, or the results of internal audits already performed, and in such instances the head of internal auditing would have a reporting relationship with the audit committee sufficient for it to perform the defined responsibilities.

This evolution suggests that for most companies the head of internal auditing will continue to be responsible to management and that the reporting relationship to the audit committee or board will develop as an additional

[16]Ibid., p. 26.
[17]*Standards,* p. 1 and pars. 110.01, 280.03.

responsibility. It therefore may be useful to study the most effective combinations of responsibilities for the internal audit function, the best balance between reporting responsibilities to top management and to the audit committee or board.

Harold Williams has said that continued responsibilities to management are inevitable. Direct communication with the board, he argued, is essential for independence, but the "realities of corporate operations . . . also dictate that the internal auditor serve management in fulfilling its particular responsibilities." "The finesse and skill with which this dual role is filled," he concluded, "will be an important determinant of the effectiveness of the internal audit staff."[18] Studies on the advantages and potential pitfalls of the dual role would augment the finesse and skill internal auditors bring to bear on this question.

Enhancing the Effectiveness of Internal Auditing

The effectiveness of internal auditing as an instrument to detect and deter management fraud can be enhanced by hastening its development as a profession. Many companies have internal audit departments staffed by highly qualified personnel, but they achieve this chiefly through their own stringent standards of hiring and administration, because there are no uniform requirements applicable to internal auditors or internal auditing departments. Since 1974, the Institute of Internal Auditors (IIA) has held examinations for certification. However, the Institute's certificate is not a requirement for employment as an internal auditor. Internal auditing departments vary significantly from company to company, and smaller companies often cannot afford a separate or elaborate internal audit function.

The IIA has research and continuing education programs to enhance the professionalism and effectiveness of internal auditors. Its publication in 1978 of *Standards for the Professional Practice of Internal Auditing* was a milestone in the developing professionalism of internal auditors. The document also defines obligations for detection of fraud and other illegalities. The guidance on professional care holds that internal auditors "should be alert to the possibility of intentional wrongdoing" and "should also be alert to those conditions and activities where irregularities are most likely to occur." The standard on scope of work defines as one of the internal auditor's tasks determining whether management's systems are adequate for ensuring compliance with laws and regulations that could have a significant impact on operations and reports and "whether the activities audited are complying with the appropriate requirements."[19]

[18]"Emerging Responsibility," p. 48.
[19]*Standards,* pars. 280.01, 320.01.

The IIA urges organizations that have an internal audit function or are planning to establish one to adopt and support the Standards.[20] Widespread adoption of the Standards would be a major advance in enhancing the professionalism of internal auditors.

Summary

Several of the proposals discussed in this chapter are controversial. Changing corporate organization structures can interfere with corporate efficiency and do a disservice to shareholders. On the other hand, the study of corporate controls over top management may open new options to corporations that wish to develop controls to ensure that management fraud is a less likely event in the future of their companies.

[20]*Standards,* pp. i–ii.

6

The Computer
and Management Fraud

I t is safe to say that far more public attention has been devoted to losses
of corporate and government assets through computer abuses than to the
potential effect of electronic data processing (EDP) technology on management misrepresentations in financial statements. The emphasis may be well
placed. Enough computer-related embezzlements have been documented to
justify the concern.[1] However, as EDP comes to play a more and more
important role in the financial reporting process, the need to understand its
potential consequences for management fraud rises.

Disguised Embezzlements

EDP can simplify the mechanics of embezzlement, thereby permitting
larger sums to be misappropriated and concealed. Managers who in this way
misappropriate sums material to the financial statements would naturally
attempt to disguise the embezzlement in the financial statements, thus render-
ing them misleading. Moreover, if the sum embezzled by an employee
through computer abuse is material to the financial statements and management learns that the embezzlement has occurred, they may be tempted to
disguise it in the financial statements. In these ways, the growth of EDP

[1]See Brandt Allen's, "The Biggest Computer Frauds: Lessons for CPAs," *Journal of Accountancy* (May 1977): 52–62. Allen analyzed 150 major cases.

systems may affect the incidence of management frauds.

A bank embezzlement of $1.4 million illustrates how EDP can facilitate the embezzlement of considerable sums. Each time the chief teller appropriated cash, he used his supervisory computer terminal to reduce by the same amount the deposit recorded in a relatively inactive account. The bank's assets then corresponded to its recorded assets. To prevent customers from discovering that their accounts had been depleted when they came to have interest entered in their passbooks, the teller took advantage of the difference between the date interest was received on day-of-deposit accounts, the last day of the quarter, and the date interest was received on time deposit accounts, two days after the last day of the quarter. Money was shifted into accounts of one type in order to receive interest in the amount the customer expected and then shifted from these accounts back to those receiving interest two days later. Donn Parker quotes the embezzler as saying, "The computer didn't make it easier to steal but it sure did make it faster."[2]

Parker speculates that as computers become more and more dominant in processing financial data, losses per incident of computer abuse will rise. He cites a bank embezzlement study that showed losses associated with computers were ten times larger than general bank embezzlement losses.[3] If this projected trend becomes a reality, disguised embezzlements could become a more common source of materially misleading financial statements.

Effective Detection of Management Fraud in EDP Environments

Auditors' detection of management fraud depends largely on inferences from evidence examined during the audit. EDP environments can affect the type and amount of evidence examined. The documentation available in EDP systems, for instance, may differ considerably from what is customarily available in manual systems. In this way EDP environments can affect the auditor's capacity to detect management fraud.

Evaluating EDP Controls. If auditors are to detect management fraud in EDP environments with the same frequency that they do in manual accounting environments, they must evaluate EDP accounting controls effectively. The auditor's evaluation of internal accounting controls relevant to specific accounts usually determines the amount of audit evidence that is examined. Fewer transactions need be tested if controls are strong than if controls are weak. Although the objectives and basic characteristics of ac-

---

[2]Donn B. Parker, *Crime by Computer* (New York: Scribner, 1976), p. 194. The case is described in chapter 16, pp. 192–203. The embezzler also used other methods to conceal his theft.

[3]Ibid., pp. 293–96.

counting controls are the same in both EDP and manual systems, the organization and procedures in each may differ.

EDP systems often consolidate several functions that would normally be segregated in manual systems. Besides the fact that the decrease in human involvement in processing transactions can obscure errors that might be observed in a manual system, EDP systems tend to combine incompatible functions. For instance, a data entry clerk may be responsible to process both invoice and payments documents, thereby facilitating a payment to a fictitious vendor. In order to reduce the likelihood that the combined functions permit errors or irregularities to occur, compensating controls must be introduced, such as independent document counts and controls over access to EDP equipment and computer files.

Most of the material in the two previous paragraphs is based on the introduction to an AICPA audit guide that provides guidance on how to study and evaluate internal controls in EDP systems. However, the same volume points out that "as EDP technology continues to expand and develop, the auditors can expect to encounter systems features not described in this guide."[4] In other words, the problem is to assure that the auditing profession's EDP auditing capabilities keep pace with the growing sophistication of EDP systems.

The Prospect of Diminished Source Documentation.   Computers are designed to reduce paper work and as systems become more sophisticated, they eliminate more and more of the backup paper documentation which can facilitate controls and audit testing. Source documentation may increasingly be eliminated by the expanded use of real-time systems for accounting. Unlike batch-operated systems, which process information when it is input from batches of source documents (e.g., sales invoices), real-time systems allow the operator to input data directly into the processing unit by a keyboard and have it processed without delay. In many situations there need be no source document.

Another potential difficulty is the trend toward larger, more integrated data bases, accessible from a multiplicity of terminals. Instead of maintaining separate files of data, they will more and more be consolidated, and the processing applications (e.g., sales ordering, inventory controls, accounts payable, accounts receivable) will be integrated. The integration of files and applications, together with continuous processing of transactions and limited generation of source documents, creates difficulties for auditors in evaluating the ramifications of a particular transaction. It becomes more difficult to trace balances back to underlying transactions and underlying transactions forward

---

[4] *The Auditor's Study and Evaluation of Internal Control in EDP Systems* (New York, 1977), p. 3.

to balances. These developments present problems both for evaluating controls and collecting suitable audit evidence.

Ensuring Auditability

EDP systems are auditable if their controls are designed to include audit trails. Audit trails are the links that enable records of transactions to be traced back to source records or documents. In many companies internal auditors routinely review all new EDP systems to make sure that they are auditable and properly controlled. Additional assurance that EDP systems are auditable is also often provided by reviews by independent auditors.

Computer vendors have taken important steps to ensure the auditability of their products. Some now build in a computer audit software capability. Burroughs, for instance, has developed the audit software package called *Audit Reporter,* and IBM has published *Auditability and Product Information Catalog,* which identifies IBM programs that can aid in auditing IBM data processing systems.

Evaluating the Present and the Near Future

It is possible to build controls into computers, to ensure that they provide audit trails, to install effective security measures, to segregate computer related duties or to introduce compensating controls for consolidated, incompatible functions, and to train an adequate number of external and internal auditors in the nuances and methods of EDP auditing. Taken together these measures would reduce the opportunities for computer fraud, increase the likelihood that those perpetrated are detected, and ensure that EDP systems are audited effectively. What is necessary is to determine the appropriate allocation of resources by auditing firms, managements and internal auditors, the AICPA, and the Institute of Internal Auditors. However, this determination is complicated by the rapid pace of technological change. It is not now clear what are the dimensions of any time lag between the advance of computer technology and the progress of control and auditing capabilities. Resolving this uncertainty would simplify the problem of determining the appropriate allocation of resources.

The uncertainty reflects varying assessments of both the new problems presented by the progress of computer technology and the responsive measures taken to date by the internal and external auditing professions. In recent years the American Institute of Certified Public Accountants has issued in a variety of documents guidance and standards to ensure that EDP Systems are audited effectively. These include Statement on Auditing Standards No. 3, "The Effects of EDP on the Auditor's Study and Evaluation of Internal Control" (1974), and the related Audit Guide *The Auditor's Study and Evalua-*

tion of Internal Control in EDP Systems (1977). *Controls Over Using and Changing Computer Programs,* an addition to the Computer Services Guideline series, was issued in 1979. This series, which includes *Management, Control and Audit of Advanced EDP Systems* (1976), is issued for the use of all interested parties, and is not devoted exclusively to the needs of independent auditors. Because unique auditing problems are presented by the accounting data processed by EDP firms for the many companies that cannot justify renting or owning a computer for their sole use, the AICPA issued the Audit Guide *Audits of Service-Center-Produced Records* in 1974.

The auditing profession has made notable advances in using computer audit software programs to audit in EDP environments. Such programs, for example, assist auditors to select exceptional transactions and accounts for examination, compare data for correctness and consistency, perform arithmetic and clerical functions, test control policies, prepare confirmations, and select and evaluate statistical samples of transactions or balances. The AICPA, which has issued an Audit and Accounting Guide on *Computer Assisted Audit Techniques,* maintains a time-sharing library of computer programs for use by CPA firms. In addition, individual auditing firms have developed their own software programs.

The Institute of Internal Auditors first issued a manual on the audit and control of computer systems in 1968. That work, *Internal Auditing of EDP Systems,* was supplanted in 1976 by *Computer Control and Audit.* The three-volume work *Systems Auditability and Control* was published by the IIA in 1977. The research was funded by IBM and performed by the Stanford Research Institute (SRI). The objective was to produce a compendium of proven EDP controls and EDP auditing techniques. As a public service, the IIA distributed 4,000 sets of the report to the chief executive officers of its members' organizations.

The initiatives noted above, and others that might be adduced, show that the external and internal auditing professions have been active in responding to the challenge posed by the development and proliferation of advanced EDP systems. But the citations say nothing about whether the response has been adequate or what is necessary in the near future. A clearer assessment of these issues could help assure that the time lag between the evolution of computer technology and the development of EDP audit and control capabilities is sufficiently narrow to maintain the level of deterrence and detection of computer fraud that society needs.

The Role of EDP Specialists

The progress of computer technology and the increasing importance of EDP systems to the financial reporting process may make EDP specialists key figures in future management frauds. Duping them or obtaining their knowing cooperation may be necessary to alter EDP data files or otherwise distort evidence underlying certain types of financial statement misrepresentations. Further study would therefore be useful of the role EDP specialists might play in the mechanics of management frauds when advanced EDP systems are employed in the financial reporting process.

If such study indicates that EDP specialists may play key roles in future management frauds, it will highlight the need for increasing the professionalism of computer scientists. The computer science field is quite young, and to date very little has been done to advance professional concepts of ethics in the field. Parker reports that a questionnaire he administered to 36 programmers and 18 managers of programmers showed considerable disagreement about what constitutes accepted legal and ethical practices.[5] There are no state requirements for licensing EDP specialists and no professional organizations with the power to discipline members. A clear sense of professionalism, of defined responsibilities in a field where one's behavior can greatly influence others, could contribute to the controls in EDP environments.

Legal Deterrents to Computer Fraud

There are now insufficient penalties for computer-related fraud because the language in current law does not apply precisely to computer technology. Senator Abraham Ribicoff, who introduced a bill to remedy this situation, described in his introductory speech two instances where current laws were inadequate. In one, the government lost a case because it could not establish that checks issued by a computer on the basis of fraudulent or manipulated data were forgeries. In another, part of an indictment was dismissed because electromagnetic impulses were determined not to be "property" as defined by the Interstate Transportation of Stolen Property Statute.[6]

The Ribicoff bill (S.1766), which was introduced in June 1977, would apply to all computers used for purposes of interstate commerce. It would make virtually all computer abuses, including frauds, punishable by up to 15 years in prison, a fine up to $50,000, or both. Hearings on the bill were held in the Senate Subcommittee on Criminal Laws and Procedures, but the bill died with the adjournment of the 95th Congress. If legislation along the lines of the Ribicoff bill is enacted, it would add to the deterrents against computer fraud.

---

[5]*Crime by Computer*, pp. 53–56. The questionnaire was administered in 1973.
[6]*Congressional Record*, June 27, 1977, S10790.

Summary

As sophisticated EDP environments become more common, they will affect the type and amount of evidence available to support business transactions. EDP environments may facilitate material embezzlements and change the techniques by which perpetrators try to mislead auditors. EDP specialists may become key figures in future management frauds. These possibilities suggest a need for further study of the impact of current and future EDP developments on the incidence of management fraud and the methods of perpetrating it.

7

Other Forces Against Management Fraud

The text has thus far focused primarily on external and internal auditors, boards of directors, and managements. These groups are not, however, society's only safeguards against management fraud. Their effectiveness in combatting management fraud is limited and augmented by other factors, such as the ethical climate in our society and the willingness of corporate personnel to report evidence of potential management fraud. Governmental oversight, regulatory, and enforcement activities contribute to the detection and deterrence of management fraud, and the role of the legal profession in the system of corporate accountability is now being reevaluated. These factors, which are described briefly in this chapter, also affect the incidence of management fraud.

The Role of the Legal Profession

The role of corporate counsel in the system of corporate accountability has received increasing attention in recent years. The Cohen Commission, for instance, wrote, "If society needs assurance on matters that are principally legal—the conformity of corporate actions with laws and regulations or information on the status of pending and future litigation—the assurance should be provided by those most capable of doing so—management assisted by its lawyers."[1] Two other aspects of lawyers' contributions to the system of corporate accountability have been widely discussed—their obligation to disclose fraud and their relationships to managements and boards of directors. These issues deserve careful consideration, particularly because they deal with the delicate question of lawyers' professional relationships to clients.

Responsibilities to Disclose Fraud.   Two recent events have focused attention on corporate counsel's obligation to disclose fraud—a petition to the SEC from the Institute for Public Representation and the SEC's suit against the law firm of Lord, Bissell & Brook for not disclosing fraud in connection with the merger of National Student Marketing Corporation and Interstate National Corporation. The merger of the two corporations was completed in 1969 without the shareholders knowing that the auditors had recommended significant changes in the National Student Marketing financial statements. Judge Barrington Parker ruled that the lawyers, who found out about the recommendation after the shareholders had voted but before the closing, were obligated to "speak out at the closing" about the significance of the information and the need to delay the closing until the information was disclosed and shareholders could vote again on the merger. By failing to speak out, Judge Parker held, the lawyers violated the antifraud provisions of the securities laws by aiding and abetting the merger. However, the judge dismissed the suit because the SEC failed to prove that the defendants, unless enjoined, were likely to continue violating the securities laws.[2] The impact of Judge Parker's opinion remains to be seen.

The petition of the Institute for Public Representation, a law institute affiliated with Georgetown University Law Center, requested the SEC to promulgate a rule clarifying the responsibilities of lawyers practicing before the Commission to disclose fraud. The petition is of interest even though the SEC has refused to act upon it. It proposed that the Commission adopt a rule that would require lawyers who learn of fraud during the course of representing a client company to disclose the information to the Commission, or to the person being defrauded, under the following circumstances: the fraud must be perpetrated with respect to a law administered or enforced by the SEC; the information about the fraud must not be protected as a privileged communication; and the client must have refused the opportunity to rectify the fraud. The petition argued that the basic obligation to make such disclosures is consistent with the Canons of Professional Ethics of the American Bar Association (if not with the Bar Association's interpretation of the Canons).

---

[1]The Commission on Auditors' Responsibilities, *Report, Conclusions, and Recommendations* (New York, 1978), p. 45.

[2]*SEC v. National Student Marketing Corp.,* August 31, 1978, CCH Federal Securities Law Reporter, Current, pp. 94,177–94,203.

The duty of confidentiality to the client, the Institute held, is owed to the corporate entity, not to management insistent upon concealing a misrepresentation.[3]

The definition of the client is obviously a key element in determining the obligations of corporate counsel to disclose management fraud. The American Bar Association's Code of Professional Responsibility treats the corporate entity as the client, but this leaves open the question of the respective obligations of counsel to the various constituencies within the corporate entity—management, the board of directors, and shareholders. It also leaves open the question of the obligations of lawyers practicing before the SEC to the investing public. As of this writing, an ABA task force is addressing the definition of the client as part of a project to review and revise the Code.[4] A more explicit definition of the corporate client may affect the way corporate lawyers view their obligations to boards of directors as well as their obligations to disclose fraud.

Relationships to Boards of Directors.   As noted in chapter 5, boards of directors cannot serve as effective top-management controls unless they have adequate information about corporate affairs. Corporate lawyers could play a larger role in providing such information. Victor H. Palmieri, an attorney and former chief executive officer of the Pennsylvania Company, has argued that they should, and in the *Harvard Business Review* he has described how corporate lawyers could perform this new role.

According to Palmieri, corporate counsel should attempt to detect and disclose to the board any material inaccuracy or nondisclosure in management's presentation of issues to the board and should be available to discuss the concerns of independent directors out of the presence of the chief executive. Corporate lawyers, he believes, should adopt the role of "officers of the board," in the same sense that trial lawyers are viewed as "officers of the court." This role need not sacrifice counsel's relationship to the chief executive, but it would require, among other things, that counsel never compromise legal judgment to satisfy the purposes of the chief executive. Bringing about this transition, Palmieri maintains, would necessitate a major shift in counsel's concept of who is the client. Because corporate counsel's tenure is typically dependent on the chief executive officer's pleasure and because counsel typically both reports to and works closely with the chief executive, it has been natural for corporate counsel to treat the chief executive as the client. Palmieri recommends that the board and chief executive take specific steps to clarify the responsibilities and func-

[3]The petition was submitted May 25, 1978. A copy was provided to us by the Institute. The SEC announced its decision to deny the Institute's request in Release No. 34–16045, July 25, 1979.

[4]*New York Times,* December 17, 1978.

tions of counsel, putting in written form what the board expects from counsel.[5]

Corporate counsel's relationship to the board might also be changed by SEC action. The Institute for Public Representation, in a petition submitted subsequent to the one referred to above, has requested that the SEC establish rules that would have the effect of requiring boards to direct corporate attorneys to communicate to the board activities they discover that they believe violate or probably violate the law. Under such directives, all violations or probable violations of laws administered or enforced by the SEC would be communicated to the board. Violations or probable violations of other laws would also be reported to the board if they could result in material financial liability to the corporation or if they call into question the quality and integrity of management. Registrants would have to report to the SEC and in annual reports to shareholders that the corporation's attorneys have indicated their compliance with the board's instructions and that the auditors were informed about violations or probable violations that the board considers material. The SEC has requested public comment on the rules proposed in this petition.[6]

Public Assurance on Corporate Conduct.   There are several ways by which lawyers could provide assurance that corporations are in compliance with laws and regulations. One way would be to add the assurance to the management report on the financial statements recommended by the Cohen Commission.[7] The report could state that corporate or outside legal counsel had evaluated the legality of the matters submitted to it by management and considers the corporation in compliance with the applicable laws and regulations. This would place on management the responsibility for bringing the relevant issues before its counsel. This proposal is controversial and has been criticized by lawyers and businesspersons as costly and unnecessary.

Another approach, which would be even more costly, is a legal audit performed by a law firm independent of the corporation. There are, of course, no standards for such audits, and developing them would be a considerable undertaking. Moreover, legal audits would put lawyers in an entirely new role, quite different from their traditional role as partisan representatives of the client.

The public image of lawyers as partisan representatives could, in fact, reduce the assurance provided by a legal audit. The public would not obtain

[5]Victor H. Palmieri, "The Lawyer's Role: An Argument for Change," *Harvard Business Review* (November–December 1978): 30–40.
[6]The supplemental petition, which was submitted November 22, 1978, was made available to us by the Institute. The request for public comment was made in SEC Release No. 34–16045, July 25, 1979.
[7]*Report*, pp. 76–77.

much assurance from lawyers' opinions about clients unless it understood the new role of legal auditors, their independence and their obligations to nonclient constituencies. Another implementation problem would be the relationship between the investigative and evaluative functions of the legal auditors. In order to evaluate the legality of an act, it must be identified, and the process of identifying such acts calls for procedures different from those used to evaluate legality. Should legal auditors have responsibility for identifying acts of questionable legality, or should they restrict their work to providing an opinion on matters brought to their attention by management? This type of question indicates how difficult it would be to flesh out a feasible plan for a legal audit.

A third possibility is a compliance audit of company policies to prevent illegal acts from occurring. Such audits could be performed by a joint team of independent lawyers and auditors or by auditing firms whose staffs had been augmented by lawyers. The accountants would supply expertise in systems analysis and compliance testing, and the lawyers would bring to bear their expertise in legal questions.

The possibilities described above show the range of alternatives that might be explored. The feasibility of the alternatives would rest largely on the relative costs and benefits of the proposals. Legal audits could prove extraordinarily expensive, and the public, which would ultimately bear the expense, might be better served from the assurances now provided by the activism of governmental regulatory and legal authorities. Moreover, it is not clear what impact, if any, legal audits would have on the incidence or detection of management frauds. Legal audits, for instance, might increase compliance with labor codes, antitrust laws, and environmental regulations, but have no effect on the likelihood of management misrepresentations in the financial statements.

Whistle-blowing and Cover-up

If corporate personnel with knowledge of wrongdoing, including management fraud, consistently informed those with the power to remedy the wrong, they would constitute an additional weapon to detect and deter management fraud. The appropriate remedial agency could be members of management with authority over the wrongdoers, the audit committee or board, or outside regulatory or law enforcement bodies. There are two basic approaches to making this weapon more effective, facilitating corporate whistle-blowing and adapting corporate institutions to inhibit cover-ups.

Whistle-blowing. It is important to distinguish the issue of protecting the rights of whistle-blowers who make justifiable allegations from the issue of encouraging whistle-blowing. The two issues are, of course, interrelated, because potential whistle-blowers who fear reprisals may be encouraged to make disclosures if they are aware that they are protected against unjust retaliation. Nevertheless, the two issues are also separable. Encouraging whistle-blowing is far more controversial than protecting whistle-blowers. It is more controversial because no one wishes to establish an atmosphere of rumor, recrimination, and unjust accusations, and measures to encourage whistle-blowing court that danger more than do measures to protect individuals who make justifiable disclosures of alleged impropriety or illegality.

Companies could establish policies prohibiting unjust reprisals against whistle-blowers and procedures to monitor the policies. If the policies were specified in corporate codes of conduct, all personnel would have reason to be aware of them. Legislation to protect whistle-blowers offers another alternative. In either case, the acts that are to be protected would have to be defined, and the breadth of the definition would determine much of the effect of the policy or law. Protecting whistle-blowers against reprisals for disclosing alleged illegalities is different from protecting them against reprisals for disclosing so-called "questionable acts," "wrongdoing," or "mismanagement." Put another way, the whistle-blower's disclosure of what is believed to be unethical but not necessarily illegal is different from disclosure of what is believed to be illegal. The broader the definition of the acts that would be protected, the more necessary it would be to build safeguards into the policy or legislation to protect the innocent from unjust accusations that damage reputations.

The cost of defending against unjust reprisals may discourage potential whistle-blowers. Therefore, a policy or law designed to encourage whistle-blowing would have to provide a mechanism to adjudicate such claims that was not prohibitively expensive. For instance, if a law prohibiting unjust reprisals against whistle-blowers put the burden of proof on the whistle-blower, or held out the prospect of burdensome attorney's fees, potential whistle-blowers would be less likely to make disclosures than if the law established a mechanism for fact finding and settlement or contained a provision for appointed legal representation or recovery of lawyer's fees.

It is unlikely that corporate whistle-blowing could be encouraged unless the policy or law protecting whistle-blowers from unjust reprisals was accompanied by a system that provided for the formal investigation of allegations made by corporate personnel. A focus on job-related rights, on whether or not a dismissal, demotion, or other job-related setback is an unjust reprisal, as opposed to a reasonable and justifiable action, is a focus solely on the whistle-blower's self-defense. Yet it is conceivable, for instance, that reorganization of a department that affects many persons as well as the whistle-blower could make it difficult to substantiate the whistle-blower's charge of unjust reprisal, whereas a separate investigation, if undertaken, might easily substantiate the whistle-blower's allegation of illegalities in business dealings. The prospect of such situations could discourage whistle-blowing unless there is a formal mechanism for investigations.

Laws and policies to encourage corporate whistle-blowing could have a deleterious effect on corporate structures—not, certainly, because of the well-based allegations that might be generated, but because of the groundless assertions that might be too frequent. There can be serious dangers in removing all—or too many—risks from accusers. Such dangers should be assessed before policies or laws are adopted. The whole question of protecting and encouraging whistle-blowing should therefore be studied.

Legislative protection for whistle-blowing has a precedent. The Civil Service Reform Act of 1978 prohibits reprisals against an employee of a government agency who discloses information that he or she "reasonably believes evidences" a violation of any law, rule, or regulation; mismanagement; gross waste of public funds; abuse of authority; or substantial or specific danger to public health or safety. The Special Counsel of the Merit Systems Protection Board is required to investigate allegations of prohibited reprisals.[8] The government's experience with these new institutions may throw light on appropriate policies with respect to corporate whistle-blowing.

Diminishing Cover-ups.   Whistle-blowing and cover-up are two sides of a single coin. To the degree that individuals disclose indications of corporate illegality, they do not participate in the collective activity of cover-up. The approach to increasing such disclosures described above is to smooth the path for the whistle-blower. Another approach is to reduce the number or effectiveness of the corporate structures that facilitate cover-up.

Jack Katz, in chapter 13, notes that organizational reforms that combat cover-up increase the number of people who are likely to know about the fraud and are therefore capable of disclosing it, or they make it more difficult for individuals to avoid knowledge about fraud, to turn their heads from the possibility of fraud and their obligation to disclose it. To the degree that proposed reforms can bring about these conditions, they can succeed in reducing cover-up. However, most reform possibilities are two-edged. For instance, rotation of personnel puts more individuals in a position to learn of impropriety, but the knowledge that they will be only temporarily in vulnerable positions, positions where they are in contact with indications of impropriety, can induce them to avoid the responsibility to report it.

Katz explores, in addition to rotation of personnel, the following organizational possibilities: turnover of personnel, overlapping jurisdictions within a hierarchical organization, and limited, joint responsibilities shared by a

---

[8]Public Law 95–454. The prohibition does not apply to disclosures specifically prohibited by law or required to be kept secret by Executive order in the interests of national defense or the conduct of foreign affairs.

team the members of which will return to their places in the organizational hierarchy when the team's defined task is accomplished (e.g., the task force). Of these, he finds turnover and the task force system most promising, but his aim is to point out a research path rather than to define conclusive solutions. The basic question is how work can be organized in ways that militate against cover-up. A full consideration of this subject would include the impact of the organizational recommendations to reduce cover-up on the efficiency of the enterprise.

The Role of Government

Legislative, regulatory, and enforcement activities by governmental bodies contribute in so many ways, directly and indirectly, to the detection and deterrence of management fraud that a chapter or more could easily be devoted to the subject. Such depth is not, however, necessary for our purposes. This section is therefore confined to four points: legal deterrents, the courts, the Securities and Exchange Commission, and congressional oversight.

Legal Deterrents.   Congress establishes, and courts apply and refine, the statutes that define illegality and serve as deterrents. The securities acts, for instance, have stood for two generations as a basic deterrent to material financial misrepresentations by SEC registrants. More recently, the Foreign Corrupt Practices Act made effective internal accounting controls a legal requirement. The basic question here is whether the deterrents established by law are adequate, in what respects they should be pruned or supplemented. We have already noted in chapter 6 that more precision in the definition of illegal acts of computer abuse would be helpful.

The Courts.   Since management fraud is a crime and also gives rise to civil remedies, the courts, which determine guilt or innocence or liability and impose penalties, serve as deterrents. The effectiveness of this deterrent could be strengthened by reducing the common perception that whenever technical issues are involved (as they invariably are in management fraud cases), there is a significant random component in the outcome of legal proceedings. This perception is based on the belief that judges and lay juries, who determine the outcomes, are often incapable of understanding technical matters at issue.

Many suggestions have been made to ameliorate this problem, but they generally share a basic concept: using experts to determine issues beyond the ken of the lay persons serving the judicial process in complex, technical cases. The most common suggestion is to use a panel of court-appointed "masters." If this is done, court decisions should be better informed and less subject to criticism. It is arguable that by thus increasing confidence in the administration of justice in management fraud cases, the courts would serve as a more effective deterrent to management fraud.

Securities and Exchange Commission.   The SEC has broad powers to administer the securities acts, including their antifraud provisions. It fulfills this responsibility both by oversight activities and enforcement actions. The Commission reviews the disclosures in documents filed by registrants and may issue letters of comment requiring that deficiencies in filings be corrected. It may bring administrative proceedings against accountants or lawyers practicing before the Commission for unethical or improper professional conduct, lack of character or integrity, inadequate qualifications, willful violations of securities laws, or aiding and abetting such violations. The penalties may include permanent or temporary denial of the privilege to practice before the Commission. The Commission also initiates civil proceedings in Federal District Courts, seeking injunctive relief for violations of the securities acts or rules promulgated under the acts. Willful violations of the securities acts may be referred to the Attorney General for criminal prosecution.[9]

The SEC's enforcement proceedings are deterrents to management fraud and provide assurance to the public that auditors and attorneys are fulfilling their responsibilities in connection with the disclosure system. Over the years the Commission has instituted many proceedings in cases of fraudulent financial statements. The methods by which the Commission detects alleged violations have not, however, been the subject of detailed study. Such a study might provide valuable information on the methods of detecting management fraud.

Congressional Oversight.   Several congressional committees have in the past few years been active in oversight of the accounting profession and the system of corporate accountability, in particular the House Subcommittee on Oversight and Investigations, the Senate Subcommittee on Reports, Accounting and Management, and the Senate Subcommittee on Governmental Efficiency and the District of Columbia.[10] Their hearings and reports have stimulated the auditing profession to reexamine its methods of self-regulation, including independence and peer review requirements and methods for disciplining accountants for unprofessional performance. Strengthened self-

[9]The Commission's enforcement powers are conveniently summarized in Table 26 of the *Annual Report* of the SEC to Congress for the fiscal year ended June 30, 1976, pp. 204–205, (House Document No. 95–21).

[10]The Subcommittee on Reports, Accounting and Management was disbanded in March 1978 following the death of its chairman, Senator Lee Metcalf, and the Subcommittee on Governmental Efficiency and the District of Columbia, was given responsibility for accounting issues.

regulatory procedures may contribute to preventing lapses in detecting management fraud, and congressional efforts to provide assurance that the procedures are effective indicate how congressional oversight, albeit indirectly, contributes to the detection and deterrence of management fraud.

Congressional oversight of the system of corporate accountability has been intermittent, rather than continuous. However, in the past few years a mechanism has developed for regular congressional oversight—annual reports by the SEC to Congress on the accounting profession and the Commission's oversight role. These reports will enable Congress to monitor on a regular basis the performance of the auditing profession and the system of corporate accountability.

Improving the Ethical Climate

It is a truism that unethical people commit unethical acts, and no one challenges the idea that the constraints imposed by personal morality are more effective in preventing fraud than policemen and punishments. However, since the attempt to raise the level of people's ethics is probably as old as mankind, it is tempting to shrug off the possibility of tailoring an ethical program to combat the unethical behavior known as business fraud. Nevertheless, clarifying the ethical issues pertaining to business fraud, removing the ambiguities that surround the subject, is an approach worth exploring.

The euphemisms attending discussions of business crime could be identified and eradicated. For instance, the ambiguous phrase, "business is business," should not be connected to incidents of corporate crime because it reduces the emphasis on the criminality of the acts. It is harder for a person to attach immorality to an act joined to an ethical behavior pattern—the everyday conduct of business—than to an act of unalloyed criminality.

This is one common example of deemphasizing the immorality of business crime. There are doubtless others that could be studied to delineate the social mechanics of deemphasizing the criminality of corporate crime. How widespread is the feeling that corporate crime is victimless crime and what is its origin? Does it spring primarily from the fact that the victims are faceless or can be thought of as well able to bear their losses? Is it because identification with a victim of business crime does not inspire the terror that occurs when identifying with a victim of violent crime? What social interests militate against a forthright treatment of business fraud as criminal behavior? What is the effect of extensive government regulation on attitudes toward business crime?

Understanding the ways in which the immorality of business crime is downplayed and the extent to which it is downplayed would contribute to making the immorality of business crime more explicit, but other measures would probably be needed to change popular attitudes. Perhaps stricter sentencing by the courts is necessary. In any case, the type of measures that might succeed should be explored.

Improving the ethical climate involves more than inculcating the will to do the right thing. It also involves inculcating knowledge of what is the right thing to do. In an increasingly complex society, with rapidly developing business forms and an expanding volume of laws and regulations, it may be becoming more difficult for individuals to be aware of the legal and ethical ramifications of both their own behavior and the activities of the institutions they serve. If so, the proposal to clarify such matters will be both more difficult and more necessary to implement.

Summary

This chapter has described briefly how factors other than auditors and corporate controls impact or may impact the detection and deterrence of management frauds. It is apparent that corporate counsel may be enlisted to play a greater role in the system of corporate accountability. Governmental legislative, regulatory, enforcement, and judicial efforts now have a great impact. Measures that increase the likelihood that corporate personnel who have knowledge of management fraud will disclose it could add to the forces for combatting misrepresentations in financial statements. Finally, the ethical climate in our society is a basic deterrent to illegality and impropriety.

The factors discussed in this chapter illustrate that combatting management fraud is a social problem, not merely a problem for external and internal auditors, managements, and boards of directors. Auditors, managements, and boards cannot control all the elements that contribute to detecting and deterring management fraud. No program for reducing the incidence of management fraud is realistic if it disregards that fact.

8

Research Needs
and Opportunities

$\mathbf{F}$uture progress in detecting and deterring management fraud is to a large extent dependent on research. A solid research base can provide the perspective and the data necessary to assess the feasibility and promise of proposals to enhance detection and deterrence. Research can also lead to the development of fresh approaches to detection and deterrence.

Many research questions have been identified in the course of the previous discussions. They are tabulated in Table 1. The tabulation does not assign priorities to the research questions. This is because it makes sense, when studying a topic so little understood as management fraud, to pursue a mixed research strategy. On the other hand, there is a higher priority on the research projects that would provide information on the nature and dimensions of management fraud and the effectiveness of current methods of detection and deterrence—the first set of projects in the tabulation. A better understanding of the current situation is essential in developing proposals for improvements and may indicate appropriate priorities for other research topics.

Some believe that the dimensions of management fraud are overestimated, others that it is underestimated. Part of the problem is that the data available are primarily based on reported crimes, a category narrower than attempted or committed crimes. This not only presents a problem for researchers attempting to assess the dimensions of management fraud, but it also limits the number of easily researchable issues. It is not unlikely that when studying management fraud, even more than other subjects, the concept "the more we know, the more we can know" will prevail. Case studies of management fraud, for instance, will make it easier to study characteristics common to events of management fraud, the auditing procedures most effective in detecting them, and the controls that could prevent them. Thus, a research program devoted to management fraud should be thought of as a long-term effort that step by step builds upon the insights and findings of previous research, gradually deepening our understanding. The need to combat management fraud would amply justify such an effort.

Table 1
Research Questions

Assessing the Problem:	*Discussed on Page:*
1. What are the dimensions (rate of incidence, social cost) of management fraud?	10
2. Does the incidence of management fraud vary according to the size, organization (e.g., centralized or decentralized), or type of business?	27
3. What is the relationship between the incidence of material management fraud and the incidence of other types of corporate illegality (e.g., price fixing)?	35–36
4. What are the psychological characteristics of perpetrators of management fraud?	36–37
5. Do some corporate officers participate in management fraud more frequently than others?	27, 52–53
6. What proportion of management frauds are cleverly concealed rather than clumsily perpetrated and easy to detect?	39
7. What proportion of management frauds involve management override of the internal accounting control system?	27, 47–57
8. Are the psychological characteristics of managers who commit fraud through materially misleading financial statements different from those of managers who commit fraud by misappropriation of company assets immaterial to the financial statements?	37
9. What is the duration of the typical management fraud? Is it typically an event that is concluded quickly or a year-to-year conspiracy, or is there	

no discernible pattern in durations of
management frauds?   27

10.   How effective are the techniques now employed
by independent auditors in deterring
management fraud?   10

11.   How effective are the techniques now employed
by independent auditors in detecting
management fraud?   10

12.   Do repeated patterns of procedures by
independent auditors affect the incidence of
either material fraud or frauds immaterial to the
financial statements?   25–26

13.   How will the mechanics of management fraud be
changed by the increasing use of advanced EDP
systems in the financial reporting process? How
will the role of EDP specialists in such
environments affect the likelihood and nature of
future management frauds?   59–60, 63–64

14.   Is the time lag between the evolution of
computer technology and the development of
EDP audit and control capabilities sufficiently
narrow to maintain the level of deterrence and
detection of computer fraud that society needs?   62–63

15.   What has been the relationship between
computer use and the incidence of management
frauds?   59–60

16.   Are laws against business fraud sufficient in their
punishments? In the breadth of their proscription
of activities?   64, 74

Auditors' Responsibilities:

17.   What is the current financial statement users'
perception of the auditor's responsibility for the
detection of management fraud?   8–10

18.   What is the relationship between the auditor's
legal responsibility to detect fraud and the
auditor's professional responsibility to detect it?   13–15

19.   How would a requirement to review and report
on the adequacy of a company's internal
accounting controls affect the independent
auditor's responsibilities for fraud detection?   45–46

20.   What would be the consequences to the audit
process of extending auditors' obligations to

include detection of immaterial frauds?   18–19

21.   What new authority, such as subpoena power or
      the power to question under oath, would be
      necessary for the auditor to detect with
      consistency frauds immaterial to the financial
      statements?   19

22.   What would be the advantages and disadvantages
      of mandatory disclosures of immaterial
      illegalities?   20–21

Auditors' Effectiveness:

23.   What new "red flags," examples of types of
      situations that might raise questions about
      potential fraud, would be helpful to auditors?   26–30

24.   What procedures now used by auditors are most
      effective in detecting management fraud?   26

25.   Do case studies of the perpetration and detection
      of management fraud reveal auditing procedures
      so effective in detecting fraud or so necessary in
      deterring it (e.g., confirmation of receivables,
      observation of inventory-taking) that they should
      be mandatory on all audits or under certain
      circumstances?   26

26.   What are the characteristics of auditors who can
      recognize with relative consistency situations
      involving fraud? How could measures of such
      characteristics be used to recruit and promote
      auditors with regard for their ability to detect
      fraud?   25

27.   Is there a need to improve communications
      among members of the audit team so that
      evidence which can indicate potential fraud when
      considered in conjunction with other evidence is
      evaluated in conjunction with that evidence? If
      so, how would communications among members
      of the audit team be improved to achieve this
      objective?   28–29

28.   Would year-to-year variations in audit procedures
      be effective in detecting and deterring fraud?
      How can such procedures be justified in terms of
      the auditors' obligation to choose the most
      efficient and effective procedures to obtain
      sufficient evidence for an opinion on the financial
      statements?   25–26

29. If auditors were to introduce annually new or
     not recently used procedures in order to improve
     their detection and deterrence of management
     fraud, how would they select the procedures and
     determine how many to use on individual audits?   25–26

30. What kind of educational background would best
     prepare auditors to assume their professional
     responsibilities with respect to management
     fraud?   23–25

31. What is the relationship between auditors'
     professional experience and their capacity to
     detect and deter management fraud?   24

32. Have compromises of audit objectivity played a
     role in successfully perpetrated management
     frauds? What circumstances occasioned the
     compromises?   31–33

33. What measures can provide assurance that
     auditors maintain their alertness to potential
     management fraud after they have had
     considerable experience with honest clients?   30–31

34. Would mandatory disclosures of material audit
     adjustments deter potential perpetrators of
     management fraud from "trying out" financial
     misrepresentations on auditors?   40–41

35. Would the employment of operational auditing
     techniques significantly enhance the independent
     auditor's effectiveness in detecting and deterring
     management fraud? If so, which techniques
     would be most effective?   41–42

36. Does the experience to date with regular
     quarterly reviews of interim financial information
     indicate that time pressures on the annual audit
     are relieved by earlier auditor involvement in the
     financial reporting process? What other measures
     can ensure that auditors are not subjected to
     excessive time pressures?   31

37. Do corporate personnel regard independent
     accountants as appropriate repositories for
     information about corporate improprieties? What
     is their attitude toward auditors as repositories
     for such information?   38

38. How does the SEC detect alleged violations of
     the antifraud provisions of the securities laws and
     what light does this throw on techniques to

The Role of the Legal Profession:

49. Should lawyers provide public assurance that corporate conduct complies with laws and regulations, and if so, what form should that assurance take (e.g., a legal audit)?   70–71

50. What are lawyers' responsibilities to disclose fraud by their clients? Should those responsibilities be expanded? How?   68–69

Whistle-blowing and Cover-up:

51. Are material management frauds commonly known by a wide circle of corporate personnel who are nonperpetrators?   39

52. What kind of legislation to protect and/or encourage whistle-blowing would be feasible and effective in combatting management fraud?   71–73

53. How can work be organized in ways that militate against cover-ups?   73–74

Ethical Climate:

54. What are the mechanisms by which the immorality of business crime is deemphasized in our society, and what measures could be taken to clarify to the public that business crime is as unethical as other types of crime?   76–77

Part II

Applying Various Disciplines
to Management Fraud

9

An Interdisciplinary Approach to the Study of Management Fraud

Myron Uretsky

New steps to improve the detection and deterrence of management fraud are largely dependent on research, and the need for such research has already been widely recognized. For instance, the November 1977 Report of the Senate Subcommittee on Reports, Accounting and Management stated, "Research into improved . . . detection of management fraud should be increased."[1] The Commission on Auditors' Responsibilities, an independent body set up by the AICPA, made a similar recommendation.[2]

This paper argues that the right approach to such research is an interdisciplinary approach that employs the behavioral sciences, such as sociology, psychology, and criminology, in conjunction with accounting and auditing research. But first, what do I mean by an interdisciplinary approach? I am referring to a coordinated effort to apply varied disciplines to the problem of understanding management fraud and how it might be detected and

[1] *Improving the Accountability of Publicly Owned Corporations and their Auditors,* U.S. Government Printing Office (Washington, D.C., 1977), p. 19.

[2] The Commission on Auditors' Responsibilities, *Report, Conclusions, and Recommendations* (New York, 1978), p. 40.

Dr. Uretsky is Professor of Accounting and Information Systems, Graduate School of Business Administration, New York University.

This paper was prepared for the Peat, Marwick, Mitchell & Co. Symposium on Management Fraud, June 1978. © *Peat, Marwick, Mitchell & Co.*

deterred. The coordinated application of these disciplines may take the form of multidisciplinary research teams or improved communications among members of several disciplines. The isolated application of individual disciplines is of course useful, and in time the knowledge gained in one field commonly permeates others. However, a coordinated effort can maximize progress, and we have reached the point where rapid progress is necessary.

I am not suggesting that scholars in different disciplines always confine their learning to their field or do not share ideas with other disciplines—far from it. My point is that in the case of research on management fraud we need a self-conscious effort to maximize the cross-fertilization of ideas from different fields, to coordinate findings, and, where possible and promising, to use multidisciplinary research teams. This approach makes sense because the ultimate objective I have described is not to contribute to a particular scholarly discipline, but to establish a body of knowledge on a socioeconomic problem that can be used to solve the problem.

The questions that must be researched in order to make significant strides in improving detection and deterrence are questions about human behavior. We must understand how management fraud is perpetrated, by what classes or types of individuals, in what types of organizations, and by what procedures. Why do some people participate in frauds and others not? Are there readily identifiable behavioral patterns that suggest proneness to fraud? Do some organizational forms create environments more conducive to fraud than others? What kinds of pressures on individuals and organizations make acts of fraud more likely? These are questions about the behavior patterns of individuals and groups. It is logical to seek answers to them by emphasizing the research techniques of the behavioral sciences.

Auditors have already based their techniques of detection and deterrence on their own answers to these behavioral questions. Although they are not now responsible to detect all business frauds, auditors are responsible to detect those frauds material to the financial statements that would be discovered through the performance with due care of professional procedures necessary to provide evidence for opinions on financial statements.[3] The procedures necessary to provide such evidence are not specifically designed to reveal fraud; quite the contrary, they are largely based on trusting various management representations. However, the auditor is responsible to be alert to possible fraud because it may affect the fairness of the financial statements.

To fulfill the latter responsibility auditors must be alert for signs that management's integrity should be viewed with additional skepticism, for conditions that may provide a motive for management fraud, and to signs that fraud has occurred. This is accomplished by their perspicacity in dealing with

---

[3]AICPA Statement on Auditing Standards No. 16, "The Independent Auditor's Responsibility for the Detection of Errors or Irregularities" (New York, 1977).

management and by so-called red-flags. Red flags are situational indicators. They indicate that the auditor should be more watchful than usual, and in combinations they may indicate that the auditor should be suspicious. The red flags now in authoritative auditing literature are based, implicitly or explicitly, on the auditing profession's answers to the behavioral questions cited above. If we are to identify new red flags and refine old ones, we must approach these questions from fresh perspectives.

There is another reason to restudy the behavioral questions that might provide new red flags. Management frauds are performed within a framework of legitimate business operations, and as these business operations evolve and new industries are formed, new patterns of management fraud may arise. New red flags may therefore be needed.

The Cohen Commission argued that because of the evolution of business practices, ongoing research is necessary on the conditions that indicate fraud and the methods of perpetrating fraud. It recommended that the AICPA set up a mechanism for regular dissemination of information on developments in the perpetration and detection of fraud.[4] In response to this recommendation early in 1978, the AICPA set up a Standing Subcommittee on Methods of Perpetration and Detection of Fraud. The subcommittee is charged to study and publish analyses of methods of perpetrating and detecting fraud and to study and publish analyses of alleged audit failures indicating a need for new or revised auditing standards. Behavioral studies on management fraud would both contribute to and augment the work of the subcommittee.

The findings from this research should be no less useful to the business community than to the auditing profession. Such findings can contribute to the development of control procedures to reduce the incidence of management fraud. Perhaps the research findings will influence hiring practices, management style, organizational structure, or the way codes of conduct are formulated. The research should also enhance the effectiveness of internal auditors in detecting and deterring fraud. The Institute of Internal Auditors has sponsored research on fraud detection, and its recent product, the useful book *Foozles and Frauds* by Harold F. Russell, acknowledges the "need for a better understanding of the multiple facets of fraud."[5]

Research on the larger question of white-collar crime suggests that the behavioral studies of management fraud may yield useful generalizations and patterns. Donald R. Cressey's study of embezzlers is a useful case in point. Cressey's study revealed a psychological process that led up to the act of embezzlement. The embezzlers first came to feel they had an unshareable personal financial problem, then ascertained a way to solve that problem by acting in secret to violate a position of financial trust, and also found a way

---

[4]*Report,* p. 40.

[5]*Foozles and Frauds* (Altamonte Springs, Fla; Institute of Internal Auditors, 1977), p. 157.

of conceiving of the act of embezzling consistent with their self-image as trusted persons. These findings indicate that a type of fraud—embezzlement —yields patterns when subjected to behavioral analysis, and suggests that management fraud will also yield patterns when analyzed by the techniques of the behavioral sciences.[6]

The application of behavioral science concepts and techniques to auditing research may not be widespread, but it is not new. For example, behavioral science techniques have been used to study the effects of audits on managerial behavior,[7] and researchers studying the auditor's evaluation of internal accounting control have used behavioral science approaches to analyze the auditor's work.[8] In addition, there have been recommendations to consider the feasibility of improving the auditor's evaluation of internal control by adapting behavioral science techniques to auditing procedures. One of these recommendations illustrates the potential behavioral science and interdisciplinary research hold for improving the effectiveness of internal and external auditors in detecting and deterring fraud. It is the recommendation first made by John J. Willingham to study the possible use of techniques from sociometry, the study and measurement of interpersonal relations.

In 1966, Willingham argued that sociological insights could be useful in the auditor's study and evaluation of internal control.[9] He pointed out that sociologists "view organizational structure in terms of norms which are behavioral prescriptions and proscriptions." These norms can be either formally derived, as is the case with a written job description assigning a designated individual a specific responsibility, or they can be informally derived —perhaps from norms supported by an unofficial group within the organization or a consensus of such groups or from the interpersonal relationships that develop as people work together. Thus, there may be differences between the person assigned to perform a task and the person who actually performs it and differences between the working relationships indicated by the formal hierarchical structure of an organization and the totality of working relationships. These differences may either strengthen or weaken a system of internal control. For instance, the formal separation of custodial and recordkeeping functions may be bridged by relationships between personnel that develop

[6]Donald R. Cressey, "Why Do Trusted Persons Commit Fraud? A Socio-Psychological Study of Defalcation," *Journal of Accountancy* (November 1951): 576–81.

[7]Neil C. Churchill, William W. Cooper, and Trevor Sainsbury, "Laboratory and Field Studies of the Behavioral Effects of Audits," in *Accounting and Its Behavioral Implications*, eds. William J. Bruns, Jr., and Don T. DeCoster, (New York: McGraw-Hill, 1969) pp. 245–57. The paper was first published in 1964.

[8]For example, R. H. Ashton, "An Experimental Study of Internal Control Judgments," *Journal of Accounting Research* Spring (1974): 143–57, and E. J. Joyce, "Expert Judgment in Audit Program Planning," Studies on Human Information Processing in Accounting, Supplement to Vol. 14 of *Journal of Accounting Research* (1976): pp. 29–60.

[9]"Internal Control Evaluation—A Behavioral Approach," *Internal Auditor* Summer (1966): 20–26.

informally and are not evident from the formal structure of the organization. This is sometimes a source of weakness. Information about any such relationships could be helpful to the auditor in the study and evaluation of internal control because it would assist in understanding the operative division of labor in the organization when it differs from the formal division of labor.

Willingham suggested that sociometric-type analysis could provide the auditor evaluating internal control with information on the operative division of labor in an organization, and he described briefly how sociometric techniques might be applied, relying largely on the methodology worked out by the sociologist James S. Coleman. Robert J. Swieringa and Douglas R. Carmichael explored this possibility further in an article published in 1971.[10] They performed a case study of the office departments of an integrated parts depot in the sales branch of a multiplant corporation, comparing actual working relationships to formally prescribed working relationships. The method they used to determine actual working relationships was originally developed by Ralph M. Stogdill and Carroll L. Shartle, behavioral scientists with doctorates in psychology.

The work by Willingham, Carmichael, and Swieringa illustrates the application of the behavioral sciences to the question of how to improve auditors' effectiveness. The research is also relevant to the problem of detecting fraud in business organizations because the techniques recommended can reveal informally assumed or shared responsibilities that are not evident from the formal organization structure and that may facilitate perpetration. Willingham recognized this explicitly, saying, "It is possible such a method [sociometric-type analysis] would enable accountants to detect fraud. . . . At a minimum, potentially collusive relationships between employees could be discovered."[11] Thus, a promising approach to improving the detection and deterrence of fraud originated from interdisciplinary scholarship employing the findings of behavioral science and can be pursued only by additional interdisciplinary studies.

In one respect the research on the use of sociometric-type analysis is not a model for the interdisciplinary studies this article has been recommending. Willingham was primarily interested in exploring a technique to improve the auditor's evaluation of internal control. The application of his findings to fraud detection was of secondary importance. What we need is an agenda of interdisciplinary studies explicitly directed toward understanding management fraud and how to detect it. It is a stone that should not in these times be left unturned.

[10]"A Positional Analysis of Internal Control," *Journal of Accountancy* (February 1971): 34–43.

[11]"Internal Control Evaluation," p. 26.

10

Classifying Acts of Fraud

Jerry L. Turner

A major problem encountered in discussing or researching a complex topic is the use of terminology open to diverse interpretations. The problem has been evident in discussions of improper acts in the business world. Terms such as "white-collar crime," "fraud," "irregularities," and "management fraud" have often been used interchangeably even though the events being described may be significantly different. This is also typically the case in debates concerning the auditor's responsibility for the detection of fraud. Much has been written concerning auditors' responsibilities, often without taking into account important differences in the types of acts being discussed. Likewise, numerous articles have been written which imply that "fraud" or "management fraud" can be readily detected by certain audit techniques or easily prevented by installation of certain internal controls or other types of procedures. Few, if any, of these articles emphasize that, because of differences in the types of acts involved, the techniques or procedures advocated would only be applicable in limited situations. With this in mind, it is apparent that certain terms need to be clarified. It is also apparent that a classification system of acts of fraud should be developed.

Mr. Turner is a Supervisor in the Department of Professional Practice—Accounting and Auditing, Peat, Marwick, Mitchell & Co.

This paper was prepared for the Peat, Marwick, Mitchell & Co. Symposium on Management Fraud, June 1978. © *Peat, Marwick, Mitchell & Co.*

Clarifying the Terms

One commonly used term for improper acts is "white-collar crime." Edelhertz defines white-collar crime in the following manner:

> . . . an illegal act or series of illegal acts committed by non-physical means and by concealment or guile, to obtain money or property, to avoid the payment or loss of money or property, or to obtain business or personal advantage.[1]

The wide range of acts this definition would encompass is illustrated in a U.S. Department of Justice publication which breaks down white-collar crime into the following categories:

A)   Crimes by persons operating on an individual, ad hoc basis for personal gain in a nonbusiness context. Examples include purchases on credit with no intention to pay and violations of federal regulations by pledging stock for further purchases or flouting margin requirements.

B)   Crimes in the course of their occupations by those operating inside business, government, or other establishments, in violation of their duty of loyalty and fidelity to employer or client. Examples include commercial bribery and kickbacks, embezzlement, and securities dealings by insiders trading to their advantage by the use of special knowledge.

C)   Crimes incidental to and in furtherance of business operations, but not the central purpose of the business. Examples include false weights and measures by retailers, submission or publication of false financial statements to obtain credit, use of fictitious or over-valued collateral, and deceptive advertising.

D)   White-collar crime as a business, or as the central activity. This is generally referred to as consumer crime, and examples include securities and commodities frauds, merchandise swindles, land frauds, insurance frauds, Ponzi schemes, and franchise frauds.[2]

Another commonly used descriptive term for improper acts is "fraud." *Black's Law Dictionary* lists one legal definition of fraud as:

---

[1] Herbert Edelhertz, *The Nature, Impact, and Prosecution of White-Collar Crime,* U.S. Department of Justice, L.E.A.A., U.S. Government Printing Office (Washington, D.C., 1970), p. 3. This definition was described as a "good working definition" in the Attorney General's first *Annual Report on Federal Law Enforcement and Criminal Justice System Assistance Activities,* U.S. Government Printing Office (Washington, D.C., 1972), p. 161.

[2] U.S. Department of Justice, Enforcement Program Division, Law Enforcement Assistance Administration, *The Investigation of White-Collar Crime,* U.S. Government Printing Office (Washington, D.C., 1977), pp. 27–31.

A generic term, embracing all multifarious means which ingenuity can devise, and which are resorted to by one individual to get advantage over another by false suggestions or by suppression of truth, and includes all surprise, trick, cunning, dissembling, and any unfair way by which another is cheated.[3]

Fraud, then, also encompasses a wide range of acts and could often be used interchangeably with the term "white-collar crime."

The auditing profession, finding the terms white-collar crime and fraud too general to be of use in describing improper acts related to a business entity in general and the accounting function in particular, began to use the term "irregularities." This concept is defined in Statement on Auditing Standards No. 16:

The term *irregularities* refers to intentional distortions of financial statements, such as deliberate misrepresentations by management, sometimes referred to as management fraud, or misappropriations of assets, sometimes referred to as defalcations.[4]

This statement contains the following definition of "management fraud":

Deliberate misrepresentations by management which result in distortions of financial statements.

For purposes of this definition, management refers to any owner or employee who is able to create a distortion of the financial statements, either because of an absence of internal accounting controls or circumvention of such controls. A distortion would result if the financial statements were not presented fairly in conformity with generally accepted accounting principles applied on a basis consistent with that of the preceding year.

A final point of clarification is needed as to when a deliberate misrepresentation would be classified as management fraud under the above definition. There are two types of deliberate misrepresentation of concern to the independent auditor. First, there are those which are included in the financial statements presented to the auditor for examination and which are *not* recognized as being misrepresentations. These undetected misrepresentations result in distortions in the final financial statements released to third parties. Second, there are those which are contained in the financial statements presented for the auditor's examination but recognized by the auditor as being misrepresentations prior to the issuance of the auditor's report. In this situation, the auditor requests that an appropriate correction be made and, if this is done, no mention of the misrepresentation is made in the final financial statements released to third parties.[5]

[3]Henry Campbell Black, *Black's Law Dictionary,* Revised Fourth Edition, (St. Paul, Minn.: West Publishing, 1968), p. 788.
[4]AICPA Statement on Auditing Standards No. 16 (New York, 1977), par. 3.
[5]A discussion of the procedures an auditor is to follow when an examination indicates that errors or irregularities may exist is contained in SAS No. 16, par. 14–15.

For purposes of this paper, *both* situations will be considered to constitute management fraud (even though if the auditor obtains a correction of the misrepresentation, the fraud does not actually occur). That is, management fraud has occurred if the financial statements presented to the auditor for examination contain deliberate, material misrepresentations, regardless of whether such misrepresentations eventually distort financial statements released to third parties.

Although the definition given above may suffice for purposes of this paper, it is necessary to recognize that it still leaves many areas open to judgment. For example, it does not include matters that involve management's legitimate discretion in the selection and application of generally accepted accounting principles, including appropriate disclosure. It should also be noted that although this definition of management fraud includes intent, intent does not necessarily have to be present for fraud in a legal sense to take place. The AICPA Commission on Auditors' Responsibilities has pointed out that "as a result of litigation, errors in judgment or mistakes in applying accounting principles have sometimes been found to involve constructive fraud."[6] Since this can be established only after the fact, however, constructive fraud will not be regarded as management fraud.

A Classification System

Examples of management fraud are given in Statement on Auditing Standards No. 16 as "misrepresentation or omission of the effects of events or transactions; manipulation, falsification, or alteration of records or documents; omission of significant information from records or documents; recording of transactions without substance; [or] intentional misapplication of accounting principles. . . . Such acts may be accompanied by the use of false or misleading records or documents and may involve one or more individuals among management, employees, or third parties."[7] Clearly, any combination of the listed actions could be used as a part of an act of management fraud. Therefore, it would appear that an attempt to develop a classification system for acts of management fraud might not be fruitful. However, in reviewing a broad spectrum of fraudulent acts, a logical system of classification does emerge. It is based on two factors—the function of the financial statements in the perpetration of an act of fraud, and whether the company or the perpetrator (management) receives the direct benefit of the results of the act. Such a classification system is shown in Table 1.

To attempt deliberately to distort financial statements, the perpetrator

[6]The Commission on Auditors' Responsibilities, *Report, Conclusions, and Recommendations* (New York, 1978), p. 33.
[7]SAS No. 16, par. 3.

TABLE 1. Classification of Acts Involving Management Fraud

Function of Financial Statements in the Fraud	Recipient of Direct Benefit	Typical Purposes of Act
I. Deliberately distorted financial statements are the instrument used to *commit* an act of fraud by misleading users or a class of users about company financial results or position.	A. Company	1. To obtain credit, long-term financing, or additional capital investment based on distorted financial information or the omission from the financial statements of information required to be disclosed under GAAP. 2. To conceal inadequate performance by company. 3. To evade legal tax liability.
	B. Perpetrator	1. To manipulate company stock value. 2. To conceal inadequate performance by management.
II. Deliberately distorted financial statements are the instrument used to *disguise* an act of fraud. If users or a class of users are misled as to company financial results or position, it would be incidental to the intent of the initial act and would constitute a separate act of fraud in itself.	A. Company	1. To conceal the sale or assignment of fictitious or misrepresented assets. 2. To conceal prohibited business activities. 3. To conceal improper payments.
	B. Perpetrator	1. To conceal the misappropriation of company funds or assets.

must have some idea as to the part the distorted financial information will play in the act of fraud. Basically, there are two ways distortions can be used. First, the deliberately distorted financial statements can be the actual instrument needed to *commit* an act of fraud by misleading users or a class of users about company financial position or results (Type I Act). In this instance, the financial statements must be made available to third parties to accomplish the act. This creates a difficult situation for the auditor in that future users of the financial statements may not be known by the auditor at the time of the audit.

Second, the deliberately distorted financial statements can be the instrument to *disguise* an act of fraud (Type II Act). In this case, if the users or a class of users are misled as to company financial results or position, it would be incidental to the intent of the initial act and would constitute a separate act of fraud itself. The financial statements are not made available to third parties until after perpetration of the act being disguised.

The types of rewards expected as a result of deliberately distorting the financial statements can vary in two basic ways. Either the perpetrator expects direct benefits as a result of the act of fraud or the perpetrator expects indirect benefits through acts of fraud perpetrated for the direct benefit of the company.

Direct benefits to the perpetrator are immediately usable or readily convertible to use, such as money or appreciated stocks, or they improve or maintain the perpetrator's position within the company. Examples of direct benefits to the perpetrator resulting from an act of fraud are the following:

1. Enhanced value of personal holdings of company stock
2. Company assets appropriated for personal benefit
3. Increased compensation (raises, bonuses, shares in profits)
4. Promotion or retention of present position within the company

Direct benefits to the company are those which make the company survive or appear to prosper. Perpetrators seeking direct benefits for the company are aware that, if successful, they will eventually obtain some direct benefits as a result of their actions. Examples of direct benefits to the company resulting from an act of fraud would be:

1. Surviving a temporarily bad situation such as inadequate cash flow or the need to meet terms of existing loan agreements
2. Obtaining credit, long-term financing, or additional capital investment not otherwise obtainable
3. Supporting presently unprofitable ventures
4. Maintaining the company's prestige

As shown in Table 1, the functions of the financial statements and the types of benefits can be combined into four subcategories as follows:

I–A—Financial statements are used to commit an act of fraud; company is recipient of direct benefits.

I–B—Financial statements are used to commit an act of fraud; perpetrator is recipient of direct benefits.

II–A—Financial statements are used to disguise an act of fraud; company is recipient of direct benefits.

II–B—Financial statements are used to disguise an act of fraud; perpetrator is recipient of direct benefits.

Examples of typical acts in each subcategory follow.

Type I–A Acts

1. To obtain credit, long-term financing, or additional capital investment not otherwise obtainable.   When a company's performance has been subpar, sources of funds become more difficult to find. Moreover, that is generally the time the company has the greatest need for sources of fresh funds. To alleviate this problem, the company's actual performance can be made to appear more successful by inflating the company financial results or position in the financial statements. The distorted financial statements can then be used to convince potential creditors or investors of the soundness of the company, and needed funds can be obtained.

Type I–A acts can also be perpetrated by withholding significant information from financial statements when such disclosure would be required under generally accepted accounting principles (GAAP). There are several types of significant information which would fall in this category:

A. RELATED PARTY TRANSACTIONS.   The AICPA Statement on Auditing Standards No. 6 defines a related party as "the reporting entity; its affiliates; principal owners, management, and members of their immediate families; entities for which investments are accounted for by the equity method; and any other party with which the reporting entity may deal when one party has the ability to significantly influence the management or operating policies of the other, to the extent that one of the transacting parties might be prevented from fully pursuing its own separate interests."[8]

Statement on Auditing Standards No. 6 states that examples of related-party transactions include "transactions between a parent company and its subsidiaries, transactions between or among subsidiaries of a common parent, and transactions in which the reporting entity participates with other affiliated businesses, with management or with principal stockholders. Trans-

---

[8]AICPA Statement on Auditing Standards No. 6 (New York, 1975), pp. 1–2.

actions between or among the foregoing parties are considered to be related party transactions even though they may not be given accounting recognition. For example, an entity may provide services to a related party without charge."[9]

It must be noted that certainly not all, and possibly only a small number of related-party transactions are part of a plan to mislead users of financial statements. Such transactions may occur when one party receives some benefit not obtainable from a nonrelated party. Examples of such transactions are:

(1) Borrowing or lending on an interest-free basis or at a rate of interest significantly above or below current market rates

(2) Buying or selling real estate at a price that differs significantly from its appraised value

(3) Exchanging property for property of a different value in a non-monetary transaction

(4) Making or receiving loans with no scheduled terms as to when or how the funds will be repaid[10]

Another form of related-party transaction involves transfer pricing. Transfer pricing is the term used to describe the process of valuing goods exchanged between related entities (e.g., a parent corporation and the related subsidiaries). These are non-arm's-length transactions, and, as a result, the controlling entity may be able to improve the results of operations of one company involved in the transaction to the detriment of the other company. For example, if the benefiting company is small and a related company is large, transfer pricing may create significant artificial profits relative to its size for the small company while having no noticeable effect on the profits of the large company. The problem becomes more complex if more than two entities are involved (i.e., transactions between a parent company and a subsidiary, using a second subsidiary as an intermediate agent) or if the entities are in different countries.

B. ACTIVITIES WITH NONRELATED PARTIES. Examples include lawsuits or pending lawsuits against the company, commitments and contingencies, long-term contracts or leases, nonmonetary transactions, and pension plans.

2. To conceal inadequate performance by company. In some situations, a company may obtain benefits by appearing larger or more profitable than it actually is. For instance, in awarding contracts, some buyers consider, in addition to other factors, the financial condition of the bidder. A bidder might, therefore, distort information in the financial statements, or fail to

[9]Ibid., p. 2.
[10]Ibid., p. 4.

disclose potentially damaging information, in order to improve its chances of obtaining a contract.

3. To evade legal tax liability.   This is one of the more common types of fraud in which the perpetrator attempts, through manipulation of the accounting records, to improperly evade, avoid, or defer income taxes owed by the company. Tax fraud can take many forms, including failure to record income, overstatement of expenses, or generation of improper investment tax credits by recording fictitious purchases of assets.

Type I–B Acts

1. To manipulate company stock value.   Financial statements are sometimes distorted in order to create a desired fluctuation in the company's stock price. Most frequently, the desired fluctuation would be an increase in value allowing management to sell personal holdings of the stock, while knowing that the value was artificially inflated. The manipulation may be accomplished using some of the Type I–A techniques above, but the desired goal is to achieve a direct benefit for the perpetrator and if the company also benefits, it is incidental to the intent of the act. The desired fluctuation may also be a temporary depression in value, allowing management to purchase additional stock for their own portfolio at a bargain price while knowing that the low price is only temporary.

2. To conceal inadequate performance by management.   Management may conceal inadequate or unacceptable performance on their part by manipulation of the accounting records. Generally this occurs when management has made a poor business decision and they are concerned about maintaining their position within the company. They feel that if they can "weather the storm," future profitable decisions will allow them to disguise the bad decisions and they will eventually triumph. Acts such as this often continue until the company is "suddenly" forced into bankruptcy.

Type II–A Acts

1. To conceal the sale or assignment of fictitious or misrepresented assets.   The most widely publicized occurrence of this type of fraud in recent years was the Equity Funding incident in which fictitious insurance policies were sold to other insurance companies. Much effort was expended by Equity Funding management to create fictitious policies and to disguise the bogus policies from both the purchasing companies and the independent auditors.[11] A similar type of fraud involves assigning accounts receivable to an outside party with the assigned accounts showing balances larger than are actually due from customers. Another variation is to fail to report receipts on an

[11]See *Report of the Special Committee on Equity Funding,* AICPA (New York, 1975), pp. 21–22.

account receivable which has been assigned to an outside party.

Companies often use their inventories as collateral on loans, and frauds can occur in this area. For instance, counterfeit or altered public warehouse receipts may be used as collateral, or the actual goods listed on the receipts may be replaced with other items of lesser value.

2. To conceal prohibited business activities.   There are many types of prohibited business activities. Some of the activities are prohibited by government regulations, while others are prohibited by some forms of contractual agreement. Examples of organizations for which various regulations restrict the variety of transactions the organization might be involved in include banks, savings and loan associations, and governmental agencies themselves. Banks are prohibited by law from speculating in equity securities such as common stock. Management may feel, however, that there are opportunities for quick profits by dealing in such securities and may improperly invest depositors' funds. Banks also have a limit as to the maximum amount that can be lent to any one customer. Management may intentionally exceed that limit in seeking unusual gains or providing "special" services for a preferred customer, often with unfavorable results. Savings and loan associations are governed by regulations specifying guidelines for the make-up of their loan portfolios (e.g., private residential, commercial residential, schools, business). Management may intentionally violate the guidelines in an effort to increase profits. Governmental agencies themselves generally work under very specific restrictions as to how funds may be disbursed or invested. The agency management may try to circumvent the regulations by operating unallowable side enterprises or improperly investing excess funds.

3. To conceal improper payments.   There has been much publicity recently on the subject of improper payments, particularly with respect to political contributions and to the conduct of United States companies doing business in foreign countries. Examples of improper payments include payments made or received by a company which

a.   Violate a law or regulation or are of questionable legality (e.g., certain political contributions)

b.   Are falsified or not recorded in the accounting records (e.g., payments from "slush funds")

c.   Represent bribes, kickbacks, and payoffs to customers, suppliers, government officials, either foreign or American, or intermediaries of such government officials

Type II–B Acts
1. To conceal the embezzlement of company funds or assets.   Embezzlement involves appropriating fraudulently to one's own use, money or property

entrusted to the perpetrator's possession. Embezzlements range from a salesperson pocketing cash received and not recording the sale to highly involved schemes for diverting income on investments to the embezzler. Typical examples include overstating expense accounts, concealing misappropriated negotiable securities, and transferring inactive bank deposits to the perpetrator's own account. Product inventories may be embezzled at any stage of production from raw materials to finished goods, detection of the misappropriation being prevented or delayed through manipulation of the accounting records.

Other Types of Fraud Not Involving Management Fraud

Many acts by management which may legally be fraud may not be misrepresented in the financial statements, and, therefore, may not involve management fraud as defined. Examples of these types of acts are included here because such acts sometimes come to the attention of the auditor, who must then decide the appropriate action to take and whether management fraud is involved. Typical examples are:

1. Consumer fraud. Consumer fraud is a form of fraud generally referred to as "con games," in which members of the general public are the primary victims. The varieties of consumer fraud are limitless and may range from individual operations to large corporate ventures. Some of the more highly publicized consumer fraud schemes in recent years have involved misrepresented foreign commodities futures, misrepresented real estate developments in swamps or deserts, and sales of counterfeit securities.

2. Diversion to management of a potentially profitable transaction that would normally create profits for the company. Some members of management are frequently in a position to have special knowledge of potentially profitable transactions of which other members of management or the company owners are unaware. Examples include requests for bids to supply some product or service, real estate transactions, and government contracts. Using this special knowledge, the members of management can establish their own independent company or act as individuals and acquire the rights to the potential transaction. As a result, the individual management members stand to make significant personal profits, whereas the company where they are employed and, in turn, the owners of that company are deprived of those profits.

3. Acceptance of bribes or kickbacks. This type of fraud occurs when the management of a company receives direct benefits from an outside party in return for some special consideration. The special con-

sideration might be proprietary information, the award of a purchase contract to a party other than the low bidder, special discounts, or acceptance of inferior or overpriced merchandise.

Conclusion

Acts of fraud can be separated into distinct subsets, each subset having its own effect on the entity and each having its own method of perpetration. This is important to the auditor because a unique set of audit procedures may be required to detect each subset.

Management may be involved with any act of fraud, but management involvement does not in itself clearly define "management fraud." "Management fraud" represents only those subsets which include intentional misrepresentations that may lead to the inclusion of false amounts in, or the omission of accounts or disclosure from, financial statements. Future discussions and research on management fraud should bear this in mind, and acts which do not fit within this definition should be viewed as other improper acts.

11

Psychological Perspectives on Management Fraud

David R. Saunders

There are many industrial psychologists who feel they know a great deal about "management." Managers at all levels, and certainly this includes top-level executives, have been the subject of dozens of studies, reported in the professional literature by dozens of psychologists. On the other hand, psychologists can claim to know very little about "fraud." In the psychologists' professional literature, fraud appears almost exclusively in the phrases "experimental fraud" and "scientific fraud." A few psychologists have expressed concern that certain other psychologists—notably ESP researchers—are perpetrators of fraud, but no one has seriously confronted the obvious psychological questions raised by the existence of fraud—neither management fraud nor scientific fraud.

This state of affairs comes as no surprise. Psychologists—even clinical psychologists—tend to regard themselves as empirical scientists. Editors of psychological journals will sometimes publish case studies, based on intensive examination of a single individual, but they much prefer to publish reports based on larger numbers of subjects, and they especially prefer reports of so-called experiments. This simply means that the editors have indirectly influenced the psychologists' plans for gathering observational data. In order

Dr. Saunders is Manager, Behavioral Sciences Department, Mathtech.
This paper was prepared for the Peat, Marwick, Mitchell & Co. Symposium on Management Fraud, June 1978. © *Peat, Marwick, Mitchell & Co.*

to do experimental research on fraud, the psychologist would require a sample of at least one and preferably many persons in which the incidence of fraud was demonstrably above average. Since such samples are obviously very difficult to assemble, psychologists have devoted their attention elsewhere.

The essence of any true psychological perspective on management fraud would be a discussion of the way(s) in which perpetrators and potential perpetrators of fraud differ from other people, and the way(s) in which various factors in the environment (including other persons in the environment) may interact to facilitate or inhibit expression of any such traits. The central concepts would be concepts of "individual differences." It *is* the case, though, that ideas and even relatively well-formed hypotheses about such individual differences have come from certain nonpsychologists, who happen to be close to the practical problem. So long as we all understand that we are discussing speculations, there is no reason why a psychologist should not comment on these ideas.

It is customary to classify management fraud as a form of criminal behavior. This immediately suggests that a psychologist should look for "criminal traits" in the perpetrators. However, even leaving management fraud aside, there probably is no universal psychological common denominator to criminal behavior—beyond the fact that it is socially disruptive and therefore disapproved. Certainly not all socially disruptive behavior is criminal, and sometimes it is only history that is even in a position to make a judgment. Psychologists have argued for years whether tendencies to insanity and criminality represent a *qualitative* abnormality, or whether they can be accounted for as merely *quantitative* abnormalities. In other words, do such persons as thieves and schizophrenics possess qualitatively unique traits, or do they merely possess the same traits as so-called normals but in some unusual degree or configuration? There are arguments favoring each view, but I suspect that the latter view is generally the more helpful one.

Thus, management fraud can, in many instances, be conceptualized as merely a perversion of effective management behavior. Nobody would deny that our system of economic incentives rewards imagination applied in the pursuit of profit, and that it rewards managers who exploit profit opportunities. Nobody would deny that this should be so. Yet this often has the effect of encouraging managers to operate as closely as possible to the borderline between legality and illegality—the borderline between what is ethical and what is unethical. And it follows, in turn, that for any of a variety of reasons, an individual manager or management group may cross over the line. Perhaps the line is ill-defined. Perhaps managers' perception in this area is dull. Perhaps they simply reason that the probable benefits outweigh the probable costs. Perhaps they simply like to live dangerously.

From this psychologist's perspective, there are many types of persons who become managers, but principally two types that frequently find their way into executive-level, leadership positions. Strictly as a caricature, we may label one of these the "super-competitor" and the other one the "super-physician." The fundamental psychological assets that these two types bring to their role are essentially opposite.

Super-competitors are fundamentally gregarious; their "real" world is the external world, and they need to be truly involved with other people in that world in order for life to be interesting. At the same time, though, they are afflicted with an innate unattractiveness, so that other people do not spontaneously grant them the involvement they seek. In becoming competitors, they have learned that they can "earn" the involvement they seek—that they can acquire points by performing valued services, and then spend these points to buy their own satisfaction. In the extremity of becoming a "super-competitor," they lose any awareness of this mechanism they may have had, having become obsessed with point-winning at the expense of point-spending. They are effective in their jobs, but it is stressful to them and they are unhappy.

I could easily believe that such persons could believe they had "unshareable problems." Even as children, "super-competitors" have found it difficult or impossible to express their true feelings without engendering hostility and rejection. They have been taught that "good" children don't have such feelings, and they have learned to conceal them by one mechanism or another. They are particularly prone to employ psychological projection as a defense mechanism, justifying their own attitudes on grounds that they are really the same as everyone else's, and that it is only hypocrisy to deny this. I could easily believe that "management fraud" is primarily a perversion of the "super-competitor."

Though they share the executive suite with super-competitors, and talk the same language and jargon with them, "super-physicians" are psychologically different animals. By nature they are ideationally self-sufficient, and their "real" world is their own internal world of thoughts and ideas. Actual involvement with other people is a psychological distraction. At the same time, though, they are afflicted with an innate attractiveness which causes them to be the target of involvement attempts by other people. In learning the "physician" role, they have essentially struck a deal whereby the external world will grant them time alone in return for a commitment to spend that time solving an externally relevant problem. In the extremity of becoming "super-physicians," their primary dedication is to make the external system work, so that it will continue to afford them their personal intellectual freedom. They are effective in their jobs and gain satisfaction from their awareness of doing it well, even though it may be (realistically) stressful on occasion.

It may seem difficult at first to see the difference between the competitor and the physician, because obviously they are both dealing with many of the same developmental issues. Indeed, this is why they are attracted to the same environments (including each other) and why they find it easy to communicate with each other even when they do not agree. The essential difference between them is that the competitor and physician start from opposite psychological poles and, initially moving toward each other, eventually trade places. Thus, the initially gregarious competitor has become (for practical purposes) very self-centered, whereas the initially self-sufficient physician has become very other-directed.

If motivation were the only prerequisite for fraud, either of these types might be a willing perpetrator. However, capacity and opportunity must be equally essential. Given sufficient intelligence, either type could have the capacity. Opportunity, though, will exist for either type only at a relatively advanced developmental stage, by which stage the physician seems relatively unlikely to be willing. Thus, we are left with a prediction that instances of fraud will be primarily associated with competitor and super-competitor personality types.

Within the psychological classification system that recognizes the "competitor" and the "physician," there are three other pairs of types we could discuss. Since this means we are sorting everybody into one of only eight groups, we are obviously employing a very coarse classification scheme. We do not mean to imply that these are the only important facets of individual differences. Quite the contrary, there must remain wide individual differences within each of the eight groups. However, the differences I am highlighting are to be regarded as immutable, whereas most of what is left is theoretically changeable and even reversible. In other words, the eightfold classification is seen as essentially innate, whereas the remnant variability results from differences in learned aspects of behavior. Learning can be undone, but heredity can only be masked—not altered.

It would be useful to discuss two of the additional pairs—first, the "idealist" and the "cynic."[1] "Idealists" are a little bit like "competitors," in that they begin life with the same dilemma. They want to be involved (for similar reasons), and they experience rejection (for similar reasons). They differ in that they are innately far more sensitive persons and have a much lower threshold for confusion. They are therefore relatively unable to ignore significant aspects of reality and to focus their efforts in the manner of competitors. Rather, their best line of development is to make a virtue out of necessity. They can be effective as psychologists or historians, for example, exploiting their intuitive understanding of human motivations. (They may

---

[1]The third additional pair, the "super-responsible individual" and the "super-dependent individual," is not of particular interest in discussing psychological types that might perpetrate or detect management fraud.

have difficulty, though, as counseling psychologists, primarily because they can't leave their clients' problems behind at the office when they go home in the evening.) They are also likely to turn up as chief administrators of nonprofit enterprises catering to human need, such as United Way. They have the easiest time of any of the eight types with the problems of aging; it is as if they were born with the problems of old age, and they have been able even as children to begin to learn to cope with them.

"Cynics" start out at the other end of this dimension and move in the opposite direction, i.e., toward the "idealists." Like physicians, they are self-sufficient and simultaneously attractive to other people. Unlike physicians, they are lacking in sensitivity and integrative capacity. Thus, left alone, they are capable of a "see-no-evil" brand of idealism. However, following one or more experiences with unwanted involvements they are prone to conclude that the world is out to take advantage of them. They have several options, and a great deal depends on how they comprehend what is happening. They may set out to "beat the world at its own game." They may develop exaggerated mechanisms to fend off further involvements. They may, if they have been indoctrinated with a strong social conscience, set out with every intention of reforming the world—and they may even succeed to some degree.

The only actual example of a person involved in "management fraud" that I am currently able to classify happens to illustrate the tension between the cynic and the idealist very well. He was the manager of a branch office of a loan company, located in an ethnically mixed area and himself a member of a minority. While he was involved in embezzlement, he was evidently using the money to promote the welfare of his own group rather than for personal purposes. It seems clear that his ethnic identification helped him to get the manager's job. It also seems possible that, from the viewpoint of his own culture, he was merely exercising one of the perquisites of the job. This case may be unique rather than typical.

It is true, though, that many garden-variety criminals—and now I am thinking of nonviolent crime against property rather than violent crime against persons—come from what I am calling the cynic group. It is a childish and Utopian ideal to suppose that we live in a Garden of Eden, capable of fulfilling all our wants and whims without requiring anything in return. If, as adults, we act out such an ideal, society may well define our behavior as criminal. If, knowing this, we persist, we deserve to be called cynics, at least. Certainly, if such persons happen to land in management positions, any expression of such "criminal" attitudes may be further defined as "management fraud."

The third pair of types I wish to discuss here comprises the "generalist" and the "specialist." Once again we are dealing with two essentially opposite patterns whose development deals with the same set of "personality" issues.

The major issue for both these types is role-definition. At one extreme, this issue arises because the individuals are so role-versatile and so defenseless against the attractions of the external environment that they can adopt virtually any role effortlessly and "effectively." They have to be taught that some roles are "bad," and they have to learn mechanisms to defend themselves against inappropriate involvements. If and when they accomplish this, we are likely to see that they have developed a "professional" role. "Unprofessional" behavior may result from lowered defenses. At the other extreme, this issue arises because the individuals are so role-inept and so unconcerned about the external environment that they truly have no role at all until they are taught one; with strong guidance, they become mirror images of their teachers, but they are unlikely ever to surpass their teachers in anything. On occasion, they may do something "dumb" simply because they have never been taught how dumb it is, or why. Each of these persons tends to envy the other for being naturally the thing he or she has to learn to be.

It does not seem particularly likely that one or the other of these will be a perpetrator of management fraud. However, if we view it as a responsibility of an auditor to *detect* such fraud, the difference between these two types is very significant. Psychologically, an auditor plays a professional role. Some auditors bring to this role only what they have been taught, and only to the extent that they have learned it. Other auditors bring much more, but normally given only what is deemed conventional and proper. If the role is redefined and enlarged to include responsibility to detect fraud, the former group is at a relative disadvantage because they really have no basis on which to proceed. The latter group does have certain aptitudes that can be put to use; however, these aptitudes are likely to be operating only at an intuitive level, so that it will be very difficult for them to specify to the first group how it is possible to do the job.

What emerges here is the prediction that even within a group of auditors who are uniformly well qualified to perform the role up to existing standards, there will be important individual differences in the skills required to detect fraud. This depends on the assumption that detection of possible fraud is a necessary preliminary to the investigation and possible verification of such fraud. It also depends on the further assumption that the ability to suspect fraud by some means that is better than pure guessing is an intuitive process, not subject to predictable forms of logical reasoning. This prediction is potentially verifiable at a statistical level. If it is sustained, we will certainly want to study the distribution of this ability among practicing auditors, and devise strategies for staffing audit engagements that will maximize the use of this possibly scarce resource.

In the course of a year, we read about hundreds of discovered incidents of fraud, just at management levels, and the rate of such reports seems to be increasing from one year to the next. Just as with medical statistics on the incidence of various diseases, we must be cautious in interpreting such observations. Perhaps the real rate of fraud is increasing. Perhaps our methods of detection are improving. Perhaps the press is becoming more inclined to spread the information. I would guess, by analogy with other topics, that the press is actually increasingly difficult to impress, and that a necessary condition for the increasing publicity is an increasing frequency of really large-scale incidents. Except that a large fraud is intrinsically harder to conceal than a small one, I know of no reason to believe that our methods of detection are improving at all. It seems very likely, then, that management fraud is truly a growth industry.

What can be done to reverse such a trend? From a more precise psychological viewpoint, how can we structure a system of rewards, punishments, and opportunities that will minimize the problem of fraud? There are no obvious solutions.

If we assume for the moment that fraud is a "rational" crime, embarked upon because the expected rewards exceed the expected punishments or other costs, since there is little that we can do to reduce the expected reward side of this comparison, this would seem to imply that we should establish severe punishments and implement strategies that maximize the probability of detection. The problem is, though, that the potential rewards have become so great, at least in some cases, that it is literally impossible to propose any commensurate penalty that is generally within the power of an individual or group conceivably to deliver. Potential rewards for fraud (at least as subjectively perceived) will continue to grow, whereas potential punishments are subject to limits. Evidently, starting from this assumption, no permanent solution is possible.

If we regard fraud as an "irrational" crime, economic costs and benefits and/or psychological "utility" are hardly relevant. We need to concentrate on prevention, which can be accomplished through control of opportunity. One approach to this is through the invention of more sophisticated accounting systems, and this is an approach that auditors have traditionally pursued. A complementary approach is through psychological screening of the individuals who control the accounting systems; this approach would certainly be politically very difficult, but it may nevertheless merit consideration. The analogy here might be to the launching controls at an ICBM site; not only do we design a system that requires coordinated action by several operators acting "independently," but we also select those operators in an effort to minimize the chances of conspiracy or "irrational" behavior. The social cost of management fraud may not yet be equal to that of a miscalculated ICBM launch, but the principle is the same.

The foregoing sections of this paper attempt to discuss the topic of management fraud from a particular psychological vantage point, while invoking a minimal amount of jargon. The immediate purpose is simply to elicit discussion, and there are obviously a lot of details that have been glossed over.

The particular vantage point is known as the Personality Assessment System, or simply PAS. A recent technical statement of the PAS may be found in the Journal of Clinical Psychology Monograph Supplement No. 38 (1973).[2] This monograph not only includes a bibliography of over 100 other PAS-oriented papers, but also provides a much more extensive definition and discussion of the central PAS concepts and indicates quite precisely how the information essential to a PAS personality description can be extracted from a profile of subtest performances on the Wechsler Adult Intelligence Scale. Superficially, this is a battery of only 11 subtests but, because statistical interaction effects play such a major systematic role in the PAS, this test battery is capable of providing information on literally hundreds of linearly independent dimensions. Again superficially, subjects accept the Wechsler battery as appropriately measuring a range of abilities, aptitudes, and achievements, so that there is consensus on what represents "good" performance. Faking is possible only at the expense of reducing the IQ score, and a seriously misleading profile can be produced only at great apparent cost. The major disadvantage of the Wechsler battery is that it requires face-to-face administration, and nearly two hours of time from a skilled tester to handle one case.

Of course, the Wechsler battery is useful only to the extent that it really does agree with other modes of observation. It *is* possible to provide evidence of concordance with paper-pencil, self-report personality measures, for example, and this is very reinforcing for theoretically oriented psychologists. The catch is that these relationships are easily distorted in the absence of self-insight or in the absence of motivation to respond truthfully to the self-report inventory. Thus, while it is possible to develop PAS scoring keys for self-report tests, these keys will frequently disqualify themselves when the tests are applied in practical situations. Some useful screening of a group can be accomplished, but such tests cannot be relied upon when it is important to assess a particular individual.

On the other hand, it *is* possible to provide evidence of concordance between Wechsler-based PAS descriptions and ratings based on formal or informal observation of behavior. If the subjects are willing to cooperate, the testing approach is actually more time-efficient and more reliable. However, when they are not willing to cooperate, the observational approach can be remarkably effective. By employing the theoretical model of the PAS, it is possible to identify the behaviors which are observable with particular in-

[2]John F. Winne and John W. Gittinger, *An Introduction to the Personality Assessment System.* Journal of Clinical Psychology, Monograph Supplement No. 38 (Brandon, Vermont, April 1973).

teraction effects existing within the individual's hypothetical Wechsler profile. If several aspects of behavior are observed—not necessarily critical ones —they often suffice to identify the complete profile. Once the profile is known, the direction of reasoning may be reversed in order to derive inferences about as yet unobserved behavior in some critical area.

Two main avenues of possible psychological research lead out of the foregoing discussion. One of these would focus on the attributes of auditors that might relate to their aptitude for the detection of management fraud. The other would focus on the attributes of the perpetrators themselves.

Given that there has never been any psychological study aimed at management fraud, the need for the latter is obvious. Given the currently increasing awareness of the problem of management fraud, the difficulty of identifying an appropriate sample of individuals for study can probably be overcome. A reasonable proportion of *identified* perpetrators might even cooperate in face-to-face procedures of psychological evaluation. However, it will be desirable to consider what could have been known observationally, anticipating that this is the channel through which useful information must come if the research is ever to be applied. I would suggest a modest but immediate effort in this direction; immediate because this is the "critical path," but modest because we are still trying to determine what the real issues are. It would be helpful just to have a few more real cases assessed in PAS terms.

A study aimed at the psychological characteristics of auditors would be much easier to design and carry out. Its payoff would be more immediate, but more limited. Such a study should be planned carefully, so that it can be done right the first time.

12

Management Fraud,
Accounting Controls,
and Criminological Theory

Donald R. Cressey

To sociologically oriented criminologists, there is not a shadow of doubt that management fraud is America's principal crime problem. Ordinarily called "white-collar crime," it is in part responsible for inflation, unemployment, international political incidents, bankruptcies, and even ill health. So far as costs to the nation are concerned, income tax evasion alone probably dwarfs all street crimes put together. As recurrent newspaper stories remind us, payoffs, bribes, illegal political contributions, kickbacks, and other frauds by corporation executives are part of the American way of life.

Although increased knowledge about management fraud does not necessarily mean that crime and chicanery in executive offices will be eliminated, valid knowledge is, in the long run, the most effective basis for control. In the short run, we can try to reduce management fraud and other types of crime by defensive measures and punitive measures—close controls, minimization of trust and freedom, certain punishment of those who deviate. Sooner or later, however, crime must be controlled in the way diseases have been controlled—by developing valid knowledge about its causes and then using that knowledge to eliminate the causes. Put another way, the most practical

Dr. Cressey is Professor of Sociology, University of California, Santa Barbara.
This paper was prepared for the Peat, Marwick, Mitchell & Co. Symposium on Management Fraud, June 1978. ©Peat, Marwick, Mitchell & Co.

program for reducing crime is one which concentrates on and employs criminological theory.

Nevertheless, I shall show that one body of such theory makes good sense of management fraud but cannot be readily applied to the task of "doing something" about such offenses. This set of theory, generally called "differential association," can be interpreted to mean that if management fraud is to be reduced significantly, the ethics and morality of business personnel will have to change significantly. Such change has been the object of clergymen and other moral entrepreneurs for centuries, but we continue to produce a good crop of backsliders every year.

The differential association principle tells us that people violate the law because the world, the nation, and even the family have multiple moralities, not a single morality.[1] The principle also points out that learning to behave in terms of a morality which could land you in jail is as easy as learning how to drive your car faster than 55 miles an hour. But once this is said, we are faced with the task of changing morality by eliminating some of the alternative moralities.

This task is beyond the capabilities of the criminologist and sociologist. In dealing with management fraud, for example, the control problem is largely a matter of getting business people (including some fictitious persons called "corporations") to take collective action toward development of a single morality. That is not an easy task for anyone, let alone social scientists. As indicated, theologians have been trying it for years. They have done so principally by calling for a brotherhood of all humans. Perhaps American business people can join in this worthy cause by learning something about the differential association theory of criminal behavior, and then using this knowledge as a base for developing their own "brotherhood" ethic.

After reviewing some ideas about white-collar crime—especially embezzlement—which have developed over the years, I shall try to illustrate what I mean by "differential association" and "multiple moralities." In doing so, I shall also try to show what is incorrect about several popular explanations of management fraud (and of criminality generally). In the course of all this, I shall try to demonstrate the naivete of the popular notion that management fraud should be reduced by substituting bureaucratic accounting controls for trust, and the preposterousness of the popular notion that auditors and other accountants should be made responsible for the morality of the corporation managers and executives employing them. Finally, I shall argue that a "war on management fraud" which focuses our energy on defense and on deterrence through punishment will be as fruitless as is the more general "war on

[1]Edwin H. Sutherland and Donald R. Cressey, *Criminology.* 10th ed. (Philadelphia: J. B. Lippincott, 1978), pp. 77–98.

crime" which focuses on defense and punishment rather than on what causes crime in the first place.

White-Collar Crime and Criminological Theory

My own interest in management fraud and other white-collar crimes goes back to my days as a graduate student at Indiana University after World War II. I was an assistant to Edwin H. Sutherland, who was conducting a study of crimes committed by the seventy largest nonfinancial corporations in America.[2] He invented the term white-collar crime as a means of calling attention to the fact that most of the popular criminological theories of the time were faulty. These theories emphasized poverty, poor education, broken homes, and emotional disturbances as causes of crime. Sutherland noted that corporation executives who violate the law do not have such characteristics. He reasoned that a good theory would explain the crimes of rich people as well as poor people. He therefore asked criminologists, criminal-justice workers, and laymen as well to reexamine the generalizations traditionally made about crime and criminals. One outcome was a strengthening of his idea that among the rich and the poor alike some people *learn* to become criminals in perfectly normal ways, regardless of personal and social pathologies.

Sutherland's study of the laws pertaining to certain business practices—restraint of trade, infringement of patents, fraudulent advertising, and unfair labor practices were among them—convinced him that these are indeed criminal laws. The procedures used for dealing with juveniles who rob and steal differ from the procedures used for dealing with adults who do the same things, but that does not mean that the juveniles' offenses are not crimes. Similarly, the procedures used for processing violators of antitrust laws (e.g., "cease and desist" orders and "consent decrees") differ from the procedures used for processing burglars and robbers, but the procedures do not change the fact that the antitrust violator has engaged in a practice which is punishable by law. And because behavior which is punishable by law is criminal behavior, violations of antitrust laws and other white-collar crimes are real crimes and must be included in any generalization about crime and criminals.

Sutherland found that, in a period covering about forty years, every one of the seventy corporations had violated one or more criminal laws. The average was about thirteen violations per corporation, with a range of from one to fifty violations. The corporations had a total of 307 adverse decisions on charges of restraint of trade, 222 adverse decisions on charges of patent infringements, 158 decisions under the National Labor Relations Act, 97

[2]Edwin H. Sutherland, *White Collar Crime* (New York: Holt, Rinehart & Winston, 1949); reissued, with an introduction by Donald R. Cressey, 1961.

adverse decisions under the laws regulating advertising, and 196 adverse decisions on charges of violating other laws. Thus, the official records revealed that all but four of the corporations were "hardened," "unreachable," "habitual," or "recalcitrant" delinquents in the sense that they had shown up at least three times in the legal settings designed for controlling corporation crime. Moreover, this enumeration of corporation crimes probably missed many adverse decisions. Even a complete enumeration of all the decisions against all corporations would be only a crude index of the total amount of crime perpetrated by them.

Sutherland defined a white-collar criminal as a person of respectability and high social status who had committed crimes in connection with business. This definition stressed his idea that criminologists and others must seek the causes of crime in something other than personal and social pathologies. But Sutherland's position was confused by the fact that he studied corporations rather than individual white-collar criminals. I tried to correct this by making a study of embezzlers. As expected, I found that the social and personal pathologies commonly attributed to criminals are rarely present in the backgrounds of embezzlers.[3] I therefore sought a different explanation, and I found one which, it developed, is quite consistent with a principle which makes good sense of blue-collar crime and white-collar crime alike. This is the principle of differential association, mentioned above, which also was developed by Sutherland. I shall return to this principle after discussing more specific ideas about embezzlement and management fraud. Here, it need only be noted that differential association theory tells us to view criminals more as conformists than as deviants.

Popular Explanations of Embezzlement

As a first step in my embezzlement study, I turned to the existing literature to see what explanations had been proposed.[4] I found three major explanations, and I expect that all three are now being used to explain management fraud—bribery, illegal payoffs, kickbacks, and so on. Nevertheless, all three explanations are quite weak. The weakness of the third one, especially, we shall see, is quite damaging to the contemporary argument that auditors and accountants ought to be held liable for the detection and disclosure of management crime.

[3]Donald R. Cressey, *Other People's Money: A Study in the Social Psychology of Embezzlement,* (Glencoe, Ill.: The Free Press, 1953), reissued, with a new introduction (Belmont, Calif.: Wadsworth, 1971 and Montclair, New Jersey: Patterson Smith, 1971).

[4]The following review summarizes arguments made in Donald R. Cressey, "Prevention of Defalcations," chapter 4 in *J. K. Lasser's Standard Handbook for Accountants,* edited by J. K. Lasser Tax Institute (New York, 1956), pp. 30–45; and in Donald R. Cressey, "The Respectable Criminal," *Transaction,* vol. 2 (1965): 12–15. See also Donald R. Cressey, "Why Do Trusted Persons Commit Fraud? A Social-Psychological Study of Defalcators," *Journal of Accountancy* (November 1951): 576–81.

According to the first explanation, embezzlements are the product of a variety of factors, any one of which or any combination of which may produce the crime. At the turn of the century, E. P. Moxey, a bank examiner for the United States Department of Justice, studied bank embezzlements and concluded that the defalcations of bank officers could be traced to the following list of "causes": promoting enterprises in which the officers have a financial interest; speculation; gambling and extravagant living; the advancement of political ambitions; negligence of directors in allowing officers to use funds, under the guise of loans, to a criminal extent; lack of diligence on the part of the bank's clerical force.[5]

Except for "gambling and extravagant living," this list is a *description* of embezzlement by managers (and of management fraud generally), not an *explanation* of it. Embezzlements by the clerical force were said to be due to the above "causes" and also to temptations offered by loose methods of conducting business and of keeping accounts; to lack of proper supervision by officers and directors; and to the criminal use of the bank's funds by its officers without detection and punishment, encouraging clerks to do likewise.

In the years since this pioneering study was conducted, the list of such alleged "causes" has been elaborated. Bonding companies have stressed gambling, drinking, loose living, extravagance, and whoring as factors in embezzlement, probably because such lists might convince employers that "anyone" might embezzle, thus convincing them to bond all their employees. But this type of explanation is based on the doubtful assumption that describing the motives, traits, and working conditions of embezzlers will help us understand why honest people steal. It seems obvious, however, that ascribing bad motives to behavior does not explain that behavior.

According to a second explanation, embezzlement is a product of a constitutional or moral weakness in the offender. An explanatory system of this kind was developed by Lester A. Pratt, a certified public accountant who derived his statement from observation of thousands of cases of bank embezzlement encountered in his profession.[6] Embezzlement, he said, is the result of faulty or illogical reasoning. The evidence for this is that all persons seek happiness and crime is not conducive to happiness, that embezzlers in many instances operate on the mistaken theory that the sum taken is merely a loan, and that embezzlers believe they can long cover up the fraud. However, the argument goes, whatever the faulty reasoning which leads to the crime, the crime is accompanied by moral weakness on the part of the individual: "A man of strong character has a steadfastness and he abides by what he knows to be right." The majority of embezzlements result not so much from inherent dishonesty as from weakness in resisting temptation. It is therefore the

[5]E. P. Moxey, "Bank Defalcations—Their Causes and Cures," *Annals of the American Academy of Political and Social Science,* vol. 25 (1905): 32–42.
[6]Lester A. Pratt, *Bank Frauds, Their Detection and Prevention* (New York: Ronald Press, 1947), pp. 8–11.

duty of the bank to eliminate loose methods of operation which tempt the weak individual. Pratt's complete theory, then, is that a combination of illogical thinking, weakness on the part of the individual, and loose accounting methods causes officers and employees to defraud their banks.

This explanation, like the first one, continues to be popular. It is the explanation of rising crime rates used by politicians and "elder statesmen" everywhere. Aristotle used it. Embezzlement, this theory holds, is increasing because young business personnel do not have the moral fiber of their forefathers.[7] "Permissiveness" is on the loose. Dr. Spock has raised a generation of immoral hedonists. But explanation in terms of weakness, moral depravity, natural dishonesty, strength of moral fiber, and so on, is always "after-the-fact" explanation. Such hidden variables can be said to cause almost any kind of behavior even before the behavior has been observed. Ascribing hidden weaknesses to fraudulent managers and others merely indicates moral disapproval of their behavior and in no sense explains the behavior. An evil result need not have something evil as its cause.

The third popular explanation of embezzlement attributes the crime to poor defense measures. For generations, auditors and other accountants have been using the "inadequate defense" argument about embezzlement even as they have on occasion attributed some influence to immoral living and weak character. Their basic point has been that accountants are desperately needed in any corporation's war on internal crime. Like American police leaders, accountants have exploited fears of crime in order to gain budgetary support, high status, and immunity from outside interferences with their activities. Twenty-five years ago, for example, an accountant melded internal controls and audits into a single system of police surveillance, then noted that close surveillance of company employees is a reasonable way to stop crime:

> The object of a sound audit program is to prevent defalcations rather than find them after they have occurred. . . . I will not contend that an audit program can be so complete as to eliminate thefts entirely, but I do believe that thefts can be made more difficult to accomplish, and the knowledge on the part of the average employee that his work is subject to review and examination will reduce the number who might otherwise dip into the till. The preventive medicine of sound internal control is its best recommendation.[8]

More recently, Barrett, Baker, and Radde (a team of accountants employed, respectively, by the University of Minnesota, Northwestern Bell Telephone, and Investors Diversified Services) elaborated on this theme after noting that

[7] In the early 1950s, an accountant put the matter this way: "[For more than a decade] personnel acquisitions have been comprised of a different stock and fibre than the 'cream of the crop' graduates from various schools who were employed a generation ago." John L. Nosker, "Audits and Controls," *Auditgram,* vol. 28 (1952): 29–33.
[8] Edward T. Shipley, "Audits and Controls," *Auditgram,* vol. 28 (1952): 26–28.

most investors believe that locating fraud is a principal function of audits. They attribute the recent increase in top management misdeeds to the following:

> A permissive investment climate, innovative financing, novel contractual arrangements, creative accounting, performance appraisal systems that offer incentives for achieving financial performance targets, and immediate dismissals for nonperformance were causes. The fact that certain illegal political activities were fostered by aggressive fund solicitors and candidates who used direct or subtle hints of retribution has also been ignored.[9]

The authors then propose a comprehensive, three-level, defense system extending to all levels of management. At the top level is a program of "climate" or operating environment controls, including a corporate audit committee, an effective and extensive internal audit charter, and a sound security program. Next, "transactional" controls would be placed on managers' activities. Included are rigorous pre-disbursement approval review procedures, quantitative analytic review procedures by internal auditors, and audits of managers' securities trading activities. Finally, the behavior of managers would be closely scrutinized by "personal" defenses such as lie-detector tests, preparation of income tax returns by external auditors, and periodic assessments of each person's net worth. All of this, it is implied, should be done by accountants: "Internal and external auditors must stop wringing their hands and disclaiming responsibility. As internal auditors, let's do something about fraud—now!"

Generally speaking, when auditors and other accountants say that defalcations and management fraud should be "prevented" or "controlled," they use a conception of "cause" similar to the one seemingly used by Barrett, Baker, and Radde. They insist, as do all good soldiers in a war on crime, that persons in positions of trust are given too much freedom from surveillance by accountants, thus allowing them to violate the trust criminally. A variant of this theme is that weak accounting systems and audits fail to detect embezzlements in their early stages. From these observations it is reasoned that laxity in accounting methods causes embezzlement and fraud—"cause" being used to refer to any condition which allows embezzlement and fraud to occur. The explanation is not inconsistent with statements attributing burglary to poor locks and inadequate alarm systems. Burglary, in this view, is caused by failure to control (locks) and failure to detect (alarms) burglars. A substitute for locks and alarms, of course, is a gun. The implication is that armed police officers are to keep citizens under such close surveillance that burglary without detection and arrest is impossible. Few people would commit burglary if there were a police officer at every person's elbow, and few

---

[9]Michael J. Barrett, Donald W. Baker, and Leon R. Radde, "Top Management Fraud: Something Can Be Done Now!" *Internal Auditor* (October 1976): 25–33.

people would commit embezzlement if there were a sharp auditor looking over every trusted person's shoulder. Stated in extreme form, the causal logic here makes liberty into an evil—if no one had any freedom, then no one would be free to commit a crime of any kind. More specifically, if no executives, managers, and employees of a corporation were trusted, then none of these personnel could violate a position of trust.

I contend, however, that the accountants' "inadequate defense" argument has been wrong all along, and they should not be held to it. This should be clear from a short study of the history of embezzlement and from a short analysis of why police officers are not held responsible for the crime rates of their communities.

Trust, Modern Business, and the Accountant

Several years ago, I argued against the "weak accounting controls" explanation of embezzlement by noting that modern society, with all its complexities, presupposes business transactions based upon a considerable amount of trust.[10] No matter what the degree of restriction imposed on trusted persons (including managers) in modern business, it is still true that an element of trust must remain. Even in this day of computer accounting and computer auditing, auditors and other accountants must *necessarily* give managers and employees enough freedom to do business, which means giving them enough freedom to commit management frauds as well as embezzlements. A brief review of the history of embezzlement as a crime should make this point clear.

When commerce was beginning to expand in the sixteenth century, there were two simple rules pertaining to financial relations between English masters, servants, and third persons.[11] These rules pertained to trust, and they determined what could be a larceny from a master and what could not. First, property received by a servant from a master remained in the *master's* possession, the servant receiving "mere charge or custody" of it. A necessary element in the common law of larceny was taking property from the possession of another, so a servant in charge of his master's horse could be convicted of larceny if he sold the horse and pocketed the money. Second, property received by a servant from a third person for the master was in the *servant's* possession, and the servant therefore was not guilty of larceny if he converted it to his own use. Thus, a servant who sold a horse he had received from a man from whom the master had bought it committed no crime—he had not taken the horse from the master's possession. These rules were

---

[10]"Prevention of Defalcations," pp. 36–37.
[11]Jerome Hall, *Theft, Law and Society,* 2nd ed. (Indianapolis, Ind.: Bobbs-Merrill, 1952), p. 35.

reasonable in an age when servants were servants and masters were masters. When one master sold a horse to another, there was no need for the services of a servant as an intermediary.

With the coming of the commercial revolution, however, "servants" became in fact clerks and cashiers. Under the second rule, servants bilked their masters right and left but were not criminals. Servants who clerked in shops and who put into their own purses the money they received from customers committed no crimes—the money never got into the master's possession. For example, in 1799 a bank teller who credited a hundred pound note to a customer's account and then put it directly into his pocket was prosecuted for larceny and found not guilty. He had not taken the money from anyone's possession. Gradually, this loophole was plugged up. First, the concept of possession was modified. It became the rule that if a servant received money from a third person and put it into a cash drawer, it thereby came into the possession of the master. So if the servant subsequently took the money from the cash drawer to keep, this act was larceny.

Then, in 1799, the first English general embezzlement statute was passed. This law, recognizing the new nature of business, made it a crime for a servant to violate the trust the master put in him; the servant was guilty of the new crime of embezzlement if the servant converted to his or her own use any money that was received from a third person for the master. But even this law was strictly construed—in 1812 a stockbroker (an "agent" not a "servant") took money given to him to invest and converted it to his own use; the court held that the general embezzlement law did not cover this act. New legislation to cover brokers, agents, and factors was passed. In the next fifty years, as the nature of business continued to change, embezzlement statutes were expanded to criminalize more and more violations of financial trust.

From this brief history it may be observed that as trade and commerce increased, and as modern business practices arose, merchants and bankers had impressed upon them the fact that the common law of larceny and fraud had been designed for a relatively simple economy in which there was no need to trust servants with business transactions. In essence, they found that third-party business transactions could not be completed unless employees were trusted, yet trust violation was no crime. Their new embezzlement statutes filled this breach by inventing a new crime, violation of financial trust.

During the twentieth century, business became increasingly dependent on trusted employees, agents, brokers, factors, and other fiduciaries. Therefore, to argue that embezzlement and management fraud can be prevented by rigid accounting methods is to overlook the pertinent point: If strict controls were imposed on all corporation personnel, then embezzlement, management fraud, and other trust violations would be greatly reduced, but very little business would be done. Indeed, if business were guided by the implications of the notion that trust violation is to be eliminated by not trusting people, there would be no need for statutes which declare embezzlement, management fraud, and similar behavior to be crime. Removing "the temptation, the opportunity, and even the suggestion to violate the solemn trust which has been placed in officers and employees," as one accountant has proposed,[12] would be to eliminate both "solemn trust" and a large percentage of all modern business transactions.

It seems reasonable to conclude that accountants never should have argued that they can institute surveillance and detection measures so tight that no embezzlements, frauds, and concealments can possibly occur. "Weak" accounting controls are essential to modern business, just as "weak" police controls are essential to modern democracy. Indeed, the fundamental problem of human rights is that of minimizing police controls and maximizing personal liberty.

Police Officers and the Crime Rate

There is a second reason why accountants should not argue that they are capable of keeping corporate personnel under surveillance, thus keeping the crime rate low: They are technically incapable of doing so. Police executives have, over the years, quite effectively convinced the public that it is not reasonable to hold police officers accountable for rising crime rates. In the first place, they argue, the community never provides them with enough money. Even if costs to civil liberties are ignored, the "crime fighter" image of police officers cannot be fulfilled. The money allocated to police departments must be spent on many functions that cannot be considered "law enforcement" in the strict sense of the term.[13] The perpetual shortage of funds makes it necessary for police departments to be "reactive" rather than "proactive," that is, police officers, like fire departments, must wait for citizens to call them for help; they cannot afford many proactive routines in which police go out looking for trouble, acting as detectives on their own initiative. In the second place, police executives argue, some criminals are smarter than police officers. It follows that the police should not be expected to detect and catch them, let alone stop them from committing crimes in the first place.

These arguments, which have been analyzed by an expert on police operations[14] and an expert on administrative law,[15] among others, are highly

---

[12]"Audits and Controls," p. 29.

[13]James Q. Wilson, *Varieties of Police Behavior: The Management of Law and Order in Eight Communities* (Cambridge, Mass.: Harvard University Press, 1968).

[14]Herman Goldstein, *Policing in a Free Society* (Cambridge, Mass.: Ballinger, 1977).

[15]Kenneth Culp Davis, *Police Discretion* (St. Paul, Minn.: West Publishing, 1975).

relevant to the problem of management fraud and to the argument that accountants are capable of keeping corporation personnel under close surveillance. The fact is that considerations of economy and efficiency make it impractical for accountants to maintain checks on all personnel and procedures, just as considerations of economy and efficiency make it impractical for police officers to detect all crimes and apprehend all criminals. One accountant long ago advanced four reasons for doubting that standard accounting and auditing methods are infallible tools for detecting defalcations:

> First, the majority of defalcations occur in the level of business transactions not normally subjected to the auditor's detailed scrutiny.
>
> Second, the perfect system of internal control has never been invented, and probably never will be.
>
> Third, the versatility of embezzlers is astounding, and greatly underestimated.
>
> And finally, in my opinion, the emphasis of auditing education and techniques has been placed on routine factual verification rather than upon analytical study and inquisitive reflection.[16]

Close attention must be given to this rebuttal of the idea that embezzlements and management frauds are caused by inadequate defenses. The four points merely summarize the two principal arguments used by police executives bent on showing that they cannot be held responsible for rising crime rates. Further, it should be noted, these points are, in one way or another, used by police executives specifically to deny their responsibility for management fraud, thus shifting the responsibility from their shoulders.

There is no legal reason why crime among business personnel should not be a grave concern of regular, uniformed, police officers. Nevertheless, Americans have organized their police services in ways which make ordinary police departments extraordinarily ineffective in the white-collar crime area. In the first place, as indicated, police departments respond to calls for help. But most of the people being harmed by white-collar crimes do not call because they do not know they are being harmed. For example, citizens rarely call their local police with a complaint alleging that they have just lost $2.00 because some corporation is engaging in price fixing. Moreover, if individuals were to call a police department with complaints about white-collar crimes, or about some injustice a corporation had done to them, the chances are good that the officers answering the telephones would politely tell them to get lost.

Police departments are organized to display a "crime fighter" image. One consequence is extreme concentration on "street crimes" rather than the crimes of corporations and their executives. As a pioneering American soci-

---

[16]William W. McCullogh, "Embezzlement, A Rising Menace," *The California Accountant*, vol. 2 (1949): 7–13.

ologist put it, business offenses "lack the brimstone smell" associated with long-standing Biblical proscriptions.[17] Few police departments employ accountants, lawyers, or business specialists who are knowledgeable about management fraud. And even in police departments—such as the FBI—with some expertise in this area, the "crime fighter" priorities remain. A Los Angeles FBI agent once pointed out to me that when a bank robbery occurs, the Bureau is likely to send fifty agents out to swarm all over the bank; but when a banker allegedly engages in a multimillion dollar stock swindle, the Bureau sends a solitary officer out to peck away at the case, sometimes for years. Perhaps it is this negligence on the part of regular police departments which has focused the attention of Congress, the SEC, and others on private auditors.

Why Honest People Steal

I have been arguing that considerations of freedom, money, and politics limit the accountant's effectiveness as a police officer, as does the fact that the versatility of criminals is astounding. But there is an even better ground. The fact is that management frauds, like other crimes, are generated by general cultural conditions over which accountants do not have, and cannot have, very much control.

My research on embezzlement approached the problem of cause in a manner consistent with the notion that concentrating attention on defense measures is not enough. Given the fact of trust, made necessary by the nature of modern business, why is it that only some trusted people violate that trust? Given the fact that audits and internal controls are not infallible, why is it that only a minority of the persons possessing the freedom to deviate do in fact deviate?

In seeking answers to these questions, I spent about a year at the Illinois State Penitentiary at Joliet interviewing embezzlers. I then moved to California and talked to more embezzlers in the Institution for Men at Chino. I also was able to gather a considerable number of cases from other studies. But I was disturbed because my sample of embezzlers included only a few bankers; this because bank embezzlement is a federal offense and most of my interviews had been conducted in state prisons. So I spent a summer interviewing embezzlers in the United States Penitentiary at Terre Haute, Indiana.

From the interview materials, I developed, after several unsuccessful attempts, a generalization which I think applies to all the embezzlers I talked to. I see no reason to believe that it does not apply to all embezzlers, although I realize that one should not generalize beyond the data. It is possible, too, that the *principle* involved in the generalization, if not the generalization

---

[17]Edward Alsworth Ross, "The Criminaloid," *Atlantic Monthly,* vol. 99 (1907): 44–50.

itself, can be used to make good sense of management fraud generally. It even seems to have something to say about blue-collar crime as well as white-collar crime.

What I came up with was the idea that embezzlement involves a psychological process made up of three steps or phases:

1. The feeling that a personal financial problem is unshareable.

2. The knowledge of how to solve the problem in secret, by violating a position of financial trust.

3. The ability to find a formula which describes the act of embezzling in words which do not conflict with the image of oneself as a trusted person.

Individuals have *unshareable financial problems* if it appears to them that they cannot turn to ordinary, legitimate sources for funds. To an outsider, the situation may not seem so dire; what matters is the psychological perspective of the potential embezzler. Because, in the embezzler's words, the trusted person is "ashamed" or "has too much false pride" to share the problem with people ordinarily available for help in financial matters, the problem must be kept secret. A few years ago I found an example of this state of mind in a newspaper letter to Ann Landers. The writer was a bookkeeper who had taken $75 from petty cash to pay some long-overdue personal bills. "I could have gone to my boss and received a loan for this amount with no trouble, but I had too much pride. My husband makes a small salary, and I was ashamed to admit that we were having a difficult time financially." The writer, who signed herself "Ashamed," had not been caught, was paying the money back, and was terrified that she might succumb to the temptation again.[18]

After I had formulated this unshareable problem notion, I tested it by asking fifty embezzlers about an imaginary financial problem. I asked them to suppose that for some reason their fire insurance policy had lapsed and then, through no fault of their own, there was a short circuit in the wiring, or lightning struck, and their home burned down. The family lost everything they owned in the fire. My question was, "Do you think that in a situation like this you would have been tempted to embezzle to get the money you would need?" Sixty percent of the cases indicated clearly that this situation did not seem to them unshareable, and that therefore they would not embezzle. The reasoning is clear in responses like these:

Case 42. I don't believe I would. I think that in a case like that folks would have sympathized with me and helped me out. There would be outside aid. But in my own case, they didn't know about it and so they couldn't help.

[18]"Ask Ann Landers," *Santa Barbara News Press,* January 9, 1963.

Case 57. Well, I don't doubt that I would if I couldn't borrow the money or something of the sort. There are people or relatives that have money. I've never got along with them, but if it was a necessity like that I would go to them. I'd do anything to give my wife and children what they needed. (He indicated earlier that he had been too proud to go to his relatives for help at the time when he had embezzled.)

The unshareable-problem concept helps to make understandable the reported high incidence of "gambling," "other women," "improvident investment," "drink," "living above his or her means," "poor business manager," and so on in the behavior of embezzlers, but these modes of behavior are not used as explanatory principles. None of these factors can be located in even a majority of cases of trust violation and, therefore, the word "cause" is hardly applicable to them. The unshareable-problem concept shows how the various factors might "work" to motivate embezzlement. It should be emphasized, however, that the possession of an unshareable problem is not alone the cause of embezzlement. Almost all persons have unshareable problems at one time or another, but most of us, of course, do not violate positions of financial trust we might hold.

The second part of my generalization, the *realization* that the problem can be solved in secret by violating a trust, is a problem in the psychological perception of opportunities to embezzle. As I have already suggested, everyone in a genuine position of trust has an objective opportunity to violate that trust. Were this not the case, the word "trust" would not be appropriate. Yet many persons in trusted positions do not perceive that their unshareable problems can be resolved by violating the trust. Before they can do so, they must have certain general information about trust violation, and must be able to apply that general information to their own conduct in the present circumstances. Let me give just one illustrative statement, made by an embezzler (an accountant) about the opportunity and techniques of embezzlement:

In my case, I would say that I learned all of it in school and in my ordinary accounting experience. In school they teach you in your advanced years how to detect embezzlements, and you sort of absorb it. . . . It is just like a doctor performing abortions. . . . I did not use any techniques which any ordinary accountant in my position could not have used; they are all known by accountants, just like the abortion technique is known by all doctors.

The third element in my generalization about the embezzlement process, *verbalization,* is the crux of the matter. I am convinced that the *words* the potential embezzler uses in conversations with himself or herself are the most important elements in the process which gets the trusted person in trouble, or keeps the person out of trouble. If a person sees a possibility for embezzlement, it is because he or she has defined the relationship between the unshareable problem and an illegal solution in language that lets the person look on trust violation as something other than trust violation. If the person cannot do this, he or she does not become an embezzler.

To illustrate, let us imagine a man who is a pillar of the community, a respected, honest employee, a man with a background no more criminal than that of most of us. This man finds himself with an unshareable problem, and an objective opportunity to steal money from his company. The chances are very good that if in that situation I walked up to him and said, "Jack, steal the money from your boss," he would look at me in horror, as if I had suggested that he could solve his problem by going down and sticking a pistol into the face of the local liquor store owner. "Jack, steal the money from your *company,*" probably would bring about less of a horror reaction. Still, honest and trusted persons "just don't do such things." However, honest and trusted persons do "borrow," and if I were to suggest that Jack secretly "borrow" some money from his firm, I would have helped him over a tremendous hurdle. Then he can tell himself that he is borrowing the money and can continue to believe that he is an honest citizen, even as he is stealing the boss blind. Because he wants to remain an honest citizen, the "borrowing" verbalization becomes the key to his dishonest conduct.

I do not wish to overemphasize the idea of "borrowing." There are many verbalizations used, some of them quite complex. The "borrowing" verbalization is but a simple example of a vocabulary that can adjust two contradictory roles—the role of an honest person and the role of a crook. I call the use of such a vocabulary a rationalization, which is different from the way psychoanalysts use the term. A rationalization is not merely an *ex post facto* justification for behavior which has been prompted by some deeply hidden psychological motive. It is itself a motive, a set of words formulated *before* the act takes place, and which are themselves the person's reasons for acting. The rationalizations used by embezzlers vary with the position of trust which is involved and, also, significantly, to some extent with the precise manner in which the trust is violated.

Trusted employees and managers who embezzle relatively small amounts over a long period of time often use the "borrowing" rationalization, but independent businesspersons, factors, and agents who convert "deposits" of various kinds usually use a rationalization which enables them to look upon the embezzled funds as their own. Absconders almost always use a "don't care" or "to hell with it" rationalization which enables them to abscond with funds or property without giving up their ideal of honesty—they view themselves as special kinds of criminals whose criminality is somehow justified, much in the manner of terrorists and other political criminals. Embezzlers report the use of other rationalizations, such as the notion that theirs is a case of "necessity," or that their families are in a precarious position, or that their employers are cheating them, but these rationalizations are almost always used in conjunction with the "borrowing," "ownership," and "don't care" verbalizations. Norman Jaspan, president of a management engineering firm bearing his name, has noted the increasing importance in embezzlements of a rationalization to the effect that "I have it coming to me," a variety of the "ownership" idea. He believes that this verbalization has accompanied the recent wave of mergers and acquisitions occurring in the corporate world. Some mergers have created unshareable problems in the form of insecurity and unfulfilled expectations, including broken promises. In one case, for example, the executive vice-president of a company lost his title and the promise of a share in the business when his boss had a heart attack and decided to sell out. A new executive crew was moved in by the new owners. The former vice-president embezzled nearly $100,000 before he was caught. He said he had the money coming, practically as a promise from the old boss.[19]

Verbalizations and Cultural Ideologies

Vocabularies of motive are not something invented by embezzlers on the spur of the moment. Rather, embezzlers' rationalizations are reflections of cultural ideologies pertaining to the propriety of committing crime under certain circumstances. For this reason, the rationalization component is by far the most important of the three elements making up the embezzlement process. Further, the fact that verbalizations exist as group definitions of situations in which crime is *appropriate* makes understandable the behavior of most criminals, not just embezzlers. These criminals include corporation managers and executives who are involved in fraud and in deception of stockholders.

Among some groups in the United States, unscrupulous and even criminal behavior is rationalized in terms of an ideology which begins and ends with the assertion that "Honesty is the best policy but business is business." The last part of the slogan neutralizes the first part. The ideology is common among business personnel. Half the 1,700 corporation executives polled in one study agreed with the following statement: "The American business executive tends to ignore the great ethical laws as they apply immediately to his work. He is preoccupied chiefly with gain."[20] In opting for gain ("business is business"), corporate directors and managers sometimes use methods which are in violation of ethical laws ("honesty is the best policy"). They do so, quite simply, because almost everyone uses the same methods—they are a part of the business culture.

Among other American groups, or in other situations, criminal behavior

[19]Reported by Robert J. Cole, "Sees Corporate Mergers as Causing More Crime," *The New York Times,* February 8, 1970, Section 3, p. 35.

[20]Raymond C. Baumhart, "How Ethical Are Businessmen?" *Harvard Business Review,* vol. 39 (1961): 6–19, 156–76.

is common because persons apply to their own conduct some variation of the ideology that "It is not wrong to steal a loaf of bread when you are starving." In groups where such ideologies exist—and these groups are very extensive —the individual using them has a sense of support and sanction. If individuals have learned that "All people steal when they get into a tight spot," it will not be surprising to find them stealing when they get into what they define as a tight spot. Another person might use the same ideology by saying, "I have tried to live an honest life, but I'm having nothing but troubles, so to hell with it." An anthropologist has given us an example from another culture:

> The Burmese are Buddhists, hence must not take the life of animals. Fishermen are threatened with dire punishment for their murderous occupation, but they find a loophole by not literally killing the fish. "These are merely put on the bank to dry, after their long soaking in the river, and if they are foolish and ill-judged enough to die while undergoing the process it is their own fault.". . . When so convenient a theory had once been expounded, it naturally became an apology of the whole guild of fishermen.[21]

Another common ideology, highly relevant to embezzlement and to management fraud as well, is the idea that "Some of our best people got their start in life by using other people's money for a time." This statement, which probably is true, can be used as a motive for illegal as well as legal use of other people's money. Once the ideology has been assimilated and internalized by individuals, it is likely to take a form such as the following: "Because I'm only borrowing other people's money, not stealing, I'm doing what some of our best people have done." This verbalization is not an "after-the-fact" justification given to police officers or others in an effort to minimize the subject's responsibility for the crime. Instead, it is a real and valid motive for acting in the first place. People who use it are not deterred by cultural prohibitions and admonitions about committing crime, for they have convinced themselves that their behavior is not crime "really," and "after all."

The Importance of Talking to Oneself

The verbalization process helps make sense of the secondary behavior of some criminals, as well as of the criminal behavior itself. For example, many of my embezzlers who used the "borrowing" rationalization eventually lost it. Some recognized that they were "in too deep" and then admitted to themselves that they had been stealing, not borrowing, all along. Others read a newspaper account of an embezzlement and as a consequence admitted to themselves that they had been stealing not borrowing. Loss of the "borrow-

---

[21]Robert H. Lowie, *An Introduction to Cultural Anthropology,* enl. ed. (New York; Holt, Rinehart, 1940), p. 379.

ing" verbalization had significant consequences for their behavior. They were faced with the unpleasant fact that they, who considered themselves honest and honorable, had slipped into a category of persons whose behavior they disapprove, criminals. The embezzlers I interviewed reported that at this point they were extremely nervous, tense, and emotionally upset, and a few said they had contemplated suicide.

There are two paths out of this unpleasant situation. One path, taken by the great majority, is to do everything possible to maintain the ideal of honesty and the conception of self as an honest and reputable citizen. Speaking generally, embezzlers who take this path behave toward themselves precisely as honest citizens behave when they find a criminal in their midst. Thus, embezzlers who have used the "borrowing" rationalization and then lost it may report their dishonest behavior to their trustors or to the police. They may go to great lengths to show their bosses exactly what they did so that the boss will be able to keep others from doing it. The embezzlers are likely to be concerned because they have not had time to get the company's books in order before going off to prison. They resemble law-abiding citizens interested in justice. In a recent interview, Norman Jaspan said that 90 percent of those who embezzle on the white-collar level will admit most of their wrongdoing "if psychologically handled with intelligent probing without lie detectors or threats of police action. Once they believe you know of their wrongdoings—they don't consider these wrongdoings a crime at the moment—they want to unburden themselves."[22]

The second path involves abandoning the conception of self as a reputable person, rather than the conception of self as a criminal. A few of my embezzlers said that by slipping into criminality they had made themselves unworthy of membership in groups which condemn criminality. After they lost the "borrowing" verbalization they identified with criminals and began behaving like criminals, becoming reckless in their peculations, deliberately taking funds with no intention of repaying them, or absconding.

Some violators, of course, are arrested before they recognize that they are "in too deep," so that they never have an opportunity to abandon the "borrowing" verbalization. Many of these persons insist, even after apprehension, trial, and imprisonment, that their behavior is not criminal. They say their intent was merely to use the trustor's money temporarily, to "borrow" it for a time. Seemingly inconsistent and variable behavior among embezzlers, then, becomes understandable in the light of the verbalizations they use.

As I suggested above, the differential association principle makes good sense of blue-collar crime and white-collar crime alike. I also have suggested that my generalization about embezzlement is consistent with this principle,

[22]Quoted by Cole, p. 35.

and that it can be used to make good sense of most management fraud, not just embezzlement. The rationalization aspect of the generalization is the critical one, both with reference to differential association and with reference to management fraud.

Differential Association and Multiple Moralities

In his statement of the theory of differential association, Sutherland stressed the fact that criminal behavior is learned behavior. Moreover, he said, the principal part of the learning occurs in intimate, personal groups, and it includes "the specific direction of motives, drives, rationalizations, and attitudes."[23] Some individuals are surrounded by persons who define the legal codes as rules to be observed, thus teaching the individual to be non-criminal, even anticriminal. Others are surrounded by persons whose definitions are favorable to violation of the legal codes, thus in subtle ways teaching the individual to act criminally.

But most persons, of course, are surrounded both by definitions unfavorable to law violation and by definitions favorable to law violation. We become criminals, or not, depending upon the ratio of these two kinds of behavior patterns in our life experiences. For example, most American children are likely to learn that "honesty is the best policy," but they also are likely to learn—in an extraordinarily complex and subtle process—that this moral axiom has many loopholes of the sort we have already mentioned—"business is business," "it is all right to steal under some circumstances," and so on. Whether a given child will grow up to become a criminal, then, depends on the balance between these two kinds of behavioral directives.

Sutherland's theory is much more sophisticated than this simple statement implies. For example, it really pertains to specific kinds of crimes rather than to crime in general. A person thus may learn to be highly anticriminal with reference to, say, burglary, but highly procriminal with reference to, say, income tax evasion. A woman to whom holding up a liquor store is unthinkable will smuggle jewelry into the country when returning from her European vacation and will brag to her friends about her crime. A man who would not dream of pimping for a prostitute will enthusiastically engage in restraint of trade. Thomas Lynch, when he was Attorney General of California, put the matter this way: "Some of our greatest criminals would be shocked at the sight of a gun. All they need is a pen. More major crimes today involve ink stains than blood stains."[24] But such complexities cannot be discussed in detail here. The important point is this: Sutherland told us that as we try to understand white-collar crime or any other kind of crime we should stop

[23]*Criminology,* p. 81.
[24]Quoted in *The Los Angeles Times,* March 2, 1967.

looking for emotional disturbances, defective personalities, and other personal and social pathologies, which are secondary, and start looking at the verbalizations of groups in which individuals participate, which are primary.

In telling us to study social participation when we try to explain why most people are noncriminals and only a small proportion are criminals, Sutherland aligned himself with social scientists who view "social organization" and "personality" as two facets of the same thing. The person is seen as part of the kinds of social relationships and values in which he or she participates. We obtain our essence from participation in values, norms, rules, and customs of various kinds which surround us. Persons (personalities) are not separable from the social relationships in which they live. They behave according to the rules (which are sometimes contradictory) of the groups in which they participate; they cannot behave in any other way.

This is to say that criminal behavior is, like other behaviors which a person exhibits, the *property of groups,* not of individuals. Criminal behavior is not just a *product* of an individual's contacts with certain groups; it is in a very real sense "owned" by groups rather than by individuals. Management fraud, for example, is owned by businesspersons in much the way the French language or the English language is owned by a collectivity rather than by individuals.

This "ownership" and "participation" point was long ago documented by Shaw and McKay, who showed that children moving into a neighborhood take on the delinquency rate of that neighborhood, whether it be high, low, or somewhere in between.[25] Despite methodological critiques, this research has stood the test of time. By the same token, we should expect corporations moving into an industry to take on the crime rate of the industry. I have not been able to locate corporation histories which either support or negate this hypothesis. But Shaw and McKay demonstrated essentially the same point by showing that boys in similar neighborhoods have similar recidivism rates. I recently reanalyzed Sutherland's data on restraint of trade and found that corporations in the same industry, like boys in the same neighborhood, have similar recidivism rates.[26] For example, neither of the two mail order houses included in Sutherland's study were repeaters of the restraint of trade offense —Sears Roebuck had no adverse decisions against it, and Montgomery Ward had only one. But all three motion picture companies had high recidivism rates—Paramount and Warner Brothers each had 21, and Loew's had 22. Two dairy companies, Borden and National Dairy Products, had middle-range rates of 7 and 8.

[25]Clifford R. Shaw and Henry D. McKay, with the collaboration of Norman S. Hayner, Paul G. Cressey, Clarence W. Schroeder, T. Earl Sullenger, Earl R. Moses, and Calvin F. Schmid, *Juvenile Delinquency and Urban Areas* (Chicago: University of Chicago Press, 1942).

[26]Donald R. Cressey, "Restraint of Trade, Recidivism, and Delinquent Neighborhoods," chapter 8 in *Delinquency, Crime and Society,* ed. James F. Short, Jr. (Chicago: University of Chicago Press, 1976), pp. 216–18.

Such patterning suggests that restraint of trade and other management crimes are neighborhood (industry) phenomena, and that—as in the case of delinquent boys—criminality is not merely a product of the individual characteristics of isolated actors. The patterning can be attributed to conspiracy among the involved corporations, to diffusion of illegal practices, to the policies of trade associations, and, generally, to the sharing by managers in the same industry of ideologies relevant either to law obedience (mail order houses) or to law violation (motion picture companies).

"Participation" in "social relationships" is, of course, the subject matter of all of anthropology, sociology, and social psychology. Nevertheless, "participation in social relationships" is rather meaningless as an explanatory concept when it stands alone, for it serves only to indicate in a general way, to oversimplify, and to dramatize social interactions which are so confused, entangled, complicated, and subtle that even the participants are unable to describe their own involvements clearly. Sutherland's criminological principle, and my embezzlement generalization as well, tell us what to look for after we have moved toward considering the specific effects that "participation in social relationships" has on individual conduct. In a word, what we should look for is *words*.

Cultures and subcultures consist of collections of words that are used in prescribed ways. These words make it proper to behave in a certain way toward an object designated by the word, "cat," and improper to behave in the same way toward an object designated by the word "cabbage." They also make it "wrong" and "illegal" to behave in certain ways, and "right" or "legal" to behave in other ways. Significantly, as noted earlier, words also make it "all right" to behave in some situations in a manner which also is "wrong" or "illegal." In short, words exist as group definitions of what is appropriate; they necessarily are learned from persons who have had prior experience with them.

Some Relevant Studies

A great deal of evidence supporting the importance of verbalizations to both criminal and noncriminal behavior is found in psychological and sociological journals, but it has not been systematically collected and summarized. Here, I can give just a few examples, drawn from the criminological literature.

Stated in oversimplified form, Lindesmith long ago found that if persons who are habituated to drugs talk to themselves in certain ways, they will become addicts, while if they talk to themselves in other ways, they will avoid addiction entirely.[27] Lindesmith's most general conclusion was that persons

[27]Alfred R. Lindesmith, *Opiate Addiction* (Bloomington, Ind.: Indiana University Press, 1947).

can become addicts only if certain kinds of verbalizations are available to them. More recently, Coleman found that even the idea that addicts are "forced to steal" is learned by some addicts and not by others, with the result that the former steal and the latter do not.[28] Consistently, Becker's studies of marijuana users showed that perception of the effects of marijuana is determined by the kinds of words given to smokers by users.[29]

Another example is found in the work of Sykes and Matza, who, in a study of delinquents, followed up the "rationalization" idea suggested by my embezzlement studies.[30] They concluded that because all youths accept conventional values to some degree, they must "neutralize" these conventional values before they can commit delinquencies. As illustrations of the "techniques of neutralization" used by delinquents, they cite use of verbalizations which blame parents or misfortune for one's theft, define the victim as worthless, justify offenses as a duty toward one's friends, and note the faults of those who condemn delinquency. Possessing these verbalizations makes delinquencies seem reasonable to boys and girls who would otherwise reject them.

Consistently, when Smigel asked people whether they approve or disapprove of stealing from organizations under certain circumstances, he found morality to be associated with size of the victim organization.[31] Thus, half of his sample strongly disapproved of specified acts of stealing from a small business, but only 34 percent and 31 percent, respectively, disapproved of specified kinds of stealing when the victim was large business or government. When 212 persons were asked to choose the type of organization from which they would steal "if in need" and if they felt "they had no other choice," 30 (14 percent) refused to steal under any circumstances and three would not answer the question. Of the 179 who responded, 57 percent preferred to steal from large business, 30 percent from government, and 6 percent from small business. (The remaining 7 percent either did not distinguish between large business and government or did not differentiate at all.) Most respondents based their choice of large business on the principle of lesser evil, feeling that stealing from big business is not as bad as stealing from small business because large business is impersonal, powerful, and ruthless. Most

[28]James W. Coleman, "The Myth of Addiction," *Journal of Drug Issues*, vol. 6 (1976): 135–41.

[29]Howard S. Becker, "Becoming a Marijuana User," *American Journal of Sociology*, vol. 59 (1953): 235–42. See also Becker, "Marijuana Use and Social Control," *Social Problems*, vol. 3 (1955): 35–44.

[30]Gresham M. Sykes and David Matza, "Techniques of Neutralization: A Theory of Delinquency," *American Sociological Review*, vol. 22 (1957): 664–70.

[31]Erwin O. Smigel, "Public Attitudes Toward Stealing as Related to the Size of the Victim Organization," *American Sociological Review*, vol. 21 (1956): 320–27. See also Smigel, "Public Attitudes Toward 'Chiseling' with Reference to Unemployment Compensation," *American Sociological Review*, vol. 18 (1953): 59–67.

used verbalizations similar to that of a respondent who said, "Big business has tremendous capital, a part of which they've cheated from me." Some of those who preferred to steal from the government used the "Robin Hood" principle, some deplored the "socialism" of government, and some used other verbalizations which neutralized the immorality of the act.

More directly relevant to management fraud are extensive and detailed studies of violations of price-control and rationing regulations during World War II.[32] These studies found, in essence, that businesspersons violated the regulations because they did not "believe in" them. Put another way, they possessed verbalizations which made the criminal law seem irrelevant. A dislike of government regulation in general was joined with dislike for price-control and rationing laws in particular. The result was verbalizations which attacked the very legitimacy of government and which, therefore, made black market operations seem almost patriotic. The bureaucrats in Washington stood for socialism, the idea went, while landlords and meat and poultry dealers stood for free enterprise and the American way of life. Clearly, the idea continued, the government is considering as a crook every businessperson who tries to make a profit; it is the government that is wrong, not the businessperson. The late Senator Robert Taft of Ohio put the matter this way: "The attitude of O.P.A. [Office of Price Administration] today, as I get it from everybody who comes to me, is that the businessman is presumably a crook; that if he is trying to make a profit he is greedy."[33] The businesspersons who entered the black market were persons who accepted and applied to their own conduct this notion that the "bad guys" are government lawmakers and the "good guys" are free enterprise merchants.

A study of crimes among New England shoe manufacturers similarly showed the important role that antigovernment attitudes play in crimes committed by management.[34] In the eight New England communities studied, there were wide variations in the number of shoe firms violating labor relations laws. In Haverhill, Massachusetts, for example, 7 percent of the shoe firms violated these laws, while in Auburn, Maine, 44 percent violated them. The author concluded that one of the reasons for the differences among the towns was differences in "attitudes toward the law, the government, and the morality of illegality." Those shoe manufacturers who associated with people whose attitudes favored violation were more likely to break the law; those who were isolated from these attitudes were less likely

[32]Marshall B. Clinard, "Criminological Theories of Violations of Wartime Regulations," *American Journal of Sociology*, vol. 11 (1946): 258–70. Frank E. Hartung, "White-Collar Offenses in the Wholesale Meat Industry in Detroit," *American Journal of Sociology*, vol. 56 (1950): 25–34; and Marshall B. Clinard, *The Black Market: A Study of White-Collar Crime* (New York: Holt, Rinehart, 1952).

[33]Quoted by Clinard, p. 332.

[34]Robert E. Lane, "Why Businessmen Violate the Law," *Journal of Criminal Law and Criminology*, vol. 44 (1953): 151–65.

to break the law. This influence on attitudes was evident even in the reading habits of the manufacturers—those who violated the law had immersed themselves in a segment of the daily press so hostile to government that violation of the law seemed quite appropriate to them. Thus, even the newspapers were sources of verbalizations that made crime "all right." Lane predicted, on the basis of such observations, that managers of companies located in bigger cities, with a cosmopolitan press, diversified social life, and greater tolerance for heterodoxy, would accept legal restrictions on how they conducted their businesses more readily than would small town management. This prediction was borne out; firms located in small towns violated the laws much more frequently than did similar firms located in larger cities. The small town atmosphere, as compared to that of bigger cities, more frequently provided a rationale which made this crime seem reasonable, even patriotic—government shouldn't tell a person how to run his or her business; "that man" in Washington is no good anyway; labor unions are corrupt.

Differential Association and Business Ethics

Fred T. Allen, Chairman and President of Pitney-Bowes, in 1975 became troubled by the almost daily revelations of corporate bribes and payoffs in the United States and abroad, and by the steep decline in the public's esteem for business and its practitioners. He thought that he and other corporation executives were beginning to be perceived as "little more than manicured hoodlums."[35] To get a line on prevailing attitudes among corporation personnel, his company commissioned a survey by The Opinion Research Corporation. The objective was to find out how some 531 top and middle managers, from a representative selection of all business sectors, viewed bribing foreign officials to attract and retain contracts. The results are a sad commentary on the state of American business ethics, but they came as no surprise to students of white-collar crime. Fifty percent said that bribes should not be paid to foreign officials, but 48 percent said they should be paid if such practices are prevalent in a foreign country. Of those who accepted the practice, 68 percent said it was a cost of doing business in certain countries. And 38 percent said it was an established practice, inferring that there was no way to get around it. Some consolation was available from the fact that 64 percent of those who would not pay bribes said they would refuse on moral grounds.

Mr. Allen was startled by these findings. He asked corporate leaders to set realistic sales and profit goals, to spell out ethical codes, and to demonstrate that they "will not tolerate wrongdoing of any kind by anyone." It is

[35]Fred T. Allen, "Corporate Morality: Is the Price Too High?" *The Wall Street Journal,* October 17, 1975, p. 14.

a bit ironic, therefore, to find that when the managers of his own company, Pitney-Bowes, were surveyed anonymously in early 1977, the majority said they feel pressure to compromise personal ethics to achieve corporate goals.[36] Similarly, a 1976 study by Uniroyal and University of Georgia professor Archie B. Carroll III, found that 70 percent of Uniroyal managers and 64 percent of a random sample of corporate managers perceived company pressure on personal ethics. "Most managers believed that their peers would not refuse orders to market off-standard and possibly dangerous products (although an even larger majority insisted they would personally reject such orders), and a majority thought young managers automatically go along with superiors to show loyalty."[37]

These little studies of corporate morality probably apply equally well to price fixing, illegal allocation of markets, false advertising, illegal use of inside information, shareholder ripoffs, illegal campaign contributions, and other management frauds. Especially relevant is the finding that young managers "go along" with the questionable practices of their superiors. This is exactly what anyone familiar with the differential association principle would have predicted. President Johnson's Commission on Law Enforcement and Administration of Justice might well have been using the differential association principle when it declared that corporate leaders influence the rest of us:

> Derelictions by corporations and their managers, who usually occupy leadership positions in their communities, establish an example which tends to erode the moral base of law and provide an opportunity for other kinds of offenders to rationalize their conduct.[38]

Put in common sense terms, the differential association principle says that criminality is a matter of morality. A person's ethics, sense of decency, or sense of morality determines whether that person will commit crime. As suggested earlier, the sense of decency and morality possessed by some persons makes it wrong to commit burglary and robbery but does not make it equally wrong to commit more genteel crimes such as restraint of trade. In turn, the differential association principle notes that one's sense of morality is a set of learned attitudes and behavior patterns. In interaction with other people, who collectively possess and exhibit a wide variety of moralities, each person develops a morality which includes a sense of what is and what is not "really" crime. It is to be expected, therefore, that persons who interact with

---

[36]Study cited by *Business Week,* January 31, 1977, p. 107.

[37]Reported by Carl Madden, "Forces Which Influence Ethical Behavior," chapter 1 in *The Ethics of Corporate Conduct,* ed. Clarence Walton (Englewood Cliffs, N.J.: Prentice-Hall, 1977), p. 66.

[38]President's Commission on Law Enforcement and Administration of Justice, *Task Force Report: Crime and Its Impact—An Assessment,* U.S. Government Printing Office (Washington, D.C., 1967), p. 104.

and look up to business personnel who make profits unethically are likely to become unethical themselves. In other words, if I associate frequently and intimately with persons whose ethics are summarized in the phrase "Honesty is the best policy *but* business is business," it would be surprising indeed if my ethics could be summarized by the simple phrase, "Honesty is the best policy."

Moreover, the differential association principle invites us to seek the origins of multiple moralities and alternative ethical principles. How does it happen that business personnel put qualifiers on such maxims as "Honesty is the best policy," thus providing procriminal verbalizations for persons participating in the set of social relationships called "business"? How did the institution of business come to get into conflict with the institution of government, resulting in widespread business practices which, from the standpoint of government, are unethical, immoral, criminal?

Proposed Solutions to the Management Fraud Problem

Implied in recent discussions of management frauds (including this one) are three quite divergent ideas about how to prevent these offenses. Two of the proposed prevention programs stress defense and punishment. One would make auditors and other accountants into police officers, responsible for bringing malefactors before a bar of justice. The second would make these professionals into private security guards, responsible for protecting individual companies from the crimes of insiders and outsiders alike. The third proposed program would put the emphasis on improving the ethics of managers—fraud would be prevented by making it morally unthinkable.

The Auditor as Police Officer.   The present trend toward holding auditors responsible for revealing the dishonest practices of management is based, implicitly at least, on the assumption that dishonesty and other immoralities will decrease if every offender is detected, apprehended, convicted, and punished. The books and articles written on this subject stock thousands of feet of library shelves, and they cannot be summarized here. There seems to be no doubt that certain and severe punishment deters and that, further, imposing punishments has long-range effects on morality.[39] But there seems to be no question, either, that a machinelike system for punishing all violators of criminal codes smacks of totalitarianism.[40] What is at issue is not the question of whether punishment deters. The sticky question is whether a system of swift, certain, and uniform punishments can be just.

[39]See Johannes Andenaes, *Punishment and Deterrence* (Ann Arbor, Mich.: University of Michigan Press, 1974).

[40]See Donald R. Cressey, "Criminological Theory, Social Science and the Repression of Crime," *Criminology,* vol. 16 (1978): 171–91.

Those who would make auditors and other accountants responsible for revealing questionable management practices to stockholders are assuming, without saying much about it, a popular "war on crime" (deterrence) posture. Thus, it is assumed that publication by auditors of the amount of money a company has used to bribe foreign officials will lead to reprimands from stockholders and others, leading to abandonment of the practice. From this assumption it is but a short logical step to the conclusion that accountants shall be responsible for detecting and publicizing all crimes committed by management. It is this step that makes auditors into police officers, deputized to serve the state without pay.

I have already shown why it is not reasonable to hold regular police officers responsible for rising crime rates. They are not, and cannot be, capable of detecting and arresting all criminals. I have argued, consistently, that auditors and other accountants are not capable, and cannot be capable, of detecting dishonest managers who are dedicated to eluding them. Consider advertising fraud. When a company advertises that there are 700 parsley seeds in a package, must the auditor count the seeds, perhaps finding (as one consumer did) that the package contains only 416 seeds?[41] Such frauds increase profits, and these profits are summarized in figures which the auditor certifies. Is the day coming when the auditor must certify that all the profits are crime free? Smogging, like mugging, increases profits. Is the auditor—internal or external—to be responsible for reporting that a certain percentage of a firm's profits came from smogging?

In one famous case, police officers from the Food and Drug Administration staked out a warehouse of a company which marketed "pure orange juice." They found that sugar, vitamin C, and other substances not permitted in pure orange juice were being brought into the plant. It was estimated that the adulteration practices of the company cost consumers about a million dollars in lost value, thereby increasing the company's profits by that amount.[42] The question now being raised is whether the company's accountants and auditors should have been required by law to stake out the company's purchase orders and then to tell consumers that a company selling "pure orange juice" had bought, say, twenty tons of sugar.

Suppose there is collusion between a trucking firm and a driver to disregard regulatory rules forbidding the employee to drive more than a certain number of hours a day. Should the auditor be liable for injuries to persons hurt in driving accidents by such employees? Consider product liability. Is it reasonable to hold the auditor liable if an aircraft corporation sells planes

---

[41]James MacGregor, "Short-Weighting Often Leaves the Customer Paying More for Less," *The Wall Street Journal,* July 2, 1972.

[42]Reported by Gilbert Geis, "Deterring Corporate Crime," chapter 9 in *Corporate Power in America,* ed. Ralph Nader and Mark J. Green (New York: Viking, 1973), pp. 182–97.

with a defective fuel system that causes crashes and numerous deaths?[43] After all, such things are done to increase profits, profits are stated in financial statements, and if auditors are made into police officers they will be responsible for the methods used to make profits as well as for the authenticity of the summary statements of profits and losses.

My point is this: It is quite silly to think that auditors are capable of preventing management fraud by smoking it out. Unethical managers who are able to conceal their frauds from both special and uniformed police officers surely are also able to hide them from accountants, too.

In addition to this "inefficiency" argument, there is a political argument against holding auditors and other accountants responsible for the morality of the American way of doing business. Clifford A. Graese, a partner of Peat, Marwick, Mitchell & Co., recently made this political point as follows:

> If any government agency can, without the judicial process, use pressure tactics to call on third parties, including the company's auditors, to disclose anything and everything they know about the company's operation, such third parties are literally turned into an investigative arm of the government. Imposing such a role is completely inconsistent with a free democratic society.[44]

The Accountant as Security Guard.   Industrial plants, business firms, schools, and universities have organized private police forces because their executives feel they are not adequately protected by the public police. These security personnel are privately selected, financed, and controlled, although they are sometimes licensed or commissioned as public agents. They protect company or institutional property from outsiders, but they also try to detect and apprehend employees who steal tools from the plant, take merchandise from the store, and so on. A decade ago about 290,000 persons (excluding part-time workers) were employed as private detectives, investigators, and guards, as compared to about 400,000 sworn public police officers and about 120,000 personnel employed as government guards.[45] The number of private police has probably increased more rapidly than the number of public police since that time. About 40,000 firms such as Pinkerton's, Burns, Brink's, and Wackenhut provide contract guard and investigative services in the United States.

Auditors and other accountants have always functioned as private police officers. Nevertheless, such police work has been only a peripheral part of

[43]See G. Christian Hill and Barbara Isenberg, "Documents Indicate Four Beech Models Had Unsafe Fuel Tanks," *The Wall Street Journal,* July 30, 1971.

[44]Clifford E. Graese, "Accounting, Accountants, and Managers," chapter 5 in *The Ethics of Corporate Conduct,* ed. Clarence Walton (Englewood Cliffs, N.J.: Prentice-Hall, 1977), p. 154.

[45]James S. Kakilik and Sorrel Wildhorn, *Private Police in the United States: Findings and Recommendations* (Santa Monica, Calif., 1971), p. 31.

their total function. They do not look upon themselves as security guards and probably resent the implication that their duties are more analogous to the activities of security guards than to the duties of vice-presidents.

In the effort to curtail management fraud, an alternative to making auditors into unpaid public police officers is to assign them to a company's private security force. The executives and managers of any firm doing so would necessarily be asking their security department to be responsible for minimizing fraud by managers as well as for minimizing thefts by employees and outsiders. As things now stand, company security guards rarely have anything to do with corporate morality.

Two principal advantages would accrue to companies which assigned accountants to keep an eye on corporate officers. In the first place, companies would get more assistance from uniformed police and, moreover, from the special police officers working for government regulatory agencies. Private police are expected to be concerned with private interests, and their major functions are said to be prevention and detection of crime on private property and the gathering of information for private purposes. Public police, on the other hand, are said to be primarily concerned with public interests such as keeping the peace and protecting consumers. But private police also serve what may be called public interests, and public police, when acting as guards and when on patrol, and even when making arrests for thefts and burglaries, serve private interests.[46] For this reason, perhaps, cooperative arrangements between private and public police are common. Public police provide security forces with arrest records and FBI rap sheets, operate nightly call-in services for security agencies and dispatch patrol cars to check on those guards who fail to call in regularly, complete investigations begun by private police, provide private police with radios preset to the police frequency, and permit, require, or even pay for the installation of direct-dial alarms and central alarms that notify the police department of burglaries, robberies, or prowlers. It seems reasonable to expect that a corporation showing a sincere interest in cutting down management fraud by adding accountants to its security force would receive similar assistance.

In the second place, and more importantly, assigning accountants to the security crew would necessarily require board members and managers to think seriously about the morality of their conduct and to publish a code of ethics, that is, if an accountant were made chief security officer, with the duty, among other things, of detecting and reporting management misconduct to the board, then the board would necessarily have to set explicit policy regarding what is and what is not proper management conduct. For example, suppose one company stated explicitly that bribing foreign politicians or

[46]See Theodore M. Becker, "The Place of Private Police in Society: An Area of Research for the Social Sciences," *Social Problems,* vol. 21 (1974): 438–55.

marketing dangerous products or advertising falsely is against company policy, and then explicitly assigned to some accountants the job of trying to police it, while another company did not take these two steps. Surely the stockholders of the two companies would be able to make logical deductions about the ethics of management, even if the first company's accountants were not capable of detecting all instances of code violations. Over the years, a corporation board that published and enforced a code of ethics might even come to believe in it.

Changing the Ethics of Managers.   In the long run, as I said at the beginning, crime is best controlled by first understanding its causes and then intervening in the causal process. To scientists, that is what "control" means. Government policy regarding the control of malaria did not become effective until scientists came to understand malaria. And the scientists who came to understand malaria were dependent on the nineteenth-century scientists who developed the "germ theory" of disease, a set of general propositions about the cause of illness. We are still far from an understanding which would make it possible to control crime in this scientific sense. We have not yet developed an accepted general theory which is comparable to the "germ theory" of disease in scope, let alone derivative theories about the specific conditions causing management fraud or any other crime. We do know, however, that the differential association principle has put us on the right track.

This principle, to repeat, holds that it is not enough to try to prevent management fraud by strengthening defenses against it, as politicians, police officers, government regulatory agencies, and even accountants would have us do. It is true, of course, that we must defend. Given the present state of behavioral and social science, and given the present state of politics, there seems to be no alternative to hit-or-miss attempts at repressive and bureaucratic control of crime and criminals. Politicians interested in reducing the crime rate are in the same boat as were the government officials interested in reducing the malaria rate. The latter could not afford to wait for the results of the search for the cause of malaria. They had to try to control malaria by defending against it—encouraging people to drink tonics and to stay away from night air. They did not know what else to do.

But, in the case of management fraud, putting the emphasis on defense has a dangerous side to it. The danger is that continuing to stress defense will continue to distract from the need to develop and use interventionist methods which will cut off the sources (causes) of the evil. It is ridiculous to let management fraud take root and grow in fertile soil and then to try to frustrate it rather than trying to do something about its breeding grounds. Doing so is like ignoring the causes of malaria and putting all time, money, and energy into an "avoid night air" campaign. Stated positively, the differential association principle implies that any real program for preventing management fraud will try to reduce the cultural conditions which encourage it. These cultural conditions, we have seen, include verbalizations ("rationalizations") which make management fraud seem "all right" or even appropriate.

Any program to reduce verbalizations favorable to management fraud is, when it comes down to it, a program for improving the ethics of business personnel. This is no easy task. Because "honesty" and "morality" and "ethics" cannot be precisely defined, a pure society free of management fraud will never be attained. But, some business leaders are observing, if managers tried harder to be honest, moral, and ethical, then management fraud surely would decline.

I have not been able to locate any organized campaigns aimed precisely at making management fraud so immoral that it is unthinkable. However, there are straws in the wind. Business ethics is now a popular topic of conversation in schools of business administration and in businessmen's clubs and executive suites all over the nation. Earlier I referred to a survey commissioned by Pitney-Bowes, Inc. When the respondents were asked if legislation —presumably calling for stronger defenses and punishments—would be effective in preventing bribery of foreign officials by United States nationals, 92 percent said it would not. They thought such bribery would continue despite such legislation, and they thought that publicity would be much more effective in discouraging bribery. What they had in mind, I think, was a need for publicizing unethical behavior to a degree such that bribery will become immoral.

An American business leader has asked business executives to get involved in a management fraud prevention program of this kind. He warns that the issue of ethics is critical to the very survival of capitalism:

> It is, of course, easy for me or any executive to sound forth with a litany of high-minded principles. It is far more difficult to imbue an organization with the ideals behind the words. And it is most difficult of all for an executive to make sure that those ideals—once spelled out—are also carried out by employees at all levels.
>
> And yet that is exactly what we must do. Business organizations take their cues from their leaders. It is up to the leader to make sure that ethical behavior permeates the entire company. Employees must know exactly what is expected of them in the moral area and how to respond to warped ethics. . . .
>
> As businessmen, we must learn to weigh short-term interests against long-term possibilities. We must learn to sacrifice what is immediate, what is expedient, if the moral price is too high. What we stand to gain [by immorality] is precious little compared to what we can ultimately lose.[47]

---

[47]"Corporate Morality" p. 14. See also George Cabot Lodge, "Managerial Implications of Ideological Change," chapter 2 in *The Ethics of Corporate Conduct,* ed. Clarence Walton (Englewood Cliffs, N.J.: Prentice-Hall, 1977), pp. 79–105.

13

Concerted Ignorance: The Social Psychology of Cover-up

Jack Katz

The gift Jim Smith, EFLIC vice president, Lloyd Edens, the treasurer, and Art Lewis, the actuary, have given their boss, Fred Levin, to commemorate the completion of the annual statement, was meant to be a gag. It was a photograph of the three of them seated in a row. Smith had his hands over his ears. Edens had his over his eyes, and Lewis's were over his mouth. Hear no evil, see no evil, speak no evil. Frank Levin liked the picture so much he hung it on his wall.[1]

That people can and do keep a silence about things whose open discussion would threaten the group's conception of itself, and hence its solidarity, is common knowledge. It is a mechanism that operates in every family and in every group which has a sense of group reputation. To break such a silence is considered an attack against the group; a sort of treason, if it be a member of the group who breaks the silence. This common silence allows group fictions to grow up, such as, that grandpa was less a scoundrel and more romantic than he really was. And I think it demonstratable that it operates especially against any expression, except in ritual, of collective guilt.[2]

---

[1] Raymond L. Dirks and Leonard Gross, *The Great Wall Street Scandal* (New York: McGraw-Hill, 1974), p. 58.

[2] Everett C. Hughes, "Good People and Dirty Work," in *The Other Side,* ed. H. S. Becker (New York: The Free Press, 1964), p. 28.

Dr. Katz is Research Associate, Yale White Collar Crime Research Program, Yale Law School.
This paper was prepared for the Peat, Marwick, Mitchell & Co. Symposium on Management Fraud, June 1978. ©*Peat, Marwick, Mitchell & Co.*

Introduction

Recent exposés of management fraud raise a central issue in the social psychology of occupational life: How do insiders arrange cover-ups? Whatever the importance of individual motive (greed, conflict of interest, character fault) and societal context (capitalism/socialism, booming or static economy), cover-up itself is a complex collective act requiring explanation.

The premise of this paper is that an examination of the social arrangement of cover-ups in formal organizations should be useful for understanding management fraud, but it must be noted that "cover-up" and "management fraud" are far from equivalent. Management frauds always entail secret knowledge and deception, but not all involve the *collective* activity that I will treat as cover-up. My focus is on organizational deviance:

> . . . for a person's actions to be organizational (rather than individual) deviance, they must be supported by the person's fellow workers or fellow members. This peer support may be active (as when all employees at a particular level engage in it) or passive (as when colleagues are aware of deviant action but tolerate it). Acts of embezzlement are thus deviant, but not organizationally deviant, since peers are typically unaware of them and do not support them.[3]

Some types of management fraud require collective guilt by definition: commercial bribery, kickback conspiracies, and price-fixing. Other frauds may be of such large scale or long duration that they require the complicity of numerous insiders in order to keep suspicion off the books. Examples include false advertising, conversion of company assets for personal benefit, sale of fictitious assets, improper valuation of assets or liabilities, failure to disclose significant information, and improper related-party transactions.

If some instances of management fraud will escape a focus on "cover-up," it must also be noted that not all cover-ups by managers will be "fraud." But the history of attempts to study white-collar crime suggests an important reason for choosing cover-up rather than fraud as the phenomenon to be explained. Very soon after it began with Sutherland's writings,[4] the academic discussion of white-collar crime bogged down in definitional controversy. Too often one person's white-collar crime is another's civil fraud is another's legitimate business practice. White-collar crime in general, and management fraud in particular, are inherently harder to define than crimes of violence and overt property theft. Legislation and enforcement policies change with

[3]David Ermann and Richard J. Lundman, "Overview," in *Corporate and Governmental Deviance,* eds. David Ermann and Richard J. Lundman (New York: Oxford University Press, 1978), p. 8.
[4]Edwin H. Sutherland, "White-Collar Criminality," *American Sociological Review,* vol. 5 (1940): 1–12; *White Collar Crime* (New York: Holt, Rinehart & Winston, 1949).

political winds, and what was not crime yesterday may be officially treated as criminal today, or vice versa.

It was once suggested that a subjective definition should be used, i.e., that the study of white-collar crime should include only those who consider themselves to be criminals.[5] Surely this is too narrow. Just as surely, "fraud" would lose all meaning if any allegation of inaccurate representation would trigger the classification. We might instead focus on behavior felt by actors to require cover-up. One might try to cover up an act or activity because one knows it is criminal, because unprincipled adversaries might try to get enforcement officials to treat it as criminal, because revelation might lead to legislation making it criminal, or merely because it might appear improper to a public audience. In any case we have a common subject for study.

Perspectives on Cover-ups

How are cover-ups established and maintained in large-scale organizations? Social scientists have argued that collective forms of deviance derive significantly from routine expectations of ignorance. By definition, subordinates are expected to carry out orders without understanding the implications as well as do their superiors. We have been warned about the tendency in large organizations toward the "bureaucratic personality,"[6] the subordinate who, having abandoned an autonomous, creative orientation to work, follows orders too literally. We have also been warned of the overly great respect paid to "expertise" in our highly technological, specialized society. Deference to the expert supposedly undermines the will of subordinates to resist even those orders which would visibly cause others pain.[7] Writing in a similarly pessimistic vein in a previous paper, I depicted several ways external audiences routinely legitimate domains of organizational secrecy.[8] Bureaucratic structures and ideologies of professionalism facilitate large-scale complicity in deviance by conditioning subordinates toward passive compliance. Institutions of organizational privacy provide covers.

There is too much pathos and too little drama in this perspective.[9] To be sure, complex organizations are based on expectations of ignorance separating occupants of different ranks and specializations and separating insiders from outsiders. Yet people are rarely if ever completely passive in respond-

[5]Ernest W. Burgess, "Comment" and "Concluding Comment," in *White-Collar Crime*, ed. Gilbert Geis (New York: The Free Press, 1977), pp. 164–65, 167.

[6]Robert K. Merton, *Social Theory and Social Structure*, (New York: The Free Press, 1968), pp. 249–60.

[7]See the experiments of Milgram. Stanley Milgram, *Obedience to Authority: An Experimental View* (New York: Harper and Row, 1974).

[8]Jack Katz, "Cover-up and Collective Integrity," *Social Problems*, vol. 25 (1977): 3–17.

[9]Cf. Alvin F. Gouldner, "Metaphysical Pathos and the Theory of Bureaucracy," *American Political Science Review*, vol. 49 (1955): 496–507.

ing to expectations, perhaps especially to the expectation that they remain ignorant.[10] Descriptive accounts of cover-ups do not square with the theoretician's image of the subordinate who does not dare or care to understand the large implications of a small role in an overall collective act. Rather than secrecy being maintained by the structures of organizational boundaries, we see difficult and often daring maneuvers to create and protect myths that boundaries between hierarchical levels and between insiders and outsiders have blocked knowledge and limited culpability.

One striking feature of many organizational frauds is that insiders often participate even though they anticipate that the fact of crime ultimately will be revealed and they will be questioned. Operators of Ponzi or pyramid sales schemes, which use new "investments" to pay returns promised to previous investors, accumulate new income arithmetically and new obligations geometrically. At some point they know that the pyramid will inevitably collapse and fraud will be alleged. More generally, insiders to cover-ups of war atrocities, price-fixing arrangements, and political kickback collusions have reason to hope that the cover might never be blown. But they also anticipate that it might. They plan no physical "getaway"; they take up positions for a metaphysical escape.

The explanation of cover-up is not completed by answering the question, How can insiders rely on outsiders not to inquire? In some cases that is sufficient, but it is not a necessary condition. A more fundamental question is how insiders manage to cover themselves, to take anticipatory positions that will protect them from being tied into the cover-up if it is revealed. This is a question about the cover-up of cover-up. It is addressed in the next section on strategic ignorance.

Strategic ignorance may insulate the individual from the group's culpability, but it is not an individual achievement. Superordinates and subordinates, insiders and outsiders, have common interests in limiting the knowledge each obtains about the other. In what are often quite tacit ways, bargains are struck as to what each will require the other to know. Without doubting for a moment that some insiders clearly and explicitly share an understanding of mutual culpability, we must also appreciate that unspoken arrangements of concerted ignorance are essential to widespread organizational deviance. I examine this collective aspect in the second section.

The final section examines some variations in the social organization of work that might make it more difficult for members collectively to keep deviance secret. Organizational conditions differ in the extent to which they encourage one to assume that others will join in a cover-up, and they differ in the degree they enable one to avoid guilty knowledge about others. The

[10]On the negotiated character of roles, see Anselm Strauss, *Negotiations* (San Francisco: Jossey-Bass, 1978).

analysis does not pretend to be conclusive, but it may at least point a way toward continuing study.

Strategic Ignorance

Strategic ignorance may be constructed with infinite ingenuity, but several symbolic resources are commonly used. I will note three, "enemy propaganda," "resignation," and the "human relations" ideology, and I will illustrate the multiple layers of cover-up that each can construct over an initially secret act of group deviance.

In March 1968:

> U.S. Army troops of the American Division massacred a large number of noncombatants (comprised almost exclusively of old men, women, and children) in two hamlets of Son My Village (known as My Lai), Vietnam. The precise number of Vietnamese killed was at least 175 and may exceed 400. . . . At every command level within the American Division, actions were taken both wittingly and unwittingly which effectively suppressed information concerning the war crimes committed.[11]

To cover their culpability, the soldiers at My Lai had to rely on the efficacy of the standard response that dismissed allegations of American atrocities as enemy propaganda. If their superiors failed to shield them effectively against even a minimal inquiry, the field soldiers would be vulnerable.[12] Their superiors also ran a risk by being vulnerable for their part in the cover-up, but they had two lines of defense. Like the field soldiers they could maintain that the allegations were enemy propaganda, and they did.[13] But unlike the field soldiers, the superiors could also claim to have been taken in by "enemy propaganda." This would explain their role in deflecting suspicion in the event the cover was removed and the allegations were subsequently credited. Thus, they might make credible disingenuous claims of ignorance and maintain the cover on their role in constructing the cover-up.

In the context of civilian conflicts, the defense of "enemy propaganda" is often presented by the public relations offices of large corporations. Cynicism about public relations is in fact so institutionalized that it itself provides a third layer of insulation. Even if one admits having known that charges made by outsiders were true, and that corporate denials were false, the claim that leaders routinely deceive outsiders may be exculpating:

> In 1946, General Electric had first issued a directive, number 20.5, which spelled out the company's policy against price fixing in terms stronger than

---

[11]Peers report, quoted in Joseph Goldstein, Burke Marshall, and Jack Schwartz, *The My Lai Massacre and Its Cover-up: Beyond the Reach of Law?* (New York: The Free Press, 1976), p. 1.
[12]*My Lai Massacre*, p. 313.
[13]Ibid., pp. 307–08.

those found in the anti-trust laws. A considerable number of the executives believed, in the words of one, that the directive was only for "public consumption" and not to be taken seriously.[14]

The executives begged lenience on a claim that they were only following orders by *not* following orders. The plea is that "everyone knows" that the picture of organizational morality presented to outsiders is a strategic myth. Similar ambiguities and equally rich resources for insulating organizational deviance have been built up around the process of terminating employees. We know that a "resignation" may not be voluntary. Professionals, political appointees, and business managers are usually dismissed without suffering the indignity of being "fired."

One layer of secrecy may be created by the manipulation of "resignation" that Erving Goffman analyzed.[15] An offer to accept a "resignation" as an alternative to an embarrassing firing is a common technique for "cooling out" troublesome insiders who have incriminating knowledge. A second layer may be constructed by members who wish to continue to enjoy the profits of organizational deviance but with reduced personal vulnerability. By threatening to "resign" and thereby suggest to outsiders that something is wrong, insiders with incriminating knowledge can negotiate for transfers away from the core conspiracy to positions of more strategic ignorance.

A third obfuscating layer is available due to the very fact that manipulations of labels for terminations are so institutionalized. Outsiders are commonly cynical about the definition used, and this cynicism may be manipulated by leaders who realize that a (real) resignation-in-protest has become unavoidable. Because firings are so often masked as resignations, resignations can be masked as firings.

After Pat Hopper, an Equity Funding manager who had strong if not conclusive evidence of the massive insurance fraud, resigned and left the organization,

> he began to receive reports that indicated his resignation had not been made public. Fred Levin (a top Equity executive) was telling people that Hopper was on vacation. An office had even been set aside for him. It was said that he would function as a consultant. Then the rumors changed to grumbling. Hopper was flaking off. He wasn't coming to work.[16]

Surprised by the "resignation," Levin needed time to prepare a context that would support the interpretation that it was a euphemism—Hopper had been fired. At this time in the fraud the cover might have been blown if suspicious

[14]Gilbert Geis, "The Heavy Electrical Equipment Antitrust Cases of 1961," in *White-Collar Crime,* ed. Gilbert Geis (New York: The Free Press, 1977), p. 124.
[15]Erving Goffman, "On Cooling the Mark Out: Some Aspects of Adaptation to Failure," *Psychiatry,* vol. 15 (1952): 473–502.
[16]*Great Wall Street Scandal,* pp. 73–74.

outsiders got the message that Hopper had resigned in protest, or if insiders who were concerned about the viability of the cover-up got the message that Hopper had concluded he could no longer remain and cover himself.

A third set of resources for covering up fraud, and for covering up participation in the cover-up, inheres in the ambiguous diffusion of policing responsibilities in management roles. Outsiders may counsel that, "The key to the elimination of corruption is the existence of elite corps who are not amenable to manipulation,"[17] but those giving advice on business organization argue against such social distance. Sayles describes the cost to rational business organization from too much distance in the relationship between internal auditors and those audited, and calls for "changing the traditional interaction pattern associated with auditing relationships, where all the interaction comes from the auditor—and on a highly irregular basis—to a bilateral pattern with greater frequency." He quotes Simon in support:

> On the other hand, if a definite program is set up, involving regular assignments for accounting personnel requiring them to contact operating supervisors for information, the accountant may begin to arouse the interest of the operating executives' needs for data. When this occurs, the operating heads will generally encourage or seek out more frequent contacts with the accountants. Each begins to gain a more thorough understanding of the other. This cycle continues until a fairly high degree of communication and use of accounting data is attained.[18]

If "bilateral" relations reduce the possibility of antagonistic collusions *within* superordinate and subordinate ranks, they increase the risk that the hierarchy will become integrated against outsiders. When managers take on oversight responsibilities, and when oversight specialists take on management concerns, they develop interests in not "enforcing" their authority; deviance in their domains would reflect failure in their leadership. Mechanic notes a pattern in studies of prison guards, officers in the Armed Services, and foremen in industry:

> To the extent that they require formal sanctions to bring about cooperation, they are usually perceived by their superiors as less valuable to the organization. For a good leader is expected to command obedience, at least, if not commitment.[19]

Multiple layers of strategic ignorance may develop when subordinates at each level of a long hierarchy sense that their superiors may compromise policing responsibilities in order to avoid losing face. Kermit Vandivier had the

---

[17]Guy Benvenista, *Bureaucracy* (San Francisco: Boyd & Fraser, 1977), p. 119.

[18]Leonard Sayles, *Managerial Behavior,* (New York: McGraw-Hill, 1964), pp. 93–94.

[19]David Mechanic, "Sources of Power of Lower Participants in Complex Organizations," in *Readings in Managerial Psychology,* eds. H. Leavitt and L. Pondy (Chicago: University of Chicago Press, 1973), p. 338.

responsibility to issue a formal qualification report on the A7D aircraft wheel brake which B. F. Goodrich was developing for LTV in 1967. In his confessional account, Vandivier describes how he overcame his reluctance to report test data fraudulently.[20] He learned that numerous engineers and managers were aware that the brake had repeatedly failed tests, that the purchaser's test flights would immediately prove the brake unqualified and might kill the test pilot, and that if the purchaser learned that a new brake design was necessary, Goodrich would probably lose the valuable contract. He inquired of the other insiders how they could go along with the fraud that was apparently developing. He was told that by maintaining a "cover your tail" file containing evidence that he had not been negligent, and by putting a negative conclusion on a substantially misleading report, he might pass the responsibility to others in the hierarchy. One manager well versed in office politics gave him strategic information: everyone up the line would do the same on the conviction that their management reputations would be destroyed if they reported fraud by their subordinates. They all knew that in the end company representatives, in order to protect *their* reputations, would have to deny that their organization *could have* engineered an elaborate cover-up. As a result, when near-disasters in test flights made the brake's incurable defects undeniable, the only participants whose guilty knowledge was provable were those who had confessed in an attempt to "blow the whistle."

Concerted Ignorance

When surveyed, managers say that they feel great pressure from superiors to compromise ethics.[21] As business periodicals might put it, the message is: It's up to the boss to set an example.[22] Some analyses of organizational deviance comport with this view. Auto dealers are said to be pressured toward systematic service fraud by auto manufacturers, who can exploit oligopolistic profits from sales but not service. Manufacturers cancel dealers for failure to meet sales quotas, but never for inadequate service facilities or poor service performance.[23] The claim is that the manufacturers not only know of and condone service fraud, they compel it by confining profit mar-

[20]Kermit Vandivier, "Why Should My Conscience Bother Me?" in *Corporate and Governmental Deviance,* eds. M. D. Ermann and R. J. Lundman (New York: Oxford University Press, 1978).
[21]See, for example, Archie Carroll, "A Survey of Managerial Ethics," *Business and Society Review,* Spring (1975): 58–60.
[22]See S. J. Baumhart, "How Ethical Are Businessmen?" *Harvard Business Review,* vol. 39 (1961): 6–31.
[23]William N. Leonard and Marvin Glenn Weber, "Automakers and Dealers: A Study of Criminogenic Market Forces," *Law and Society Review,* vol. 4 (1970): 138. See also Harvey Faberman, "A Criminogenic Market Structure: The Automobile Industry," *Sociological Quarterly,* vol. 16 (1975): 438–57.

gins to sales. The dealers figure the manufacturers figure the dealers will adapt by cutting corners in the service end.

Subordinates sometimes comply with pressures toward deviance emanating from above. They also sometimes initiate demands for cover-up. The "pressure from above" perspective is made questionable by evidence that subordinates involved in major management frauds are often far from merely compliant. There are many examples of participants at all levels who are "on the make." In fact, it is not uncommon for lower level insiders to use their incriminating knowledge as protection when stealing from the thieves.[24] Some of those who were responsible for fabricating insurance policies subsequently sold by Equity Funding to reinsurers as genuine, started manufacturing fictitious death certificates and cashing in as beneficiaries.[25]

Subordinates who now claim they only passively went along often were far from diffident in demanding less exposed positions. Despite the "awesome" reputation of Stanley Goldblum, President of Equity Funding, managers repeatedly said "no" to orders that put them too much at risk. Aware that a Bahamian corporation was being used to "launder" contributions, Gulf Oil treasurers dared to demand extraordinary written authorizations for payments from executive chiefs. At one point in Gulf Oil's political payments operation, Joseph Bounds, then a vice-president of Gulf, complained to William Whiteford, then Chairman of the Board and Chief Executive Officer of Gulf,

> that he did not like "the Bahamian set-up," indicating uneasiness as to his vulnerability. Whiteford told him that was what he was getting paid for and he had better do it or be fired. Bounds' discontent led to a confrontation with Whiteford in Pittsburgh on October 4, 1961. To persuade Bounds to transfer from Tulsa to Pittsburgh in 1955, Whiteford had apparently promised Bounds that if Bounds accomplished four tasks while in Pittsburgh he could take early retirement with full benefits. At the October 1961 meeting at the Duquesne Club, where some spirits were consumed, Bounds reminded Whiteford of the promise, pointed out that he had just accomplished the fourth task with the acquisition of Wilshire Oil Company in California, and said he now wanted early retirement. A violent argument ensued in the course of which Bounds, according to his account of the affair, "decked" Whiteford. The next day Whiteford told Bounds he should fire him except for the difficulty of explaining such a move to Mr. R. K. Mellon (representing the largest stockholder). Instead, Whiteford "exiled" Bounds to the West Coast to run Wilshire Oil Company. Bounds continued writing requests for transfers (of funds to the Bahamas) to Moorhead (Treasurer) and receiving deliveries (of over $650,000 in laundered money) from Viglia (a

[24] See Melville Dalton on "symbiotic" and "parasitic," vertical and horizontal cliques, *Men Who Manage* (New York: John Wiley & Sons, 1959), p. 59.

[25] Robert E. Dallos and Richard L. Soble, *The Impossible Dream: The Equity Funding Story* (New York: New American Library, 1975), pp. 134–35.

courier) after he moved to California and until his early retirement from Gulf in August 1964.[26]

Clearly there is no consistent pattern that would support the assignment of causal and moral responsibility to one place in the hierarchy. What is consistent is a particular kind of collective symbolic work, a concerted, although often conflictual, effort to the end that each might avoid apparent possession of guilty knowledge. A key resource in this collective achievement is the mythical nature of organizational boundaries. Three will be briefly examined: the boundaries between superordinates and subordinates, between work and personal life, and between insiders and outsiders.

Conceptions of hierarchical authority sometimes obscure the fact that people in organizations negotiate what will be expected of them. A central issue in the negotiations is what each will know about the performance of the other. Subordinates often exercise strategic control over what their superiors will know about them, and to this end they manage what they will know about superiors. Deviance that is not detected will avoid sanction; orders that have not been understood cannot be flouted. For their part, superordinates manage subordinates' perceptions of what they, the superordinates, know so as to control obligations to make decisions. When executive leaders want to develop policy or sanction personnel, they will often seek out the knowledge that will justify the desired decision. When they are not ready to act, they may avoid knowledge that would force a decision.[27]

Because superordinates will be assumed to have exercised control or policing responsibilities, they must seek cooperation from subordinates in order to reduce the burden of avoiding undesired knowledge. In his study of "Milo Fractionating Center," Dalton describes various ways that the need for ignorance was satisfied. One common solution, a happy one because it conferred benefits on both parties, was to tip off subordinate managers on the timing of "surprise" safety and health inspections.[28]

With the possible exception of "total institutions,"[29] all organizations draw limits on their responsibilities to police members' personal lives. The legitimacy of this boundary on the responsibility of organizational authority is well institutionalized. In Weber's classic analysis, the rationality of bureaucracy is dependent on "ignorance of 'irrelevant' personal characteristics, and . . . [requires] ignorance whenever knowledge would impair impersonal fulfillment of duties."[30]

[26]John J. McCloy, *Report of the Special Review Committee of the Board of Directors of Gulf Oil Corporation,* Securities and Exchange Commission v. Gulf Oil Corporation, Claude C. Wild, Jr. Civil Action No. 75-0324, United States District Courts, District of Columbia, (1975), p. 44.

[27]See Norman H. Martin and John Howard Sims, "Power Tactics," *Harvard Business Review,* vol. 34 (1956), 25–29.

[28]*Men Who Manage,* chapter 2, "Power Struggles in the Line."

[29]Erving Goffman, *Asylums* (Garden City, New York: Doubleday, 1961).

[30]Wilbert E. Moore and Melvin Tumin, "Some Social Functions of Ignorance," *American Sociological Review,* vol. 14 (1949): 792.

Limitations on organizational oversight of spheres of personal privacy are useful for hiding individual deviance and for constructing several layers of collective cover-up. Crimes by individuals against organizations often grow out of private miseries. Cressey found that financial need from an unshare-able personal problem (costs of divorce and remarriage, gambling debts) is an important motive for embezzlement.[31] At a collective level, suppliers often bribe purchasing agents to cheat their organizations with gifts, enter-tainment, and payments to relatives.[32]

Institutions of personal privacy also figured in second-order cover-ups, in which organizational authorities remain strategically ignorant of a member's deviance. On tacit understandings of mutual benefit, superordinates wink at deviance by subordinates that only harms outsiders. Andrew Tobias, in a humorous account of his moral education as a twenty-one-year-old vice-president at National Student Marketing Corporation, provides an example:

> I learned from a classmate that his employer, a highly respectable major publishing company, gives its employees substantial weekly expense accounts knowing full well that most of the money is not used for business expenses, but as *untaxed* salary instead.[33]

In many cases, the subordinate will not know that the superordinate consents. A third order of cover-up is so implicitly arranged that neither party realizes that both are cooperating in concerted ignorance. Perhaps more important to the maintenance of cover-ups than an organization's restraint in investigat-ing its members' personal lives is the converse restraint. A member's personal associates do not feel free to make independent inquiry into his or her business life. Burns has written on "confidant relations": More reliable and durable than most relations at work, they are useful for obtaining "absolution from having done the dirty on somebody." Confidant relations exist where "revelations that would be too embarrassing between people of equal status (in the organization) . . . can flow in one direction only," for example, "between husbands and 'career wives.' "[34] A wife's distance from the busi-ness setting sets the stage for rehearsals and debriefings in which both part-ners can agree that the manager's presentation of self at work does not reflect his "real self."[35]

As with the boundaries between subordinate and superordinate and be-tween work and personal life, so with the distinction between insiders and

[31]Donald R. Cressey, *Other People's Money* (Belmont, Calif.: Wadsworth, 1971).

[32]A list of such methods of payoff is given in Neil H. Jacoby, Peter Nehemkis, and Richard Eells, *Bribery and Extortion in World Business* (New York: The Free Press, 1977), pp. 98–99.

[33]Andrew Tobias, *The Funny Money Game* (Chicago: Playboy Press, 1971), p. 58.

[34]Tom Burns, "The Reference of Conduct in Small Groups: Cliques and Cabals in Occupa-tional Milieux," *Human Relations,* vol. 8 (1955): 483–84. See also Rosabeth Moss Kanter, *Men and Women of the Corporation* (New York: Basic Books, 1977), pp. 116–26.

[35]Turner contrasts folk conceptions which locate "the real self" in and outside of a person's experience in institutions. Ralph Turner, "The Real Self: From Institution to Impulse," *American Journal of Sociology,* vol. 81 (1976): 989–1016.

outsiders. The principle of moral limitations is well institutionalized: *organizational leaders have a greater responsibility to police members than nonmembers.* The most prominent current example is transnational bribery. While admitting "sensitive" payments, corporation leaders have often taken the position that, questions of disclosure aside, the legality of contract inducements paid to foreign officials is properly not a matter of their concern, but a difficult question best left to the foreign legal system.

Particular line drawings are often unclear. Whether collective behavior is properly characterized as the product of a relationship between insiders or between insiders and outsiders may become a matter of negotiation and dispute. Accountants acting as independent auditors may enter negotiations in which their objective is to learn enough to demonstrate that they have made a reasonable inquiry, but not so much that they would either have to credit false statements knowingly or lose the account. In his review of the recent series of cases on the auditor's civil and criminal liability, Briloff characterizes the auditors as working not for outsiders but for top management, seeking to learn not what investors need to know but only what they need to cover themselves.[36]

Sometimes those who might acquire insider knowledge are unabashedly explicit in their desires to remain outsiders. Demands to institutionalize concerted ignorance have been made by stockholders who know of cover-ups and know they do not want to know what is under them. A SEC chairman reported:

> One large multinational corporation that had disclosed some questionable payments conducted a stockholder vote to determine whether it should disclose all foreign and political contributions. Ninety-nine percent of the stockholders voted no—they didn't want to see it.[37]

I have been considering relatively simple arrangements of concerted ignorance by two parties. Any detailed examination of a given large-scale cover-up probably would require an analysis of much greater complexity. The dimensions of concerted ignorance can be multiplied by combining different types of organizational boundaries. The transnational bribery phenomenon permits a quick example. A corporation can gain the protection of additional ignorance when the form of payment is a "commission" to a "self-employed" business agent in another country. The work/personal life boundary as well as the member/outsider line may come into play. Domestic companies can profess not to know that the "secret" partner who shared in the commission was a prominent politician.[38]

---

[36]Abraham Briloff, *More Debits than Credits* (New York: Harper and Row, 1976).
[37]Roderick M. Hills, "Doing Business Abroad: The Disclosure Dilemma," *Yale Law Report,* vol. 23 (1976): 4–5.
[38]*Bribery and Extortion,* pp. 96–97.

Concerted ignorance can be arranged with still greater complexity when several different parties participate, each invoking a different insider/outsider boundary for protection. For example, investors were primarily attracted to Home-Stake Oil as a tax-deductible drilling investment. This swindle was essentially a pyramid scheme, whereby investments that were supposed to go for developing oil reserves were in part siphoned off and in part used to pay returns. When investors started to complain, those who had media and political clout were offered a buy-back of their investment, less the tax gain they had realized, and they were offered evaluation reports stating inflated values for their investments units, which units could then be donated to charitable organizations for another tax benefit. Those investors who accepted the offers were in effect bought off for not disclosing their inside information. The tax advantages of their charitable donations would be drastically reduced or destroyed if the fraud was revealed. For their part charitable organizations

> know that they sometimes are given junk by wealthy donors. "Everybody sort of smiled when we got our Home-Stake gift," recalled an official of a Boston hospital. For fear of offending donors, however, most charities don't often turn down gifts. "You take what you can get," said an officer from a Long Island charity. "You don't bargain and say to a donor, 'We would rather have your General Motors.' "[39]

Structural Conditions

Let me begin with several caveats. The most direct treatment of the problems of overcoming the tendencies to secrecy in organizations is Harold Wilensky's *Organizational Intelligence* (1967), but neither Wilensky nor anyone else, to my knowledge, has been able to qualify ideas about the variable likelihood of cover-up under differing organizational conditions with anything recognizable as "systematic" data. As in the preceding sections, sociological analysis is typically based on well-recognized positive examples of deviance. In the nature of the case, we must be more hesitant to cite or count instances where cover-up did *not* occur.

Another bias in the literature is that the concern is usually to get information to the top of the organization. There is virtually no worry about the dangers of collusion throughout the hierarchy against outside interests. Still, deterrents to cover-ups against leaders are not necessarily inconsistent with deterrents to cover-ups against outsiders. Wilensky and others have made several suggestions that are worth considering for both concerns.

Another caveat: Obviously not all social structures are equally feasible for organizing all types of work. Some interesting research has been done on the

[39]David McClintick, *Stealing from the Rich* (New York: M. Evans, 1977), p. 206.

relation of technology to the organizational structure that can mobilize it,[40] but not a lot. For the most part, when discussing structural conditions, I will not attempt to specify the types of organizations for which they are most suitable.

A third caveat: We cannot reasonably expect to prevent attempts to cover up, nor even to decrease its profits. Like any other valued good, the rewards of cover-up increase as its incidence becomes more scarce. And as with any other form of deviance, short of redefining cover-up as proper we cannot expect to abolish the problem. This too may be obvious, but it is worth saying because the response to scandalous revelations is often that we must never let this happen again.

Fortunately, knowledge of the organizational conditions more or less conducive to cover-up is not useless simply because there are no fail-safe reforms, nor even because implementation of the most promising reforms might be politically impossible or so damaging to efficiency as to be undesirable. In order to focus our suspicions and gauge the extent of our investigations, we need ideas about the differential likelihood of misrepresentation.

The final caveat is the most distressing: Most of the organizational structures that at first glance appear to undermine the foundations of cover-up, at a second glance cut the other way. I draw ambivalent implications for most of the structural conditions I discuss, and further thought might find trade-offs in all.

To begin, the analytic questions as I see them are: Which organizational conditions would increase or decrease the number of persons with guilty knowledge and thus, presumably, the risk that the cover will be blown? Which variations in organizational conditions might affect the costs to members of revealing to outsiders knowledge about the questionable activities of other members?

Rotation of personnel has seemed to many students of organization a way of limiting the ability to keep deviance secret. Kaufman studied the United States Forest Service, an institution that has enjoyed a reputation virtually unblemished by scandals about corruption.[41] He wondered how it was that legitimate authority apparently has governed throughout the Service's extremely decentralized organizational format. The working conditions of the forest ranger, far removed from the organization's central office and extraordinarily isolated even from regional population centers, would seem to facilitate corrupt relations with locally based entrepreneurs whose interests can be severely disadvantaged by the laws rangers administer. Kaufman analyzed the deterrent value of selective recruitment and anticipatory socialization—

---

[40]Joan Woodward, *Industrial Organization* (London: Oxford University Press, 1965).
    [41]Herbert Kaufman, *The Forest Ranger: A Study in Administrative Behavior* (Baltimore: Johns Hopkins, 1960).

people who become forest rangers often dream of the occupation as youths —but his comments on rotation are probably more generalizable. If someone you have not had the opportunity to know will be replacing you in the foreseeable future, you have no opportunity to guarantee the cover-up of any traces of malfeasance that you may leave, and the outsiders who might be inclined to offer bribes will have little security for investing in corruption.

Kaufman's case study was admittedly not of an organization that typifies modern occupations, but in some respects the distinctiveness of the forest ranger's work setting argues all the more strongly for the prophylaxis of rotation. Relative to inspectors and overseers who work in urban areas, rangers deal with few outsiders. Thompson has written of the possibilities for control in the "boundary-spanning" units of organizations:

> Boundary-spanning units, engaged in direct inter-dependence with elements of the task environment, are judged in part by evidence of disappointments they cause for elements of the task environments. Boundary-spanning units are always interdependent with other units of the organization and hence are evaluated on technical or organizational rationality. . . . But elements of the task environment always have data about the capacity or performance of these units which are not directly available to the organization itself.[42]

The greater the number of outsiders in the "task environment," the greater the opportunity for outside investigators to seek evidence independent of the accounts given by organization leaders. If rotation deters forest rangers from colluding in conspiracies with the relatively few locals who would be in the know, it should be even more effective in deterring the typical urban inspector who would have to make arrangements with scores of enterprises in order to secure cover-ups.

However, casual examination of recent scandals suggests that for many "boundary-spanning" workers, the difficulties of coordinating cover-up and the potential for independent investigative review are not awesome deterrents. About two years ago in the New York City area, dozens of meat inspectors and meat wholesalers were successfully prosecuted for participating in a tightly organized payoff system that had been operating quietly for years. The inspectors rotate every few months in different parts of the city. Rotation *was* instrumental in detection: the investigation was "made" by an inspector who worked as an undercover agent and, over several months in the ordinary course of rotation, was able to map out the precise schedule of payments from over 50 wholesalers spread throughout the city's boroughs. But rotation was not effective as a deterrent.

There is an even more discouraging word about rotation. It has a distinctive positive value for cover-up. Even if rotation does increase the risk that an honest insider will come upon a cover-up, it often limits the risks that must

[42]James D. Thompson, *Organizations in Action* (New York: McGraw-Hill, 1967), p. 96.

be borne by a member who is participating in its outer reaches. As noted earlier, in Gulf Oil and Equity Funding, transfers to sites further removed from the core conspiracy can be key factors in keeping wavering insiders in line. A standard practice of rotating members to different posts might assure them that they would have to remain in vulnerable positions only temporarily.

Turnover may be a stronger deterrent to cover-up than rotation. When leaving, as contrasted to transferring to a less vulnerable internal position, members typically lose the benefit of the organization's deviance. They incur lower opportunity costs if they blow the cover.

Moreover, for an organization that is not shrinking in size turnover brings in replacements from outside the organization. Unlike rotation, which creates and fills vacancies internally, turnover means that a cover-up would have to run the risk of socializing newcomers into the conspiracy.

That this is a substantial risk is suggested indirectly by what is perhaps the most consistent finding in the sociology of organizations. Organizations maintain a public image somewhat more glorified than the view from within. Over time, they "displace" formal goals with concerns not fully stated to outsiders. As managers interact with constituencies, audiences, and pressure groups, as they realize they need the consent or at least benign neglect of client groups, government overseers, and the press, they enter private understandings, co-opt or otherwise make deals with adversaries. In Goffman's colorful phrase, all occupational settings have "back stages."[43] As a result, the socialization experience for newcomers is quite often morally stressful.[44]

Turnover appears to play an important causal role in the breakdown of cover-ups. Frank Serpico, the novice New York City policeman whose refusal to be socialized led to the Knapp Commission investigation, symbolizes this point of vulnerability for the systems of corruption. The young newcomer's sense of distance from the organizational role he or she is expected to play, and the lack of moral identification which this sustains,[45] is also symbolized by the Alice-in-Wonderland tenor of Andrew Tobias's confessional on National Student Marketing. Kermit Vandivier, who was the first to go to the FBI with allegations of B. F. Goodrich's A7D aircraft brake fraud and the first to go before a congressional investigating committee, was supported in his indignation from the start by Searle Lawson, the second to go to the FBI and testify to Congress, who was out of engineering school only a year before he came to Goodrich, a few weeks before the fraud began.

But Wilensky opines:

[43]Erving Goffman, *The Presentation of Self in Everyday Life* (New York: Doubleday, 1959), p. 112.

[44]John Van Manaan, "Breaking In: Socialization to Work," in *Handbook of Work, Organization, and Society,* ed. R. Dublin (Chicago: Rand-McNally, 1976), p. 92.

[45]See "Cover-up and Collective Integrity."

Other things being equal, high turnover of administrative leaders *discourages* the expression of critical opinion in the short run; the newcomers tend to keep quiet until they learn the "lay of the land," build confidence among superiors and subordinates, acquire a political base, or solidify their position in other ways.[46][emphasis supplied]

I would counsel the opposite. Other things equal, we should expect cover-up to be less likely where turnover is high. This is especially so where high turnover results from firing. The "disgruntled" ex-employee is a common source of revelations. (Ron Sechrist, the man credited with "blowing the whistle" on Equity Funding, did so only after he was fired in a budget cutback.) For a balanced approach to oversight, examiners might be advised to initiate investigative probes where rates of discharge are low, because they will be pressured to respond to complaints where rates are high.

Wilensky goes on:

Frequent, institutionalized succession is one reason for the reluctance of the United States government to liquidate error in such places as Cuba and Vietnam—a striking continuity of policy through a succession of men as different in viewpoint and style as Eisenhower, Kennedy, and Johnson.[47]

Again Wilensky's argument is doubtful. Is there a greater tendency to end cover-up and to confess error where leadership is more permanent? A new incumbent has an immediate interest in criticizing past administrations in order to scale down expectations, and he or she should be less encumbered by any commitments to continuity that the predecessor may have built up.

Perhaps we should qualify our faith in turnover as a threat to cover-up by the amount of experience newcomers have had in other similar organizations or in the larger institutions. Unfortunately for the deterrent promise of turnover, the higher the level of the position, the less likely a new occupant will require initial socialization into the institution. Entry to higher administrative levels tends to be correlated with age and experience in the institution.

This qualification is especially necessary to understand the incidence of collective frauds in new, fast growing companies. In new companies, all members will be new on the job. Yet they often share "latent culture," a functional equivalent to internal tenure for socialization.[48]

New companies typically do not start by obtaining upper echelon members on meritocratic, universalistic principles, through nationwide screenings on objective test criteria. More often than established firms, they draw

[46]Harold Wilensky, *Organizational Intelligence: Knowledge and Policy in Government and Industry* (New York: Basic Books, 1967), p. 87.

[47]*Organizational Intelligence,* p. 87.

[48]Howard S. Becker and Blanche Geer, "Latent Culture: A Note on the Theory of Latent Social Roles," *Administrative Science Quarterly,* vol. 5 (1960): 304–13.

managerial staff in through informal social networks. The new group will frequently share latent culture, formally irrelevant social identities they previously held in common. These may be school ties, ethnic group identifications, regional backgrounds, kinship relations, or acquaintanceships in the trade.

In new organizations, years of shared background experiences may provide the basis for the in-group feeling that might develop among colleagues within an organization only after fighting common battles over several years. Latent culture often supplies two important resources for cover-ups. It is an informal principle of association, already subterranean or invisible to outsiders. And in many cases, continuing personal debts will have been created within the prior shared relation. These debts may be drawn on to preserve the cover-up. An example is the experience of Harry Fitzgerald, the executive vice-president of Home-Stake Oil:

> Fitzgerald, the engaging James Joyce expert and reformed alcoholic playboy whom Trippet (the company president) had rescued from the gutters of Manhattan (the Winslow Hotel) in 1959, had been trying to quit Home-Stake for some time. As the company's top salesman, his attitude always had been that of the brothel pianist who claims ignorance of what goes on upstairs.

When Fitzgerald finally did resign, he wrote Trippet:

> My mental and physical condition have deteriorated to such an extent that I can't even begin to continue. . . . You have been my loyal friend and have probably done more for me than anyone I know. . . . Don't worry about me. (Remember I've been to the Winslow.)[49]

I have been discussing the potential for cover-up in different patterns of recruiting, deploying, and retaining personnel. Rotation did not fare too well, but with appropriate qualifications, turnover seems to be more promising. Variations in the nature of the authority system are also relevant.

As principles of organization, hierarchy and specialization promise efficiency. By the same token, they provide incentives for cover-ups:

> Insofar as the problem of control—coordinating specialists, getting work done, securing compliance—is solved by rewards of status, power, and promotion, the problem of obtaining accurate, critical intelligence is intensified. For information is a resource that symbolizes status, enhances authority, and shapes careers. In reporting at every level, hierarchy is conducive to concealment and misrepresentation.[50]

---

[49]*Stealing from the Rich*, pp. 175–76.
[50]*Organizational Intelligence*, pp. 42–43.

From the perspective of organizational leadership, one antidote is overlapping jurisdiction. Efficiency may be reduced, but this cost may be offset by what sociological methodologists recognize as the virtues of "triangulating" the sources of information. President Franklin D. Roosevelt, criticized by contemporaries as an inefficient administrator, is said to have been a master at this method:

> "Roosevelt's persistent effort was to check and balance information acquired through official channels by information acquired through a myriad of private informal and unorthodox channels and espionage networks." Roosevelt also attempted to generate information by recruiting strong personalities and structuring their work so that clashes would be certain: "His favourite technique was to keep grants of authority incomplete, jurisdictions uncertain, charters overlapping."[51]

For our purposes, the trouble with the principle of overlapping jurisdictions is that its virtue is only in revealing information to the top of the organization. If the leader is malevolent, "divide and rule" would be a shrewd way to orchestrate a cover-up. In a spirit of rivalry, departments would try to maintain secrecy from and report upward on each other, limiting the collective ability to assess the leader's design.

In a study of the social organization of the home-construction industry, Stinchcombe, has argued that Weber's model of bureaucracy (a preset, hierarchical definition of assignments) should not be taken as essential to rational organization.[52] The "craft" principle is a viable alternative. In contrast to bureaucracy, craft work is organized around a "project" in which participants jointly work out a temporary alignment of responsibilities as they work along. The idea of the "task force" is analogous: "a team or project of diverse specialists who are brought together to solve a limited range of problems and then are reassigned when the task is done."[53] This organizational mechanism is promising as a deterrent to cover-up, but its strengths may not be realized when craft is the exclusive format for work.

Instead of using either bureaucratic or craft principles, dual principles of organization can be used: task forces can be temporarily drawn from and laid over an ongoing, neatly bounded hierarchy. A case in point is the modern American university:

> Traditionally the American university has placed historians in one department, physicists in another, because the faculties and students of either were more

[51] Andrew M. Pettigrew, *The Politics of Organizational Decision-Making* (London: Tavistock, 1973), p. 154, quoting Schlesinger. See also Wilensky, pp. 50–53, for an earlier and more extensive discussion of President Roosevelt in this respect.

[52] Arthur L. Stinchcombe, "Bureaucratic and Craft Administration of Production," *Administrative Science Quarterly*, vol. 4 (1959): 168–87.

[53] *Organizational Intelligence*, p. 46.

interdependent with one another than with those in the other field. But as the American university has taken on new projects—liberal arts curricula, undergraduate specialization or majors, graduate curricula, adult education and public service, and interdisciplinary research efforts—its academic departments have increasingly become pools from which professional talents are allocated.[54]

Specialization of departments and hierarchy within departments remain, but instead of assigning them emergent or irregularly recurring tasks, specialized administrative units, universitywide faculty and faculty-student committees, are formed. The committees take on such responsibilities as developing policy on the rights of human subjects in research, reviewing the university's progress in hiring women and minorities, altering the grading system, and re-examining a "core" curriculum required of all students.

In contrast to unitary systems, whether craft or bureaucratic, this dual system provides distinctive deterrents to cover-up. It presumes a sharing of power across departments, plants, or offices. The hierarchy is not the sole channel and primary director of the flow of information from and to horizontal units. Because members from different sectors have practical opportunities to share perceptions of the whole organization, "divide and control" strategies for designing cover-ups from the top become problematic.

Deviance within hierarchically organized departments is also more difficult to cover up. From the standpoint of individuals who want to control those who will be in the know about their actions, there is the certainty that others will come on their turf and the uncertainty as to who they will be. A member's colleagues change from project to project, and they are not bound to the member by a history of tactful bargains made to facilitate everyday cooperation. Stable deals of the sort that might be contracted with a permanent administrative or auditing unit will be less likely. From the standpoint of the individual who is uncomfortable with moral compromise in his or her department, the dual system provides a potentially liberating set of dual loyalties. There is a regular opportunity to take distance from the primary work group in the hierarchy and to become open to other moral perspectives.

The overlay of task forces onto a continuing hierarchy also embodies advantages of rotation for deterring cover-up. A member's participation in a task force usually requires vacating his or her responsibilities in the hierarchy to some extent. If a temporary replacement is brought in, he or she may come across traces of deviance left uncovered in the haste of moving into the task force. In large law offices, for example, lawyers brought together in teams formed to handle major cases will often need temporary replacements to manage their ongoing, more routine caseloads. Replacements may be

[54]*Organizations in Action,* p. 81.

shocked by client expectations and by what they find in files. Freidson provides a compelling example from his study of a medical group practice:

> The vast majority of cases in which physicians were subjected to the ultimate stage of social pressure in the medical group—being brought up before the Executive Committee—were those in which one *physician* had complaints about another. Offending patients was not sufficient: physicians as well had to be offended. *Collective forms of professional control were brought into play primarily when the issue was that of inter-collegial relations,* not that of patient relations or relations with the administration [emphasis in the original]. . . . To have been given colleague attention, the refusal to make a housecall had to have been accompanied by more heinous crimes, such as asking for a case of Scotch, collecting a fee for the call, or filling out record forms claiming that housecalls were made when they were in fact not made. *Most important of all to the collegium was the involvement of another colleague whose patient was refused a call that the colleague then had to make himself.*[55] [emphasis supplied]

The dual system also avoids the disadvantages of rotation. Unlike rotation, members move out of their jobs in the hierarchy and into task forces with the expectation of going back. If they have been uncomfortable with their exposure to culpability for fraud involving their specialized, hierarchical unit, team participation will not provide the relief that transfer might. They will have to live with the knowledge that they will return to an uncomfortable position while working with colleagues free from its compromises.

I would like to end the discussion with two ideas about organizational conditions that militate against cover-up not yet fatally weakened by ambivalence—turnover and the dual system of task force and hierarchical authority. Again, the practical value of these ideas might be less as objectives for organizational reform than as guides to the depth of investigative probes. Were this a paper geared to recommend the most promising reforms, it would have to deal with proposals to increase legal liability for strategic ignorance. It would also have to consider such reform possibilities as creating legal protection against organizational punishment for whistle-blowing, and perhaps bounties; institutionalizing policing roles for outside directors; expanding inducements for stockholder derivative suits; and, because the transformation of conspiracies from symbiotic to parasitic often leads to their disintegration, perhaps even reducing liability for stealing from thieves.

[55]Eliot Freidson, *Doctoring Together* (New York: Elsevier, 1975), p. 232.

14

Management Fraud: Its Social Psychology and Relation to Management Practices

Martin M. Greller

S ocial psychology examines individual behavior as it is affected by other people—in ones, twos, or whole organizations. Management fraud deals with individual acts that are conducted in such a "social" environment. Social psychology should therefore provide useful perspectives on the occurrence of management fraud and how to detect and deter it. This paper makes an initial effort to develop such perspectives and to discuss the relationship between modern management practices and controls to deter management fraud.

Unfortunately, social psychology has not yet addressed management fraud. Considerable work has been done on moral development, personal judgment, and the personality and background of convicted felons, but this has not been assembled in any way that applies to management fraud in the real world. As a consequence, this paper interpolates from what is known with the goal of defining useful avenues for thought and research.

The first section describes the psychological concepts which are basic to the analysis and is followed by detailed consideration of two types of fraud

Dr. Greller was Assistant Professor of Management, Graduate School of Business Administration, New York University, at the time this paper was written. He is now a consulting psychologist with Rohrer, Hibler & Replogle, Inc.
ⓒ*Peat, Marwick, Mitchell & Co.*

(those for and against the firm). In each case the individual and organizational factors apt to promote or deter fraud are discussed. Because management itself has been influenced by social psychology, a section examines the impact of this thinking on management practices and its implications for management fraud.

Basic Concepts

Groups usually serve multiple functions. Three functions can be identified in most groups: task functions, sentient functions, and reference functions.[1] The task function is to successfully complete the group's or organization's work. However, the essence of a group goes beyond accomplishing its assigned tasks. A sentient (or socio-emotional) life develops that includes networks of friendship and mutual support. This sentient life involves protecting other group members from what are thought to be "hostile forces" in the environment (e.g., changes in market, changes in legal requirements). Sometimes it is not just an individual but the whole group that must be protected from a troublesome environment. In this case, one can actually see the group band together cohesively to take on the challenges. The reference function represents a service that groups provide to their members. The group helps members make sense of confusing situations or ill-structured decisions. The reference function explains individuals' reliance on the group for guidance, information, and interpretation.

The three functions usually work together. Thus, one finds managers in a manufacturing firm who must estimate market trends and adjust production (task) seeking each others' counsel and contributions (reference), a process facilitated by the group's maintenance of an environment in which members are confident that coworkers will come to their aid and not think them foolish or weak in asking for help (sentience). The three functions may also work together in a fraud situation where a group of perpetrators support each other's view regarding the rectitude of their actions (reference), create social support which relieves any sense of alienation (sentient), and work together to commit fraudulent acts (the group's task).

Another important social psychological concept is *identification.* It is not entirely poetic to ask whose pain will be experienced as if it were one's own. An individual who identifies with the organization will suffer empathetically with the firm. The identification of the individual with the organization will have an important impact on the *type* of fraud in which the individual is apt to become involved.

[1]W. Bion, *Experience in Groups* (New York: Basic Books, 1961); E. J. Miller and A. K. Rice, *Systems of Organization* (London: Tavistock, 1967); and M. Sherif, *Social Psychology of Norms* (New York: Harper Brothers, 1936).

Frauds may involve specific managerial actions, but they grow and are nurtured in the broader context of organizational relationships. A sensitivity to the implicit and explicit task, sentient, and referent functions, and nature of identification should help the auditor to understand and possibly detect management fraud.

Fraud Against the Company's Welfare

One may distinguish between frauds *for* the welfare of the company and those *against* its welfare. This is a useful distinction, and the two types of fraud will be considered separately.

Fraud against the company's welfare includes embezzlement, conversion of assets, or acceptance of bribes. In this situation the company joins the auditor, IRS, and society at large in the desire to detect and deter such activity. What are the conditions which foster the occurrence of the fraud?

Dynamics of the Fraud.   Many people have financial needs, even severe ones, and have the opportunity to defraud their employers, yet most refrain from doing so. It is important to begin by exploring why some individuals chose to defraud their employers. Cressey suggests two factors leading to fraud: the existence of an unshareable problem and verbalizations that reduce awareness of wrongdoing.[2] These elements are indicative of adverse social conditions, specifically, alienation from the organization and its symbolization.

What are the conditions which inhibit problem sharing? Individuals certainly do vary in their openness, and some problems are embarrassing. But if personality or the type of problem explained its unshareability, research would already have discovered the "criminal personality" or identified fraud-producing life situations, and this has not occurred. Failing to find such explanations, a third alternative becomes likely: conditions in the group may inhibit communication.[3]

A number of conditions in groups contribute to making problems unshareable. The task structure may be organized so that peers or those in reporting relationships see each other only rarely. There may be little sense

[2] See chapter 12 of this book.

[3] It would be equally appropriate to discuss the problem in terms of organizational climate; however, climate is manifested in the group anyway [e.g., R. Likert, *New Patterns in Management* (New York: McGraw-Hill, 1961)]. Discussing the group is particularly appropriate, as the individual experiences the company through the filter of a group. Furthermore, given that the auditor experiences groups within the organization rather than the whole organization in one instant, speaking of the group is more congruent with experience. When examining the conditions which support fraud, it is not clear how much of an organization will be involved (the whole firm, a single department, or three clerks in the billing department). The concept of "group" is applicable to all of these.

of psychological safety—members are often criticized or "kidded unmercifully." The group seems to have weak boundaries—no one can ever be confident that he or she is inside the group and apt to stay there. These conditions are often found in groups where people must constantly prove themselves. If there is little cohesiveness or openness on other issues, problem sharing can be inhibited. These circumstances should be evident prior to the fraud, and they should be apparent to an outsider who deals with the group over a period of time.

Another feature which may inhibit problem sharing is the sentient role structure. Groups act to defend themselves against anxiety, and often there are very explicit expectations of members—myths to be maintained. One about which we hear a lot these days is the "macho" myth for male roles. But there are many sources for unrealistic expectations of infallibility and self-sufficiency, some of which are generated in groups. While these may be quite valuable in pushing members to do their best, they also make it difficult for an individual to admit to having a problem. Simply having a problem may make the individual fear that he or she will be seen as less of a member for having failed to meet the group's expectations, making a cover-up an urgent need. In order to retain members and maintain the myth of self-sufficiency, many groups will conveniently fail to notice information indicating problems. This possibly unconscious decision not to know creates more pressure on the individual not to share problems.

Still, not everyone who is alienated, unable to share problems, and in need of money commits fraud. Many poor, lonely people moonlight, look for new jobs, or simply feel miserable. Somehow, the individual must justify aggressive action against the firm. This illustrates Cressey's second point, that most people who defraud their employers do not define themselves as criminals.[4] They must have some way of explaining to themselves why this label is not applicable. They symbolize events differently than do their coworkers.

A group is not necessary to explain away the moral implications of fraud. The individual's capacity for rationalization is not to be denied. One need not resort to others in justifying one's own behavior. In such cases, events come to hold meaning unique to the individual, causing still further alienation. However, rationalizations are more potent when supported by a group, even if this is only a small group of fellow conspirators.

There are two ways in which rationalization becomes a group activity during frauds against the company. The first is where there is direct collusion among a group to perpetrate the fraud. Such collusion may be necessary to by-pass the accounting controls. Part of the group's reference function would be to help members "understand" their actions in the most positive light.

Second, the group may covertly aid the fraud even though members

[4]See chapter 12 of this book.

obtain no monetary benefit for doing so. This seeming irrationality is explained by the sentient life of the group. Unless the perpetrator is new to the group, some sort of role and feeling will have developed. Recognition of the fraud would be disruptive and threatening to the whole group. If the group has had a felon in its midst, what other evils might the group also contain? It is easier to look the other way, to avoid knowing and thereby avoid the responsibility of taking action. A number of intra-organizational options are available. The individual can always be promoted out of the group (kicked upstairs) to a job with fewer opportunities for fraud. This can be accomplished so that the group need never recognize the transgressions.[5] Presumably, there are some bounds or rules by which the individual must abide, but within these the group may grant provisional license.

The state of the group can play an important role in laying the groundwork for fraud. However, unlike personality, the state of the group is something which the auditor can observe. While one may never know if an individual is harboring an unshareable problem, disruption of communication, demands for members to prove themselves, and isolation are observable. Understanding group dynamics may be of assistance in targeting likely settings for fraud against the company.

Dynamics of Detection.   The auditor can expect the basic cooperation of management. Even where recognition of the fraud would disrupt the sentient life of the group, there are limits to the risks others will bear. A group which is not otherwise rigid and defensive would not be expected to go too far in its defense of a defalcator.

While traditional means of control are most appropriate for fraud against the firm, there are advantages to attending to conditions within the group. Where conditions are more conducive to fraud, greater scrutiny is warranted. This raises the issues of staffing and training. The audit partner and manager are the most experienced members of the audit team, but they may not have direct, personal contact with a broad range of management groups. If junior audit staff are to be relied upon as the primary observers, they must develop the requisite skills, and hence they should receive explicit training in the analysis of groups.

Management Fraud for the Company

Frauds for the company are of a different sort. They include misrepresentations designed to create a false impression in the financial or credit markets. They may also include misrepresentations to mask any business activities

[5]"More Pressure to Punish Executive Crime," *Business Week,* December 18, 1978, pp. 104, 109.

which members feel might result in censure if known. From a social psychological view, these frauds are set apart because the perpetrators are not the main beneficiaries. The needs and circumstances which surround them are apt to differ from those associated with fraud against the firm.

Dynamics of the Fraud.   A central feature of many frauds for the company's benefit is that the perpetrators are thoroughly identified with the firm. Such frauds are feasible because the individuals have come to see the company's well-being so closely united to their own sense of well-being[6] that they choose to run personal risks for corporate benefit—an interesting inversion of the rationale for creating a corporation.

The characteristics associated with close identification to one's group are quite the opposite of those found in fraud against the firm. There is considerable confidence in the stability of membership and a clear sense of inclusion in the group.[7] Trust and cohesiveness among group members is also apt to be high. The group's boundaries are clearly defined, even to the point of xenophobia. A negative view of outsiders may well precede the fraud; it certainly is adaptive once the fraud has begun.

The closeness of the group heightens the impact of its sentient life on members. Two common sentient patterns may easily foster fraud for the company. A group oriented toward "fight/flight" is particularly vulnerable. Such a group starts with the assumption that most of their problems come from outside forces. If these forces can be vanquished or avoided, all will be well. Falsification of financial statements or covert corruption of outside agents would be one way of dealing with the outside forces.

A second group orientation to be wary of is "dependency." Here the assumption is that faithful obedience to authority will cause everything to turn out all right. In a dependency group one need not have an evil leader. The dependence of members upon the leader creates incredible pressure for the leader to pull the group through. This pressure may cause the individual to authorize the falsification of records so that the group will not be let down. Similarly, subordinates may fail to report negative results for fear of upsetting the assumptions on which this sentient structure is based.

Just as with fraud against the company, it is important that people be able to think well of themselves. Even if frauds for the firm are not entirely altruistic, they can be symbolized as selfless service. The symbolization is almost certain to be collective. It also serves a purpose beyond justifying the

---

[6]The notion of well-being used here is psychological. While the participants may ultimately benefit materially as well, it is not the key element. Even the lower level employee who receives a raise or promotion for participating will generally receive it in the normal time for "faithful service." At the point participation requires extrinsic rewards the fraud is beginning to fall apart and may turn into fraud against the firm.

[7]See chapter 13 of this book.

fraud. Here there may be very real ambiguity as to the moral value of the activities. This ambiguity increases the individual's reliance on the group both as a referent and a source of socio-emotional support. By joining together in rationalizing their actions the members of the group tighten their bonds.

There are problems built into this situation. The bonds among members are strong but not healthy. The sentient and reference functions foster the task of fraud, but get in the way of the group's main business. The fraud is supported by unrealistic beliefs and evaluations. Living as though fabrication were truth is cumbersome and becomes more problematic over time.

A major negative is that the firm itself no longer knows how well or poorly it is doing. Unless double books are kept *and* widely available within the firm, responsible individuals will not know how bad things actually are. Decisions are made on the basis of faulty information. Several people can inadvertently distort the same information in independent attempts to cover the firm.

A second negative is the effect on the group's behavior. Participation in the fraud fosters a nervous sort of cohesiveness. The ease with which the group deals with outsiders and its ability to effectively use outside resources will be diminished. Self-protection can so hang upon the continued dependability of this group that even the appearance of discord cannot be risked. At this point the group is unable to discuss issues critically. Individuals must be excruciatingly stressed before they will raise a point in contradiction to what they expect others in the group believe. The assumptions on which the fraud is based must be protected; challenges rouse anxiety and are subject to sharp attack. But just as important, the critical faculties of the group, its capacity to analyze, disagree, and discuss, have been impaired, which will adversely affect decisions totally unrelated to fraud.[8]

The characteristics most likely to be associated with fraud for the firm are loyalty, cohesiveness, trust, aggressiveness, and other attributes typically valued by an organization. Often firms go to great lengths to produce these conditions in the interest of organizational effectiveness. The inherent problems of these frauds are subtle and develop slowly. The benefits are clear and quickly apparent. There is an ambivalence built into frauds for the firm. Perpetrators may enter into such a fraud with the best of motives. Initially they may not realize they have transgressed.

Dynamics of Detection.   It is very difficult to detect fraud for the company's benefit, and the auditor can expect to receive less help from inside the company. The internal control processes are either by-passed by knowledge-

---

[8] I. Janis, *Victims of Groupthink: A Psychological Study of Foreign Policy Decisions and Fiascos* (Boston: Houghton Mifflin, 1972).

able insiders, or they are exploited to facilitate the fraud. Whistle-blowing is less likely to take place because of the group's greater cohesiveness. A different approach to detection is in order, one which focuses on the group's process and climate.

The company's cohesiveness is evidenced by a sharply defined group boundary (the boundary between insider and outsider). This boundary can cause the auditor considerable difficulty. It may mean less cooperation from members and greater restriction of information. Symptomatic of this difficulty is a high level of formality in the relationship. The formality and restrictiveness can be a previously existing condition that fostered the fraud's development.

The well-bounded group provides a second trap for the unwary auditor —co-optation. The ability to work with difficult groups is a necessary "tool of the trade" for a successful auditor. A cooperative working relationship must be developed if the audit is to proceed efficiently. The auditor learns the client's language, business, and problems and develops a role within the group other than that of complete outsider. This is useful and is not necessarily compromising. It facilitates information gathering, and it helps to secure the acceptance of recommendations. However, co-optation begins to occur when the auditor becomes responsive to social influence from the group. Co-optation may be subtle. In the process of learning the language and logic of the firm, in becoming one who is in but not of the firm, the auditor risks unwitting acceptance of the group's concepts and symbols, the same things which support the group's rationalization of its acts. As a consequence the individual's perception of the situation is subtly shifted, affecting his or her judgment.

It is important to recognize that co-optation feels good and can look like effective professionalism. In many cases the co-opted auditor will be very effective in communications with the client and in urging changes. This effectiveness is achieved through mutual trust and understanding. If this group lapses into fraud, it will try to *protect* the auditor from the knowledge. As a part-time participant in the group's sentient and referent processes, the auditor will be subtly steered away from information that might be disturbing. These dynamics can change as the fraud develops, particularly if the fraud is discovered. The group must then either push the auditor out of the group or corrupt him or her. The corruption may be an accomplished fact if the auditor would be publicly construed as having been derelict at this point.

The Audit Team.   So far "the auditor" has been characterized as an individual. In fact, there may be many people involved. Furthermore, social psychological considerations have been discussed as though they applied only to client organizations. Another factor to be considered is the social process within the audit staff. Most often the social processes here will exacerbate the problems already identified.

If the partner or manager has developed a good relationship with the client and a junior auditor finds some small, suspicious bit of information, it appears less likely it will lead to major discovery. The impact is less for a variety of reasons. If the information is reported to the partner, it will have less impact than information directly discovered. Each of the many people involved in an audit is apt to see only a small piece of what is happening. The pieces singly may not appear incriminating. This reduces the likelihood that any one part will be reported. If reported, it may be readily explained away, especially by a partner who identifies with the group. When little or no action is taken, the audit staff comes to understand that these curious little disconcerting facts "don't mean anything," and they cease to bother the partner about them. There need be neither malevolence nor intent. The audit staff divides the labor, and as a consequence no one person need ever be aware of the full importance of what is going on. It is less likely that all the pertinent facts will be assembled in observable form (e.g., they may be in the working papers, but spread on eight feet of shelf space).

Ironically the auditor's role itself may make detection of fraud for the company more difficult. On the one hand, the auditor is the embodiment of external control, demanding a fair and accurate accounting of management performance. On the other hand, the auditor is hired by the company, and effective performance requires trust and understanding. There may be no conflict when confronting fraud *against* the firm, but this is less clear when the fraud is undertaken for the firm's benefit.

Research on Social Psychology of Fraud

All of the above may be wrong! It seems reasonable enough. It is consistent with social psychological knowledge. Unfortunately, the amount of research on the social psychology of auditing—especially rigorous field research—is negligible. Unless insight and intuition are of themselves sufficient, an agenda for research is in order.

There are many specific topics which could be pursued, but three general areas seem to be particularly important: dynamics of the client group, factors affecting auditors' perceptiveness (individually or collectively), and the impact of interventions on the auditor (especially identifying training or job experiences which help them size up what is happening in a client group).

However, the methods by which research is conducted may be more important than its intended topic. The results must not only be correct but usable too. This dictates an action research approach, one in which researcher and auditor work together. The selection, operationalization, and measurement of variables should be generated jointly. Before the results are published as truths, they should be reviewed by practitioners. The action recommendations should also be a joint product. The researchers, having been educated as to the realities of the field, can help by challenging the auditors' assumptions, just as they were themselves oriented by the auditors.

The action research model can be cumbersome. It is time consuming and often generates arguments. It is far easier for the individual specialists to do their own thing. But this does not result in integrated conclusions. Action research has proved successful in implementing change in organizational practices.[9]

Modern Management and Control Systems

Social psychologists have shared auditors' concerns about organizations' control systems. Their findings on control of human systems provide a helpful context in which to consider the role of auditing. However, this involves a shift in perspective. Rather than focusing on financial integrity, individual integrity is studied, assuming that the behavior of individuals will ultimately determine the extent of financial integrity.

Much of the thinking on control starts from the mundane notion that people are inclined to do things which provide them with the greatest benefit. Whether the notion is simple, even intuitive, many organizations seem to disregard it by implementing control systems which are primarily punitive. Even where rewards are available, companies mute their effect by relying on unwieldy extrinsic rewards (i.e., raises, promotions, etc.) in lieu of the more potent sources of gratification which can be designed into the work.

Positive Control Systems.   Behavioral research clearly underscores the value of positive control systems. Such systems are based on reward. When people do what is desired, they receive some payoff. A system which is primarily punitive can have a stultifying effect. Punitive controls produce an orientation toward seeking safety. The orientation toward maximization and achievement is lost. Most accounting control systems are fundamentally negative systems: if you get caught, there will be negative consequences.

Negative control systems have a built-in irony: they are apt to produce undesirable behavior. This happens in two ways. First, given a choice, most people do not enter situations in which they will be subjected to this kind of control. When trapped in a punitive control system, they "withdraw." With luck they withdraw totally, by quitting. Somewhat less satisfactorily they become a sullen or lethargic, psychologically withdrawn work force. Carry it one step further, and you have people ready to act against the firm. The control system has undermined the individual's sense of identification

[9]H. A. Hornstein, et al., *Social Intervention* (New York: The Free Press, 1971).

with the firm. Further, it provides the basis for a self-justifying excuse (symbolization) for fraud ("the firm owes me for putting up with these conditions"). A second problem is that negative control systems are fun to "beat." Beyond simply avoiding the consequences of detection, getting around the system can be a gratifying challenge.[10] Indeed, getting around the system can be gratifying even if there is no material benefit. Even where "beating the control system" does not result in frauds to the point of materiality, it creates a climate wherein the potential defalcator will not experience any clear, restrictive norms from the group. Once the act of fraud becomes known within the group, it will be difficult for peers to take strong action, feeling their own hands not to be entirely clean.

A case can be made for the concept of a positive control system, but is it feasible?[11] After all, safeguards against fraud are defined in negative terms, and a philosophical question may be raised whether one ought to pay someone for doing that which was expected in the first place. The only thing to be said here is that in a similar situation many companies are rewarding attendance rather than punishing absence or tardiness, and the results have proved quite satisfying in terms of both employee behavior and costs.[12] It is not entirely clear just how a positive control system should be designed for deterrence of management fraud. It will have to be left as an intriguing prospect for future development. But one thing can probably be generalized from prior experience: the system will need to be compatible with the particular organization to which it is applied and will be most effective where designed with management's active participation.

Techniques of Positive Control.   In large measure modern managers have come to recognize the value of motivating people toward doing things rather than trying to scare them away. The techniques which accomplish this often result in a loss of visible external control. However, in so doing a basis is laid for a far more potent set of controls. This is evident in many of the techniques used to increase employee motivation.

Consider two current methods used to produce positive motivation. The first is job enrichment. The second is self-appraisal. These need to be considered both because they represent some important insights as to why people

[10]By way of example, consider all the effort and creativity that has been invested in beating dormitory curfews, "three feet on the floor" rules, and myriad armed forces regulations.

[11]There is a theoretical argument against positive feedback. It is based on the logical impossibility of anything being infinitely increasing. Fortunately for practical concerns, most things for which a positive control system might be used in managing organizations have a present status far from perfection or infinity. The theoretical concerns are probably saved by the existence of countervailing controls (i.e., exhaustion) which emerge as one approaches the limit.

[12]E. E. Lawler and J. R. Hackman, "The Impact of Employee Participation in the Development of Pay Incentive Plans: A Field Experiment," *Journal of Applied Psychology,* vol. 53 (1969): 467–71.

act as they do at work and because they increasingly represent managers' views of what constitutes effective management.

Job enrichment is based on the notion of "intrinsic motivation." Intrinsic motivation does not mean that people exude some unalterable drive to work, but that given the proper conditions, a large part of the work force can experience significant satisfactions from doing the job well and that these satisfactions are more potent than those available from traditional forms of compensation. The availability of these satisfactions will lead to continued effort toward successful job performance.

What are the conditions necessary to have such an intrinsically motivating environment? Three factors have been consistently identified, all of which are necessary if the job is to have much motivating potential: experienced meaningfulness, autonomy, and feedback.[13] Meaningfulness is probably the most subjective of the three because it depends on individual evaluations as well as objective job characteristics. Meaningfulness implies that a variety of valued skills are used, a potentially significant impact is perceived, and a sense of task completeness or wholeness exists. While important for job enrichment, meaningfulness does not seem to be a major issue for management fraud.

The concept of autonomy may be more troubling. From the job enrichment view, autonomy is a critical element. After all, even if you know that the job was done well (positive feedback) and view the consequences of the job as far reaching (meaningfulness), it is not apt to conjure up any sense of personal achievement unless responsibility for the work was one's own. As a consequence, most job enrichment efforts make certain that people are allowed to do their jobs and do not have others intervening, measuring, or second-guessing at stages during the process. During the early stages of job enrichment, managers must often be reminded to trust in their subordinates (or simply be restrained) so that they do not intervene and rob the individual's sense of accomplishment.

Building autonomy into a job runs counter to the notion of control held in many organizations. For some, control means no one person is allowed to make any decision: there is always someone to share responsibility, to observe, to intervene. Such an approach puts autonomy and control in opposition. But this need not be the case. Ford's study at AT&T suggests that control is often strengthened by autonomy and task identity.[14] If there is anything wrong, the people potentially at fault are far fewer and highly

[13]See A. N. Turner and P. R. Lawrence, *Industrial Jobs and the Worker*, (Boston: Research Division, Graduate School of Business Administration, Harvard University, 1965); J. R. Hackman, "Work Design," in *Improving Life at Work*, ed. J. R. Hackman and L. Suttle (Santa Monica, Calif.: Goodyear, 1977).

[14]R. N. Ford, "Job Enrichment Lessons from AT&T," *Harvard Business Review* (January-February 1973): 96–106.

identifiable. To the degree autonomy is maintained, the individual cannot deny responsibility.

Feedback represents a common ground for the auditor and those interested in capitalizing on intrinsic motivation. The auditor's concern with good internal control supports the quality of information available to managers. While the auditor may be concerned about the information's availability for external review, its value to the manager should not be underestimated. Such information can be the key to the individual's self-evaluation. The impact of feedback on the individual varies more as a function of its source than its validity. Formal management information systems (MIS) and companywide reports are among the least valued sources. While MIS are used, they are generally used selectively as a function of the indices one's superiors focus upon. The most potent sources of feedback are those under the individual's own control, ones to which the individual can attend at will and which are not confounded by the evaluations of other people.[15] Such sources include information obtained by observing the flow of work and one's own results, independent comparisons to the work of others, etc.

The finding that sources of feedback under the individual's control are the most potent raises the concern that self-evaluation may be based on standards and information different from that which the organization might wish. However, there is no cause for alarm. This does not imply a work force running amok, fueled by idiosyncratic standards and criteria. Fortunately, superiors and others in the organization have an early impact in shaping the individual's standards which will then be used in independent feedback gathering.

One implication of the feedback research for deterring management fraud is that management can be helped by adopting an informal self-monitoring scheme. CPA firms can be invaluable guides. They are the greatest help when counseling management: first, selling them on the importance of providing quality feedback to management and second, developing an information system suited to their wishes. It is critical to realize that an aesthetically pleasing system or one which meets sundry accounting or computer science criteria is of no particular benefit. The value is entirely contingent upon its being used comfortably and frequently by management. Such use is most apt to occur where management sees this as *their* information, under *their* control, answering *their* information needs.

The positive controls approach treats the manager as an active collabora-

---

[15]M. M. Greller, "What Makes You Think That's Good Enough," *Wharton Magazine,* vol. 1, no. 2 (1977): 58–62; D. M. Herold and M. M. Greller, "Feedback: The Development of a Construct," *Academy of Management Journal,* vol. 20 (1977): 142–47; L. M. Hanser and P. M. Muchinsky, "Work as an Information Environment," *Organizational Behavior and Human Performances,* vol. 21 (1978): 47–60; D. A. Nadler, P. Mirvis, and C. Cammann, "The Ongoing Feedback System," *Organizational Dynamics,* Spring (1976): 63–80.

tor. The goal is to make desired behavior more gratifying and more likely than undesired behavior. Equally important, positive controls are representative of the perspective of many managers. To the degree positive controls are consistent with management's philosophy, restrictive controls will be less readily accepted. It is likely that efforts to implement restrictive control systems will meet with greater resistance in future years. Fortunately, a positive control approach can be taken. We have not nearly explored the ways such an approach might be applied.

Summary

A social psychological look at management fraud focuses on the relationship between the individual and the organization. The nature of this relationship enhances or reduces the likelihood of fraud. It may even alter the type of fraud most apt to occur. The concern with the individual-organization relationship goes far beyond "good morale" or "positive attitude toward the company." Indeed, even positive attitudes can turn corrupt, as was noted in the discussion of frauds for the firm.

Deterrence of fraud demands attention to group and organizational processes. It would be frivolous to suggest that such sensitivities could replace traditional forms of control, but they should be considered a necessary tool in the accountant's kit. The greatest challenge may be reconceptualizing the "thou-shalt-nots" of fraud into principles usable in a positive control framework. Nowhere is this clearer than with frauds for the firm. It is not in the firm's interest to discourage the drive, commitment, and identification associated with both fraud and good performance. Rather than discourage we must find ways to better harness the energy, directing it toward more acceptable means, and in the process building greater mutual commitment between individual and organization.

15

Computer-Related Management Misdeeds

Donn B. Parker

Management misdeeds are defined as any intentional acts perpetrated by a manager in which a victim suffered or could have suffered a loss that would or could result in a gain for the perpetrator(s) or the employer. Such misdeeds are computer related if a computer was the object, if the misdeeds are identified in the unique environment of a computer, if a computer is the tool or instrument of the misdeeds, if a computer is used as a symbol for deception or intimidation, or if the computer becomes the collection vehicle and container of evidence of the misdeeds. These misdeeds represent criminal acts of fraud only when one or more individuals have been convicted of violating a criminal fraud law. For the purpose of convenience and common usage, the terms fraud and misdeeds will be used interchangeably at the small cost in precision.

Whether or not management fraud is increasing or decreasing is unknown because reliable statistics are not available. Irrespective of lack of data, the nature of management fraud is changing because of the increasing use and reliance on computer technology as computers proliferate in business and government. According to an eight-year study at SRI International, computer-related misdeeds are increasing at a rapid pace. This study conclu-

Mr. Parker is Senior Management Systems Consultant, SRI International.
This paper was prepared for the Peat, Marwick, Mitchell & Co. Symposium on Management Fraud, June 1978.©Peat, Marwick, Mitchell & Co.

sion is based on the collection of over 575 reported cases. Of these cases, over one-third involve a manager as perpetrator. It is not surprising to find that the largest losses per case are those in which a manager was the perpetrator or was one of the perpetrators in collusion with others.

A new kind of problem results from computer-related management fraud. The occupations of the managers and their co-conspirators often are new. In the past, their occupations have been accountants, salesmen, clerks, and secretaries. Now we find an increasing number of managers of programmers, computer operators, data entry clerks, and data processing managers engaged in this new kind of fraud.

The environment in which computer-related management misdeeds are conducted is changing. The change has resulted in the storage of information in electronic form inside computer systems and on magnetic media and in their transmission via telecommunications facilities. More business information is being converted close to the site of its generation into computer-readable form. Liquid assets formerly stored in vaults and cash drawers are, in a metaphorical sense, increasingly being stored inside computer systems, thereby making computers the vaults of tomorrow. If management fraud continues to focus on liquid assets, the focus will change from the manual, paper-based systems of the past onto the real-time, integrated, distributed computer systems of the present or near future.

The methods of executing fraud are also changing. The early methods of conducting fraud with paper, pencil, and typewriters are giving way to automated methods using computer programs and changing data as they enter or exit computer systems. With automated fraud, new techniques can be used that were never practical in previous manual methods. A new jargon naming a number of these methods is starting to appear. Such terms as "superzapping," "piggybacking," "trojan horse attacks," "salami techniques," "asynchronous attacks," and "logic bombs" are replacing familiar terms such as "kiting," "lapping," "fiddling," and "cooking the books."

Computers are also changing the geographic and time constraints of fraud. Some computer-related frauds can be conducted from any place in the world where a telephone and computer terminal are accessible. In the past, we have measured time for conducting fraud in terms of minutes, hours, days, months, and years. Now, however, the time scale for measuring automated fraud with computers is the same as the time frame in which we measure computer processing functions—that is, in thousandths or hundredths of seconds.

Computers have created new problems for those having the responsibility for the deterrence, prevention, detection, and recovery from fraud. Line management is barely able to cope with the complexities of computer technology, much less ensure that a computer is being used safely and free from fraudulent activities and other misdeeds. The corporate security organization is not sufficiently technically oriented to fully understand computer technology. Internal auditors assisting line management in protection from fraud have only recently started major efforts to catch up with the advancing technology.

Furthermore, the use of computers has eroded the capability of a responsible individual to independently establish the integrity of business records. Technologists invariably stand between this individual and the electronic documents of records. This person must rely on the programmer, computer operator, job set-up clerk, magnetic tape librarian, and electronic maintenance engineer and their integrity before being assured of the integrity of the electronic documents of records stored in the computer and in computer media.

Deeper insight into the nature of changing management fraud may be gained by considering specific types of misdeeds. A taxonomy of such misdeeds, developed by J. L. Turner, is given in chapter 10. It is based on two factors—the function of the financial statements in the perpetration of an act of fraud, and whether the company or the perpetrator (management) receives the direct benefit of the results of the act. Each of these types of fraud will be discussed here as it relates to the increasing use of computer technology in business.

Company Is Recipient of Direct Benefit from Financial Statement Misrepresentations

Distorting Financial Statements to Obtain Credit, Long-term Financing, or Additional Capital Investment Not Otherwise Available. Computers are commonly used to maintain records of real assets. Outside organizations, including governments and CPAs, increasingly rely on computer-produced data to accurately identify the assets. Therefore, the computer data can be changed to benefit the company without actually changing the amounts of physical assets. For example, in an alleged fraud in Chicago, the inventory of products was artificially increased in the computer system to "increase" the total value of the company by $40 million. The perpetrators planned that when the company recovered from its current financial difficulties, the false inventory would be reduced in the computer system back to actual levels by the use of the same computer programs used to increase the false inventory.

Failure to Disclose Significant Information. Computer output listings or output from a teleprocessing system through remote terminals lends legitimacy and an aura of correctness and completeness to business data. Therefore, the computer can be the instrument of deception in failure to disclose significant information to authorized parties. These people often lack the capability or the motivation to validate data they are receiving by independently examining the computer programs and the content of the computer.

Related-party transactions comprise a major set of activities that may be inadequately disclosed in the financial statements. Related party is defined here as the reporting entity, its affiliates, principle owners, management and members of their immediate families, entities for which investments are accounted for by the equity method, and any other party with which a reporting entity may deal when one party has the ability to significantly influence the management or operating policies of the other. Interest-free borrowing, selling property at nonmarket prices, exchanging property, and open-ended lending are common types of related-party fraud. The important element in this type of fraud is hiding the evidence of its perpetration. This can be done when management can direct that controls, such as journaling, exception reporting, and floor limits, not be used or be neutralized under special circumstances inside the computer system, thus obscuring the evidence of misdeeds.

When an individual manager, rather than the entire management of a company, engages in concealed related-party transactions in an EDP environment, collusion with a specific type of perpetrator is usually necessary. A manager must at least collude with technologists sufficiently familiar with the computer programming or operations to complete the misdeed.

Transfer pricing, i.e., valuing goods exchanged between related parties, plays an important role in many related-party transactions. Corporations often use large, centralized computer systems to simultaneously process business data on their divisions, subsidiaries, and related companies. This increases the ease with which management can improve the results of operations of one company to the detriment of another company in cases in which all accounting for both companies is done in the same computer. This can result in transactions that are practically impossible to detect because of the complexity of computer programs and the large volume of data processed.

Evading Legal Tax Liabilities.   Businesses are increasingly submitting tax data to taxing agencies in the form of magnetic tapes. In the near future, this will also be done by direct transmission from computer to computer. This will open new opportunities for fraud through secret manipulation of data and inadequate controls in data processing and telecommunication systems.

Perpetrator Is Recipient of Direct Benefit from Financial Statement Misrepresentation

Concealment of Inadequate Performance by Management.   Computer technology management affords new methods of concealment of evidence of inadequate performance. The performance data can be changed covertly inside the computer system, or data can be suppressed in performance reports. Again, this misdeed often requires collusion with a technologist who can perform the technical part of the acts. The financial statements, which reflect the altered performance data, can mislead readers as to the quality and effectiveness of management's leadership and decision-making.

Company Is Recipient of Direct Benefit from Financial Statements Misrepresented to Disguise an Act of Fraud

Concealment of Sale or Assignment of Fictitious or Misrepresented Assets. Businesses with increasing frequency exchange assets (not physically) in the form of assignment by description of the assets or accounting of them where the transfer is conducted between one business computer and another over telephone lines or by the exchange of electronic media such as magnetic tapes. The resale of insurance policies is commonly done in the insurance industry merely by the transfer of a magnetic tape containing the descriptions of the policies; the selling company retains the policies for servicing purposes only. The Equity Funding insurance fraud of 1973 is an example. In that case, 6,400 fake insurance policies were "created" automatically in a computer system. This could have been accomplished on such a scale only through the use of a computer system. The misrepresented financial statements disguised the sale of the fictitious policies.

Concealment of Prohibited Business Activities. Computer services represent an entirely new form of business. New laws have been enacted to prohibit banks from engaging in certain types of computer service bureau businesses. New questions are arising about related entities performing computer services for one another. The computer facilities management business adds a new dimension to questions of fair business activities. As such questions are answered and clear prohibitions are established, concealment of prohibited computer-related business activities may become a source of financial statement misrepresentations.

Concealment of Improper Payments. EDP systems may play a role in executing and concealing improper payments. Transfer of funds from one financial institution to another, both domestically and internationally, is becoming increasingly common. The accomplishment of the transfer leaves no evidence when supporting documents normally produced by the computer system are suppressed through computer program changes. The financial statements ultimately reflect the improper transactions.

Perpetrator Is Recipient of Direct Benefit from Financial Statements Misrepresented to Disguise an Act of Fraud

Embezzlement. Computers are increasingly becoming primary sites for embezzlement because they "contain" much of the liquid assets and the records of the physical assets of the company. New kinds of embezzlement schemes are possible that would have been impractical in manual environments. For example, "salami techniques" represent a category of dishonest methods that have little likelihood of being discovered. "Salami" refers to taking small amounts from large numbers of sources over an extended period of time. For example, secret code in a production computer program could be inserted to transfer small amounts of money from large numbers of accounts into a favored account. The small amounts of money in the individual accounts could be attributed to loss from errors. The total amount lost would be unknown. The perpetrator could then withdraw the money from the favored account in legitimate ways. Financial embezzlement usually requires three acts: (1) the creation of a hidden debit, (2) the creation of a hidden balancing credit to avoid violation of controls, and (3) conversion of these technical acts to financial gain. The manager must usually be in collusion with the technologist who can perform the technical act. After the technical act is accomplished, the manager is in a position to convert the act to economic gain, either directly or in collusion with other employees.

The removal of physical assets from the possession of the company is a manual act usually not involving the use of a computer. However, for the theft to remain undetected, data representing the identity, location, and form of the assets often must be changed inside a computer system. For example, in a $14 million gasoline inventory theft in San Juan, Puerto Rico, the theft involved workers, guards, and clerks. Computer operators played an essential role in the deception. They changed the contents of the computer that recorded the inventory levels of gasoline. Computer programs also represent entirely new assets of companies, and therefore are subject to theft. However, most companies have not identified their computer programs sufficiently as the objects of such theft, and controls and protection are minimal.

Other Types of Fraud Not Involving Management Fraud

Consumer Fraud. Businesses can perpetrate frauds on the general public, such as falsely advertising the use of computers or assigning to an information product an exaggerated power or thoroughness or accuracy. Computer outputs can falsely convey legitimacy to information on the basis that if it came from a computer, the information must be correct because "computers don't lie."

Diversion to Management of a Potentially Profitable Transaction That Would Normally Create Profits for the Company. Some members of management are in the position to have special knowledge of potentially profitable transactions that other members of management or the company owners do not have. The company's computer center is becoming a power center because of the information that is stored there. Data processing managers are entirely new kinds of managers with the custodianship of this center of power; therefore, they may obtain information about potentially profitable transactions which they can divert, perhaps through collusion, to their own profit instead of the company's.

Acceptance of Bribes or Kickbacks. The opportunity to accept bribes or kickbacks is made possible through industrial espionage involving the exchange of proprietary information that is increasingly being stored in computer systems. Transferring or revealing this information can be done in highly automated fashion by the use of hidden, secret computer instructions in production computer programs ("trojan horse" technique). "Narrow bandwidth data leakage" from computer systems can be accomplished in completely undetectable ways through a variety of exotic technical methods.

Audit Problems and Solutions

Business criminals most often perform fraud in the areas that they know the best and that are the least likely to be discovered. They know these areas better than anyone else in the world. This puts auditors at a disadvantage because their expertise in these areas is far more limited than that of the fraud perpetrators. The perpetrators anticipate these limitations and refrain from perpetrating the fraud unless they have confidence they can deceive or avoid the auditors. Therefore, auditors normally will be unable to detect a fraud so long as they limit themselves to expected, routine audit practices.

The use of computers substantially increases the safety of the fraud perpetrator who has sufficient computer skills, knowledge, and access but reduces the safety of the one who lacks these capabilities. The reason for this disparity is that data representing assets, accounting for assets, and controls are removed from direct observation and modification by being in electronic form in a computer. A computer program and computer hardware are required to gain access; hence, deception by the computer sophisticate is more likely to be successful, but unobservable controls make detection of the unsophisticated thief more likely.

In computer-related crime experience, the auditor has been surpassed because the perpetrators have more capability in computer technology than the auditors. Fortunately, this situation is changing as auditors specialize and become expert in the technology. However, keeping up with the race between the advancing EDP audit capabilities and fast-paced advancing technology is difficult.

It is clear that the days of the generalist auditors are numbered. Specialization in the computer field has been a necessity for many years. As the audit environment becomes more automated, the auditor must specialize to be competent enough to be effective. Auditing even for small companies, which are rapidly moving to minicomputer usage, can only be done in the EDP environment where team auditing to apply the necessary range of skills and knowledge is possible. Looking further ahead, a new level of specialization will develop. The job title "EDP auditor" will probably disappear because all auditors will have to have training similar to that of today's EDP auditors. Specialization will be more particular. Specialists will emerge in operating systems, report generators, data base management, electronic engineering, software quality assurance, payment applications, inventory applications, general ledger systems, and many more specialized applications. Each technical subject will require a specialist to match wits with those specialist employees who are included in the potential population of fraud perpetrators.

Probably the greatest impact of computer technology on auditors lies in the fact that it can lead to reliance on client specialists. Because auditors have not become sufficiently specialized, they must rely on those specialists—often the client's employees—for assurances as to the functioning of various EDP systems. There are always technologists standing between auditors and the electronic documents of records they must use. Chief among these are the programmers who write the auditor's programs and applications and operating system, the computer operators, the tape librarians, and even the electronic maintenance engineers. Any of these persons can easily deceive the generalist auditor and even the specialist EDP auditors. What EDP auditor could detect a subtle electronic hardware change? Auditors claim that substantive testing to verify the electronically stored data and appropriate reliance on the honesty of management is effective. Nevertheless, opportunity to do substantive testing independent of computers is greatly reduced as less paper and manual activities are performed and the volume of data in computers grows. Furthermore, managers also lack technical understanding of the automated mechanics of their businesses and are therefore little help to the auditor in this regard.

Several major changes must be made to solve these problems, especially in the control of the most challenging problem—dealing with the intelligent computer fraud perpetrator. First, auditors need their own independent specialized computers to reduce reliance on the client's computers. The audit computer, either stand-alone or on-line to computers to be audited, must be especially designed in both hardware and software.

Second, audit tools and techniques must be further developed beyond the present state of the art as presented in the report "Systems Auditability and Control," produced by SRI International and available from the Institute of Internal Auditors. Increasing use of minicomputers, distributed processing computer networks, and other technical advances require new tools and techniques. Research and development in this area is a new concept, and sources of funding must be found.

Third, computer systems and business application systems must become more auditable. The audit requirements must be included at the time the systems are designed to ensure full integration. Auditors must participate in systems design, and management must understand that additional expenditures in software development are essential to ensure auditability. The rationale for these requirements can be demonstrated by showing the savings possible from more reliable and safer systems and reduced costs of audits.

Fourth, specialization of the auditor and team auditing must be realized through training programs and staffing. Audit plans should be restructured. Increased or improved staffing is needed to direct the technologists to provide adequate controls and safeguards and the auditors to change their methods so as to ensure the continued safety of business and government.

Conclusion

The previous discussion has shown that the taxonomy of management fraud has not changed because of the addition of new terminology and types of fraud. Nevertheless, the changes in the occupations, the backgrounds of the perpetrators, the changing technical environment, the changing form of assets, the *modi operandi* of fraud, and the different geographic and timing constraints that are inherent in the use of computer technology for sensitive business functions make computerized management fraud an entirely new kind of fraud. Consequently, this environment requires entirely new methods of deterrence, prevention, detection, and recovery and new approaches to auditing. These new methods can be developed only by the technologists in the computer field and audit management. Hence, the need for new methods presents a challenge to management.

16

Detecting Management Fraud: Some Organizational Strategies for the Independent Auditor

James E. Sorensen and Thomas L. Sorensen

What is management fraud? Is the independent auditor responsible for detecting management fraud? What auditing tools and techniques are available for detecting management fraud? Can they be improved? Are new tools needed? Like many other professional services in today's world, audits of large corporations have undergone significant changes in recent years. While fraud detection has become an increasingly important part of the independent audit, organizing and performing complex and effective audits at a reasonable cost taxes even the most capable auditor. This paper seeks to identify how independent auditors can sharpen their approach to unearthing such fraud.

As an outgrowth of management frauds leading to audit failures, the 1970s revealed a renewed interest in the auditor's standard of care for fraud detection. Deliberate violations by management, the auditing profession's reluctance to accept expanded responsibility for detecting management fraud, only a recent emergence of systematic audit review practices by out-

Dr. James E. Sorensen is Professor of Accounting, School of Accountancy, University of Denver. Mr. Thomas L. Sorensen is Professor of Sociology, Arapahoe Community College.
This paper was prepared for the Peat, Marwick, Mitchell & Co. Symposium on Management Fraud, June 1978. ©Peat, Marwick, Mitchell & Co.

side peers, and the acknowledged weaknesses of existing audit methods to decisively reveal deliberate management frauds all have contributed to a call for new standards and methods to address a serious social problem. At stake is the future of the profession of auditing as well as an economic system. The need for dependable financial statements is widely recognized, but no one profession or group unilaterally can fulfill that need. However, increased cooperation among the various advocates for dependable financial statements can make the goal achievable. Clearly, new mechanisms are needed by which auditors, the SEC, concerned investors, and citizens can work together (instead of in opposition) to improve auditing and to assure the authenticity of financial reports.

The objective of this paper is to determine how auditors should be geared to detect management fraud. The suggested answer is complex, involving expansion and systematic testing of a behaviorally oriented "red flag" approach, and extension of the "open" systems concept of organizational behavior.

Current Auditing Approaches Used to Detect Management Fraud

The Triangle Model.   According to Hanson, "Containment of fraud is founded on three closely related functions:

(1)   a strong, involved, investigative board of directors;

(2)   a sound, comprehensive system of internal controls; and

(3)   alert, capable independent auditors.

"Like the points of a triangle, if any function is not forcefully delineated, the entire structure becomes vulnerable." When all three functions are vigorously pursued, the opportunity for sizable management fraud is significantly reduced. Frauds by management become possible when the protective functions are relaxed "because of neglect, lack of dedication, the pressure of other duties, or an over-reliance on those responsible for safeguards at any other point in the triangle."[1] Using this model, two instructive points can be identified for the auditor trying to locate potential management fraud situations:

○   Lack of active, continuous and diligent participation by board members spells problems; auditors may now need to "audit the board" to assess its overall composition (e.g., percentage of outside directors, percentage of financially disinterested directors) and operation (e.g., is critical information being provided and reviewed? are board members attending meetings?) and to test

[1]Walter E. Hanson, "Focus on Fraud," *Financial Executive,* vol. 43 (1975): p. 15.

the knowledge and understanding of its individual members (e.g., do board members understand financial statements?); new standards and procedures would be needed to guide the auditor in this important task.

○ Using the boards' audit committees (including outside directors) to assure the adequacy and effectiveness of accounting and other controls as well as the objectivity of the financial statements. Perhaps the AICPA should promulgate an auditing standard *requiring* audit committees as a condition for expressing an opinion on the financial statements of any publicly held company. (The New York Stock Exchange now requires audit committees as a condition for listing.)

Management Involvement in Material Transactions. Under ASR No. 153, issued by the SEC on February 25, 1974, Touche Ross undertook to design procedures to accomplish in all audit engagements (public and private ownership) a specific review to determine management's direct or indirect involvement in material transactions which are included in financial statements.[2] The product was a constructive step toward the development of the independent auditor's detection of management's actions which may have implications of fraud. "Red flags" are tied to conducive economic factors (e.g., lack of sufficient working capital, declining industry, extremely rapid expansion) and business structures (e.g., high turnover in key financial positions, numerous businesses each with its own accounting system, need for but a lack of internal audit staff). New procedures are to be integrated into the appropriate sections of the basic audit program to avoid unnecessary duplication of work and overauditing.

Extending the "Red Flag" Approach. Framing the discussion in a somewhat different view, Coopers and Lybrand recast the "conducive economic factors and business structures" approach into "danger signals of improper practice."[3] Many of the previous factors or structures are included, but several additional ones are cited:

Economic Factors
○ Pressure to finance expansion via current earnings rather than through equity or debt
○ A profit squeeze as a result of sales and revenues not having kept pace with increasing costs and expenses
○ The need for additional collateral to support existing obligations
○ Significant reduction in sales order backlog heralding a future sales decline

[2]Touche Ross, *Management Involvement in Material Transactions,* rev. ed. (1976), p. 10.
[3]Coopers & Lybrand, *Newsletter* (April 1977).

○ Competition from low-priced imports
○ Reluctance by management to provide additional information to improve the clarity and comprehensiveness of the company's financial statements
○ Sizable inventory increases without comparable sales increases
○ Progressive deterioration in quality of earnings, e.g., switching from sum-of-the-year's digits depreciation to straight-line without good reason

Business Structures
○ Management tendency to exert extreme pressure on executives to meet budgets
○ Executives with records of malfeasance[4]

The "red flag" approach is proposed as a cost-effective approach for the auditor. Drastic new measures to prevent management fraud can be both expensive and incapable of preventing or detecting every malfeasance. Hanson implies that devising practical measures, such as a rational and reasonable early warning system, will serve in the great majority of cases, and when fraud strikes, explore its sources, prosecute the guilty, and learn from the experience.[5]

The "red flag" approach has appeal, and some effort to identify the flags has been stimulated by SAS Nos. 6, 16, and 17. However, there appears to be a need for systematic evaluation which attempts to assess the effectiveness and costs of the "red flag" approach. A suggested approach is developed in the following section.

Researching the "Red Flag" Approach.   A general analysis strategy could begin with the observed relationship, measure by measure, of each major type of predictor (e.g., economic conditions or organizational structure, internal controls) to a series of irregularity criterion measures. Next, multiple economic or multiple organizational measures could be grouped to test for improved predictions over single variables. The interaction between major types could be explored, for example, by showing that each major type continues to be predictive while the other is held constant. Finally, combinations of various predictors should provide maximum explanatory power in predicting the existence of irregularity. A multivariable approach could be developed by a pattern analysis using nominal or interval level measures. If, for example, each measure were dichotomized (e.g., yes or no, such as in the case of Touche Ross *Technical Letter 149*), the result is a theoretically high fraud-prone group and a theoretically low fraud-prone group. If the two

---

[4]Coopers & Lybrand, *Newsletter* (March-April 1978).
[5]"Focus on Fraud," p. 18.

TABLE 1. Multivariable Fraud-Prone Measures and Prediction of Irregularities*

Patterns	Fraud-Prone Measures			Number of Clients	Irregularities	
	X	Y	Z		#	%
I Optimal pattern—minimum expected irregularities	A —	—	—	xx	xx	0
	(— = Low-fraud prone + = High-fraud prone)					
II One-variable departure—toward greater expected irregularities	B —	—	+	xx		
	C —	+	—	xx	xx	0
	D +	—	—	xx		
III Two-variable departure—toward greater expected irregularities	E —	+	+	xx		
	F +	—	+	xx	xx	3
	G +	+	—	xx		
IV Three-variable departure—maximum expected irregularities	H +	+	+	xx	xx	5

*Adapted from Richard Jessor, *et al.*, p.349.

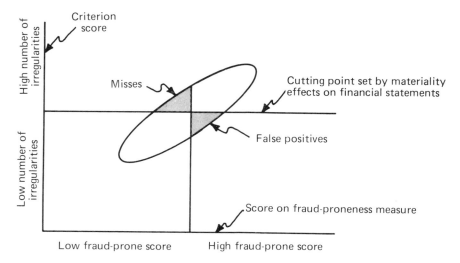

FIGURE 1.   Schematic representation of the effectiveness of a
fraud-proneness measure (Adapted from G. Helmstadter,
Principles of Psychological Measurement, Figure 19, p. 120 [New
York, 1964])

derived groups are compared on various measures, a lower percentage of
irregularities should be found in the low fraud-prone group than in the high
fraud-prone group. If multiple high-low fraud-prone predictor measures are
simultaneously combined, the group with the low fraud-proneness on all
measures should have the lowest proportion of discovered irregularities; the
group with high fraud-proneness on all measures should have the highest
proportion of discovered irregularities. Other groups with mixed high-low
patterns should be predicted to fall between the extreme high and low
groups. For example, if three fraud-prone measures were used, Table 1 could
be constructed; hypothetical percentages are inserted to identify the expected
outcome.[6]

If these patterns could be replicated within client groups within firms and
across firms, confidence in the meaningfulness of the "red flag" approach
(from SAS Nos. 6 and 16) would be significantly enhanced.

The suggested analysis is straightforward and can be applied easily by
auditors. The groups would be clear-cut by auditor definitions, and the
analysis would proceed through a discernible path; in some measure, the
analysis combines a quantitative research method with the auditor's applied

[6]The foregoing discussion is adapted from Richard Jessor, Theodore D. Graves, Robert C.
Hanson, and Shirley L. Jessor, *Society, Personality, and Deviant Behavior: A Study of a Tri-Ethnic
Community* (Huntington, N.Y.: 1968), pp. 335–63.

judgment. Other analyses are possible. One method might be Automatic Interaction Detection (AID), which searches the data for a statistical structure which might give an insight into an explanatory structure.

Expressing Empirical Validity.   Our concern is simple. There is a need to account for the differential rates of occurrence of irregularities among clients of independent audit firms or else SAS Nos. 6 and 16 have no explanatory power for the auditor. Although the variables identified earlier have some face validity, a general "red flag" approach should be tested in the natural laboratory of audit practice. A client screening approach is graphically portrayed in Figure 1.

The elipse represents a scatter plot indicative of the degree of relationship between scores of fraud-proneness measures and the criterion scores on observed irregularities (assuming interval level measures for the moment). Two problems arise: (1) clients who revealed high fraud proneness but who, after extended procedures were applied, proved to have a low number of irregularities; (2) clients who revealed low fraud proneness but, in fact, had a high number of undetected irregularities. The former may be labeled "false positives" and the latter "misses." To evaluate the "red flag" approach one should calculate the correlation between the measures and the criterion of irregularities as well as the base rate of irregularities. The base rate represents the proportion of *incorrect* decisions made about the level of irregularities *without* the use of the particular "red flag" measure. To evaluate the effectiveness of the measure(s), the proportion of incorrect decisions made when the "red flag" measure is used must be determined and compared to the base rate of irregularities.[7] Follow-up studies can help to establish the empirical or predictive validity of the "red flag" approach. Cross-validation studies using clients other than those with known irregularities produce validity generalization.[8] Evidence of construct validity can be developed, for example, through comparisons of client groupings that should reveal differences, correlational patterns among measures, and an analysis of internal consistency.

Summary on "Red Flags."   Management fraud may be the result of multiple determinants such as the opportunity to commit fraud (e.g., poor or inadequate internal controls), the environmental predisposers (e.g., outside factors bringing financial pressure on the enterprise), and supporting normative structures (e.g., survival at any cost). Such factors may explain why individuals, as well as groups, engage in management fraud. An opportunity

[7]G. C. Helmstadter, *Research Concepts in Human Behavior: Education, Psychology, Sociology* (Englewood Cliffs, N.J.: Prentice-Hall, 1970), p. 307.
[8]Ibid., p. 308.

coupled with a personal pressure and a personal belief and control structure supportive of deviant behavior converge to involve the single individual in a fraud. If the individual is highly placed, then it becomes a management fraud. Single-person frauds perpetrated by circumventing the internal control system should be detected by study and evaluation of the internal controls.[9] In any event, single-person management fraud and multiple-person management fraud may be an interactive product of economic, sociocultural, and personal determinants, and systematic research at several levels could offer a convincing theoretical and empirical synthesis.

A first step would be a careful retrospective application of the "red flag" approach on known fraud cases to sharpen the general approach for prospective validation. In the final analysis, our proposal for research of the "red flag" approach would be amply rewarded if the inferences about the likelihood of irregularities using the theory of SAS Nos. 6 and 16 can be drawn with some degree of empirical certainty. If the effectiveness of these SASs cannot be demonstrated, then the auditor must turn to some other neglected variables which should have been identified in the first place.

Emergence of a Systems Perspective

The ferment of management fraud has been paralleled by transformation of the audit approach itself. The driving conceptual force in general systems theory was initially advanced in the 1920s by Ludwig Von Bertalanffy who saw the organism as a whole or as a system.[10] Meaningful applications of the insights of this perspective are observable in the approach to and practice of auditing. A relevant current example is the audit approach by Peat, Marwick, Mitchell & Co. called the Systems Evaluation Approach (SEA). The approach is an open systems perspective and is characterized by

[9]John J. Willingham, "Discussant's Response to Relationship of Auditing Standards to Detection of Fraud," in *Contemporary Auditing Problems: Proceedings of Arthur Andersen/University of Kansas Symposium on Auditing Problems* (Lawrence, Kansas, 1974); p. 58. The auditor can become dismayed quickly about the individual level of motivation when he or she learns that one of the individuals in the Equity Funding fraud stated, "I did it for the jollies." William E. Blundell, "Equity Funding: I did It for the Jollies," in *Crime at the Top: Deviance in Business and the Professions,* eds. John M. Johnson and Jack D. Douglas (Philadelphia: J. B. Lippincott, 1978), p. 155.

[10]Eugene J. Haas and Thomas E. Drabek, *Complex Organizations: A Sociological Perspective* (New York: Macmillan, 1973), p. 83. The natural system model has evolved in an "open" system model where the latter is characterized by interacting systems within an environment (rather than being mere reactors), systems defined as interacting elements with emphasis in the relations among the interacting elements, systems which must interact to survive, system states which can be obtained from different initial conditions and in different ways, systems which have complex feedback and regulatory mechanisms to permit adaptive response to environmental change, system interaction which reflects differing layers of control and autonomy, organizations which are viewed as patterned sets of events, organizations which have boundaries that differentiate them from other various environments. See Haas and Drabek, pp. 83–93.

A client system interacting in a larger system which requires the auditor, for example, to have an understanding of the overall economy, industry, and environment in which the client operates and a general knowledge of the operations of the client's business.

Interacting systems elements such as the flow of economic transactions and the study of internal controls and the reliance to be placed on those controls.

A realization that system interaction with its environment is necessary for survival and, for example, that material undetected errors and irregularities could occur in this interaction and such detection depends heavily on the strengths and weaknesses of the internal control system.

Systems states which can be obtained by starting at varying initial conditions and through varying ways, by, for example, flowcharting to document major systems or transaction cycles enabling the auditor to understand the client's specific accounting and financial reporting system and to highlight significant internal control strengths and weaknesses.

An audit process with complex feedback and regulatory mechanisms to permit adaptation to varied environmental changes; for example, initial reliance may be placed on internal controls but subsequent tests of controls (e.g., observation tests and compliance tests of transactions) lead to no significant reliance on the internal control.

Differing layers of control and autonomy throughout the various systems; for example, in both reliance and nonreliance areas, substantive auditing procedures should be explained by linking the reliance on internal controls to the audit scope and to the extent of substantive procedures.

Other large accounting firms have also adopted systems approaches.[11]

Although the open systems theory is a helpful organizing concept, auditors (as well as behavioral scientists) find it difficult to use operationally. Several perplexing questions arise. Is the auditor simply groping in the theoretical dusk of an open system orientation by testing intuitive propositions, some of which work and some of which do not? Why has the auditor not developed the "interacting cycles" approach sooner? The end result of this analysis is the uneasy feeling that auditors are not achieving a maximum yield from the open systems perspective. The idea of the open systems concept applied to the audit needs to be better crystalized and organized to assure a more efficient and effective use of the concept.

---

[11]For example, see Arthur Andersen, *A Guide for Studying and Evaluating Internal Accounting Control* (Chicago, 1978), and Coopers & Lybrand, *Newsletter* (March-April 1978).

An Integrating Model.   A useful tack would be the formulation of a behavioral perspective which could be applied simultaneously to the organizations of the client, the auditor, and other key entities such as the SEC. Such a perspective would be a basic framework so each organization could be analyzed individually and in concert within a larger environment. One such promising model (although not yet applied to clients and auditors) is a *stress-strain* perspective developed by Haas and Drabek. The basic components of their model seek to explain patterned interaction sequences (or organizational performance structure) by reference to three explanatory structures:

1.   Normative structure—preferred and required interaction for categories of persons in kinds or types of situations

2.   Interpersonal structure—responses to other individuals as individuals rather than as incumbents of a position

3.   Resource structure—skills, physical materials, space, and information under the jurisdiction of or available to an organization

FIGURE 2.   The basic framework (Adapted from Eugene J. Haas and Thomas E. Drabek, *Complex Organizations: A Sociological Perspective*, p. 118 [New York: Macmillan, 1973])

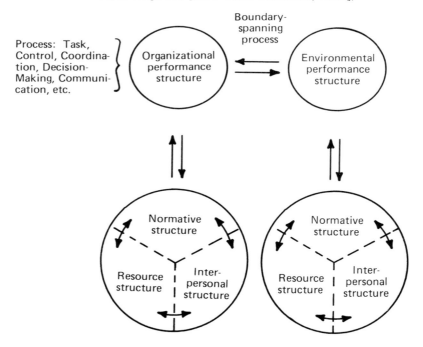

The performance structure is viewed as a series of processes such as task, control, communication, and decision-making. The explanatory structures are interactive and jointly serve to explain the varying outcomes observed in the performance structure. The interactive nature of the three explanatory structures provides a basis for understanding and predicting patterns of interaction in the performance structure of organization. The model can be applied to an individual, an organizational unit, an entire organization, or to an entire environment in which many organizations function. Figure 2 reveals the basic relationship in the Haas–Drabek formulation.

Haas and Drabek suggest that all organizations have some degree of *strain* (defined as the inconsistencies or discrepancies among the normative, interpersonal, and resource structural elements of the organization) and *stress* (defined as the degree of discrepancy between organizational demands and organizational capacity). The strain and stress are always in a state of flux and are always a matter of degree. By an insightful analogy Haas and Drabek suggest an organization is like a cracked windshield shattering as the wind pressure and rough road converge to help break it along the predetermined fractures.[12] The cracks represent the inconsistencies and discrepancies in the structure (strain), and the road combines with the wind pressure (demand) against a fixed capacity, thus creating stress and leading to the disintegration of the windshield along the pattern of cracks.

> From our perspective then, organizations are viewed as patterned interaction structures that vary in stability, both in degree and over time. Likewise, the normative, interpersonal, and resource structures that permit us to understand and predict the behavior patterns also are dynamic and interdependent. Strains within and among these structures give us clues as to how the structure will fare as demands from the environment are altered.[13]

Application of the Model to Clients, Auditors, and the SEC.   One of the direct benefits of the model is the ability of the auditor to interpret some of the traditional audit concerns within a behavioral perspective. Take internal control, for example. An auditor has a concern for internal check, and reviews how individual employees *should* interact to accomplish internal check (normative structure), how staff turnover or illness can defeat the prescription (resources impacting the normative structure), or how personal friendships among employees may abridge some essential controls (interpersonal impacting the normative structure).

Another useful dimension of the model is in predicting when management fraud is likely to occur. By identifying strains and stresses and the changes in them, the auditor may be more productive in sensing and pin-

[12]*Complex Organizations,* pp. 119–20.
[13]*Complex Organizations,* p. 120.

pointing management frauds (and other irregularities or illegal acts). For example, how does the performance structure change when there are:

1. Changes in demands where the demand
   a. was an unanticipated sharp increase in quantity?
   b. has high priority because organizational existence is threatened?
   c. previously met is now not met?
   d. was not previously met but is temporarily accepted by the organization?
2. Changes in organizational capacity such as
   a. changes in resource structure (e.g., absence or turnover of key personnel, loss of crucial information)?
   b. changes in normative structure (e.g., emergent norms contradict those previously existing)?
   c. changes in interpersonal structure (e.g., relocation of personnel develops strained relationships)?[14]

If the auditor searches for *changes* in the type of strains and levels of stress, the *kinds* of variables and the *measures* they would seek may take them down an expanded and different audit path. The recent emergence of the "red flag" approach is consistent with the stress-strain auditing approach. If the stress-strain perspective had been used in the development of auditing methods five years ago, much of the content of the Touche Ross *Technical Letter 149* would have been incorporated before the prompting effect of ASR No. 153.

Information about strain may indicate where the performance structure will crack. Sudden shifts in demand-capacity may pressure an already tight working capital. Some kind of coping behavior (including management fraud) can be predicted. The level and length of time is likely to affect performance and coping behavior. Acute stress may cause the auditor to look for different kinds of irregularities than if the stress is chronic.

We are not suggesting we need a new type of auditor, but we are suggesting that current auditors need to think about the audit in new ways. Some of the recent changes in audit methods suggest the process has started. The proposed model can focus on a single position within an organization, or it may be shifted to departments, divisions, the total organization, or its environment. Although the approach is promising, further empirical work is needed. How would the audit approach look if it were anchored in the stress-strain perspective? Can the auditor's perspective be focused to pinpoint the linkages between stress/strain and coping behavior? Would the auditor need to develop interviewing skills like those of a behavioral researcher? How can the auditor obtain useful measures? Who will do the innovation? Those who dare to imagine better auditing must be willing to translate their imagination into reality.

[14]Adapted from *Complex Organizations,* p. 252.

17

Auditor Involvement in the Detection of Fraud

W. Steve Albrecht, David J. Cherrington, I. Reed Payne, Allan V. Roe and Marshall B. Romney

C ourt decisions, criticisms by the financial press, actions by regulatory bodies, and surveys of users indicate that auditors may be required to assume increasing responsibilities for fraud detection in the future. If so, it is imperative that auditors understand the nature of fraud, the backgrounds from which it arises, its possible causes, controls and procedures that will deter fraudulent activity, as well as techniques that can be used to detect fraud once it has occurred. The only way that such an understanding can be gained is through a thorough study of fraudulent activities.

The goals of our research have been threefold:

1. To conduct an extensive review of all the fraud-related literature

2. To identify the individual and organizational factors (situations, circumstances, patterns, procedures, personality characteristics, background, etc.) that suggest a high probability of fraud

3. To summarize and document the significant fraud-related variables that can be used by auditors to develop an early warning system to detect and deter fraud.

Dr. Albrecht is Associate Professor of Accounting, Brigham Young University; Dr. Cherrington is Associate Professor of Organizational Behavior, Brigham Young University; Dr. Payne is Professor of Psychology, Brigham Young University; Dr. Roe is Criminal Psychologist, Utah State Prison; and Dr. Romney is Assistant Professor of Accounting, Brigham Young University.

The research for this paper was supported by a grant from the Peat, Marwick, Mitchell Foundation under its Research Opportunities in Auditing Program.

This paper provides a description of our research to date, some of the problems we encountered, and some tentative conclusions. They are tentative because the major portion of our research has thus far been devoted to the literature review. We expect to refine our conclusions by additional analysis of the data we have gathered.

Defining Fraud

In reviewing the fraud literature, several unexpected problems were encountered. The first problem we faced was finding an adequate definition of fraud. We found that everyone seems to define fraud differently. The FBI and other federal agencies do not compile statistics on fraud, but they do gather some statistics on white-collar crime. However, white-collar crime is not necessarily the same as fraud. For example, it has been used to describe any crime committed by anyone from the upper socioeconomic class, any crimes committed by business executives to further the financial interests of their company, or any crime committed against a company by one of its employees.[1] This may include crimes other than fraud. Another definition states that white-collar crime is

> "Illegal acts" which may be handled by civil proceedings and remedies as well as by criminal proceedings and sanctions. Such acts are characterized by fraud, deceit and concealment and not dependent on force, violence or threats. Personnel involved may act independently or in collusion with others. The objective is to obtain money, property, services or information; to avoid payment or losses; or to secure an advantage.[2]

This definition includes many criminal acts which do not concern auditors. The business literature has proposed numerous definitions of fraud. One, for example, defines fraud as improper actions that result in a material misstatement of the financial statements.[3]

After considering various definitions, it was concluded that, for our purposes, the best definition of fraud was one discussed at the Peat, Marwick, Mitchell & Co. Symposium on Management Fraud held in New York in June of 1978. Fraud is

1. Improper actions resulting in a material misstatement of the financial statements and in financial detriment to shareholders or creditors

[1] See D.C. Gibbons, *Society, Crime, and Criminal Careers—An Introduction to Criminology,* 3rd ed. (Englewood Cliffs, N.J.: Prentice-Hall, 1973), ch. 14.

[2] *Handbook on White-Collar Crime,* U.S. Chamber of Commerce (Washington, D.C., 1974), pp. 3–4.

[3] Harvey Kapnick, "Responsibility and Detection in Management Fraud," *CPA Journal* (May 1976): 19–23.

2. Improper actions resulting in the defrauding of the consumer public, such as false advertising, etc.

3. Embezzlement and defalcations perpetrated by employees against their employers

4. Other improper actions such as bribes, kickbacks, violations of regulatory agency rules, failure to maintain an adequate internal control system, etc.

While each of these four types of fraud is of interest to accountants, probably the first type, material financial misstatements, represents the kind that auditors fear most. A very significant problem in studying fraud, however, is that most of the documented data and available literature only discuss the third type of fraud (embezzlement and defalcations).

Three of the four types of fraud have different types of victims. While the victims of the first type of fraud (material misstatement of financial statements) are investors, the victims of the second type are the consuming public, and the victims of the third type are the companies. The victims of the fourth type of fraud are hard to ascertain.

Data Sources

The second difficulty we faced in our study was the inaccessibility of data. Much of the data we wanted were unavailable for one or more reasons. Some organizations (for example, the SEC, Department of Commerce, and some CPA firms) did not collect data in the form we needed it. Other organizations, because of legal considerations, would not release the data they had. Some firms were afraid of adverse publicity. Most contended that their information on current frauds could not be released because it would constitute an invasion of privacy rights or because the release of the information might bring a lawsuit or bias the outcome of a lawsuit in progress. In addition, they contended that information on past lawsuits could not be released due to the confidentiality of the information.

The following is a list of the data sources that were personally visited by our project participants during the summer of 1978:

1. Comptroller of Currency
2. CPA firms (major firms, including seven of the Big 8)
3. Department of Commerce
4. Department of the Treasury
5. Donn Parker's Computer Fraud Files
6. Federal Bureau of Investigation
7. Federal Reserve Board

8. National District Attorneys Association
9. Pinkerton's (investigative agency)
10. Securities and Exchange Commission
11. State Probation and Parole Records
12. Utah State Prison

Data were also gathered by mail and by telephone. A partial list of those sources contacted by letter and/or by telephone includes:

1. Aetna Life and Casualty
2. American Bankers Association
3. American Bar Association
4. American Institute of Certified Public Accountants
5. Apex Charitable Trust
6. Automation Training Center
7. Bank Administration Institute
8. Battelle Institute
9. U.S. Chamber of Commerce
10. Commercial Union Assurance Corporation
11. Computerworld
12. Continental Insurance Co.
13. Crum and Forster
14. Department of Housing and Urban Development
15. Department of Justice
16. Department of Treasury
17. EDP Analyzer
18. Every prison in the United States and Canada with a population of over 400 inmates
19. Every women's prison in the United States and Canada with a population of over 100 inmates
20. Federal Deposit and Insurance Corp.
21. Federal Trade Commission
22. Fidelity and Deposit Co. of Maryland
23. Fireman's Fund Insurance Co.
24. Government of Japan, Ministry of Justice
25. Hartford Insurance Co.

26. IBM Corporation
27. INA Corporation
28. Insight Services
29. Institute of Internal Auditors
30. Internal Revenue Service
31. International Association of Chiefs of Police
32. International Criminal Police Organization
33. Library Centre of Criminology, Toronto, Canada
34. Lloyds of London
35. Ministry of the Solicitor General, Research Division, Ottawa, Canada
36. National Association of Attorneys General
37. National Council on Crime and Delinquency
38. National Criminal Justice Reference Service
39. National Institute of Law Enforcement and Criminal Justice (LEAA)
40. Office of Management and Budget
41. Professor Stanton Wheeler, Yale University
42. Public Information Officer, Federal Bureau of Prisons
43. Reliance Insurance Co.
44. Research Departments of State Divisions of Corrections
45. Research Unit, U.S. Parole Commission
46. St. Paul Fire and Marine Insurance Company
47. State Parole Departments
48. State Probation Departments
49. The Surety Association of America
50. TransAmerica Corporation
51. United Nations Asia and Far East Institute for the Prevention of Crime
52. United Nations Social Defense Research Institute
53. United Pacific Insurance Co.
54. U.S. Fidelity and Guarantee Co.

Although most sources tried to be helpful by referring us to various pieces of literature or other potential sources, only a few (Donn Parker of SRI and several prisons) would share with us any documented cases or confidential information from their files. Probably the single biggest disappointment we encountered was the FBI, which flatly refused (even at the top level) to let us examine any fraud files.

Literature Review

The third and final major problem encountered in our study was the problem of "incest" in the literature. Once we realized that we would have to rely heavily on the literature, we hoped that it would be rich literature full of good empirical studies about the causes or etiology of fraud and fraud detection. What we found instead was a topic overloaded with plagiarism, undocumented conclusions, subjective observations, and "shooting from the hip." There had been very little empirical research done, and most of the speculations lacked empirical support. In addition, most authors seemed to quote Sutherland, Cressey, or Parker, or quote someone who quoted them. In most cases, authors expounded on ideas, theories, and statistics without ever recognizing the source of their information. Thus, our review of the literature [see bibliography at the end of this chapter] was personally frustrating and disappointing due to the lack of good empirical research on fraud.

Nevertheless, we conducted a thorough review of the literature in a search for relevant factors or "red flags" that could be used to signal fraud. Using the fraud theme as the unit of analysis, we compiled a master list of every item that the literature suggested might be a causal variable or predictor of fraudulent activity. (This list is presented on pages 223–226.)

After reviewing and analyzing the literature, we began to validate some of the items identified in our literature search using a content analysis of fraud cases. We selected 50 cases of fraud that were documented in the literature and/or contained in Donn Parker's files. Content analysis is a method of observing and measuring variables in a systematic, objective, and quantitative manner. Our content analysis consisted of reviewing the descriptions of each fraud case and noting the presence or absence of the "red flags." For each of the 50 cases, we gathered everything written about the case and then carefully analyzed the case materials to determine which of the "red flags" on our master list appeared to be present. At the completion of this process, each item on the master list was carefully reviewed and the master list revised.

In revising the master list, we were careful not to quickly conclude that a given "red flag" was useless just because it was not associated with any of the 50 cases. We recognized that each of the authors who wrote about the cases had a perspective that differed from ours. Therefore, just because the publicly available information was silent on a given "red flag" it did not necessarily mean that it was not a factor in the cases. Rather, all it really meant was that writers did not mention it in their writings. We realized that once a "red flag" was removed from our master list we would no longer be considering it; therefore, our revision process involved more refining than deleting. We believe this list, which contains personality, situational, and opportunity indicators of fraud, will be invaluable to auditors. Using this list, auditors can develop an audit section that will require them to explicitly consider the potential presence of fraud in each audit. Such an explicit approach would make it less likely that auditors, who seldom see a fraud case, would dismiss too quickly the possibility that fraud might exist on their audit jobs.

Understanding Fraud and White-Collar Crime

Before introducing our preliminary master list of "red flags," the various theories that have been used to explain crime in general and fraud in particular are reviewed. In spite of the diversity in the academic disciplines discussing fraud (such as psychology, sociology, criminology, moral development, and personnel administration), a generally consistent explanation of fraud has been produced. Based on our own data and a review of these theories, it is our position that fraud is caused by interaction of forces within the individual's own personality (especially the trait of honesty) and influences in the external environment. This position is consistent with our list of "red flags," which contains personality factors, situational factors (especially financial pressures), and opportunities to commit fraud.

Probably the only characteristic all criminals have in common is the fact that they have been accused of and found guilty of committing a crime. Beyond that, there do not appear to be any general characteristics that *all* criminals have in common. For example, persons who commit fraud are quite different from those who commit aggravated assault or forcible rape.

Over the past three centuries, several unsuccessful attempts have been made to determine general causes of criminality. Don Gibbons's excellent text, *Society, Crime, and Criminal Careers,* analyzed these general theories of criminality and classified them into (a) physiological explanations of crime, (b) psychological explanations of crime, and (c) social psychological explanations of crime. His review of crime concluded that no single theory can explain all the complex forms of crime. Instead, he has suggested that different forms of crime should be examined separately. Gibbons claimed that the subject matter of criminology has this in common with that of medicine: there is not one form of sickness, there are many. Furthermore, there is not just a single cause of illness, there are a number of causes, each related to a particular form of sickness. In criminology, therefore, fraud must be examined as a separate role career where the causes of fraud and the perpetrators of fraud are different from the causes and perpetrators of other crimes.[4] This conclusion of Gibbons is supported by a comparison of white-collar criminals with other criminals convicted of property offenses.

White-Collar Criminals and Property Offenders

Even though it has been suggested that white-collar criminals are different from other criminals, there does not appear to be any published evidence supporting this conclusion. The impression of some members of our research team was that white-collar offenders are more like normal citizens than like the other prisoners. Allan Roe, psychologist at the Utah State Prison, noted that most white-collar criminals incarcerated in the Utah State Prison are so completely different from other criminals that they associate more with the prison officers than with other criminals. Consequently, we decided to collect and analyze our own data comparing the demographic data and results of the Bipolar Psychological Inventory[5] for a sample of white-collar criminals and other property offenders.

White-collar criminals were selected who committed crimes against their employers which usually involved embezzlement of more than $5,000. Property offenders were those involved in burglary, theft, and robbery. The sample included 667 property offenders and 42 white-collar criminals from a national prison sample and the Utah State Prison. In analyzing these data, we found the following:

1. White-collar criminals were considerably older than other property offenders (this makes sense since they must have worked into a position where there was an opportunity to commit fraud).

2. A higher proportion of white-collar criminals were female.

3. None of the white-collar criminals were tattooed, whereas 61 percent of the other property offenders were tattooed.

4. The proportion of white-collar criminals who were divorced was much lower than the proportion of other property offenders who were divorced. It appeared that most white-collar criminals led more happy family lives.

5. White-collar criminals had much more education than other property offenders.

6. White-collar criminals were much less likely to have used drugs than other property offenders.

7. On average, a much higher proportion of white-collar offenders were members of some religion than were the other property offenders.

---

[4]*Society, Crime, and Criminal Careers,* ch. 14.
[5]R. J. Howell, I. R. Payne, and A. V. Roe, *Bipolar Psychological Inventory* (Orem, Utah, 1972).

8. The white-collar offenders had several fewer entries on their "rap" sheets (arrest and conviction records) than did other property offenders.

9. The white-collar offenders had much higher IQs than did other property offenders.

The results of the psychological tests showed that white-collar criminals scored much higher than other property offenders in measures of self-esteem, self-sufficiency, achievement motivation, social conformity, self-control, kindness, empathy, optimism, and family harmony.

We also compared the test scores of our white-collar criminals with those of a sample of college students. It was found that there were only six personality scales that produced significant differences between the incarcerated white-collar criminal and the college student. On three of the scales the white-collar criminals scored more pathologically than the students, while the students scored worse on the other three. Overall, the white-collar criminals' personality scores were much more similar to those of the students than to those of other property offenders.

In examining these results, we tentatively concluded that white-collar criminals are much more like the average person than they are like other property offenders. We admit that this sample is small and that the results may be biased, but we believe that these results help explain the view popular in the literature that white-collar criminals are really average people borrowing from the company, but who somehow reached a point where they felt a higher reward in not repaying what they had taken than in repaying it.

Contributions of Research on Moral Behavior

Although we have been critical of the lack of empirical research on fraud, we recognize that carefully controlled experiments on the causes of fraud would be very difficult to perform. Researchers would find it very difficult to contrive an artificial situation that met the necessary conditions for a study of the causes of fraud, e.g., a controlled experimental situation which appeared real, could be systematically altered, could be applied to a sample of white-collar employees, and permitted the researchers to observe the subjects' behavior when confronted with an opportunity to commit fraud.

Numerous experiments have been conducted, however, on honesty and other moral behaviors. These experiments provide considerable insight into the causes of fraud and evidence for the theoretical position presented here.

Management fraud, white-collar crime, forgery, embezzlement, kickbacks, bribes, and theft are all forms of dishonesty. When an executive misrepresents a business transaction or steals from the company, he or she is behaving dishonestly. Honesty is a "moral" behavior. Moral behaviors consist of those actions which are considered intrinsically desirable, valued, and good because of their contribution to the betterment of society. Most of the research on moral development has focused on three "moral" behaviors: honesty, aggression, and prosocial behaviors, especially altruism. Theories of moral development help explain why some people behave honestly and others dishonestly.

There are several important contributions which the moral development literature makes to an understanding of management fraud. This literature has shown that honesty is not necessarily a generalized personality trait. While some individuals can be described as honest or dishonest, most individuals are either honest or dishonest depending on their situation. Honesty is determined by a combination of personality variables and situational variables, and the moral development literature explains why individuals are honest in some situations and dishonest in other situations. Finally, the literature helps explain which forces contribute to the development of honesty and how honesty can be taught. The following is a brief review of the major contributions of the research on honesty.

Studies in Deceit.   Among the first major empirical studies in moral development were the early studies in deceit conducted by Hartshorne and May.[6] These studies examined the effects of character education and religious training on young people. During this five-year project, Hartshorne and May studied seven thousand children from 8 to 16 years of age. Several methods were used to test the honesty of the children. One method was the planted dime test. Each child was given a box containing a dime and other contents. The dime was supposed to be used in one of the puzzles. After the boxes were returned, a check was made to determine which children had "stolen" the dime.

Other methods of measuring honesty used an "improbable achievement technique" in which the child's self-reported performance on trials with the experimenter absent was dramatically greater than their performance on earlier trials with the experimenter present. In each study an attempt was made to provide a natural situation which provided a feasible opportunity to be dishonest for children who chose to cheat, but children who chose to be honest were not tricked into cheating.

These studies found that honesty was positively related to some variables (e.g., higher intelligence, greater emotional stability, higher socioeconomic backgrounds, more refined cultural backgrounds, better deportment in personal behavior) and negatively related to other variables (e.g., dishonest friends, parental discord, poor parental example, bad discipline). Other variables were unrelated to honesty or deceit: sex, physical health, religious

[6]H. Hartshorne and M. A. May, *Studies in the Nature of Character, Vol. 1: Studies in Deceit* (New York: Macmillan, 1928).

affiliation, Sunday school attendance, and academic achievement.

The most significant conclusion of these studies in deceit, a conclusion which had a major impact on later research, was that honesty is not a generalizable personality trait. The authors stated that any correlation between honesty in one series of tests and honesty in another series of tests was due to the similarities in the test situations. Behaving honestly on the different tests was attributed to the similarities in the situations and not to a consistent personality trait in people. "Our contention, however, is that this common factor is not an inner entity operating independently of the situations in which the individuals are placed but is a function of the situation in the sense that an individual behaves similarly in different situations in proportion as these situations are alike, have been experienced as common occasions for honest or dishonest behavior, and are comprehended as opportunities for deception or honesty."[7]

The conclusions of Hartshorne and May produced the doctrine of *specificity of moral behavior.* This doctrine held that each person acts in each situation according to the way he or she has been taught to act under the particular conditions. This principle implied that people would be honest in some situations and dishonest in others. A student might cheat on a reading test but not on a spelling test. Whether a person would cheat in any given situation would depend in part upon his or her intelligence, home background, emotional stability, etc., and in part on the specific factors surrounding the situation. For white-collar employees, this principle suggests that they will be honest in some situations, e.g., negotiations with customers, but dishonest in other situations, e.g., negotiations with regulatory agencies.

The opposite of the principle of behavioral specificity is the *generality of moral behavior* principle. This principle claims that individuals acquire a personality or character trait of "honesty" whereby they behave consistently at all times and in different situations. Thus, a person who is honest in school should also be honest at home, in a store, or in an athletic contest. For white-collar employees, this principle suggests that each person has developed either an honest or dishonest character, or somewhere in between and will behave consistently according to this character at all times. Thus a meticulously honest person will be honest in all situations, regardless of the temptation, whereas a person who tends to be dishonest will behave dishonestly whenever the chances of being caught are sufficiently low and the rewards of the fraud are sufficiently high.

Generality versus Specificity.   Research evidence has suggested that neither the generality nor the specificity principle of moral behavior is entirely correct, but that reality lies somewhere between these two extremes. The

[7]Ibid., p. 385.

data are not entirely consistent, however. For example, a study by MacKinnon[8] provided empirical support for the generality of moral behavior, whereas a study by Allinsmith[9] provided empirical support for the specificity of moral behavior.

Roger Burton reanalyzed the original Hartshorne and May data and concluded that honesty was not always a situationally specific measure but was a generalizable personality trait for *some individuals.*[10] Burton first examined the reliabilities of the honesty tests and decided that three of the tests were not sufficiently reliable and consistent to be considered in the analysis. When these three tests were eliminated and the remaining data were re-scored to maximize the reliabilities of the scores, it was found that the intercorrelations among the remaining tests were all positive and ranged from .10 to .45. When the correlations for these six tests were factor analyzed, Burton obtained a factor he called "honesty" which accounted for 43 percent of the variance. From this analysis Burton concluded that for some individuals there was a general trait of honesty, but not for all individuals.

Burton attributed the difference between honest and dishonest individuals to two characteristics of parental child-rearing practices. The first characteristic was the degree of parental consistency in administering positive reinforcement for honest behavior and punishment for dishonest behavior. The second characteristic was verbal labeling of situations so that all honesty situations were consistently defined and would evoke consistent responses of honesty. Thus, if parents consistently rewarded and encouraged honesty and gave verbal labels to honest and dishonest behaviors, the children would be likely to develop a general character trait of honesty. However, if parents simply punished or rewarded behavior without giving it a label or explaining a principle, and if the standard of honesty was inconsistent, then the children would also be inconsistent in their moral behavior. That is, if parents condemned dishonesty in one situation, such as stealing money, but encouraged it in another situation, such as cheating on college entrance examinations, their children would not perform consistently on the honesty test. Burton extended this analysis to account for the association of honesty with age, intelligence, and socioeconomic level. For example, older children have greater cognitive complexity for interpreting moral situations, and middle-class parents are more likely than lower-class parents to label moral situations and explain a moral principle. These reasons were used to explain why older children behaved more consistently, why the high social-class children were

[8]D. W. MacKinnon, "Violations of Prohibition," in *Explorations in Personality,* ed. H. A. Murray (New York: John Wiley, 1938), pp. 491–501.

[9]W. Allinsmith, "The Learning of Moral Standards," in *Inner Conflict and Defense,* eds. D. R. Miller and G. E. Swanson (New York: Holt, Rinehart & Winston, 1960).

[10]R. V. Burton, "Generality of Honesty Reconsidered," *Psychological Review,* vol. 70, no. 6 (1963): 481–99.

more honest, and why lower-class school children were more dishonest.

In summary, Burton agreed with Hartshorne and May that honesty is not a generalized all-or-none characteristic in which all people are consistently honest or dishonest. But Burton argued that there was a general trait of honesty for those individuals whose parents had consistently reinforced them for honesty or dishonesty and where situations of honesty and dishonesty had been consistently labeled. Considerable additional research on other moral behaviors, especially altruism,[11] has supported the same conclusion—that a specific moral behavior is a generalized personality trait for only some individuals, whereas for other individuals behavior is primarily influenced by the environment.

The implication here is that honesty consists partly of a personality trait and partly of a response to the specific situational factors. The generality of honesty in children is apparently influenced by the consistency of parental child-rearing practices and the kind of labeling or training the parents provide. Similarly, the generality of honesty in adults would probably be determined by the developmental experiences they have had both as children and during their earlier work experience. Therefore, a businessperson would not necessarily behave honestly in all situations. An executive who would not think of manipulating stock prices, financial reports, or accounting procedures might willingly participate in an illegal kickback scheme. Or, an executive who is meticulously precise in submitting his or her travel expense statements might think illegal price fixing is a good business practice. An executive would behave honestly in all situations only if he or she has learned to identify correctly the honest response and if he or she has consistently been rewarded for honesty and punished for dishonesty.

Measuring Personal Honesty

Three main approaches have been used to measure personal honesty: polygraph or "lie detector" tests, investigations of a person's background, and personality-type psychological questionnaires.

Polygraph or "Lie Detector." The polygraph has been widely used to measure the honesty of a person's answers in the United States, most European and Middle Eastern countries, and Japan. It consists of measuring an individual's autonomic responses while he or she answers a fixed set of questions. The autonomic responses include such things as pulse rate, blood pressure, electrogalvanic skin resistance, rate and depth of respiration, and

[11]M. L. Hoffman, "Altruistic Behavior and the Parent-Child Relationship," *Journal of Personality and Social Psychology,* vol. 31, no. 5 (1975): 937–43; J. P. Rushton, "Socialization and the Altruistic Behavior of Children," *Psychological Bulletin,* vol. 83, no. 5 (1976): 898–913.

restlessness. The theory behind the use of the polygraph is simple: the emotional stress created by lying is reflected by significant autonomic changes, such as accelerated pulse, elevated blood pressure, shallow respiration, etc.

Several techniques have been developed for administering and interpreting a polygraph test. The reliability of polygraph tests has been generally high. It has been estimated that polygraph examiners will be reliable—i.e., agree with themselves or others—in 75 to 95 percent of their judgments.[12]

Public acceptance of polygraph tests has not been very favorable in some instances. Furthermore, some states have passed laws forbidding companies from using polygraph tests for personnel decisions. Nevertheless, in the hands of a trained examiner, the polygraph test is a highly respected method of measuring personal honesty.

Background Investigations. A widely used method of investigation, especially of potential applicants to a new job involving a position of trust, is a background check. This is usually accomplished by gathering information from police records, retail credit bureaus, employment histories, and interviews with past associates. Personal honesty and the person's desirability as a hiring risk is inferred indirectly from this information. Background investigations are useful, but not totally reliable for detecting potential defrauders because (1) they rarely identify those whose previous crimes were undetected, and (2) many white-collar criminals are "first-time" offenders and do not have unusual backgrounds.

Psychological Questionnaires. A psychological questionnaire that shows great promise in measuring honesty is the Reid Report.[13] The Reid Report is a paper and pencil instrument designed to predict employee theft by using questions that clearly alert the examinee to the fact that theft behavior and theft proneness are being measured. The first section, for example, consists of yes-or-no questions measuring two dimensions of honesty. The first dimension is a measure of punitiveness, as reflected in attitudes toward punishment for crimes of theft (e.g., "Do you believe there are special cases where a person has a right to steal from an employer?" "An employer discovers that a long-service, trusted employee has been taking a few dollars out of the cash register every week; should the employer have him arrested?"). The second dimension is a self-reflective measure of the individual's own attitudes and behaviors relating to theft (e.g., "Did you ever think about committing a burglary?" "Are you too honest to steal?").

---

[12]F. S. Horvath, "Verbal and Nonverbal Clues to Truth and Deception During Polygraph Examiners' Diagnoses," *Journal of Police Science and Administration,* vol. 3 (1973): 138–52. F.E. Hunter and P. Ash, "The Accuracy and Consistency of Polygraph Examiners' Diagnoses," *Journal of Police Science and Administration,* vol. 3 (1973): 370–75.

[13]J. E. Reid, *The Reid Report* (Chicago: John E. Reid and Associates, 1967).

The Reid Report has been specifically developed for employers to use as a selection tool in hiring new employees who will fill a position of trust. Considerable research on over 5,000 job applicants has shown that the Reid Report is highly reliable (.90 and above) and produces scores that are correlated about .60 with polygraph test scores.[14] The validation studies of the Reid Report are quite impressive. Furthermore, the evidence seems to indicate that individuals tend to provide honest answers even when it involves admission of previous dishonesty. (Perhaps their honesty was due in part to an awareness of a subsequent polygraph test.)

In summary, our efforts to understand fraud have suggested that fraud cannot be explained by general theories of criminality. White-collar offenders have been shown in our research to differ significantly from other property offenders on demographic variables and personality traits. They are more like nonoffenders. Furthermore, honesty is both a generalized and specific characteristic. Some individuals tend to be generally honest, and many efforts are being made to measure the degree of personal honesty as a personality trait. Other individuals tend to be situationally honest, where their honesty is situationally determined by pressures and opportunities to commit fraud.

Red Flags for Fraud

Three Forces Behind Fraud.   The preceding review of the literature in moral development and criminology indicated that the causes of fraud are to be found both in the individual personality and in the situation. Using this perspective, all of the articles discussing fraud and white-collar crime were reviewed to identify variables that were thought to be associated with fraud. These variables, which we called "red flags," were classified into three major categories representing the major forces that influence the decision to commit fraud or not to commit fraud. These three factors are illustrated in Figure 1 as three separate continua; however, we postulate that it is the combination of these three forces that produces the honest or fraudulent act. We have labeled these three forces situational pressure, opportunity to commit fraud, and personality factors (e.g., personal honesty).

This model suggests that the decision to commit fraud is determined by the interaction of all three forces. A useful way to visualize the interaction

[14]P. Ash, "The Validation of an Instrument to Predict the Likelihood of Employee Theft," *Proceedings of the 78th Annual Convention of the American Psychological Association,* American Psychological Association (Washington, D.C., 1970): pp. 579–80; "Screening Employment Applicants for Attitudes Toward Theft," *Journal of Applied Psychology,* no. 55 (1971): 161–64; "The Assessment of Honesty in Employment," *South African Journal of Psychology,* no. 6 (1976): 68–79.

FIGURE 17.1

Low Amount of Situational Pressures	"Situational Pressure Continuum"	High Amount of Situational Pressures
Low Opportunity to Commit Fraud	"Opportunity to Commit Fraud Continuum"	High Opportunity to Commit Fraud
High Personal Honesty	"Personality Factors (e.g., Personal Honesty) Continuum"	Low Personal Honesty

is to picture a balance scale with three weights that can slide along three bars at the top, tipping the scales in either direction. There are three connected bars with three separate weights that can move in either direction independently. Thus, the combination of the three continua, the locations of the three weights, and their size determine which side of the scale is the heavier.

Similarly, these three forces interact to determine whether the person will or will not commit fraud. A person with a high level of personal honesty and no opportunity or pressure to commit fraud will most likely behave honestly. But fraud becomes increasingly likely as individuals with less personal honesty are placed in situations with increasing pressures and greater opportunities to commit fraud. In all probability, an individual would not be at the same place on the honesty continuum in all situations. The interesting philosophical question is whether a person's level of personal honesty can ever be so high that it is beyond the point of being overcome by situational pressures and convenient opportunities to commit fraud. On the other hand, a very practical question is whether the opportunities to commit fraud can ever be so tightly controlled that fraud will be deterred regardless of the level of personal honesty and situational pressure.

How to Detect Fraud. The list of red flags for detecting fraud is designed to help identify (a) situations where people or groups of people are placed in positions where the *pressures* to commit fraud become too great for them to handle, (b) situations where people have easy *opportunities* to commit fraud, and (c) *personality factors* which indicate that people may be less honest. The following factors were mentioned in the literature:

SITUATIONAL PRESSURE RED FLAGS

I. *Personal*
   A. Financial Pressures
      1. High personal debts
      2. Severe illnesses in family
      3. Inadequate income and/or living beyond means
      4. Extensive stock market speculation that creates indebtedness
      5. Loan shark involvement
      6. Excessive gambling
      7. Heavy expenses incurred from the involvement with other women/men
      8. Undue family, peer, company, or community expectations
      9. Excessive use of alcohol or drugs which cause indebtedness
   B. Revenge Motives
      1. Perceived inequities (e.g., underpaid, poor job assignment)
      2. Resentment of superiors
      3. Frustration, usually with the job

II. *Company*
   A. Financial Pressures
      1. Unfavorable economic conditions within that industry
      2. Heavy investments or losses
      3. Lack of sufficient working capital
      4. Success of the company is dependent on one or two products, customers, or transactions
      5. Excess capacity
      6. Severe obsolescence
      7. Extremely high debt
      8. Extremely rapid expansion through new business or product lines
      9. Tight credit, high interest rates, and reduced ability to acquire credit
      10. Pressure to finance expansion through current earnings rather than through debt or equity
      11. Profit squeeze (costs and expenses rising higher and faster than sales and revenues)
      12. Difficulty in collecting receivables
      13. Unusually heavy competition (including low-priced imports)
      14. Existing loan agreements with little flexibility and tough restrictions
      15. Progressive deterioration in quality of earnings

16. Significant tax adjustments by the IRS
17. Long-term financial losses
18. Unusually high profits with a cash shortage
19. Urgent need for favorable earnings to support high price of stock, meet earnings forecast, etc.
20. Need to gloss over a temporary bad situation and maintain management position and prestige
21. Significant litigation, especially between stockholders and management
22. Unmarketable collateral
23. Significant reduction in sales backlog indicating future sales decline
24. Long business cycle
25. Existence of revocable and possibly imperiled licenses necessary for the continuation of business
26. Suspension or delisting from a stock exchange
27. Fear of a merger

OPPORTUNITY RED FLAGS

I. *Personal*
   A. Personally Developed Opportunities
      1. Very familiar with operations (including cover-up capabilities)
      2. In a position of trust
      3. Close association with cohorts, suppliers, and other key people
   B. Firm Environments Which Foster and/or Create Opportunities
      1. A firm which does not inform employees about rules and disciplines of fraud perpetrators
      2. A firm in which there is rapid turnover of key employees—quit or fired
      3. A firm in which there are no annual vacations of executives
      4. A firm in which there are no rotations or transfers of key employees
      5. A firm which does not use adequate personnel screening policies when hiring new employees to fill positions of trust
      6. A firm in which there is an absence of explicit and uniform personnel policies
      7. A firm which does not maintain accurate personnel records of dishonest acts or disciplinary actions for such things as alcoholism and/or drug use
      8. A firm which has no documented code of ethics
      9. A firm which does not require executive disclosures and examinations

10. A firm which has weak leadership
11. A firm which has a dishonest management and/or environment
12. A firm which has a dominant top management (one or two individuals)
13. A firm which is always operating on a crisis basis
14. A firm which pays no attention to details
15. A firm in which there is too much trust in key employees
16. A firm in which there are relatively few interpersonal relationships
17. A firm which does not have viable dissatisfaction and grievance outlets
18. A firm which lacks personnel evaluations
19. A firm which does not have operational productivity measurements and evaluations

II. *Company*
   A. Nature of Firm
      1. A firm which has related party transactions
      2. A firm which has a very complex business structure
      3. A firm which does not have an effective internal auditing staff
      4. An extremely large and decentralized firm
      5. A highly computerized firm
      6. A firm which has inexperienced people in key positions
   B. Relationship with Outside Parties
      1. A firm which uses several different auditing firms
      2. A firm which has a reluctance to give auditors needed data
      3. A firm which changes auditors often
      4. A firm which hires an auditor that lacks expertise
      5. A firm which persistently brings unexpected information to the auditors' attention
      6. A firm which changes legal counsel often
      7. A firm which has a reluctance to give accounting information to their legal counsel
      8. A firm which has several different legal counsels
      9. A firm which uses several different banks, none of which can see the entire picture
      10. A firm which has continuous problems with various regulatory agencies
   C. Accounting Practices
      1. A firm which has large year-end and unusual transactions
      2. A firm in which there are many adjusting entries required at the time of the audit

3. A firm which supplies information to auditors at the last minute
4. A firm which has a poor internal control system or does not enforce internal control procedures
5. A firm which has unduly liberal accounting practices
6. A firm which has poor accounting records
7. A firm which has inadequate staffing in the accounting department

PERSONALITY RED FLAGS

I. *Personal Traits*
   1. A person lacking in the development of personal moral honesty
   2. A person without a well-defined code of personal ethics
   3. A person who is a "wheeler-dealer," i.e., someone who enjoys feelings of power, influence, social status, and excitement associated with rapid financial transactions involving large sums of money
   4. A person who is neurotic, manic-depressive, or emotionally unstable
   5. A person who is arrogant or egocentric
   6. A person with a psychopathic personality
   7. A person with threatened self-esteem
   8. A person who is intrigued by the personal challenge of subverting a system of controls

II. *Personal Demographics*
   1. A person with a criminal history
   2. A person who has questionable associates
   3. A person with poor references

At the present time, our research team is continuing the effort to validate these "red flags" on our sample of 50 available cases of fraud. Because we are still in the process of conducting that validation, we have presented the "red flag" list in this paper without documenting it. It appears from these cases, however, that the situational pressure and opportunity "red flags" are more significant than the personality red flags.

Auditors can include in their audit procedures an examination of personal factors, company factors, or both. Certainly, it would be a new approach to auditing if auditors sought satisfactory answers to all of the above "red flags." If auditors took the more extensive approach, we envision a checklist of questions auditors would ask themselves about the company, and a checklist of questions they would ask key employees. Although we realize the behavioral problems inherent in such a direct approach to fraud detection, if pressures on auditors to detect fraud grow, they may eventually find it cost-benefit effective to employ these kinds of extensive procedures.

BIBLIOGRAPHY

Books and Pamphlets

American Bar Association. *Section of Criminal Justice—Committee on Economic Offenses; Final Report,* 1976.

Anatomy of a Crime—Final Report. Burbank, Calif.: Lirol Productions, 1974.

Appleton, D. *The Young Child in the Home: A Survey of Three Thousand American Families.* Report of the Committee on the Infant and Preschool Child, New York, 1936.

Arens, A. and Loebbecke, J. K. *Auditing: An Integrated Approach.* Englewood Cliffs, N.J.: Prentice-Hall, 1976.

Aronfreed, J. *Conduct and Conscience; The Socialization of Internalized Control Over Behavior.* New York: Academic Press, 1968.

Audit Guide. Evanston, Ill.: American Group of CPA Firms, 1970.

Axelrod, R. *Conflict of Interest.* Chicago: Markham, 1970.

Bailey, F. *Defending Business and White-Collar Crimes.* Rochester, N.Y.: Lawyers Co-op, 1969.

Baldwin, J. M. *Social and Ethical Interpretations in Mental Development.* New York: Macmillan, 1906.

Bandura, A. and Walters, R. *Adolescent Aggression.* New York: Ronald Press, 1959.

Bennet, G. E. *Fraud: Its Control Through Accounts.* New York: Century, 1930.

Bequai, A. *Computer Crime.* Lexington, Mass.: Lexington Books, 1978.

Bigelow, R. and Nycum, S. H. *Your Computer and the Law.* Englewood Cliffs, N.J.: Prentice-Hall, 1975.

Bloch, H. A. and Geis, G. *Man, Crime and Society: The Forms of Criminal Behavior.* New York: Random House, 1962.

Blumberg, A. S. *Current Perspectives on Criminal Behavior—Original Essays on Criminology.* New York: Alfred A. Knopf, 1974.

Bosly, H. D. *Bad Checks and Credit Cards.* Washington, D.C.: National Institute of Law, 1975.

Brombert, W. *Crime and the Mind.* Westport, Conn.: Greenwood Press, 1972.

Bryant, C. D. *Deviant Behavior.* Chicago: Rand McNally, 1974.

Carmichael, D. R. and Willingham, J. J., eds. *Perspectives in Auditing.* New York: McGraw-Hill, 1975.

Carson, C. R. *Managing Employee Honesty.* Los Angeles: Security World, 1977.

Clarke, T. *Dirty Money—Swiss Banks, The Mafia, Money Laundering, and White-Collar Crime.* New York: Simon and Schuster, 1975.

Clinard, M. B. *The Black Market: A Study of White-Collar Crime.* New York: Rinehart and Company, 1952.

———. *Criminal Behavior Systems: A Typology.* 2d ed. New York: Holt, Rinehart & Winston, 1973.

———. *Sociology of Deviant Behavior.* New York: Holt, Rinehart & Winston, 1963.

Cohen, A. K., et al. *The Sutherland Papers.* Bloomington, Ind.: Indiana University Press, 1956.

Colclough, W. P. *Constitutional Limitations on the Production of Documentary Material in Civil Cases.* Washington, D.C.: Law Enforcement Assistance Administration, 1977.

Cole, R. B. *Protection Management and Crime Prevention.* Cincinnati: Anderson Publishing, 1974.

Comer, M. J. *Corporate Fraud.* Maidenhead, Berkshire, England: McGraw-Hill, 1977.

Commission on Auditors' Responsibilities, The. *Report, Conclusions, and Recommendations.* New York, 1978.

Conklin, J. E. *Illegal But Not Criminal—Business Crime in America.* Englewood Cliffs, N.J.: Prentice-Hall, 1977.

Cook, F. J. *The Corrupted Land: The Social Morality of Modern America.* New York: Macmillan, 1966.

Corporate Crime—Proceedings of the Institute of Criminology—University of Sydney. May 9, 1974, Sydney, Australia.

Cosson, J. *State—Victim of Organized Crime—NCJRS Translation.* Washington, D.C.: National Institute of Law Enforcement and Criminal Justice, 1975.

Cost of Crimes Against Business, The. U.S. Department of Commerce, Bureau of Domestic Commerce, U.S. Government Printing Office, Washington, D.C., 1976.

Cressey, D. R. *Other People's Money: The Social Psychology of Embezzlement.* New York: The Free Press, 1953.

————. *Theft of the Nation.* New York: Harper and Row, 1969.

————. *White-Collar Crime.* New York: Holt, Rinehart & Winston, 1961.

Crime in Retailing. U.S. Department of Commerce Domestic and International Business Administration, U.S. Government Printing Office, Washington, D.C., 1975.

Crime in Service Industries. U.S. Department of Commerce Domestic and International Business Administration, U.S. Government Printing Office, Washington, D.C., 1977.

Crime Prevention and Control—The Challenge of the Last Quarter of the Century. Ministry of Finance, Printing Bureau, Tokyo, 1975.

Crimes Against Business: A Management Perspective. U.S. Department of Commerce, Bureau of Domestic Commerce, U.S. Government Printing Office, Washington, D.C., 1976.

Crimes Against Business: Proceedings of Phoenix Seminar Held April 23, 1976. U.S. Department of Commerce, Bureau of Domestic Commerce, U.S. Government Printing Office, 1976.

Criminal Investigations—Agreement Between the United States of America and Belgium. U.S. Department of Justice, Washington, D.C., 1976.

Criminal Investigations—Agreement Between the United States of America and Greece. U.S. Department of Justice, Washington, D.C., 1976.

Curtis, S. J. *Modern Retail Security.* Springfield, Ill.: Charles C. Thomas, 1960.

Dentinger, D. *Crimes Against Business—Crime Prevention Manual for Business.* Kentucky Department of Justice, Frankfort, Ky., 1977.

DePalma, D. J. and Foley, J. M. *Moral Development: Current Theory and Research.* Hillsdale, N.J.: Halsted Press, 1975.

Dewey, J. *Moral Principles in Education.* Boston: Houghton Mifflin, 1911.

Dirks, R. L. and Gross, L. *The Great Wall Street Scandal.* New York: McGraw-Hill, 1974.

DiTullio, B. *Horizons in Clinical Criminology.* Littleton, Colo.: Fred B. Rothman, 1969.

Douglas, J. D. *Official Deviance—Readings in Malfeasance, Misfeasance, and Other Forms of Corruption.* Philadelphia: Lippincott, 1977.

Drapkin, I. *Victimology—A New Focus, Exploiters and Exploited.* Lexington, Mass.: Lexington Books, 1975.

Dunn, D. H. *Ponzi: The Boston Swindler.* New York: McGraw-Hill, 1975.

Durkheim, E. *Moral Education.* Glencoe, Ill.: The Free Press, 1961.

Duska, R. and Whelan, M. *A Guide to Piaget and Kohlberg.* New York: Paulist Press, 1975.

Dwivedi, I. C. *Combatting White-Collar Crimes in India. (From UNAFEI, United Nations Asia and Far East Institute for the Prevention of Crime and Treatment of Offenders— Report for 1975 and Resource Material Series N 11),* 1976.

Economic Crime Project Newsletter. May, June, July, 1974, National District Attorneys Association, Chicago.

Edelhertz, H., Walsh, M., and Brintnal, M. *San Francisco—Development of an Economic Crime Response Capability—Technical Assistance Report for the District Attorney's Office —Criminal Courts Technical Assistance Project.* Washington, D.C., 1976.

———. *The Nature, Impact and Prosecution of White-Collar Crime.* National Institute of Law Enforcement and Criminal Justice, Washington, D.C., 1970.

Ernstine, B. I. *Profitability Through Loss Control.* Cincinnati: Anderson Publishing, 1977.

Farr, R. *Electronic Criminals.* New York: McGraw-Hill, 1975.

Ferguson R. J., Jr. *The Polygraph in Private Industry.* Springfield, Ill.: C. C. Thomas, 1966.

———. *The Scientific Informer.* Springfield, Ill.: C. C. Thomas, 1974.

Financial Analysis as an Audit Tool. New York: Touche Ross, 1975.

Finn, P. and Hoffman, A. R. *Exemplary Projects Prosecution of Economic Crime.* U.S. Government Printing Office, Washington, D.C., 1976.

Finn, P. and Hoffman, A. R. *Prosecution of Economic Crime—San Diego and Seattle Fraud Divisions—Exemplary Projects.* Cambridge: ABT Associates, 1976.

Frank, M. *Underestimation and Tax Fraud in Belgium—Cost to the Treasury for 1970 (from Frontiers of Repression, Part 1, Negligence, Economic and Social Law, Eastern-Bloc Countries).* Bruxelles, Belgium, 1974.

Frankel, E. *White-Collar Rip-Off.* New York: NBC News, Inc. 1975.

Fraud Bulletin. Nos. 58–60, Bank Administration Institute, New York.

Gardiner, J. A. *Theft of the City—Readings on Corruption in Urban America.* Bloomington, Ind.: Indiana University Press, 1974.

Gartner, M. *Crime and Business.* Princeton, N.J.: Dow Jones, 1971.

Gasper, L. C. *Principles of Criminal Economics. An Introduction to the Analysis, Measurement, and Economic Control of Criminal Activities.* Springfield, Va.: NTIS, 1971.

Geis, G. and Meier, F. *White-Collar Crime: Offenses in Business, Politics and Professions.* New York: The Free Press, 1977.

Geisert, H. A., ed. *White-Collar Criminal: The Offender in Business and the Professions.* New York: Atherton Press, 1968.

Gibbons, D. C. *Society, Crime, and Criminal Careers—An Introduction to Criminology,* 3d ed. Englewood Cliffs, N.J.: Prentice-Hall, 1977.

Glick, R. G. and Newsom, R. S. *Fraud Investigation—Fundamentals for Police.* Springfield, Ill.: C. C. Thomas, 1974.

Glueck, S. and Glueck, E. *Unraveling Juvenile Delinquency.* New York: Commonwealth Fund, 1950.

Goffman, E. *The Presentation of Self in Everyday Life.* Garden City, N.Y.: Doubleday, 1959.

Goldwasser, D. L. and Mushkin, M. *Accountant's Liability: Law and Litigation.* New York: Practising Law Institute, 1975.

Goring, C. *The English Convict: A Statistical Study.* His Majesty's Stationery Office, London, 1913.

Gorrill, B. E. *How to Prevent Losses and Improve Profits with Effective Personnel Security Procedures.* Homewood, Ill.: Dow Jones-Irwin, 1974.

Graham, G. A. and Reining, H., Jr. *Regulatory Administration.* New York: John Wiley & Sons, 1943.

Green, G. *Introduction to Security.* Los Angeles: Security World, 1975.

Gross, E. *Work and Society.* New York: Thomas Y. Crowell, 1958.

Guide to Security Investigations, rev. ed. American Society for Industrial Security, Washington, D.C., 1975.

Hall, J. *Theft, Law and Society.* Indianapolis, Ind.: Bobbs-Merrill, 1935.

Handbook on White-Collar Crime: Everyone's Problem, Everyone's Loss. U.S. Chamber of Commerce, Washington, D.C., 1974.

Hanna, T., Swerin, L. and Amos, B. *States Combat White-Collar Crime.* National Conference of State Legislators, Washington, D.C., 1977.

Hare, R. M. *The Language of Morals.* New York: Oxford University Press, 1952.

Harries, K. *White-Collar Crime Issues in Crime and Justice.* Oklahoma City, Oklahoma: Humanities Committee, 1976.

Harris, D. R., Maxfield, M. and Holladay, G. *Basic Elements of Intelligence—A Manual for Police Department Intelligence Units,* rev. ed. Arlington, Va.: CACI, 1976.

Hartshorne, H. and May, M. A. *Studies in the Nature of Character. Vol. 1, Studies in Deceit.* New York: Macmillan, 1928.

Haskell, M. R. and Yablonsky, L. *Criminology—Crime and Criminality.* Chicago: Rand McNally, 1974.

Hathaway, S. R. and Monachesi, E. D., eds. *Analyzing and Predicting Delinquency with the MMPI.* Minneapolis: University of Minnesota, 1953.

Heidenheimer, A. J. *Political Corruption.* New York: Holt, Rinehart & Winston, 1970.

Heilbroner, R. L., et al. *In the Name of Profits.* New York: Doubleday, 1972.

Herling, J. *The Great Price Conspiracy: The Story of the Antitrust Violations in the Electrical Industry.* Washington, D.C., 1962.

Hernon, F. E. *White-Collar Rip-Off.* Akron, Ohio: Management, Inc. 1975.

Hills, S. L. *Crime, Power and Morality—The Criminal Law Process in America,* New York: Harper & Row, 1971.

Hodges, L. *The Business Conscience.* Englewood Cliffs, N.J.: Prentice-Hall, 1963.

Hollinshead, A. and Redlich, F. C. *Social Class and Mental Illness.* New York: John Wiley, 1958.

Hooton, E. A. *The American Criminal: An Anthropological Study.* Westport, Conn.: Greenwood Press, 1939.

————. *Crime and the Man.* Cambridge, Mass.: Harvard University Press, 1939.

Hormachea, C. *Sourcebook in Criminalistics.* Reston, Va.: Reston Publishing, 1974.

Horton, P. B. and Leslie, G. R. *The Sociology of Social Problems,* 3d ed. New York: Appleton-Century-Crofts, 1965.

Howell, R. J., Payne, I. R., and Roe, A. V. *Bipolar Psychological Inventory.* Orem, Utah, 1972.

Hughes, M. M. *Successful Retail Security—An Anthology.* Los Angeles: Security World, 1974.

Inhelder, B. and Piaget, J. *The Growth of Logical Thinking: From Childhood to Adolescence.* New York: Basic Books, 1958.

Investigation of White-Collar Crime, A Manual For Law Enforcement Agencies, The. U.S. Department of Justice, Law Enforcement Assistance Administration, Washington, D.C., 1977.

Jaspan, N. *Mind Your Own Business.* Englewood Cliffs, N.J.: Prentice-Hall, 1974.

———— and Black, Hillel. *The Thief in the White Collar.* New York: J. B. Lippincott, 1960.

Johnson, Lawrence Todd. *The Auditor's Responsibility for the Detection of Management Fraud: Selected Cases.* Unpublished Ph.D. dissertation, 1972.

Josephson, M. *The Robber Barons: The Great American Capitalists.* New York: Harcourt, Brace, 1934.

Kaiser, G. *Criminology—An Introduction into the Fundamentals.* Karlsruhe, West Germany: C. F. Mueller Juristischer Verlag, 1976.

————. *Enterprise Justice—Research on Social Control of Deviance in Industrial Enterprise.* Berlin, West Germany: Duncker and Munblot, 1976.

Katona, G. *Price Control and Business.* Bloomington, Ind.: Principia Press, 1945.

Kerner, H. J. *Professional and Organized Crime—A Stock-Taking and a Report on New Development Tendencies in the Federal Republic of Germany and in the Netherlands.* Wiesbaden, West Germany, 1973.

Kohlmeier, L. M., Jr. *The Regulators.* New York: Harper and Row, 1969.

Krebs, R. *The Development of Moral Judgment in Young Children.* Master's Thesis, University of Chicago, 1965.

Kroy, M. *The Conscience: A Structural Theory.* New Brunswick, N.J.: Transaction Books, 1974.

Lane, R. E. *The Regulation of Business: Social Conditions of Government Economic Control.* New Haven, Conn.: Yale University Press, 1954.

LaPiere, R. T. and Farnsworth, R. *Social Psychology.* New York: McGraw-Hill, 1949.

Lasser, J. K. *J. K. Lasser's Standard Handbook for Accountants.* Tax Institute Edition, New York, 1956.

Lee, N. H. *The Search for an Abortionist.* Chicago: University of Chicago Press, 1969.

Leibholz, S. W. and Wilson, L. D. *User's Guide to Computer Crime: It's Commission, Detection and Prevention.* Radnor, Penn.: Chilton, 1974.

Leininger, S., ed. *Internal Theft: Investigation and Control—An Anthology.* Los Angeles: Security World, 1975.

Lepera, P. A. *Memoirs of a Scam Man: The Life and Deals of Patsy Anthony Lepera.* New York: Farrar Strauss, 1974.

Lipman, M. *Stealing, How America's Employees Are Stealing Their Companies Blind.* New York: Harpers Magazine Press, 1973.

Lock, D. and Mathews, K. E. *Seattle (WA)—Evaluation of the Consumer Crime Prevention Project, November 1973–June 1975.* Seattle Law and Justice Planning Office, Seattle, 1975.

McClellan, J. L. *Crime Without Punishment.* Westport, Conn.: Greenwood Press, 1976.

McKnight, G. *Computer Crime.* New York: Walker, 1973.

McNew, B. B. and Prather, C. L. *Fraud Control for Commercial Banks.* Homewood, Ill.: Richard D. Irwin, 1962.

Mack, J. A. *Business-type Crime on the Increase?* International Center for Comparative Criminology Symposium, Versailles, 1971.

Mack, J. A. and Kerner, H. J. *Crime Industry.* Farnborough, England, 1975.

Management Involvement in Material Transactions, rev. ed. Touche Ross & Co., February 1976.

Mannerheim, H. *Criminal Justice and Social Reconstruction.* London: Routledge, 1946.

Meyer, P. S. *Swindling on Credit.* National Institute of Law Enforcement and Criminal Justice, Washington, D.C., 1976.

Middlebrook, P. N. *Social Psychology and Modern Life.* New York: Knopf, 1974.

Mileski, M. *Policing Slum Landlords: An Observation Study of Administrative Control.* Ph.D. Dissertation, Yale University, 1971.

Miller, N. C. *The Great Salad Oil Swindle.* New York: Coward McCann, 1965.

Mintz, M. and Cohen, J. S. *America, Inc.* New York: The Dial Press, 1971.

Mirgus, R., preparer. *The Thief You Pay.* Los Angeles: Security World Publishing Co., 1969.

Moffat, E. M. *White-Collar and Sexual Offender Project in 1975—A Report of the Work of Project 2.* London: Apex Charitable Trust, 1975.

Molditt, D., ed. *Swindled.* Princeton, N.J.: Dow Jones, 1976.

Moran, C. J. *Preventing Embezzlement.* U.S. Small Business Administration, U.S. Government Printing Office, Washington, D.C., 1973.

Mortimer, H. E. *Consumer Credit, 1977—Current Developments and Trends.* New York: Practising Law Institute, 1977.

Muehlen, R. *Computer Crime.* Frieburg Im Breisgav, West Germany: Verlan Herder KG, 1974.

Mullan, W. C. *Theft and Disposition of Securities by Organized Crime.* Huntsville, Tex.: Sam Houston State University, 1975.

National District Attorneys Association—Economic Crime Project—Year-End Report, 2D, 1976. National District Attorneys, Chicago, 1976.

New York—Temporary Commission of Investigation of the State—Annual Report to the Governor and the Legislature, 15th, New York State Temporary Commission of Investigation, New York, 1973.

North, S. E. *Fraud in Industry—Detection, Prevention and Prosecution.* London: Industrial and Commercial Techniques, Ltd., 1973.

Nossen, R. A. *Seventh Basic Investigative Technique—Analyzing Financial Transactions in the Investigation of Organized Crime and White-Collar Crime Targets.* National Conference on Organized Crime, Law Enforcement Assistance Administration, Washington, D.C., 1975.

Opinion Research Corporation. *Public Accounting in Transition.* Arthur Andersen & Co., Chicago, Ill., 1974.

Osterman, P., et al. *White-Collar Crime—A Selected Bibliography.* National Institute of Law Enforcement and Criminal Justice, Washington, D.C., 1977.

Ostrow, N. S. *White-Collar Crimes: Defense Strategies.* New York: Practising Law Institute, 1977.

Ottenberg, M. *The Federal Investigators.* Englewood Cliffs, N.J.: Prentice-Hall, 1962.

Oudin, B. *Crime and Money.* Paris, France: Editions Robert Laffont, 1975.

Oughton, F. *Fraud and White-Collar Crime.* London: Elek Books, 1971.

Pace, D. and Styles, J. C. *Handbook of Narcotics Control.* Englewood Cliffs, N.J.: Prentice-Hall, 1975.

Parker, D. B. *Computer Abuse Assessment.* Menlo Park, Calif.: Stanford Research Institute, 1975.

———. *Computer Abuse Perpetrators and Vulnerabilities of Computer Systems.* Menlo Park, Calif.: Stanford Research Institute, 1975.

———. *Computer Abuse Security and Auditing.* Menlo Park, Calif.: Stanford Research Institute, 1976.

———. *Crime by Computer.* New York: Scribner, 1976.

———. *Ethical Conflicts in Computer Science and Technology.* Montvale, N.J.: AFIPS Press, 1978.

———, Nycum, S., and Oura, S. *Computer Abuse.* Menlo Park, Calif.: Stanford Research Institute, 1973.

Pearce, F. *Crimes of the Powerful: Marxism, Crime and Deviance.* London: Pluto Press, 1976.

Peterson, R. W., ed. *Crime and the American Response.* New York: Facts on File, 1973.

Piaget, J. *The Moral Judgment of the Child.* M. Worden, translator. New York: Harcourt, Brace, 1932.

Placing of the White-Collar Offender and the Sexual Offender During 1973. Apex Charitable Trust, London, 1974.

Plate, T. G. *Crime Pays!* New York: Ballantine, 1977.

Porteus, S. D. *Porteus Maze Test: Fifty Years' Application.* Palo Alto, Calif.: Pacific Books, 1968.

Post, R. S., ed. *Combatting Crime Against Small Business.* Springfield, Ill.: C. C. Thomas, 1971.

Pratt, L. A. *Bank Frauds: Their Detection and Prevention.* New York: Ronald Press, 1947.

Prosecutor's Manual on Economic Crime, The. National District Attorney's Association, Washington, D.C., 1977.

Rawson, H. E. *The Relationships of Moral Value Dimensions and Unethical Behavior Under Varying Conditions of Risk.* Ph.D. Dissertation, Ohio State University, 1961.

Reach, S. and Deloatch, B. *Crime in Service Industries.* U.S. Department of Commerce, U.S. Government Printing Office, Washington, D.C., 1977.

Reasons, C. E., ed. *The Criminologist: Crime and the Criminal.* Santa Monica, Calif.: Goodyear, 1974.

Reckless, W. C. *The Crime Problem,* 5th ed. Englewood Cliffs, N.J.: Prentice-Hall, 1973.

Redden, E. A. *Embezzlement: A Study of One Kind of Criminal Behavior with Prediction Tables Based on Fidelity Insurance Records.* Ph.D. Dissertation, University of Chicago, 1939.

Reform of the Federal Criminal Laws—Hearings Before the Senate Subcommittee on Criminal Laws and Procedures on S. 1 and S. 1400, Part 11—Civil Rights Offenses, etc., June 13, 17, July 19, 22 1974. U.S. Congress, Washington, D.C., 1975.

Reid, J. E. *The Reid Report.* John E. Reid and Associates, Chicago, 1967.

Reiss, A. J. *The Police and the Public.* New Haven, Conn.: Yale University Press, 1971.

Renfrew, C. B. *ALI-ABA Course of Study on Defense of White-Collar Crime.* Los Angeles, September 26, 1975.

Report of the Securities and Exchange Commission on Questionable and Illegal Corporate Payments and Practices. Senate Banking, Housing and Urban Affairs Committee, U.S. Government Printing Office, Washington, D.C., May 12, 1976.

Report on the Role of Sanctions in Tax Compliance. U.S. Government Printing Office, Washington, D.C., 1968.

Rich, B. A. *State Regulation and the Antitrust Laws—Conflicting Roles for Attorneys General.* National Association of Attorneys General, Raleigh, 1975.

Roberts, M. *Thief's Manual,* 2d ed. Stone Mountain, Ga.: Dosh Printers and Associates, 1975.

Robin, G. D. *Employees as Offenders: A Sociological Analysis of Occupational Crime.* Ph.D. Thesis, University of Pennsylvania, 1965.

Rose, N. *Balance Sheet Offenses.* Law Enforcement Administration Association, Washington, D.C. 1975.

———. *Computer Crime: Some Marginal Notes on Recent Literature Regarding a New Phenomenon.* Law Enforcement Administration Association, Washington, D.C., 1975.

Rudnitsky, C. P. and Wolff, L. M. *How to Stop Pilferage in Business and Industry.* New York: Pilot Books, 1961.

Russell, H. *Foozles and Frauds.* Alamonte Springs, Fla.: Institute of Internal Auditors, 1977.

Saint-Jours, Y. *Criminal Law Concerning Social Security—France.* Paris: Presses Universitaries de France, 1973.

San Luis, E. *Office and Office Building Security.* Los Angeles: Security World, 1973.

Schaeger, H. *Economic Crime—White-Collar Crime—West Germany.* Hamburg, West Germany: Steintor Verlag, 1974.

Schafer, S. *Readings in Contemporary Criminology.* Reston, Va.: Reston Publishing, 1976.

Schur, E. M. *Our Criminal Society: The Social and Legal Sources of Crime in America.* Englewood Cliffs, N.J.: Prentice-Hall, 1969.

Sears, R., Maccoby, E., and Levin, H. *Patterns of Childrearing.* Evanston, Ill.: Row, Peterson, 1957.

Seidler, L. J., Andrews, F., and Epstein, M. J. *The Equity Funding Papers: The Anatomy of a Fraud.* New York: John Wiley, 1977.

Servadio, G. *Mafioso: A History of the Mafia from Its Origins to the Present Day.* New York: Stein and Day, 1976.

Seymour, W. N. *Fighting White-Collar Crime—A Handbook on How to Combat Crime in the Business World.* New York Office of the Attorney for the Southern District of New York, New York, 1972.

Shapiro, S. *Background Paper on White-Collar Crime—Considerations of Conceptualization and Future Research.* Law Enforcement Assistance Administration, National Institute of Law Enforcement and Criminal Justice, Washington, D.C., 1976.

Sheldon, W. H., Stevens, S. S., and Tucker, W. B. *Varieties of Human Physique.* New York: Harper and Row, 1940.

Shoplifting, and Thefts by Shop Staff—Report of a Working Party on Internal Shop Security. Great Britain Home Office, London, 1973.

Sidgwich, H. *Methods of Ethics.* London: Macmillan, 1901.

Sieben, G., Matschke, M., and Neuhaeuser, H. J. *Balance Sheet Offenses—Summary.* National Institute of Law Enforcement and Criminal Justice, Washington, D.C., 1975.

Simon, R. J. *The Contemporary Woman and Crime.* National Institute of Mental Health, 1975.

Smigel, E. O., ed. *The Violators Vocabularies of Adjustment in Crimes Against Bureaucracy.* New York: Van Nostrand Reinhold, 1970.

———and Ross, H. L. *Crimes Against Bureaucracy.* New York: Van Nostrand Reinhold, 1970.

Snead, E. E. *Governmental Promotion and Regulation of Business.* Englewood Cliffs, N.J.: Prentice-Hall, 1969.

Sobel, L. A., ed. *Corruption in Business.* New York: Facts on File, 1977.

Sobel, R. and Dallos, R. *The Impossible Dream, The Equity Funding Story: The Fraud of the Century.* New York: Putnam, 1975.

Special Task Force to the Secretary of Health, Education and Welfare. *Work in America.* Prepared under the auspices of the W. E. Upjohn Institute for Employment Research, Cambridge, Mass., 1973.

Spillman, N. Z. *Consumers: A Personal Planning Reader (For You and Me).* St. Paul, Minn.: West Publishing, 1976.

Stapes, F. *Auditing Manual.* Thiersville, Wis.: Counting House, 1972.

Stearns, L. *Economic Crime.* Scandinavian Research Council for Criminology, Stockholm, Sweden, 1976.

Stone, Christopher D. *Where the Law Ends: The Social Control of Corporate Behavior.* New York: Harper and Row, 1975.

Stotland, E., Walsh, M., and Weinberg, M. *Investigation of White-Collar Crime—A Manual for Law Enforcement Agencies.* Battelle Human Affairs Research Centers, Seattle, Wash., 1977.

Suchan, H. J. *Insurance Fraud, The Shapes It Takes and Criminal Code Reform.* National Institute of Law Enforcement and Criminal Justice, Rockville, Md., 1975.

Summary of the White Paper on Crime, 1972. Research and Training Institute, Ministry of Japan, Government of Japan, Printing Bureau, Tokyo, 1977.

Sutherland, E. H. *White-Collar Crime.* New York: Holt, Rinehart and Winston, 1949.

———and Cressey, D. R. *Criminology,* 10th ed. Philadelphia: Lippincott, 1978.

Sykes, Gresham M. *Criminology.* New York: Harcourt Brace, 1978.

Taft, D. R. and England, R. W., Jr. *Criminology,* 4th ed. New York: Macmillan, 1964.

Tappan, P. W. *Crime, Justice and Correction.* New York: McGraw-Hill, 1960.

Task Force Report: Crime and Its Impact—An Assessment, U.S. President's Commission on Law Enforcement and Administration of Justice, U.S. Government Printing Office, Washington, D.C., 1967.

Taylor, I. *Politics and Deviance.* Baltimore, Md.: Penguin Books, 1973.

Tiedemann, K. and Cosson, J. *Crime and the Criminal Law in Germany and French Banking and Credit.* Cologne, West Germany: Carl Heymanns Verlag, 1973.

Tomkins, D. *White-Collar Crime, A Bibliography.* Berkley: Institute of Government Studies, University of California, 1967.

Vetter, H. J. *Introduction to Criminology.* Springfield, Ill.: C. C. Thomas, 1974.

Viano, E. *Social Problems and Criminal Justice.* Chicago: Nelson-Hall, 1975.

Von Ungern-Sternberg, J. *Economic Crime—Dealings in Foreign Securities.* National Institute of Law Enforcement and Criminal Justice, Washington, D.C., 1976.

Wallace, J. R. *Distribution of Antitrust Class Action Proceeds.* Law Enforcement Assistance Administration, Washington, D.C., 1977.

———. *Government Purchasing and the Anti-Trust Laws.* Law Enforcement Assistance Administration, Washington, D.C., 1977.

Walsh, M. E. *Fence—A New Look at the World of Property Theft.* Westport, Conn.: Greenwood Press, 1977.

Walton, C., ed. *The Ethics of Corporate Conduct.* Englewood Cliffs, N.J.: Prentice-Hall, 1977.

Wheeler, P. G. *State Antitrust Laws and Their Enforcement.* Law Enforcement Assistance Administration, Washington, D.C., 1974.

White-Collar Crimes: Defense and Prosecution. New York: Practicing Law Institute, 1971.

Whiteside, T. *Computer Capers.* New York: Crowell, 1978.

Wilensky, H. L. *Organizational Intelligence.* New York: Basic Books, 1967.

Wolf, A. *American Consumers: Is Their Anger Justified?* Englewood Cliffs, N.J.: Prentice-Hall, 1977.

Workplace Crime—Proceedings and Resources of Internal Business Theft Conference. Chicago, October 19–22, 1975, Vol. 1 and 2, National Council on Crime and Delinquency, Hackensack, N.J., 1976.

Workplace Crime—Systems in Conflict. National Council on Crime and Delinquency, Hackensack, N.J., 1976.

Wright, B. L. *North Dakota—Attorney General's Office—Consumer Fraud Division—An Evaluation.* University of North Dakota Institute for the Study of Crime and Delinquency, Grand Forks, N. Dak., 1973.

Zimring, F. E. and Hawkins, J. *Deterrence: The Legal Threat in Crime Control.* Chicago: University of Chicago Press, 1973.

Articles

Adams, D. L. "Computer Fraud Goes to the Dogs." *EDPACS* (January 1978): 8, 9.

———. "Who Is Responsible for Computer Fraud?" *Journal of Accountancy* (February 1975): 35–39.

Adams, F. L. and Hochfelder, O. "Securities Regulation—Courts Disagree Whether

SEC Must Allege and Prove Scienter in Injunctive Actions Under Section 10(b) and Rule 10b-5." *Vanderbilt Law Review* (March 1977): 282–95.

Adelberg, A. and Feld, S. "Illegal Payments: Who's to Tell." *C.A. Magazine* (April 1977): 31–33.

"AICPA Sets Auditors' Responsibility for Fraud Detection." *SEC Accounting Report* 2 (July 1976): 3–4.

Akers, R. L. "The Professional Association and the Legal Regulation of Practice," *Law and Society Review* (May 1968): 463–82.

Albrecht, R., Barlow, J., and Richins, R. "Some Insights into Management Fraud for Auditors." Unpublished paper, Brigham Young University, December 13, 1977.

Alderman, T. "Computer Crime." *Journal of Systems Management* (September 1977): 32–35.

Alexander, T. "Waiting for the Great Computer Rip-Off." *Fortune* (July 1974): 143–46, 148, 150.

Allen, B. "Embezzler's Guide to the Computer." *Harvard Business Review* (July/August 1975): 79–89.

―――. "The Biggest Computer Frauds: Lessons for CPAs." *Journal of Accountancy* (May 1977): 52–62.

Allen, F. "Criminal Justice, Legal Values and the Rehabilitative Ideal." *Journal of Criminal Law, Criminology, and Police Science* 50 (1959): 226–32.

Allinsmith, W. "The Learning of Moral Standards." In *Inner Conflict and Defense,* edited by D. R. Miller and G. E. Swanson. New York: 1960.

Andenaes, J. "The General Preventive Effects of Punishment." *University of Pennsylvania Law Review* 114 (1966): 949–83.

―――, Christie, N., and Skirbekk, S. "A Study in Self-reported Crime." *Scandinavian Studies in Criminology* 1 (1966): 86–116.

Anderson, G. S. "Computer Manipulation Robs Our Firms of Millions of Dollars a Year." *Management World* (July 1977): 7.

Andreder, S. S. "Equity Funding Aftermath for Ray Dirks, the Ugly Story Isn't Over." *Barron's* (June 23, 1975): 3, 8, 12, 14, 16, 18.

"Are Auditors Ever Free of Liability? Equity Funding Case Equates Negligence with Fraud." *SEC Accounting Report* (July 1975): 1–2.

Arson, E. and Carlsmith, J. M. "Effect of the Severity of Threat on the Devaluation of Forbidden Behavior." *Journal of Abnormal and Social Psychology* 66 (1963): 584–88.

Ash, P. "The Assessment of Honesty in Employment." *South African Journal of Psychology,* no. 6 (1976): 68–79.

―――. "Screening Employment Applicants for Attitudes Toward Theft." *Journal of Applied Psychology,* no. 55 (1971): 161–64.

―――. "The Validation of an Instrument to Predict the Likelihood of Employee Theft." *Proceedings of the 78th Annual Convention of the American Psychological Association,* The American Psychological Association, Washington, D.C., 1970, 579–80.

Aubert, V. "White-Collar Crime and Social Structure." *Journal of Sociology* (1968): 173–84.

"Auditors Admit Responsibility to Search for Fraud." *SEC Accounting Report* (April 1977): 1–2.

Baker, D. I., Dershowitz, A. M., and Wheeler, S. "Paper Lable Sentences—Critiques." *Yale Law Journal* (March 1977): 619–44.

Baker, Donald W., Barrett, Michael J., and Radde, Leon R. "Top Management Fraud: Something Can Be Done Now!" *Internal Auditor* 33 (1976): 23–33.

Ball, H. V. "Social Structure and Rent-Control Violations." *American Journal of Sociology* 65 (1960): 598–604.

—— and Friedman, L. M. "The Use of Criminal Sanctions in the Enforcement of Economic Legislation: A Sociological View." *Stanford Law Review* (January 1965): 197–223.

Bandura, A. "Social-Learning Theory of Identification Processes." In *Handbook of Socialization Theory and Research,* eds. D. A. Goslin and D. C. Glass. Chicago: Rand McNally, 1968.

—— and McDonald, F. J. "Influence of Social Reinforcement and the Behavior of Models in Shaping Children's Moral Judgments." *Journal of Abnormal and Social Psychology* 67 (1963): 274–83.

"Bank Fraud and Embezzlement." *F.B.I. Law Enforcement Bulletin* (February 1975): 7.

"Bankers See Better Staff Training Biggest Need in Combatting Crime." *Crime Control Digest* (March 7, 1977): 2–4.

Barefoot, J. K. "Combatting White-Collar Crime." *Office* (August 1973): 50–52, 117.

Barnett, C. "Turning the Pros into Cons." *PSA California Magazine* (May 1978): 62–66.

Baron, C. D.; Johnson, D. A.; Searross, D. C.; and Smith, C. H. "Uncovering Corporate Irregularities: Are We Closing the Expectation Gap?" *Journal of Accountancy* (October 1977): 56–66.

—— et al. "Corporate Irregularities: Bankers' Expectations and the New Audit Standards." *Journal of Commercial Bank Lending* (July 1977): 45–58.

Barrus, W. R. and Paxman, M. J. "Management Styles as a Crime Deterrent." *Security World* (January 1978): 28–9.

Baumhart, R. C. "How Ethical Are Businessmen?" *Harvard Business Review* (July/August 1961): 6–9, 156–76.

Bechtold, M. L. "Validation of the K. D. Scale and Check List as Predictors of Delinquent Proneness." *Journal of Experimental Education* 32 (1964): 413–16.

Bell, R. Q. "A Reinterpretation of the Direction of Effects in Studies of Socialization." *Psychological Review* 75 (1968): 81–95.

Bensman, J. and Gerver, I. "Crime and Punishment in the Factory: The Function of Deviancy in Maintaining the Social System." *American Sociological Review* 28 (1963): 588–98.

Benson, G. S. C. "Business Ethics in American Society." *Journal of Contemporary Business* (Summer 1975): 59–74.

Bentley, T. J. "Auditability and Control of Computers." *Management Accounting* (January 1977): 13–14.

Bequai, A. "Crooks and Computers." *Trial* (August 1976): 48–49.

——. "Computer Fraud: An Analysis for Law Enforcement." *Police Chief* (September 1976): 54–56.

——. "Forty Billion Dollar Caper." *Police Chief* (September 1977): 66–68.

Berner, R. L., Franklin, R. M., and Hochfelder, O. "Scienter and Securities and Exchange Commission Rule 10b-5 Injunctive Actions: A Reappraisal in Light of Hochfelder." *New York University Law Review* (November 1976): 769–98.

Besser, A. G. and Hochfelder, O. "Privity?—An Obsolete Approach to the Liability of Accountants to Third Parties." *Seton Hall Law Review* (Spring 1976): 507–42.

Bettauer, Arthur. "Extending Audit Procedures—When and How." *Journal of Accountancy* 142 (1975): 69–72.

"Bibliography on White-Collar Crime." *American Criminal Law Review* (Summer 1973): 1011–13.

Billings, C. A. "Private Action Against a Securities Fraud Aider and Abettor: Silent and Inactive Conduct." *Vanderbilt Law Review* (October 1976): 1233–69.

Binns, J. "The Internal Auditor's Role in Questioning Fraud Suspects." *The Magazine of Bank Administration* (October 1977): 38–41.

Black, D. J. "The Social Organization of Arrest." *Stanford Law Review* 23 (1971): 1087–1111.

————. "The Mobilization of Law." *The Journal of Legal Studies* 2 (1973): 125–49.

Blinn, M. "Detecting Management Fraud: Putting One Past the Auditors." *Management Accounting* (May 1977): 20–22.

Bloomberg, M. "On the Relationship Between Internal-External Control and Morality." *Psychological Reports* 35 (1974): 1077–78.

"Blue Chip Stamps v. Manor Drug Stores: The Future of Standing Under Rule 10b-5." *Iowa Law Review* 61 (1975): 497–544.

Blustein, P. "Richard Marx: A Crook's Best Friend Is His Lawyer." *Forbes* (May 1, 1978): 70–72.

Boehm, L. "The Development of Conscience: A Comparison of Students in Catholic Parochial Schools and in Public Schools." *Child Development* 33 (1962): 591–602.

Bride, E. J. "Loopholes Said to Exist in All Systems." *Computerworld* (December 3, 1975): 1.

Brief, R. P. "The Accountants' Responsibility for Disclosing Bribery: An Historical Note." *The Accounting Historian's Journal* (Fall 1977): 97–100.

Brodsky, E. "Self-Incrimination in White-Collar Fraud Investigations—A Practical Approach for Lawyers." *Criminal Law Bulletin* (March/April 1976): 125–39.

Bromberg, W. and Thompson, C. B. "The Relation of Psychosis, Mental Defect and Personality Types to Crime." *Journal of Criminal Law and Criminology* (May/June 1937): 70–89.

Brown, R. G. "Changing Audit Objectives and Techniques." In *Readings in Auditing*, ed. J. T. Johnson, pp. 1–8. Cincinnati, Ohio: South-Western, 1962.

Bullard, R. and Caldwell, R. T. "Current Developments in the Civil Liability of Accountants." *Internal Auditor* (June 1977): 18–26.

"Burden of Control: Derivative Liability Under Section 20(a) of the Securities Exchange Act of 1934." *Securities Law Review* (1974): 616–39.

Burgess, E. W. "Comment on Hartung, 'White-Collar Offenses in the Wholesale Meat Industry in Detroit.'" *American Journal of Sociology* 56: 32–34.

Burgess, R. L. and Akers, R. L. "A Differential Association—Reinforcement Theory of Criminal Behavior." *Social Problems* 14 (1966): 128–47.

Burn, C. "Auditing the Computer, A Time for Reappraisal." *The Accountant* (June 30, 1975): 131–33.

Burnstein, H. "Not So Petty Larcency." *Harvard Business Review* 37 (May/June 1959): 72–78.

Burton, R. V. "Honesty and Dishonesty." In *Moral Development and Behavior,* ed. T. Lickona. New York: Holt, Rinehart and Winston, 1976.

———. "Generality of Honesty Reconsidered." *Psychological Review* 70 (1963): 481–99.

———, Maccoby, R. R., and Allinsmith, W. "Antecedents of Resistance to Temptation in Four-Year-Old Children." *Child Development* 32 (1961): 689–710.

Byrne, D. R. and Scott, G. M. "Closing the Computer Audit Gap." *Internal Auditor* (April 1977): 27–32.

"Can Accountants Uncover Management Fraud." *Business Week* (July 10, 1978): 92.

"Can Management Frauds Be Detected? AICPA Has Suggestions on Related Party Transactions." *SEC Accounting Report* (May 1975): 1–3.

"Capitalism, Class, and Crime in America." *Crime and Delinquency* (April 1973): 163–86.

Carmichael, D. R. "Carmichael Cites 'Red Flags' for Fraud Prevention." *Journal of Accountancy* (June 1975): 16–18.

———. "Corporate Accountability and Illegal Acts." *Journal of Accountancy* (January 1977): 77–81.

———. "What Is the Independent Auditor's Responsibility for the Detection of Fraud?" *Journal of Accountancy* (November 1975): 76–79.

Carroll, A. B. "Managerial Ethics: A Post-Watergate View." *Business Horizons* (April 1975): 75–80.

Carson, W. G. "White-Collar Crime and the Enforcement of Factory Legislation." *British Journal of Criminology* (October 4, 1970): 383–98.

Castruccio, L. M. and Tischler, R. B. "Developments in Federal Securities Regulation —1975." *Business Lawyer* (July 1976): 1855–87.

Catlett, G. R. "Relationship of Auditing Standards to Detection of Fraud," in *Arthur Andersen/University of Kansas Symposium on Auditing Problems,* Lawrence, Kans., 1974, 47–56.

Causey, Denzil Y. "Newly Emerging Standards of Auditor Responsibility." *Accounting Review* 51 (1976): 19–30.

Chambliss, W. J. "Types of Deviance and the Effectiveness of Legal Sanctions." *Wisconsin Law Review* (1967): 703–19.

Chapman, T. G. "Criminal Liability of Public Accountants: A Lurking Nightmare." *Journal of Criminal Law & Criminology* (March 1976): 32–45.

Chazen, C. "Move Over Sherlock Holmes . . . Here Come the Auditors." *Laventhol & Horwath Perspective* (Spring/Summer 1977): 6–8.

Cheatham, C. "Is the Polygraph a Valid Internal Control Device?" *Internal Auditor* (January/February 1974): 39–43, 46–48.

Chun, K. T. and Campbell, J. B. "Notes on the Internal Structure of Wrightsman's Measure of Trustworthiness." *Psychological Reports* 37 (1975): 323–30.

———, Campbell, J. B., and Yoo, J. H. "Perceived Trustworthiness of Occupations:

Personality Effects of Cross-Cultural Generalizability." *Journal of Cross-Cultural Psychology* (December 1975): 430–43.

Clark, J. L. *Selected Documents in the Matter of United States of America v. Jack L. Clark, et al., Defendants (Four Seasons Nursing Centers of America, Inc.)*, Arthur Andersen & Co., Chicago, 1973, 401.

Clark, J. P. and Hollinger, R. "On the Feasibility of Empirical Studies of White-Collar Crime." Presented at the 28th Annual Meeting of the American Society of Criminology, Tucson, Ariz., November 4–7, 1956.

Clarke, W. V., and Hasler, K. R. "Differentiation of Criminals and Non-Criminals with a Self-Concept Measure." *Psychological Reports* 20 (1967): 623–37.

Clifford, W. "New and Special Problems of Crime—National and Transnational." *International Review of Criminal Policy,* no. 32 (1976): 3–7.

Clinard, M. B. "Criminological Theories of Violations of Wartime Regulations." *American Sociological Review* 11 (1946): 258–70.

———. "White-Collar Crime." In *International Encyclopedia of the Social Sciences,* ed. D. E. Sills, pp. 483–90. New York: Macmillan, 1968.

Coley, R. C. "Securities Law—Securities Fraud—Proof of Causation in 10b-5 Non-disclosure Cases Involving Trading on Impersonal Markets." *Vanderbilt Law Review* (January 1977): 122–30.

"Commerce Lists Government Publications on Crimes Against Businesses." *Security Systems Digest* (March 9, 1977): 3–4.

"Computer Crime Is Now Big Business." *Protection Management* (February 1, 1977): pp. 3–5.

"Computer Crime Laws Inadequate." *Crime Control Digest* (February 21, 1977): 9–11.

"Computer Crime, Privacy Act Discussed by EFTS Commission." *Crime Control Digest* (November 1, 1976): 4–5.

Cooper, K. and Flory, S. "Lessons from McKesson and Equity Funding." *CPA Journal* (April 1976): 19–24.

Cowan, P. A.; Langer, J.; Heavenrich, J.; and Nathanson, M. "Social Learning and Piaget's Cognitive Theory of Moral Development." *Journal of Personality and Social Psychology* 11 (1969): 261–74.

Cox, J. D. "Fraud Is in the Eyes of the Beholder: Rule 10b-5's Application to Acts of Corporate Mismanagement." *Securities Law Review* (1973): 636–62.

"The CPA as Detective or Are Those Bloodstains?" *Forbes* (September 15, 1973): 65–66.

Cressey, D. R. "Application and Verification of the Differential Association Theory." *Journal of Criminal Law* (May/June 1952): 43–52.

———. "The Criminal Violation of Financial Trust." *American Sociological Review* (December 1950): 738–43.

———. "Epidemiology and Individual Conduct: A Case from Criminology." *Pacific Sociological Review* 3 (1960): 47–58.

———. "The Language of Set Theory and Differential Association." *Journal of Research in Crime and Delinquency* 3 (1966): 22–26.

———. "The Respectable Criminal: Why Some of Our Best Friends Are Crooks." *Transaction* (March/April 1965): 12–15.

————. "Why Do Trusted People Commit Fraud? A Social-Psychological Study of Defalcators." *Journal of Accountancy* (November 1951): 576–81.

"Criminal Liability for Violations of the Federal Securities Laws." *American Criminal Law Review* (Summer 1973): 883–958.

Curnow, D. P. "Economic Crimes: A High Standard of Care." *Federal Bar Journal* (Winter 1976): 21–33.

"Danger Signals of Improper Practices." *CPA Journal* (August 1977): 76–77.

Dash, S. "Means and Methods Employed in Penal Law." *Criminal Law Bulletin* 10 (1974): 571–88.

DeFleur, M. L. and Quinney, R. "A Reformation of Sutherland's Differential Association Theory and a Strategy for Empirical Verification." *Journal of Research in Crime and Delinquency* 3 (1966): 1–22.

Defliese, P. L. "The 'New Look' at the Auditor's Responsibility for Fraud Detection." *Journal of Accountancy* (October 1962): 36–44.

De Gouw, C. "Data Processing Crimes." *EDPACS* (January 1978): 1–8.

Delmas-Marty, M. "Business Crime." *Revue de la Science Criminelle et de Droit Penal Compare* (January/March 1974): 45–65.

DeMarco, V. "How Internal Auditors Can Help CPAs Stamp Out Illegal Acts." *Internal Auditor* (February 1978): 60, 62, 64.

Dershowitz, A. M. "Increasing Community Control Over Corporate Crime: A Problem in the Law of Sanctions." *Yale Law Journal* 71 (1961): 289–306.

"Detection of Errors and Irregularities." *The Week in Review,* Haskins & Sells (May 14, 1976): 2.

"Deterrence Held Key to Reducing Business Crimes." *Crime Control Digest* (February 28, 1977): 8.

"Deterrence Held Key to Reducing Crimes Against Business." *Security Systems Digest* (February 23, 1977): 3–4.

Devlin, G. "Internal Control Is Not Optional." *Management Accounting* (August 1975): 49–51.

Dickerson, R. "Are Auditors Responsible for Fraud Detection?" *C. A. Magazine* (February 1975): 61–62.

————. "Legal Cases." *C. A. Magazine* (August 1977): 67–69.

Dickinson, W. B. "Business Morality." *Editorial Research Reports* (June 2, 1961): 401–18.

Diczok, P. "10b-5 Liability Expanded Against Accountants." *Securities Regulation Law Journal* (Summer 1975): 183–85.

Dienstbier, R. A. "The Role of Anxiety and Arousal Attributing to Cheating." *Journal of Experimental Social Psychology* 8 (1972): 168–79.

———— and Munter, P. O. "Cheating as a Function of the Labeling of Natural Arousal." *Journal of Personality and Social Psychology* 17 (1971): 208–13.

————, Hillman, D.; Lehnoff, J.; Hillman, J.; and Valkenaar, M. C. "An Emotion-Attribution Approach to Moral Behavior: Interfacing Cognitive and Avoidance Theories of Moral Development." *Psychological Review* 85 (1975): 229–315.

Dixon, A. J. "CPA's Face Their Responsibilities." *CPA Journal* (June 1975): 21–24.

Doherty, D. P. "The SEC's Management Fraud Program." *The Business Lawyer* (March 1976): 1279–83.

Dunham, W. H. "The Schizophrene and Criminal Behavior." *American Sociological Review* 4 (1939): 352–61.

Dupiellet, L. "Economic and Financial Crime." *Police Nationale* (February 1975): 19–31.

Earle, V. M. "The Fairness Myth." *Vanderbilt Law Review* (January 1975): 147–63.

Eccard, W. T. "Securities Law—Securities Fraud—Proof of Reliance is Unnecessary in Open Market Transactions Under 10b-5." *Vanderbilt Law Review* (January 1976): 287–99.

Egeman, H. "Economic Criminality and the System of Electronic Data Processing—Poland." *Studia Kryminologiczne Kryminal Istyczne I Penitencjarne* 4 (1976): 25–49.

Ehrlich, I. "The Deterrent Effect of Criminal Law Enforcement." *Journal of Legal Studies* 1: 259–79.

Eldridge, M. B. "SEC v. National Student Marketing Corporation, Attorneys as Aiders and Abetters of Securities Frauds: Is There a Limit?" *Journal of Corporation Law* (Fall 1976): 162–73.

Elkins, J. R. "Corporations and the Criminal Law—An Uneasy Alliance." *Kentucky Law Journal* 65 (1976–77): 73–129.

Ellison, Ray. "The Changing Face of the 'Fraudsman.' " *CPA Journal* (January 1976): 5–6.

Englebrecht, T. D. "The Auditor's Expanding Legal Liability to Third Parties: An Analysis." *The National Public Accountant* (April 1976): 18, 19, 22, 23.

Eysenck, H. J. "The Development of Moral Values in Children: The Contribution of Learning Theory." *British Journal of Educational Psychology* 30 (1960): 11–31.

Eysenck, S. B. G., Rust, J., and Eysenck, H. J. "Personality and the Classification of Adult Offenders." *British Journal of Criminology* (April 1977): 169–79.

Farrand, J. R. "Ancillary Remedies in SEC Civil Enforcement Suits." *Harvard Law Review* 89 (1976): 1779–1814.

Feshbach, N. D. "Empathy in Children: Some Theoretical and Empirical Considerations." *The Counseling Psychologist* 5 (1973): 25–30.

———— and Feshbach, S. "Children's Aggression." *Young Children* (August 1971): 364–77.

————. "Punishment: Parent Rites Versus Children's Rights." In *Children's Rights and the Mental Health Professions,* ed. G. P. Koocher, pp. 149–70. New York: John Wiley, 1976.

————. "The Relationship between Empathy and Aggression in Two Age Groups." *Developmental Psychology* 1 (1969): 102–7.

Fiflis, T. J. "Current Problems of Accountants' Responsibilities to Third Parties." *Vanderbilt Law Review* (January 1975): 31–145.

Finch, J. H. "Espionage and Theft Using Computers." *Assets Protection* (Winter 1976): 32–38.

Finckenauer, J. O. "Theory and Practice in Sentencing the Political Criminal—A Comment." *Criminal Law Bulletin* (October 1974): 737–48.

Fink, Robert S. "The Role of the Accountant in a Tax Fraud Case." *Journal of Accountancy* 141 (1976): 42–48.

Fitzpatrick, Christopher. "Securities Law—Rule 10b-5—Compliance with Generally Accepted Accounting Principles Will Not Insulate Accountants from Civil Liability for Fraud. Herzfeld v. Laventhol, Krekstein, Horwath and Horwath (SDNY 1974)." *Catholic University Law Review* 24 (1975): 343–52.

Fodor, E. M. "Delinquency and Susceptibility to Social Influence Among Adolescents as a Function of Moral Development." *Journal of Social Psychology* 82 (1972): 257–60.

————. "Moral Judgment in Negro and White Adolescents." *Journal of Social Psychology* 79 (1969): 289–91.

Fonyo, A. "Economy and the Law—Aspects of Criminal Law—Hungary." *Revue de la Science Criminologie et de Droit Penal Compare* (January-March 1974): 68–78.

Fooner, M. "Vulnerable Society—Crisis in Technology, Terror, and Victimization." *Police Chief* (February 1974): 26–27.

Form, W. H. "Occupations and Careers," *International Encyclopedia of the Social Sciences,* vol. 11, ed. D. E. Sills, pp. 245–54. New York: Macmillan, 1968.

Foster, W. "Related Party Transactions—Some Considerations." *CPA Journal* (May 1975): 15–19.

Frank, M. "Tax Evasion and Concessions in Belgium—Methods, Extent and Remedies." *Revue de L'Institute de Sociologie,* no. 1–2 (1975): 29–70.

"Fraud: A Growing Problem for Banks." *Business Week* (September 8, 1975): 30.

"Fraud Detection." *The Week in Review,* Haskins & Sells, July 19, 1974.

"Fraud Spotting." *European Business* (Spring 1975): 6–7.

Freed, R. "Computer Fraud—A Management Trap." *Business Horizons* (June 1969): 25–30.

Freedman, M. S. "A Primer on Fraud and Embezzlement." *Management Accounting* (October 1973): 35–40.

Freedman, M. V. "Liability of Professionals Under Rule 10b-5." *Practical Lawyer* (June 1, 1977): 45–59.

————. "The Legality of the SEC's Management Fraud Program." *Business Lawyer* (March 1976): 1295–1300.

Fuller, C. "Morals and the Criminal Law." *Journal of Criminal Law and Criminology* (March/April 1942): 624–30.

Gallo, K. "All Deposits, No Returns—The Story of Suzie's Bank." *Security World* (February 1977): 34–37.

Galvin, T. "The Cost of Crime." *Michigan Economic Record,* Bureau of Business and Economic Research, Michigan State University, November 1965, 1–24.

Gardiner, J. A. "Politics of Corruption in an American City." In *White-Collar Crime —Offenses in Business, Politics, and Professions,* rev. ed., eds. G. Geis and R. F. Meier. New York: Free Press, 1977.

Garrett, R. "Chairman Garrett Proposes Increased Role for Profession." *Journal of Accountancy* (December 1973): 14–18.

Geerds, F. "Relationship Between the Economic and Public Safety from a Criminological Point of View." *Archiv Fuer Kriminiologie* (September/October 1976): 65–79.

Geis, G. "Avocational Crime." In *Handbook of Criminology,* ed. D. Glaser, pp. 273–98. Chicago: Rand McNally, 1974.

————. "Criminal Law and Consumer Fraud—A Sociolegal View." *American Criminal Law Review* (Summer 1973): 989–1010.

————. "Criminal Penalties for Corporate Criminals." *Criminal Law Bulletin* (June 1972): 377–92.

————. "The Heavy Electrical Equipment Antitrust Cases of 1961." In *Criminal Behavior Systems,* eds. M. B. Clinard and R. Quinney, pp. 139–50. New York: Holt, Rinehart & Winston, 1967.

————. "Toward a Delineation of White-Collar Offenses." *Sociological Inquiry* (Spring 1962): 160–71.

————. "Upperworld Crime." In *Current Perspective on Criminal Behavior—Original Essays on Criminology,* ed. A. S. Blumberg. New York: Alfred A. Knopf, 1974.

Geisert, H. A. "Victimization Patterns in White-Collar Crime," in *Victimology: A New Focus,* eds. I. Drapkin and E. Viano, vol. 5, pp. 89–105. Lexington, Mass.: Lexington Books, 1975.

————. "Criminal Penalties for Corporate Criminals." In *Crime and Justice 1971–1972,* An AMS Anthology, ed. J. Susman. New York: AMS Press, 1974.

————. "Deterring Corporate Crime." In *Corporate Power in America,* eds. R. Nader and M. Green, pp. 182–97. New York: Viking, 1973.

Gellman, H. S. "Using the Computer to Steal." *Journal of Systems Management* (October 1974): 28–32.

Giacoletti, R. R. "The Auditor's Liability for Fraud." *Management Accounting* (July 1977): 29–32.

Gibson, H. B. "The Validation of a Technique for Measuring Delinquent Association by Means of Vocabulary." *British Journal of Social and Clinical Psychology* 5 (1966): 190–95.

Gillis, J. G. "Equity Funding Revisited." *Financial Analysis Journal* (March/April 1977): 10–11, 72–73.

Gilson, M. "Computer Assisted Fraud." *Data Management* (April 1975): 22–23.

Goldfarb, W. "Psychological Privation in Infancy and Subsequent Adjustment." *American Journal of Orthopsychiatry* 15 (1943): 247–55.

Goldstein, T. "Business and the Law: The White-Collar Group at Rikers." *New York Times* (June 2, 1978): D-4.

Gordon, D. M. "Capitalism, Class and Crime in America." *Crime and Delinquency* (April 1973): 163–86.

Gottheimer, D. "Those Hidden 'Opportunities' for Computer Crime." *Administrative Management* (January 1978): 65–66, 68, 72, 74, 76, 78.

Gough, H. G. "Cross-Cultural Validation of a Measure of Asocial Behavior." *Psychological Reports* 17 (1965): 379–87.

————. "Theory and Measurement of Socialization." *Journal of Consulting Psychology* 24 (1960): 23–30.

———— and Peterson, D. R. "The Identification and Measurement of Predispositional Factors in Crime and Delinquency." *Journal of Consulting Psychology* 16 (1952): 207–12.

Granof, M. H. and Smith, C. H. "Equity Funding, Home-Stake Production and Penn Central: Benchmarks for an Expanded Legal Liability." *Chartered Accountant in Australia* (October 1974): 19–21.

Griffin, C. H. "The Beleaguered Accountants: A Defendant's Viewpoint." *Journal of Accountancy* (January 1977): 81–85.

———. "Fraud in Business." *National Public Accountant* (October 1976): 30–34.
———. "How to Define the Limits of Responsibility." *Touche Ross Tempo.* 22: 3–5.
Grim, P., Kohlberg, L., and White, S. "Some Relationships Between Conscience and Attentional Processes." *Child Development* (1966): 37.
———. "Some Relationships Between Conscience and Attentional Processes." *Journal of Personality and Social Psychology* 8 (1968): 239–52.
Grossman, N. C. "How to Audit a Known Fraud." *Touche Ross Tempo.* 22: 12–18.
Groves, H. M. "An Empirical Study of Income-Tax Compliance." In *Crimes Against Bureaucracy,* eds. E. O. Smigel and H. L. Ross, pp. 86–96. New York: Van Nostrand, 1979.
"Guarding Against Computer Fraud." *Banking* (April 1976): 36, 57.
Gugas, C., Sr. "Computer Crimes." *Security World* (February 1978): 40–42.
Gurry, E. J. "Locating Potential Irregularities." *Journal of Accountancy* (September 1975): 111–14.
Gutermuth, W. D. "Securities—Aiding and Abetting Under Rule 10b-5." *Vanderbilt Law Review* (April 1976): 880–91.
Haan, N., Smith, B., and Block, J. "Moral Reasoning of Young Adults: Political-Social Behavior, Family Background and Personality Correlates." *Journal of Personality and Social Psychology* 10 (1968): 183–201.
Haas, P. C., Jr. "Closing the Door on Internal Bank Fraud." *The Personnel Administrator* (November 1978): 45–50.
Hachensack, M. J. "White-Collar Crime: Legal Sanctions and Social Control." *Crime and Delinquency* (July 1977): 290–303.
Hadden, T. "The Origin and Development of Conspiracy to Defraud." *The American Journal of Legal History* 11 (1967): 26–40.
———. "A Study of Offenses of Breach of Trust and Fraud with Special Reference to Offenses Committed in Business and Commerce." *Crime and Delinquency Abstracts* 4 (1964): 329.
Haimoff, L. and Hochfelder, O. "Holmes Looks at Hochfelder and 10b-5." *Business Lawyer* (November 1976): 147–75.
Hannay, W. M. "Introduction." *The American Criminal Law Review* (1973): 817–19.
———. "White-Collar Crime—A Symposium." *The American Criminal Law Review* (Summer 1973): 820–35.
Hanson, W. E. "Focus on Fraud." *Financial Executive* (March 1975): 14–19.
———. "Focus on Fraud: The New Ethic." *World,* Peat, Marwick, Mitchell & Co., (Autumn 1974): 3–5.
———. "The Role of the Internal Auditor Is Changing." *Internal Auditor* (October 1977): 19–24.
Harrel, W. and Hartnagel, T. "The Impact of Machiavelianism and the Trustfulness of the Victim on Laboratory Theft." *Sociometry* 39 (1976): 157–65.
———. "White-Collar Crime: Its Significance for Theory and Practice." *Federal Probation* (June 1953): 31–36.
———. "White-Collar Offenses in the Wholesale Meat Industry in Detroit." *American Journal of Sociology* (July 1950): 25–34.
Hartung, F. E. "The White-Collar Thief." In *Crime, Law and Society.* Detroit: Wayne State University Press, 1965.

Havinghurst, R. J. and Davis, A. "A Comparison of the Chicago and Harvard Studies of Social Class Differences in Child Rearing." *American Sociological Review* 20 (1955): 438–42.

Hawkins, D. H., "Deliberate Fraud and Unintentional Error Can Be Avoided if Security Routines Are Part of Your System." *Computer Decisions* (June 1972): 18–20.

Hazard, L. "Soviet Socialism and Embezzlement." *Washington Law Review* (November 1951): 301–20.

———. "Are Big Businessmen Crooks?" *The Atlantic* (November 1961): 57–61.

Hemphill, C. F. "Limiting Loss Potential from Employee Theft." *Security World* (February 1975): 28–29.

Henshel, A. M. "The Relationship Between Values and Behavior: A Developmental Hypothesis." *Child Development* 42 (1971): 1997–2007.

Henshel, R. L. and Carey, S. H. "Deviance, Deterrence and Knowledge of Sanctions." In *Perceptions in Criminology,* eds. R. L. Henshel and R. A. Sullivan, New York: Columbia University Press, 1975.

Hermann, D. H. "Conspiracy, The Business Enterprise, White-Collar Crime and Federal Prosecution—A Primer for Practice." *Creighton Law Review* (June 1976): 647–76.

Hernon, F. E. "Industrial Purchasing Safeguards: Reducing Criminal Frauds." *Financial Executive* (May 1976): 20–25.

Hershman, A. "The Gumshoe Accountants." *Dun's Review* (January 1974): 29–31, 82–84.

———. "The War Over Corporate Fraud." *Dun's Review* (November 1974): 51–55.

Hess, H. "Repressive Crime and Criminal Typologies—Some Neglected Types." *Contemporary Crises* (January 1977): 91–108.

Hewitt, W. H. "Combatting the White-Collar Criminal." *Law and Order* (February 1963): 14–16.

Hill, C. G. "Large Loan Swindles Spread with Reliance on Central Data Bank. *Wall Street Journal* (March 12, 1976): 1.

Hirschi, T. and Rudisill, D. "The Great American Search: Causes of Crime, 1876–1976." *Annals of The American Academy of Political and Social Sciences* (January 1976): 14–22.

Hochfelder, O. "Supreme Court Eases Auditor's Liability for Client's Fraud." *Journal of Accountancy* (May 1976): 20–21.

Hoffman, J. H. and Vinyard, J. W. "Undetected Industrial Losses." *Security World* (January 1978): 27, 92.

Hoffman, M. L. "Altruistic Behavior and the Parent-Child Relationship." *Journal of Personality and Social Psychology* 31 (1975): 937–43.

———. "Childrearing Practices and Moral Development: Generalizations from Empirical Research." *Child Development* 34 (1963): 295–318.

———. "Moral Development." In *Carmichael's Manual of Child Development,* ed. P. H. Mussen, 3d ed., vol. 2. New York: John Wiley, 1970.

———. "Moral Internalization, Parental Power, and the Nature of the Parent-Child Interaction." *Developmental Psychology* 2 (1975): 228–39.

————. "Parent Discipline and the Child's Consideration for Others." *Child Development* 34 (1963): 573–88.

———— and Saltzstein, H. D. "Parent Discipline and the Child's Moral Development." *Journal of Personality and Social Psychology* 5 (1957): 45–57.

Hogan, R. A. "A Dimension of Moral Judgment." *Journal of Consulting and Clinical Psychology* 35 (1970): 205–12.

Holmes, G. "Roadships, Ltd.—Yet Another Lesson for Auditors." *Accountancy* (December 1976): 78–83.

Holstein, C. B. "The Relationship of Children's Moral Judgment Level to That of Their Parents and to Communications Patterns in the Family." In *Readings in Child Development and Relationships,* eds. R. C. Smart & M. S. Smart. New York: Macmillan, 1972.

"The Home-Stake Case: Where Was the SEC?" *Fortune* (September 1974): 95, 98, 104.

Hoover, J. E. "Embezzlements, Their Causes and Consequences." *Certified Public Accountant* (August 1963): 540–48.

Hopwood, W. S. and Stone, W. E. "Computer Fraud—An Audit Risk." *South African Chartered Accountant* (January 1977): 15–16.

Horne, J. M. "EDP Controls to Check Fraud." *Management Accounting* (October 1974): 43–46.

Horvath, F. S. "Verbal and Nonverbal Clues to Truth and Deception During Polygraph Examinations." *Journal of Police Science and Administration* (June 1973): 138–52.

Hunter, F. E. and Ash, P. "The Accuracy and Consistency of Polygraph Examiners' Diagnoses." *Journal of Police Science and Administration* 3 (1973): 370–75.

Ichamura, J. "Ten Year Follow-up Study on the Early Prediction of Juvenile Delinquency by Means of the Rorschach Test." *Japanese Psychological Research* 8 (1966): 151–60.

"Ineffectiveness of the Criminal Sanction in Fraud and Corruption Cases—Losing the Battle Against White-Collar Crime." *American Criminal Law Review* II (Summer 1973): 959–88.

"Ink Analysis—Weapon Against White-Collar Crime." *Identification News* (June 1977): 13–15.

Jacobs, A. S. "Birnbaum in Flux: Significant 10b-5 Developments." *Securities Law Review* (1975): 403–27.

————. "Role of Securities Exchange Act Rule 10b-5 in the Regulation of Corporate Management." *Cornell Law Review* (November 1973): 27–105.

Jaspan, N. "Eight Billion Dollar Rip-Off." *Management Accounting* (June 1973): 49–50.

————. "Problem—People—Prevention." *National Public Accountant* (May 1972): 27–33.

Jeffrey, C. Ray. "Criminal Behavior and Learning Theory." *Journal of Criminal Law, Criminology and Police Science* (September 1965): 294–300.

————. "The Structure of American Criminological Thought." *Journal of Criminal Law, Criminology and Police Science* (1956): 658–72.

Jeffery, W. J. "The Forty Thieves." *FBI Law Enforcement Bulletin* (excerpt), Baltimore, Indiana, 1970: 16–19, 21–25.

Jensen, W. "White-Collar Crime—A Challenge to the RCMP." *Canadian Chartered Accountant* (December 1973): 21–25.

Johnson, H. "The Thief from Within." *Savings and Loan Laws* (February 1972): 38–41.

Johnston, J. M. "Punishment of Human Behavior." *American Psychologist* 27 (1972): 1033–54.

Joseph, A. M. "Combatting Computer Crime." *Retail Control* (April/May 1975): 28–32.

———. "Computer Fraud and Sales Audit, Part One." *Retail Control* (June/July 1976): 36–41.

———. "Computer Fraud and Sales Audit, Part Three." *Retail Control* (June/July 1977): 25–30.

———. "Preventing Computer Fraud." *Retail Control* (March 1977): 55–64.

———. "Psychology of the Computer Crook." *Retail Control* (January 1975): 25–28.

Judge, M. "Progress in the War on Medicaid Fraud." *Social and Rehabilitation Record* (May 1977): 24–27.

"Judge Reviews Impact of 'Alternative' Sentences for White-Collar Crimes." *The Criminal Law Reporter: Court Decisions and Proceedings* (January 19, 1977): 2337–38.

Jung, B. L. "Right of a Beneficial Shareholder to Bring a 10b-5 Action: Heyman v. Heyman." *Securities Law Review* (1975): 429–50.

Kadish, S. H. "Some Observations on the Use of Criminal Sanctions in Enforcing Economic Regulations." *University of Chicago Law Review* (Spring 1963): 423–49.

Kahalas, H., Groves, D. L., and Bonham, T. W. "Importance of Honesty as a Value Factor for Business Students." *College Student Journal* 11 (1977): 112–17.

Kahl, M. "The Increasing Concern with Internal Crimes." *Bank Administration* (April 1975): 55–56.

Kapnick, H. "Management Fraud and the Independent Auditor." *Journal of Commercial Bank Lending* (December 1975): 20–30.

———. "Responsibility and Detection in Management Fraud." *CPA Journal* (May 1976): 19–23.

Karpeles, L. "A Further Investigation of the Porteus Maze Test as a Discriminative Measure in Delinquency." *Journal of Applied Psychology* 16 (1932): 427–37.

Kay, R. "How to Detect Illegal Activity." *Touche Ross Tempo.* 22: 7–10.

Keasey, C. B. "Social Participation as a Factor in the Moral Development of Preadolescents," *Developmental Psychology* 5 (1971): 216–20.

Kelley, C. M. "Accounting and Auditing vs. White-Collar Crime." *Internal Auditor* (June 1976): 35–39.

———. "Criminal Attacks on Financial Institutions." *The Magazine of Bank Administration* (September 1975): 21–23.

———. *White-Collar Crime,* Excerpts from Testimony of Clarence M. Kelley, Director, Federal Bureau of Investigation, before the House Subcommittee on Appropriations, February 20, 1976.

Kenley, W. J. "Proposed Review of Auditing Standards as a Result of the Equity Funding Case." *Australian Accountant* (October 1974): 534–36, 539–40.

Kevan, Q. et al. "The Role of Criminalistics in White-Collar Crimes." *Journal of Criminal Law, Criminology and Police Science* 62 (1971): 437–49.

Keysor, C. W. "Do You Have an Embezzler on Your Payroll?" *Commerce Magazine* (November 1954): 19–20.

Kintzele, P. L. and Kintzele, K. D. "Fraud: Its Prevention and Detection." *The National Public Accountant* (April 1976): 11–16.

Kirkpatrick, W. W. "The Adequacy of Internal Corporate Controls." *Annals of the American Academy of Political and Social Science* (September 1962): 75–83.

Klein, D. J. and Densmore, M. L. "Improving Internal Control to Curb White-Collar Crime." *The National Public Accountant* (November 1977): 11–16.

Kline, G. L. "Economic Crime and Punishment." *Survey* (October 1965): 67–72.

Kluever, M. H. "Ten Reasons Why Employees Steal." *Burroughs Clearing House* (May 1978): 14–15, 51–52.

Klutzmick, P. M. "Reducing Crime and Assuring Justice—A Businessman's Guide." *Vital Speeches of the Day* (February 15, 1973): 279–81.

Kohlberg, L. "The Child as a Moral Philosopher." *Psychology Today* 2 (1968): 25–30.

————. "The Development of Children's Orientations Toward a Moral Order: I. Sequence in the Development of Moral Thought." *Vita Humana* 6 (1963): 11–33.

————. "The Development of Modes of Moral Thinking and Choice in the Years Ten to Sixteen." Unpublished Doctoral Dissertation, University of Chicago, 1958.

————. "Development of Moral Character and Moral Ideology." In *Review of Child Development Research,* eds. M. L. Hoffman and L. W. Hoffman, vol. 1. New York: Russell Sage Foundation, 1964.

————. "Kohlberg Moral Judgment Situations," (Test), University of Chicago, 1958.

————. "Moral and Religious Education and the Public Schools: A Developmental View." In *The Role of Religion in Public Education,* ed. T. R. Sizer. Boston: Houghton Mifflin, 1967.

————. "Moral Development and Identification." In *Yearbook of the National Society of the Study of Education: Pt. 1,* ed. H. W. Stevenson, *Child Psychology,* Chicago: University of Chicago Press, 1963, pp. 227–332.

————. "Moral Education in the Schools: A Developmental View." *The School Review* 74 (1966): 1–30.

————. "Stage and Sequence: The Cognitive-Developmental Approach to Socialization." In *Handbook of Socialization Theory and Research,* ed. D. Goslin, pp. 347–480. Chicago: Rand McNally, 1969.

———— and Kramer, E. "Continuities and Discontinuities in Childhood and Adult Moral Development." *Human Development* 12 (1969): 93–120.

Kohn, A. and Garrett, R. D. "Interview with Chairman Ray D. Garrett, Jr." *SEC 1975,* New York, 1975, pp. 19–29.

Kramer, A. and Hochfelder, O. "The Significance of the Hochfelder Decision." *The CPA Journal* (August 1976): 11–14.

Krause, S. "Business Frauds: Their Perpetration, Detection and Redress." *The National Public Accountant* (November 1965): 8–34.

Kriesberg, L. "National Security and Conduct in the Steel Gray Market." *Social Forces* 34 (1956): 268–77.

Kriesberg, S. M. "Decision-Making Models and the Control of Corporate Crime." *Yale Law Journal* (July 1976): 1091–1129.

Krueger, R. J. and Dillon, W. B. "The ACH: A Perspective on the Need for Controls and Review." *The Magazine of Bank Administration* (December 1976): 17–20.

Kuitenbrouwer, F. "Computer Crime—Some Marginal Notes on Recent Literature Regarding a New Phenomenon." *Delikt en Delinkwent* (March 1975): 133–48.

Kurtines, W. and Greif, E. B. "The Development of Moral Thought: Review and Evaluation of Kohlberg's Approach." *Psychological Bulletin* 81 (1974): 453–70.

Kwan, Q. Y.; Rajeswaran, P.; Parker, B. P.; and Amir, M. "The Role of Criminalistics in White-Collar Crimes." *The Journal of Criminal Law, Criminology and Police Science* 62 (1971): 437–49.

Laing, P. P. "Hidden Crime, the Store of Embezzlement." *Police* 4: 58–60.

Lane, R. E. "Why Businessmen Violate the Law." *Journal of Criminal Law, Criminology and Police Science* (July/August, 1953): 151–65.

Layton, L. and Perry, W. "The Auditor's Responsibility." *Internal Auditor* (February 1977): 12–15.

Lazere, M. R. "Swindles & Frauds." *Dun & Bradstreet Reports* (July/August 1977): 15–19.

Leavitt, D. "Physical DP Tampering Discounted in Bank 'Shuffle.' " *Computerworld* (April 25, 1973): 4.

Leonard, W. N. and Weber, M. G. "Automakers and Dealers: A Study of Criminogenic Market Forces." *Law and Society Review* 4 (1970): 407–24.

Lepper, M., Green, R. D., and Nesbitt, R. E. "Undermining Children's Intrinsic Interest with Extrinsic Reward: A Test of the 'Overjustification' Hypothesis." *Journal of Personality and Social Psychology* 28: 129–38.

Levens, G. E. "101 British White Collar Criminals." *New Society* (March 26, 1964): 6–8.

Levine, M. "Legal Liability and the Auditing Profession." *Michigan CPA* (May/June 1977): 33–38.

Levine, S. R. " 'Computer Fraud' Is a Fraud." *Datamation* (May 1975): 204–6.

Liggio, C. D. "The Expectation Gap: The Accountant's Legal Waterloo?" *CPA Journal* (July 1975): 23–29.

Little, R. "Phonies, Frauds and Flakes." *Viewpoint,* Main Lafrentz & Co., 1974: 18–21.

Long, R. H. "Will Massive Systems Bring Massive Fraud?" *The Magazine of Bank Administration,* 11–12.

Lopez-Rey, M. "Criminological Manifesto." *Federal Probation* (September 1975): 18–22.

Lottier, S. F. "Tension Theory of Criminal Behavior." *American Sociological Review* (December 1942): 840–48.

Lundell, E. D. "DA Charges DP Used to 'Shuffle' $1.5 Million Out of N.Y. Bank." *Computerworld* (April 4, 1973).

————. "DP Implicated in $40 Million Fraud." *Computerworld* (December 27, 1976): 1.

Lyman, G. M. "Subject Matter Jurisdiction in Transnational Securities Frauds." *Ohio Northern University Law Review* 3, No. 4A (1976): 1305–31.

McAdams, T. and Miljus, R. C. "Growing Criminal Liability of Executives." *Harvard Business Review* (March-April, 1977): 1–4.

McCarthy, C. "Worst Criminals Are the Ones In . . ." *Canadian Police Chief* (April 1975): 36, 40.

McCord, W., McCord, J., and Howard, A. "Familial Correlates of Agression in Nondelinquent Male Children." *Journal of Abnormal and Social Psychology* 61 (1961): 79–93.

McDonald, M. F. "Controls and Coverages Against Dishonesty Loss," (Insurance Series No. 85), Panel Session, American Management Association, New York, 1950.

McGeorge, C. "Susceptibility to Faking of the Defining Issues Test of Moral Development." *Developmental Psychology* 11 (1975): 108.

MacKinnon, D. W. "Violation of Prohibition." In *Explorations in Personality,* ed. H. A. Murray, pp. 491–501. New York: John Wiley, 1938.

McLaughlin, R. A. "Equity Funding: Everyone Is Pointing at the Computer." *Datamation* (June 1973): 88–91.

McMullen, M. "A Theory of Corruption." *Sociological Review* (July 1961): 181–201.

MacRae, D., Jr. "A Test of Piaget's Theories of Moral Development." *Journal of Abnormal and Social Psychology* 49 (1954): 14–18.

Mace, M. L. "Strengthening the Functions of Internal Auditors." *Harvard Business Review* (July/August, 1977): 46–47.

Mack, J. A. "Full-Time Miscreants, Etc." *The British Journal of Sociology* 10: 38–43.

————. "Professional Crime and the Organization of Crime." *Revue de Science Criminelle et de Droit Penal Compare,* no. 1 (January-March 1977): 5–18.

Majumdar, A. K. and Roy, A. B. "Latent Personality Content of Juvenile Delinquents." *Journal of Psychological Research, Madras* 6 (1952): 4–8.

Maller, J. B. "General and Specific Factors in Character." *Journal of Social Psychology* 5 (1934): 97–102.

Maltz, M. D. "On Defining 'Organized Crime'—The Development of a Definition and a Typology." *Crime and Delinquency* (July 1976): 338–46.

————. "Policy Issues in Organized Crime and White-Collar Crime," in *Crime and Criminal Justice, 1975,* eds. J. A. Gardiner and M. A. Mulkey. Lexington, Mass.: Lexington Books, 1975.

Mangold, K. M. "Comparison of Delinquents and Non-Delinquents on the IES Test." *Perceptual and Motor Skills* 22 (1965): 317–18.

Manley, P. S. "Clarence Hatry." *Abacus* (June 1976): 49–60.

Mannerheim, H. "Our Criminogenic Society III: White-Collar and Other 'Non-Working-Class' Crimes." In *Comparative Criminology,* vol. 2, ed. H. Mannerheim, pp. 469–98. London: Routledge and Kegan, 1965.

Mathews, A. F. and Sullivan, W. P. "Criminal Liability for Violations of the Federal Securities Laws—The National Commission's Proposed Federal Criminal Code, S. 1, and S. 1400." *American Criminal Law Review* (Summer 1973): 883–958.

Mathews, A. F. "SEC's 1974 Enforcement Record Assessed." *SEC 1975* (1975): 31–61.

Meier, R. F. "Corporate Crime as an Organizational Behavior." Paper presented at annual meeting of American Society of Criminology, Canada, October 30–November 2, 1975.

Meyer, A. J. "The Computer Bandits." *Accountant's Digest* (September 1976): 15–16.

Meyer, J. C., Jr. "An Action-Orientation Approach to the Study of Occupational Crime." *The Australian and New Zealand Journal of Criminology* (March 1972): 35–48.

Meyers, E. "Computer Criminals Beware." *Datamation* (December 1975): 105–7.

Moorman, W. H. "Proof Tapes and Audits." *Journal of Accountancy* (March 1976): 84–85.

Morgenson, D. F. "White-Collar Crime and Violation of Trust." *Personnel Journal* (March 1975): 154–55, 176.

Morris, A. "Criminals of the Upper World," in *Criminology,* ed. A. Morris, New York, 1935, pp. 152–58.

Moszynski, W. "Criminological, Penal, and Legal Problems of Inventiveness—Poland." *Studia Kryminologiczne Kryminalistyczne 1 Penitencjarne* 4 (1976): 51–65.

Mukherjee, K. "Personality of Criminals: A Rorschach Study." *Council of Social and Psychological Research Bulletin,* Calcutta, No. 5 (1965): 15–18.

Murray, A. "Role of the Internal Auditor." *Accountant,* England (October 2, 1975): 393–94.

Muse, A. "Firmly Stated." *Internal Auditor* (August 1977): 24–27.

"NCLS Study Finds State Progress in Combatting White-Collar Crime." *Crime Control Digest* (February 21, 1977): 3–7.

Nelson, E. A., Grinder, R. E., and Mutterer, M. L. "Sources of Variance in Behavioral Measures of Honesty in Temptation Situations: Methodological Analyses." *Developmental Psychology* 1 (1969): 265–79.

Nettler, G. "Embezzlement Without Problems." *British Journal of Criminology* 14 (1974): 70–77.

"New Breed of Criminal Is Surfacing in Wake of Computer, Experts Warn." *Security Systems Digest* (December 8, 1976): 4–5.

"New Commerce Bibliography Lists Government Publications on Crimes Against Businesses." *Crime Control Digest* (November 29, 1976): 10–13.

Newman, D. J. "Legal Norms and Criminological Definitions." In *Sociology of Crime,* ed. J. S. Roucek, pp. 55–89. Westport, Conn.: Greenwood Press, 1961.

———. "Public Attitudes Toward a Form of White-Collar Crime." *Social Problems* 4 (1953): 223–32.

———. "White-Collar Crime." *Law and Contemporary Problems* (Autumn 1958): 735–53.

———. "White-Collar Crime—An Overview and Analysis." In *White-Collar Crime—Offenses in Business, Politics, and Professions,* rev. ed., eds. G. Geis and R. F. Meier. New York: Free Press, 1977.

Nolan, J. "FBI Agent Accountants Intensify Campaign Against 'White-Collar' Crime." *Journal of Accountancy* (October 1974): 26, 28, 30.

Norman, A. "Computer Frauds—Are They a Manageable Risk?" *Accountancy* (October 1976): 78–79, 81.

Nottingham, C. "Conceptual Framework for Improved Computer Audits." *Accounting and Business Research* (Spring 1976): 140–48.

Nycum, S. H. "Computer Abuses Raise New Legal Problems." *American Bar Association Journal* (April 1975): 444–48.

Ogren, R. W. "The Ineffectiveness of the Criminal Sanction in Fraud and Corruption Cases: Losing the Battle Against White-Collar Crime." *The American Criminal Law Review* 11 (1973): 959–88.

"Only One of Six Cases Fits Cressey's Model Comparative Profile of White-Collar vs. Employee Theft." *Criminology & Delinquency* 20 (1974): 251–62.

O'Sullivan, E. "Equity Funding Scandal." *Accountancy Ireland* (June 1975): 21–28.

Pantages, A. "The Price of Protection." *Datamation* (March 1976): 143–44.

Panton, J. H. "MMPI Profile Configurations Among Crime Classification Groups." *Journal of Clinical Psychology* 15 (1959): 305–08.

Parker, D. B. "Computer Security—Some Easy Things to Do." *Computer Decisions* (June 1974): 17–19.

———. "Further Comment on the Equity Funding Insurance Fraud Case." *EDPACS* (January 1975): 16.

———. "A Look at Computer Fraud and Embezzlement in Banking." *The Magazine of Banking Administration* (May 1976): 18–23.

———. "New Criminal." *Datamation* (January 1974): 56–58.

———. "The Round-Down Fraud." *Banker's Magazine* (Spring 1977): 28–30.

Paul, L. and Montgomery, R. E. "The Porteus Maze Test as a Discriminative Measure of Delinquency." *Journal of Applied Psychology* 13 (1929): 145, 151.

Pearce, F. "Crime, Corporations and the American Social Order." In *Politics and Deviance,* eds. I. Taylor and L. Taylor. Harmondsworth, England: Taylor and Taylor, 1973.

Pecar, J. "White-Collar Crime and Social Control." *International Journal of Criminology and Penology* (May 1975): 183–99.

Pennington, W. J. "Embezzling: Cases and Cautions." *Journal of Accountancy* (July 1964): 47–51.

Pepinsky, H. E. "From White-Collar Crime to Exploitation: Redefinition of a Field." *Journal of Criminal Law and Criminology* 65 (1974): 225–33.

Peter, M. "Federal Administrative Criminal Procedures and Cantonal Jurisdiction." *Kriminalistik* (November 1974): 509–11.

Peterson, V. W. "Why Honest People Steal." *Journal of Criminal Law* (July/August 1947): 94–103.

Podgus, C. "Outwitting the Computer Swindler." *Computer Decision* (September 1973): 12–16.

Pomeranz, F. and Cancellieri, A. "Management Fraud—What Business Can Do for Itself." *Financial Executive* (September 1977): 18–23.

Porter, A. C., Hochfelder, O., and Herzfeld, G. L. "Securities Regulation—Rule 10b-5—Accountants Derivative Liability for Negligence in Conducting an Audit Under Section 17(a) of the Securities Exchange Act of 1934: Hochfelder v. Ernst & Ernst." *Case Western Reserve Law Review* (Fall 1975): 252–82.

Porteus, S. D. "Q-Scores, Temperament, and Delinquency." *Journal of Social Psychology* 21 (1945): 81–103.

"Postwar Embezzler Is Younger, Lives Faster, Is Less Inclined to Suicide." *Journal of Accountancy* (October 1950): 344.

Prentice, N. M. "The Influence of Live and Symbolic Modeling on Promoting Moral Judgment of Adolescent Delinquents." *Journal of Abnormal Psychology* 80 (1972): 157, 161.

President's Commission on Law Enforcement and Administration of Justice. "White-Collar Crime." *Task Force Report: Crime and Its Impact—An Assessment,* U.S. Government Printing Office, Washington, D.C., 1967, pp. 102–15.

"Problems of Fighting White-Collar Crime." *Kriminalistik* (August 1974): 346–49.

Pucheus, J. "New Law of January 3, 1972, Regarding the Prevention and Punishment of Offenses in Connections with Checks—France." *Revue de Droit Penal et de Criminologies* (November-December 1973): 89–101.

"Pyramid or Chain Referral Schemes." *International Criminal Police Review* (May 1975): 144–49.

Quinney, R. "Occupational Structure and Criminal Behavior: Prescription Violations by Retail Pharmacists." *Social Problems* 11 (1964): 179–85.

———. "The Study of White Collar Crime: Toward a Reorientation in Theory and Research." *Journal of Criminal Law, Criminology and Police Science* (June 1964): 208–14.

Rabin, R. L. "The Exercise of Discretion by the Justice Department in Handling Referrals for Criminal Prosecution from Federal Agencies and Departments." Preliminary draft of report to the Administrative Conference of the United States, March 1972.

Rabinowitz, D. L. "Use Immunity and Self-Regulation in the Securities Industry." Paper prepared for seminar in white-collar crime, Yale Law School, December 1974.

Ramos, G. "Multinational Enterprises—White-Collar Crime at the Supranational Level." *Criminologico,* No. 3 (1975): 131–38.

Rauchlin, N. S. "Managing Your Practice—How to Tell Your Clients that Fraud Is Their Responsibility." *The Practical Accountant* (May/June 1977): 34–35.

Reed, J. P. and Reed, R. S. "Doctor, Lawyer, Indian Chief—Old Rhymes and New on White-Collar Crime." *Australian and New Zealand Journal of Criminology* (September 1974): 145–56.

Reeve, J. T. "Lessons from Equity Funding." *Internal Auditor* (October 1976): 20–23.

Refia, U. "Moral Behavior and Moral Judgment of Children." *Journal of Abnormal and Social Psychology* 47 (1952): 463–74.

Reid, K. E. "Non-Traditional Crime and Countermeasures." *Police Chief* (June 1977): 47, 50–51.

Reiss, A. J. "The Study of Deviant Behavior: Where the Action Is." *Ohio Valley Sociologist* (Autumn 1966): 1–12.

———. "Surveys of Self-Reported Derelicts." Paper prepared for the Symposium on Studies of Public Experience, Knowledge and Opinion of Crime and Justice, Washington, D.C., 1973.

————— and Bordua, D. J. "Environment and Organization: A Perspective on the Police." In *The Police: Six Sociological Essays,* ed. D. J. Bordua, pp. 25–55. New York: Krieger, 1967.

Renfrew, C. B. "Paper Label Sentences—An Evaluation." *Yale Law Journal* (March 1977): 590–618.

Rest, J. R. "The Hierarchical Nature of Moral Judgment: A Study of Patterns of Comprehension and Preference of Moral Stages." *Journal of Personality* 41 (1973): 86–109.

—————, Cooper, D.; Manaz, J.; and Anderson, D. "Judging the Importance of Issues in Moral Dilemmas—An Objective Measure of Development." *Developmental Psychology* 10 (1974): 491–501.

—————, Turiel, E., and Kolberg, L. "Level of Moral Development as a Determinant of Preference and Comprehension of Moral Judgments Made by Others." *Journal of Personality* 37 (1969): 225–52.

Riemer, S. "Embezzlement: Pathological Basis." *Journal of Criminal Law and Criminology* (November/December 1941): 411–23.

Riley, J. H. C. "Computer Fraud and Embezzlement." *Newspaper Controller* (October 1972): 6–9.

Robin, G. D. "White-Collar Crime and Employee Theft." *Crime and Delinquency* (July 1974): 251–62.

Roemer, J. "Economic Criminality and Its Repression by the Creation of Central Prosecutor's Offices (Schwerpunkt-Staatsanwaltschaften)." *Revue de Droit Penal et de Criminologie* (December 1974): 227–38.

"Role of Criminalistics in White-Collar Crimes." *Criminologist* 7 (1972): 12–23.

Romney, M. "Detection and Deterrence: A Double Barreled Attack on Computer Fraud." *Financial Executive* (July 1977): 36–41.

—————. "Fraud and EDP." *CPA Journal* (November 1976): 23–28.

Rose-Ackerman, S. "The Economics of Corruption." *Journal of Public Economics* 4 (1975): 187–203.

Rosenbaum, R. W. "Predictability of Employee Theft Using Weighted Application Blanks." *Journal of Applied Psychology* 61 (1976): 94–98.

Rosenstein, J. "Computer Security: Rx for Ripoffs, Goofs, Other Maladies." *Laventhol & Horwath Perspective* (Spring/Summer 1977): 16–17.

Ross, E. A. "The Criminaloid." *The Atlantic Monthly* (January 1907): 44–50.

Rothschild, D. P. "Criminal Consumer Fraud—A Victim-Oriented Analysis." *Michigan Law Review* (March 1976): 661–707.

Rotter, J. "Generalized Expectancies for Internal Versus External Control of Reinforcement." *Psychological Monographs* 80 (1966): 1–28.

Rubin, K. H. and Schneider, F. W. "The Relationship Between Moral Judgement, Egocentrism and Altruistic Behavior." *Child Development* 44 (1973): 661–65.

Ruder, D. S. "Factors Determining the Degree of Culpability Necessary for Violation of the Federal Securities Laws in Information Transmission Cases." *Washington and Lee Law Review* (Summer 1975): 571–96.

—————. "Multiple Defendants in Securities Law Fraud Cases: Aiding and Abetting, Conspiracy, in Pari Delicto, Indemnification, and Contribution." *Securities Law Review* (1973): 573–95.

Ruma, E. H. and Mosher, D. L. "Relationship Between Moral Judgement and Guilt in Delinquent Boys." *Journal of Abnormal Psychology* 72 (1967): 122–27.

Rushton, J. P. "Generosity in Children: Immediate and Long-Term Effects of Modeling, Preaching, and Moral Judgement." *Journal of Personality and Social Psychology* 31 (1975): 459–66.

———. "Socialization and the Altruistic Behavior of Children." *Psychological Bulletin* 83 (1976): 898–913.

Russell, H. "Facing the Problem—Fraud." *Internal Auditor* (July/August 1975): 13–23.

Saltzstein, H. D., Diamond, R. M., and Belenky, M. "Moral Judgment Level and Conformity Behavior." *Developmental Psychology* 7 (1972): 327–36.

Sawyer, L. "What's the Internal Auditor's Responsibility for Preventing and Detecting Fraud, Grandfather?" *Internal Auditor* (May/June 1974): 69–77.

Scantlebury, D. L. "Can the Auditor Survive the Computer Age?" *GAO Review* (Fall 1974): 11–14.

——— and Schultz, J. R. "Lessons We Can Learn from the Equity Funding Scandal." *GAO Review* (Spring 1976): 35–45.

Schabeck, T. A. "Computer Crime Investigation, Part 1." *Assets Protection* (Spring 1977): 11–16.

———. "Investigators Tackle Computer Crime." *Security World,* (February 1977): 31–34.

"Schedule D. Swindle—An Oil and Natural Gas Wells Investment Fraud." *FBI Law Enforcement Bulletin* (May 1977): 14–15.

Schilder, P. "The Cure of Criminals and Prevention of Crime." *Journal of Psychopathology* (October 1940): 152–60.

Schmid, N. "White-Collar Offender—Results of a Zurich Switzerland Study—Implications for the Prevention and Repression of Economic Crimes." *Schweizerische Zeitschrift Fuer Strafrecht* 92 (1976): 51–97.

Schnepper, J. A. "The Accountant's Liability Under Rule 10b-5 and Section 10(b) of the Securities Exchange Act of 1934: The Hole in Hochfelder." *Accounting Review* (July 1977): 653–65.

Schuessler, K. F. and Cressey, D. R. "Personality Characteristics of Criminals." *American Journal of Sociology* 55 (1950): 476–84.

Schwartz, S. H.; Feldman, K. A.; Brown, M. E.; and Heingartner, A. "Some Personality Correlates of Conduct in Two Situations of Moral Conflict." *Journal of Personality* 37 (1969): 41–57.

Sears, R. "Relation of Early Socialization Experiences to Aggression in Middle Childhood." *Journal of Abnormal and Social Psychology* 63 (1961): 466–92.

Sechter, R. J. "Human Aspects of Fraud Are Among Worst Pitfalls." *Internal Auditor* (November/December 1974): 33–35.

Selman, R. L. "The Relation of Role Taking to the Development of Moral Judgement in Children." *Child Development* 42 (1971): 79–91.

Seymour, W. N. "Social and Ethical Considerations in Assessing White-Collar Crime." *American Criminal Law Review* (Summer 1973): 821–34.

"Sharper Definition of the Auditor's Job, A." *Business Week* (March 28, 1977): 55, 56.

Sherwin, R. "White-Collar Crime, Conventional Crime and Merton's Deviant Behavior Theory." *Wisconsin Sociologist* 2 (1963): 7–10.

Shoemaker, D. and South, D. R. "White-Collar Crime." In *Deviant Behavior,* ed. C. D. Bryant, pp. 189–200. Chicago, Ill.: Rand McNally, 1974.

Simon, R. J. "Women and Crime Revisited." *Social Science Quarterly* (March 4, 1976): 658–63.

Siverston, E. "Swindlers I Have Known." *Credit and Financial Management* (March 1975): 15–16.

Slavin, N. S. "The Elimination of 'Scienter' in Determining the Auditor's Statutory Liability." *Accounting Review* (April 1977): 360–68.

Smalheiser, M. and Ward, P. "System Stops $902,000 Fake Check." *Computerworld* (December 18, 1974).

Smith, C. H. "What Security, Order and Laws Must Achieve." *Security Management* (January 1974): 47–51.

Smith, R. A. "The Incredible Electrical Conspiracy." *Fortune* 63 (1961): 132–37, 161–64.

Smith, R. C. "Equity Funding—Implications for Auditing and Data Processing." *EDPACS* (October 1974): 1–7.

Sneath, C. "An Auditing Viewpoint." *Accountant* (October 2, 1975): 388–91.

Solomon, K. I. and Muller, H. "Illegal Payments: Where the Auditor Stands." *Journal of Accountancy* (January 1977): 51–57.

Sommer, A. A., Jr. "Accountants, A Flexible Standard." *Journal of Accountancy* (December 1974): 76–80.

————. "The Disclosure of Management Fraud." *Business Lawyer* (March 1976): 1283–93.

Soothill, K. "If You Must Steal, Steal Big." *University of Lancaster, Lancaster News Society* 38 (1976): 249–50.

Sorenson, R. C. "Review of Sutherland, White-Collar Crime." *Journal of Criminal Law, Criminology and Police Science* (May/June 1950): 80–132.

"Soviet Methods of Character Education: Some Implications for Research." *American Psychologist* 17 (1962): 550–65.

Speiser, S. M. "Abolish Paper Money and Eliminate Most Crime." *American Bar Association Journal* (January 1975): 47–49.

Spencer, J. C. "White-Collar Crime." In *Criminology in Transition,* eds. T. Grygier, H. Jones, and J. C. Spencer, pp. 251–64. London: Tavistock, 1965.

"Standing Under Rule 10b-5 After Blue Chip Stamps." *Michigan Law Review* (December 1976): 413–44.

Steffen, R. "How I Embezzled $1.5 Million . . . and Nearly Got Away With It." *Bank Systems and Equipment* (June 1974): 24–28.

Stinchcomber, A. L. "Institutions of Privacy in the Determination of Police Administrative Practice." *The American Journal of Sociology* 69 (1963): 150–60.

Stone, J. "Professional Deprivation Tied to DP Crime?" *Computerworld* (January 9, 1978): 27.

————. "DP Crooks Couple Basic Skills, Craftiness." *Computerworld* (January 23, 1978): 21.

———— and Mason, I. "DP Crooks Going Unnoticed, Undiscouraged." *Computerworld* (January 16, 1978): 17.

————. "Precautions Can Help Deter DP Criminals." *Computerworld* (May 30, 1978): 19.

Stone, R. L. "Who Is Responsible for Computer Fraud?" *Journal of Accountancy* (February 1975): 35–39.

Stone, W. E. and Hopwood, W. S. "Computer Fraud." *South African Chartered Accountant* (October 1975): 333–34.

————. "Public Auditor's Increasing Responsibilities for the Detection of Fraud." *South African Chartered Accountant* (January 1976): 25–27.

Strauss, R. D., Morris, E. L., Hochfelder, O. "Securities Law—Private Cause of Action for Damages Under Rule 10b-5 Requires Scienter—Ernst & Ernst v. Hochfelder." *Emory Law Journal* (Spring 1976): 465–77.

Strother, R. S. "Crime by Computer." *Research Digest* (May 1976): 143–48.

———— and Royce, E. "Crime by Computer." *Chartered Accountant of India* (May 1977): 739–40.

Stuart, R. B. "Decentration in the Development of Children's Concepts of Moral and Causal Judgement." *The Journal of Genetic Psychology* 111 (1967): 59–68.

Sutherland, E. H. "Crime and Business." *The Annals of the American Academy of Political and Social Science* 217 (1941): 112–18.

————. "Crime of Corporations." In *The Sutherland Papers,* eds. A. Cohen, A. Lindesmith, and K. Schuessler. Bloomington, Ind.: Indiana University Press, 1956.

————. "Is 'White-Collar Crime' Crime?" *American Sociological Review* (April 1945): 132–39.

————. "The White-Collar Criminal." In *Encyclopedia of Criminology,* eds. V. C. Branham and S. B. Kutash, pp. 511–15. New York: Philosophical Library, 1949.

————. "White Collar Criminality." *American Sociological Review* (February 1940): 1–12.

Sweeney, L. "Are Internal Auditors Responsible for Fraud Detection?" *Internal Auditor* (August 1976): 10–16.

Tappan, P. W. "Who Is the Criminal?" *American Sociological Review* (February 1947): 96–102.

Taylor, R. C. "Methods of Embezzlement and Protective Measures." *NACA Bulletin* (February 1953): 747–54.

Tennenbaum, D. J. "Personality and Criminality: A Summary and Implications of the Literature." *Journal of Criminal Justice* 5 (1977): 225–35.

Teufel, M. "Criminology and White Collar Crime." *Archiv Fuer Kriminologie,* (May/June 1975): 129–47.

Tiedemann, K. "Fraud in the Area of Subsidies—Criminology and Criminal Justice Policy—West Germany." *Revue de Droit Penal et de Criminologie* (November 1975): 129–40.

————. "Multinational Enterprises and Tax Delinquency." *Anuario de Derecho Penal y Ciencias Sociales* (September/December 1976): 487–503.

————. "White Collar Crime in the Modern Economy." *Revue Internationale de Criminologie et de Police Technique* (April/June 1975): 147–58.

Traini, R. "How Employee Dishonesty Can Drain Business Resources—And How Firms Seem to 'Invite Theft.' " *Security Gazette* (May 1974): 189–90.

Trites, J. D. and Grant, B. M. "Set the Watchdog Free." *C. A. Magazine* (January 1975): 22–26.

Turiel, E. "An Experimental Test of the Sequentiality of Developmental Stages in the

Child's Moral Judgments." *Journal of Personality and Social Psychology* 3 (1966): 611–18.

———— and Rothman, G. R. "The Influence of Reasoning on Behavioral Choices at Different Stages of Moral Development." *Child Development* 43 (1972): 741–56.

Tyler, H. R., Jr. "An Address Presented to the American Society of Criminology," Toronto, Ontario, October 31, 1975.

Ungern-Sternberg, J. V. "Economic Crime in Dealings in Foreign Securities—West Germany." *Kriminalistik* (March 1975): 100–05.

Van Graafeiland, E. A. and Hochfelder, O. "Forward: Lawyer's Observations on Hochfelder." *St. John's Law Review* (Winter 1977): 239–48.

Varga, J. "Safeguarding Your Computer Resources." *Cornell Hotel and Restaurant Administration Quarterly* (November 1975): 56–60.

Vold, G. B. "White-Collar Crime." In *Theoretical Criminology,* ed. G. B. Vold, pp. 243–61. New York: Oxford University Press, 1958.

————. "Fraudulent Business Practices." *International Criminal Police Review* (June/July 1975): 158–65.

Voris, J. W. "How the Computer Can Be Used to Commit Fraud." *Practical Accountant* (March/April 1975): 63–64.

"Vulnerable Computer, The." *Protection Management* (January 1, 1977): 3–6.

Waldo, G. P., and Dinitz, S. "Personality Attributes of the Criminal: An Analysis of Research Studies, 1950–1965." *Journal of Research in Crime and Delinquency* 4 (1967): 185–202.

Walker, L. J. and Richards, B. S. "The Effects of a Narrative Model on Children's Moral Judgements." *Canadian Journal of Behavioral Science* 8 (November 2, 1976): 169–77.

Waller, R. R. "Computer Fraud." *The Accountant* (October 2, 1975): 392–93.

Wasserman, J. J. "Computer Systems Must be Audited." *The Office* (August 1974): 49–52.

Watkins, J. C. "White-Collar Crime, Legal Sanctions, and Social Control—'Idols of the Theatre' in Operation." *Crime & Delinquency* (July 1977): 290–303.

Weinstein, E. "A Time of Travail and Challenge." *CPA Journal* (December 1974): 29–31.

Weiss, H. "Rebuttal to Equity Funding Implications." *EDPACS* (October 1974): 8–11.

Wells, J. T. "Accountant's Role in the FBI." *Law Enforcement Journal* (April/June 1975): 9–10, 22.

"What the Courts Decided." *The Banker* (September 1976): 1077, 1079.

Wheeler, S. "Trends and Problems in the Sociological Study of Crime." *Social Problems* (June 1976): 525–34.

"When Accountants Hire Private Detectives." *Business Week* (June 30, 1975): 105.

"White-Collar Crime—A Symposium." *American Criminal Law Review* 11 (Summer 1973).

"White-Collar Crime Strikes Home: FHA-Related Frauds." *FBI Law Enforcement Bulletin* (December 1975): 12–15

Whiteside, T. "Annals of Crime—Dead Souls in the Computer, Part 1." *New Yorker* (August 22, 1977): 35–65.

Wilensky, H. L. "Organizations: Organizational Intelligence." In *International Encyclopedia of the Social Sciences,* Vol. 11, ed. D. E. Sills, pp. 319–34. New York: Macmillan, 1968.

Williams, J. R. and Davis, J. R. "Implications of the Audit Report for Financial Statement Users." *The Journal of Commercial Bank Lending* (February 1975): 9–18.

Willingham, J. J. "Discussant's Response to Relationship of Auditing Standards to Detection of Fraud." *Cooperative Accountant* (Summer 1975): 69–75.

Willmer, M. A. P. "A Mathematical Approach to Complex Fraud Problems." *Accounting and Business Research* (Spring 1977): 120–23.

Wolman, B. "Auditor's Report—Society's Expectation v. Realities." *South African Chartered Accountant* (December 1974): 421–24.

Wolfe, R. N. "Trust, Anomie, and Locus of Control Alienation in U.S. College Students in 1964, 1969, and 1974." *Journal of Social Psychology* (October 1976): 151–52.

Woolf, E. "The Astonishing Story of the 'Salad Oil Swindle.'" *Accountancy* (June 1976): 78–83.

———. "Lesson of Equity Funding." *Accountancy* (January 1977): 30–40.

Wornham, T. V. A. "How I Launched a $540,000 Check Kite from an Honest Business Background." *Bank Systems and Equipment* (July 1975): 28–31.

Wyndham, R. "Those Daring Young Con Men of Equity Funding." *Fortune* (August 1973): 81–85, 120–32.

Yarrow, M. R., Scott, P. M., and Waxler, C. Z. "Learning Concern for Others." *Developmental Psychology* 8 (1973): 240–60.

Yeager, M. G. "Gangster as White Collar Criminal—Organized Crime and Stolen Securities." *Issues in Criminology* (Spring 1973): 49–73.

Yoder, Stephen A. "Criminal Sanctions for Corporate Illegality." *Journal of Criminal Law and Criminology* 69 (1978): 40–58.

Zaleski, M. L. "It Takes More than Guns—White-Collar Crime Enforcement." *Police Chief* (September 1977): 60–61.

Zeitlin, L. R. "A Little Larceny Can Do a Lot For Employee Morale." *Psychology Today* (June 1971): 22–26.

Appendix

Clarifying Responsibility for the Detection of Fraud*

Fraud is an ever-present threat to business corporations and other entities in society. Management, operating outside the controls over the accounting system, may either misappropriate or misuse assets or intentionally mislead financial statement users. Assets may be misappropriated or misused by non-management employees who circumvent the controls over the accounting system.

No major aspect of the independent auditor's role has caused more difficulty for the auditor than questions about his responsibility for the detection of fraud. In the last ten years, a number of major frauds that independent auditors failed to detect have focused unfavorable attention on this aspect of the audit function.

The Expectations of Users

Independent auditors have always acknowledged some responsibility to consider the existence of fraud in conducting an audit. Nevertheless, the nature and extent of that responsibility have been unclear. Court decisions, criticisms by the financial press, actions by regulatory bodies, and surveys of

*Copyright © 1978 by the American Institute of Certified Public Accountants. Reprint of chapter 4 from *Report, Conclusions, and Recommendations* by the Commission on Auditors' Responsibilities.

users indicate dissatisfaction with the responsibility for fraud detection acknowledged by auditors.[1]

Opinion surveys in this and other countries indicate that concerned segments of the public expect independent auditors to assume greater responsibility in this area. Significant percentages of those who use and rely on the auditor's work rank the detection of fraud among the most important objectives of an audit.[2]

The SEC has consistently taken the position that the detection of fraud is an important objective of an audit. In Accounting Series Release No. 19, "In the Matter of McKesson & Robbins, Inc.," issued in 1940, the Commission stated,

> Moreover, we believe that, even in balance sheet examinations for corporations whose securities are held by the public, accountants can be expected to detect gross overstatements of assets and profits whether resulting from collusive fraud or otherwise. We believe that alertness on the part of the entire [audit] staff, coupled with intelligent analysis by experienced accountants of the manner of doing business, should detect overstatements in the accounts, regardless of their cause, long before they assume the magnitude reached in this case. Furthermore, an examination of this kind should not, in our opinion, exclude the highest officers of the corporation from its appraisal of the manner in which the business under review is conducted. Without underestimating the important service rendered by independent public accountants in their review of the accounting principles employed in the preparation of financial statements filed with us and issued to stockholders, we feel that the discovery of gross overstatements in the accounts is a major purpose of such an audit even though it be conceded that it might not disclose every minor defalcation.

This position was reiterated in 1974 in exactly the same terms in ASR No. 153.[3]

---

[1]Descriptions of the auditor's responsibility in authoritative literature have led to conflicting interpretations. The AICPA's special committee on Equity Funding concluded that the then current description in the official literature of the auditor's responsibility for the detection of fraud, with its greater emphasis on the limitations rather than on the positive aspects of the matter, "may contribute to the risk of disparity in understanding, between the public at large and the public accounting profession, as to what an auditor's responsibility is with respect to the detection of fraud." (*Report of the Special Committee on Equity Funding* [New York: AICPA, 1975], p. 40).

[2]A survey conducted for Arthur Andersen & Co. indicated that 66 percent of the investing public believes that "the most important function of the public accounting firm's audit of a corporation is to detect fraud." (Opinion Research Corporation, *Public Accounting in Transition* [Chicago: Arthur Andersen & Co., 1974], p. 48.) See also G. W. Beck, *Public Accountants in Australia: Their Social Role* (Ph.D. diss., University of Queensland, Brisbane, Australia, 1972), and T. A. Lee, "The Nature of Auditing and Its Objectives," *Accountancy* (England) 81 (April 1970): 292–96.

[3]SEC Accounting Series Release No. 153, "In the Matter of Touche Ross & Co.," February 25, 1974.

The courts have also shown a readiness to hold auditors responsible for material misrepresentations in financial statements and have recognized that failure to detect fraud can indicate a failure to exercise the standard of care society expects of independent auditors.[4]

The viewpoint of various groups of users, the SEC, and the courts was expressed well in an article in *Accountancy* on the role of the independent auditor: "The first object of an audit is to say that the accounts can be *relied on,* that they are 'all right'; it is absurd to say that they are all right subject of course to the possibility that undetected fraud may have made them all wrong."[5]

The Concept of Fraud and the Auditor's Evolving Approach to Its Detection

Viewed broadly, any intentional act designed to deceive or mislead others is fraud. Fraud in the business environment with which the auditor is concerned has a more specialized meaning.

Fraud from the Auditor's Viewpoint.   Fraud may occur at the employee or management level. Frauds by nonmanagement employees are generally designed to convert cash or other assets to an employee's own benefit. Management fraud may differ significantly. Often direct theft is not involved. It may be a "performance fraud"—the use of deceptive practices to inflate earnings or to forestall the recognition of either insolvency or a decline in earnings.

The auditor's concern about the possibility of fraud relates primarily to intentional misrepresentations in or omissions from financial statements. These misrepresentations are undertaken by management to mislead users, but at the same time necessitate actions to mislead the auditor. The auditor is also concerned with misappropriations or misuse of assets and other irregularities that constitute fraud.

Fraud at the management level includes intentional misrepresentations that may lead to improper selection of accounting principles or inclusion of false amounts in, or the omission of amounts from, financial statements. It is usually accompanied by acts of concealment, such as omission of entries,

---

[4]For example, see the discussion of an Australian court's decision on the auditor's responsibilities with regard to fraud in W. J. Kenley, "Legal Decisions Affecting Auditors: Comments on the Pacific Acceptance Corporation Case." *The Australian Accountant* 41 (May 1971): 153–61. Our staff analyses (described in appendix B) include cases in which auditors were held responsible for failure to detect material fraud. Also, the Commission's consideration of the legal environment of independent auditors demonstrates that such failures in audit performance subject the auditor to liability to an expanding group of users.

[5]A.M.C. Morison, "The Role of the Reporting Accountant Today—II," *Accountancy* (England) 82 (March 1971): 122.

manipulation of documents (including forgery), or collusion among individuals inside or outside the company. It may take several forms, including

Fictitious transactions—nonexistent transactions recorded to overstate revenue or assets. For example, the Equity Funding fraud involved recording fictitious loans receivable and issuing bogus insurance policies.

Transactions without substance—transactions arranged by management with related parties (with the relationship not adequately disclosed) so that substantial undisclosed risks are retained by the company. ASR No. 153 (1974), for example, describes several real estate transactions of U.S. Financial, Inc., alleged to have been fashioned by management to make it appear that income had been earned when in fact it had not.

Intentional misapplication of accounting methods to actual transactions to produce misleading results—income measurement methods, such as realization or the assignment of transactions to periods, misapplied to recognize revenue without evidence of realization, to misclassify assets, liabilities, revenue, or expenses, or to record transactions in the wrong period. For example, the practices alleged to have been followed by Stirling Homex (as described in ASR No. 173)[6] in recognizing sales of modular dwelling units illustrate alleged management misrepresentations to the auditor of the circumstances of transactions and the validity of relevant documents to support recognition of income.

Management fraud does not include matters that involve management's legitimate discretion in the selection and application of generally accepted accounting principles, including appropriate disclosure, when the independent auditor knows the relevant facts and concurs with management's judgment. However, the distinction between intentional misapplication of accounting principles and management's appropriate exercise of discretion is complex and may often be resolved only through litigation. As a result of litigation, errors in judgment or mistakes in applying accounting principles have sometimes been found to involve constructive fraud. If the independent auditor knows the relevant facts, however, questions that might then arise concern his responsibility for judging the appropriateness of accounting principles, not his responsibility to detect fraud.

The Evolution of an Unclear Description of the Auditor's Concern with Fraud. The auditor's concern with detecting fraud was clearly expressed in

---

[6]SEC Accounting Series Release No. 173, "In the Matter of Peat, Marwick, Mitchell & Co.," July 2, 1975.

works such as Dicksee's *Auditing*, first published in the nineteenth century, when the threefold object of an audit was said to be the detection of fraud, the detection of technical errors, and the detection of errors of principle.[7]

The straightforward recognition, in early literature, of the detection of fraud as an object of an audit has been steadily eroded. This erosion is evident in the descriptions of audit objectives in successive editions of Montgomery's *Auditing*[8] and in professional standards. In the first three editions (1912, 1916, and 1923), Montgomery acknowledged that in the formative days of auditing "students were taught" that "the detection or prevention of fraud" and "the detection or prevention of errors" were the "chief objects" of an audit. He went on to explain that the former "chief objects" must be relegated to a subordinate position because those who retain auditors "have enlarged their demands and now require a vastly broader and more important class of work." Subsequent editions gave less and less emphasis to the detection of fraud until, in the eighth edition (1957), it was described as a "responsibility not assumed," with the observation that, "The American Institute has properly pointed out that if an auditor were to attempt to discover defalcations and similar irregularities he would have to extend his work to a point where its cost would be prohibitive."

In Montgomery, this disavowal of responsibility clearly relates to the detection of "defalcations and similar irregularities" (misappropriation or misuse of assets with no material effect on financial statements); Montgomery's position on the detection of management fraud is not clear.

From the beginning, auditing pronouncements have tended to emphasize the limitations on the auditor's ability to detect fraud rather than the positive aspects. *Verification of Financial Statements*, a booklet on auditing procedures prepared by the American Institute of [Certified Public] Accountants and published in 1929 under the auspices of the Federal Reserve Board, stated that the recommended procedures "will not necessarily disclose defalcations nor every understatement of assets concealed in the records of operating transactions or by manipulation of the accounts."[9]

In 1933, a letter from the New York Stock Exchange's Committee on Stock List to its Governing Committee recognized and accepted the limitation in *Verification of Financial Statements*.

[7]Lawrence R. Dicksee, *Auditing: A Practical Manual for Auditors*, 3d ed., rev. and enl. (London: Gee & Co., 1898), p. 8.

[8]Robert H. Montgomery, *Auditing, Theory and Practice* (New York: The Ronald Press, 1912, 1916, 1923, and 1957). Obviously, many other sources could have been used to document the erosion. However, the several editions of this book comprised the most significant series of auditing texts in the United States for many years. They provide a continuous source, widely regarded by accountants as highly authoritative, particularly in the period before official bodies issued formal pronouncements.

[9]Federal Reserve Board, *Verification of Financial Statements*, 1929, also published in the *Journal of Accountancy* (May 1929): 321–54.

Your committee is satisfied that the detailed scrutiny and verification of the cash transactions of large companies can most efficiently and economically be performed by permanent employees of the corporation . . . and that it would involve unwarranted expense to transfer such work to independent auditors or to require them to duplicate the work of the internal organization. Your committee, however, feels that the auditors should assume a definite responsibility for satisfying themselves that the system of internal check provides adequate safeguards and should protect the company against any defalcation of major importance.

The letter goes on to discuss other responsibilities that the auditor should assume.

. . . The auditor should recognize a responsibility to verify and, if necessary, to report to the shareholders upon any transactions affecting directors or officers of the corporation in respect of which there might be a conflict of interest between such directors and officers and the general body of shareholders.[10]

Thus, the independent auditor was expected to be concerned with management's accountability for corporate assets and to guard against the possibility of material misrepresentations in financial statements caused by fraud. Auditors were not expected to be concerned with the possibility of immaterial frauds that would not significantly distort financial statements or that would not result in a major loss of assets.

Subsequent pronouncements, however, placed primary emphasis on the lack of concern for immaterial frauds, such as defalcations. These pronouncements contributed significantly to an evolving attitude among auditors of minimal concern for detection of fraud. The position of the American Institute of [Certified Public] Accountants in Statement on Auditing Procedure No. 1, *Extensions of Auditing Procedure,* issued in 1939, emphasized "defalcations and other similar irregularities" and stressed the limitations on the auditor. The position slightly modified was carried forward in a codification of auditing pronouncements issued in 1951.

The ordinary examination incident to the issuance of an opinion respecting financial statements is not designed *and cannot be relied upon* to disclose defalcations and other similar irregularities, although their discovery frequently results. In a well-organized concern reliance for the detection of such irregularities is placed principally upon the maintenance of an adequate system of accounting records with appropriate internal control. If an auditor were to attempt to discover defalcations and similar irregularities he would have to extend his work to a point where its cost would be prohibitive. It is generally recognized that good internal control and surety bonds provide

[10]*Audits of Corporate Accounts* (New York: American Institute of [Certified Public] Accountants 1934; reprint ed., 1963), p. 19.

protection much more cheaply. On the basis of his examination by tests and checks, made in the light of his review and tests of the system of internal control, the auditor relies upon the integrity of the client's organization unless circumstances are such as to arouse his suspicion, in which case he must extend his procedures to determine whether or not such suspicions are justified.[11]

This position seemed to many readers to disavow all but an incidental concern for fraud detection, even though the disavowal pertained to "defalcations and other similar irregularities." It remained in the official literature for over twenty years and played an important part in shaping the attitude of auditors. By 1960, however, the negative and defensive tone of the official position on fraud detection was no longer acceptable to the profession, and it was amended to read in part as follows:

> In making the ordinary examination, the independent auditor is aware of the possibility that fraud may exist. Financial statements may be misstated as the result of defalcations and similar irregularities, or deliberate misrepresentation by management, or both. The auditor recognizes that fraud, if sufficiently material, may affect his opinion on the financial statements, and his examination, made in accordance with generally accepted auditing standards, gives consideration to this possibility. However, the ordinary examination directed to the expression of an opinion on financial statements is not primarily or specifically designed, and cannot be relied upon, to disclose defalcations and other similar irregularities, although their discovery may result. Similarly, although the discovery of deliberate misrepresentation by management is usually more closely associated with the objective of the ordinary examination, such examination cannot be relied upon to assure its discovery. The responsibility of the independent auditor for failure to detect fraud (which responsibility differs as to clients and others) arises only when such failure clearly results from failure to comply with generally accepted auditing standards.[12]

Many in the profession felt this position put the auditor's concern for the detection of fraud, particularly management fraud, in proper perspective. It was not limited to "defalcations and other similar irregularities." A greater concern for management fraud was acknowledged, but the nature and extent of concern were still unclear to some and were hedged by negative language.

Increased Attention in Present Standards for the Detection of Management Fraud. The American Institute of Certified Public Accountants has

---

[11]*Codification of Statements on Auditing Procedure* (New York: American Institute of [Certified Public] Accountants, 1951), pp. 12–13.

[12]Statement on Auditing Standards No. 1 (November 1972), section 110.05. Originally issued as Statement on Auditing Procedure No. 30 in September 1960, this material was superseded by Statement on Auditing Standards No. 16 in January 1977 (AICPA, *Professional Standards,* vol. 1, AU section 327).

recently taken positive actions to clarify and strengthen auditing standards related to the detection of fraud. For example, Statement on Auditing Standards No. 6 on related party transactions, issued in July 1975, requires the auditor to search for transactions with related parties and to probe the details of material transactions to determine whether management is involved. Statement on Auditing Standards No. 16, on the detection of errors and irregularities, issued in January, 1977, clarifies existing guidance for directing an auditor's attention to possible management fraud.

The Auditing Standards Executive Committee and the Commission studied the issue of the auditor's responsibility for fraud detection at approximately the same time and had access to much of the same background information. However, the two positions were developed independently, and the Commission agreed on its conclusions before Statement on Auditing Standards No. 16 was issued. Although the positions are not significantly different, we believe our report presents a more positive description of and rationale for the auditor's responsibility.

A Suggested Explanation of the Auditor's Responsibility for the Detection of Fraud

The essential basis for an explicit statement on the independent auditor's responsibility for the detection of fraud is that users of financial statements should have the right to assume that audited financial information is not unreliable because of fraud and that management maintains appropriate controls to safeguard assets.[13] An audit should be designed to provide reasonable assurance that the financial statements are not affected by material fraud and also to provide reasonable assurance on the accountability of management for material amounts of corporate assets.[14]

In an audit of financial statements, an independent auditor is concerned with the adequacy of controls and other measures designed to prevent fraud, has a duty to search for fraud, and should be expected to detect those frauds that the exercise of professional skill and care would normally uncover.

This description of the auditor's responsibility includes the responsibility to see that the financial statements report and explain adequately the nature and effects of material frauds discovered. It is a general description of responsibility, however, and, standing alone, it does not provide adequate guidance

[13]Other aspects of the auditor's concern with management's accountability for corporate assets are considered in section 5.

[14]All references to fraud in the Commission's explanation of the auditor's responsibility should be understood to apply only to material fraud. However, in connection with subsequent discussions in this section on the review of internal controls bearing on fraud prevention, materiality should be considered in relation to the possible aggregate effect of fraud that might result because of an internal control weakness.

for independent auditors nor an adequate standard by which their performance may be judged by others. Explicit guidance on the appropriate exercise
of professional skill and care is necessary.

The concept of "due professional care" is part of generally accepted
auditing standards.[15] That standard provides only a broad guide for judging
performance. Nevertheless, it can form the basis for an elaboration of the
elements of skill and care that should govern the performance of auditors.

In *The Philosophy of Auditing,* Mautz and Sharaf propose the development
of

> a concept of professional care which indicates in more or less specific terms
> the considerations which must govern the performance of an examination by
> an auditor. If his examination is conducted with the care required by this
> concept he will discover certain types of irregularities, should they be present.
> Thus he is neither excused from discovering any and all irregularities nor
> charged with an examination so extensive that it will uncover any and all
> irregularities. Practitioners are expected, under this concept, to make a
> reasonable search for irregularities, to provide their clients and business
> generally with an important service and some effective protection; they are
> not held for an examination unreasonably extensive or rigorous. At the same
> time, the concept gives some useful guidance as to the extent of the search
> they should make.
>
> Of course the statement of such a concept has implications for those
> outside the profession as well. To the extent that laymen understand the
> concept they have a satisfactory standard by which to establish their
> expectations and to measure the results of audit work. The general usefulness
> of such a concept should be apparent. Even more apparent should be the
> conclusion that formulation of such a concept is an appropriate, even an
> essential undertaking for a profession, to state fairly and clearly the
> responsibility which its members accept without equivocation or
> understatement.[16]

An auditor cannot be expected to detect all frauds. He cannot detect certain
types of fraud, such as collusion between management and other parties
whom he has no reason to suspect of duplicity. The need to provide audits
at a rational cost imposes limits. Society does not require perfect performance
of any professional. Thus, a standard of professional skill and care is needed
to evaluate the performance of auditors.[17]

[15]The third general standard is, "Due professional care is to be exercised in the performance
of the examination and the preparation of the report" (Statement on Auditing Standards No.
1, section 150.02 [AICPA, *Professional Standards,* vol. 1, AU section 150.02]).

[16]R.K. Mautz and Hussein A. Sharaf, *The Philosophy of Auditing* (Sarasota, Fla.: American
Accounting Association, 1961), p. 131.

[17]Statement on Auditing Standards No. 16, *The Independent Auditor's Responsibility for the
Detection of Errors and Irregularities* (January 1977) (AICPA, *Professional Standards,* vol. 1, AU
section 327), explains several factors that make the detection of some frauds impossible.

Recommendations on a Standard of Care for Fraud Detection

The recommendations in this section are intended to add to the substance of the standard of care for fraud detection and improve the effectiveness of independent auditors in performing this important aspect of the audit function. These recommendations, offered as an illustrative, rather than an exhaustive, explanation of the changes in professional standards, auditing practice, and support activities of the AICPA, will be helpful in achieving these ends.

Many of the recommendations are not original. Some public accounting firms already apply a number of the recommended practices. Several of the subjects of the recommendations have been placed on the agenda of the AICPA's Auditing Standards Executive Committee. But while many of these recommendations may not be new, the emphasis on directing the auditor's attention to an active and affirmative responsibility for the detection of material fraud is a significant departure from the prevailing attitude of many independent auditors.

Establish an Effective Client Investigation Program. The relationship between an independent auditor and his clients makes it essential that the auditor exercise care in deciding to accept new clients and to retain clients. A systematic approach to investigating a prospective client before accepting a new engagement and a periodic review of continuing engagements are essential tools of independent auditors. The reputation and integrity of a company and its management are critical factors in determining whether a company is auditable. An auditor is under no obligation to accept or retain a client about whose integrity he has reservations; indeed, such clients should be rejected.

Take Immediate Steps if Serious Doubts Arise about Management's Integrity. The exercise of professional skill and care requires healthy skepticism—a disposition to question and test the validity of all material management representations. The independent auditor should approach an examination with an open mind about the integrity and good faith of management. He should neither assume that management is dishonest nor take management's integrity and good faith for granted. The auditor's tests of the validity of transactions and resulting financial statement amounts or other evidence may cause him to question management's honesty or good faith.

The Commission's review of significant cases involving auditors and of other evidence makes it amply clear that when management is untrustworthy, there is a significant chance that a valid independent audit cannot be performed.[18] A dishonest management group that is determined and innovative has the ability, under the right circumstances, to perpetrate fraud and avoid detection by an auditor for a significant period of time.

Thus, if at any point serious doubts arise concerning the honesty, integrity, or good faith of management, the auditor should take all reasonable actions to resolve the doubts to his satisfaction. If the auditor is unable to satisfactorily resolve his doubts, he should consider resignation or other appropriate responses.

Observe Conditions Suggesting Predisposition to Management Frauds. In planning and conducting his examination, the auditor should take into account unusual circumstances or relationships that may predispose management to commit frauds. While it is impossible to catalog such conditions completely, some of the more obvious situations can be identified. For example, the auditor might find that a company is operating under economic conditions that motivate management to misrepresent earning power or solvency. He may find, among other things, that the industry is declining or experiencing a large number of business failures, the company lacks sufficient working capital or credit to continue operations, or is expanding at a rapid rate through new business or product lines, that the industry is overbuilt or its market is otherwise saturated, the company urgently needs a favorable earnings record to support the price of its stock, or is subject to restrictive covenants in bank or indenture agreements, or depends on a single or relatively few products, customers, or transactions for continued success.[19] Similarly, though it is not a predisposition to fraud, the lack of an effective internal audit function when the size or economics of the business would normally dictate one should suggest to the auditor the increased possibility that fraud will fail to be detected.

The auditor should be alert for these and similar conditions. On observing them, he should give due consideration in the audit to their existence—including a judgment as to the necessity for extending his audit procedures, or other appropriate measures.

Maintain an Understanding of a Client's Business and Industry. Independent auditors recognize that an understanding of a client's business and the industry of which it is a part is critical to a proper audit. The required knowledge encompasses economic conditions, inherent internal control problems, and peculiarities of the industry. Although virtually all auditors would agree that having knowledge of a company and its industry is a

[18]The Commission's research is described in appendix B.
[19]SAS No. 16 on errors and irregularities identifies similar and other conditions that may increase the auditor's concern about the existence of fraud.

necessary condition for a proper audit, that responsibility is not explicitly recognized in professional standards. Current professional standards provide the auditor little guidance on how to fulfill that responsibility. Consequently, the standard of professional skill and care should be sharpened to require specifically that the auditor have an understanding of the nature of the business of the company under examination, its methods of operations, and significant practices and regulatory requirements peculiar to the company or the industry of which it is a part. The Commission's research indicated that lack of knowledge of a client's business or industry was often a problem.[20]

Awareness of specific financial and business-related risks of an entity is essential to the application of informed judgment necessary for a proper audit. Thus, independent auditors should make every effort to acquire all readily available knowledge that might lead to perception of substantial financial or business-related risks deliberately or unwittingly accepted by the company under examination.

Extend the Study and Evaluation of Internal Control.   The study and evaluation of internal control is an important aspect of an audit.[21] However, under present generally accepted auditing standards, it is performed solely to determine the extent of other procedures that the auditor must perform. The standard of professional skill and care should be amplified to require a study and evaluation of controls that have a significant bearing on the prevention and detection of fraud.[22] The auditor should report material weaknesses to the proper level of management, including, if appropriate, the audit committee or the full board, and should follow up to determine whether the weaknesses have been eliminated.[23] It should be noted, however, that internal controls may not be effective in preventing or detecting many types of management fraud. As noted in Statement on Auditing Standards No. 1, section 320.34, "Procedures designed to assure the execution and recording of transactions in accordance with management's authorizations may be ineffective against either errors or irregularities perpetrated by management with respect to transactions or to the estimates and judgments required in the

[20]The Commission's research is described in appendix B.

[21]The second standard óf field work included in the ten generally accepted auditing standards states, "There is to be a proper study and evaluation of the existing internal control as a basis for reliance thereon and for the determination of the resultant extent of the tests to which auditing procedures are to be restricted" (Statement on Auditing Standards No. 1, section 320.01 [AICPA, *Professional Standards,* vol. 1, AU section 320.01]).

[22]Under present standards, the auditor's study and evaluation may exclude controls that are not relied on in determining the nature, timing, or extent of other audit procedures.

[23]The question of the auditor's responsibility for public reporting on internal control is explored in section 6. Statement on Auditing Standards No. 20, *Required Communication of Material Weaknesses in Internal Accounting Control* (August 1977) (AICPA, *Professional Standards,* vol. 1, AU section 323), which was issued after the Commission's *Report of Tentative Conclusions,* now requires such reporting to management or the board of directors.

preparation of financial statements." As discussed in section 6, the existence of such weaknesses in internal control need not preclude the auditor from expressing an opinion on the financial statements, so long as it is possible to make appropriate extension of audit tests.

Develop and Disseminate Information on Frauds and Methods of Detecting Fraud. A prudent auditor will seek knowledge of methods of perpetrating, concealing, and detecting fraud. Conditions indicating fraud and the methods of perpetrating fraud are not always obvious and change as the business environment changes. Auditors should recognize those changing conditions and be knowledgeable about the latest methods of perpetration and detection.

Methods and procedures should be adopted for public accounting firms to exchange information on developments in the perpetration and detection of fraud. The AICPA should establish means for regular dissemination of that type of information. For example, the initiative shown by the AICPA in studying and reporting on the Equity Funding case should become the norm rather than the exception.[24]

Be Aware of Possible Deficiencies in Individual Audit Techniques and Steps. The Commission's review of significant cases involving auditors disclosed several instances in which certain traditional audit steps did not produce the assurances they were intended to provide. For example, direct confirmation with parties outside the company is an important method of substantiation of both financial statement amounts and other management representations. However, in several cases, outsiders either ignored incorrect information that was clearly shown in confirmations or actively cooperated with management in giving incorrect confirmation. Constant attention should be given by both auditors and the AICPA to the effectiveness of conventional auditing techniques and to the development of new ones.

Understand the Limitations of Incomplete Audits.   Auditors frequently undertake special, limited engagements at the request of clients. Such engagements are desirable. Auditors should have the ability to offer services tailored to the needs of clients. While an audit does contain a variety of interrelated steps and tests, which *will* often disclose frauds, limited engagements, directed only toward specific steps or evidence, provide far less assurance of fraud detection.[25]

---

[24]The nature of the effort that should be undertaken in studying and reporting on suspected cases of audit failure is discussed further in section 11.

[25]For example, the auditor of one reinsurance customer of Equity Funding was requested only to examine support for a limited number of policies. Testimony indicated that the client intended this special examination (at least in part) to detect fraudulent policies. Needless to say,

Both auditors and clients should be fully aware of the limitations of the engagement. Auditors, in particular, should beware of undertaking special engagements that contain an element of fraud detection, without assuring full understanding, by themselves and their clients, of the inherent limitations of such engagements.

---

the limited examination did not detect the fraud, nor, in the absence of a host of other tests of related records and documents which were not requested (or permitted), could it have.

Corporate Accountability and the Law*

Recent publicity and activities of governmental bodies, particularly the Securities and Exchange Commission, concerning illegal or questionable corporate acts—such as bribes, political payoffs, and kickbacks—have focused attention once again on aspects of the accountability of management for corporate assets and the auditor's traditional concern with management's stewardship.[1]

Suggestions have been made by several congressional committees, the SEC, and others, that independent auditors should assume more responsibility for detection and disclosure of illegal or questionable acts by management. This section of the report of the Commission considers the implications of these suggestions and recommends actions that should be taken by various parties, including independent auditors.

Current attention has been devoted to certain types of illegal or questionable acts—primarily covert payments—but the auditor's responsibility for the detection and disclosure of the entire range of illegal acts that might be committed by clients needs to be explored. In addition, the present under-

---

[1]The auditor's traditional concern with misappropriation or misuse of corporate assets and related aspects of management's accountability are discussed in section 4.

*Copyright © 1978 by the American Institute of Certified Public Accountants. Reprint of chapter 5 from *Report, Conclusions, and Recommendations* by the Commission on Auditors' Responsibilities.

standing by users of auditors' responsibilities for disclosure of litigation and claims is unclear.[2]

This section of the report suggests a framework within which the auditor, commensurate with his abilities, can respond to increasing calls for his assistance in improving corporate accountability. At the same time, it suggests increased responsibilities for lawyers in matters that are primarily legal in nature.

An Evolving Public Concern

Society has always been concerned with illegal and questionable acts involving business, although as Beard noted, "Few really horrid crimes, without rational motive, may be imputed to businessmen. Seldom have they put out the eyes of competitors with hot irons or burned rival salesmen at the stake."[3]

Laws governing the conduct of business were developed in each society virtually as soon as business activities began.[4] In the United States, there have been several periods when particular attention was given to the conduct of businessmen and legislation was adopted to define and provide punishment for improper business activities.

Agitation by farmers and owners of smaller businesses in the last quarter of the nineteenth century produced the Interstate Commerce Act (1887) and the Sherman Antitrust Act (1890). After the turn of the twentieth century, the writings of "muckrakers" such as Ida Tarbell and Professor William Ripley inflamed public sentiment and combined with the activism of Presidents Theodore Roosevelt and William Taft to bring antitrust activity to a peak.[5] The Clayton Act (1914) was enacted and the Federal Trade Commission was established during the Wilson administration. Nevertheless, the combination of less activism under Wilson and restrictive court decisions ended the progressive movement's campaign against business.

It was not until the administration of Franklin Roosevelt, spurred by public sentiment that blamed business for the depression, that another period of development of legislation and regulation of business started. In 1973, the Watergate scandal provided revelations of another form of questionable

---

[2]The auditor's role in reporting on uncertainties is discussed in section 3.

[3]Miriam Beard, *A History of the Businessman* (New York: The Macmillan Co., 1938), p. 3.

[4]The first law defining an illegal business act may be the biblical prohibition, "Ye shall do no unrighteousness . . . in measures of length, or weight, or of quality" (Leviticus 19:35–36). The first accusation of a financially oriented illegal or questionable business act may well have occurred when the prophet Amos denounced the corrupt court of Israel for "making the ephah small, and the shekel great, and dealing falsely with balances. . . ." (Amos 8:5–6).

[5]For discussions of these periods, see Richard Hofstadter, *The Age of Reform* (New York: Knopf, 1956); and William Z. Ripley, ed., *Trusts, Pools and Corporations,* rev. ed. (Boston: Ginn and Co., 1916).

corporate conduct: payments made to the Committee to Reelect the President that were illegal under U.S. law.

Investigations and further disclosures stimulated by these initial revelations covered a wider spectrum of conduct. Attention shifted from domestic political payments to foreign political payments, then to other payments made in foreign countries and, more recently, to bribes paid within the United States to obtain business.[6] Although the specific types of conduct receiving attention will probably continue to change, it does not appear that the heightened concern with corporate accountability will diminish, nor should it.

Unclear Expectations of Society.   The expectations of users of financial information with respect to the auditor's detection and disclosure of illegal or questionable acts are unclear. However, a number of regulatory and legislative initiatives are under way that may provide some clarification of society's expectations.

Hearings have been held and reports have been issued by government bodies and agencies such as the Subcommittee on Multinational Corporations, chaired by Senator Frank Church, the Subcommittee on Oversight and Investigations, chaired by Congressman John Moss, and the President's Task Force on Questionable Corporate Payments. The SEC has made proposals that have been incorporated in some of the proposed legislation.[7] The SEC also encouraged corporations to make internal investigations to determine whether they had made illegal or questionable payments and, in some cases, brought suit against corporations to require disclosure. The SEC's efforts resulted in extensive publicity and revelations of illegal or questionable payments ranging from extremely small amounts to millions of dollars.

The current attention paid to illegal or questionable corporate payments emphasizes the widespread concern over corporate accountability. It seems clear that this concern will not remain confined to the actions that stimulated the initial interest. As noted earlier, the SEC has already indicated its interest in domestic commercial bribery and similar corrupt promotional activity.

Several interested groups have expressed the view that independent auditors should act in some way to improve corporate accountability in the areas of concern. Some have suggested that auditors should have a direct, active

[6]The first SEC proceeding involving domestic commercial practices was SEC v. Emersons Ltd. et al. (Civ. No. 75-0808 [D.D.C. May 11, 1976]), concerning promotional payments made by beer brewers and distributors to a restaurant chain (SEC Litigation Release No. 7392, May 11, 1976 [CCH Fed. Sec. L. Reptr., paragraph 95,544]).

[7]SEC Securities Exchange Act Release No. 34-13185, "Promotion of the Reliability of Financial Information, Prevention of the Concealment of Questionable or Illegal Corporate Payments and Practices and Disclosure of the Involvement of Management in Specified Types of Transactions," January 19, 1977. Proposals related to illegal payments are also included in S. 305, *Foreign Corrupt Practices Act of 1977.*

role in *enforcing* corporate accountability. For example, members of the staff of the SEC have asserted in speeches and articles that independent auditors should report illegal or questionable client conduct directly to the SEC.

The expectations of users, regulators, and legislators as to the appropriate responsibilities of the independent auditor are clouded by the lack of a clear definition of prohibited corporate conduct. Some illegal acts, such as tax evasion, have been well defined and are easily recognized by experienced auditors. Other illegal corporate acts, such as price fixing and price discrimination, are less clearly defined and less susceptible to detection in an audit. Also important, particularly for clarifying the auditor's responsibility, many of the illegal or questionable corporate acts are based on unspecified standards of business conduct. These standards are sometimes defined after the fact, and the notion of what is questionable appears to be in a process of continual evolution.

The recent revelations of corporate misconduct have generated significant reaction from many sectors of the United States political and economic system. Given the apparent widespread nature of such corporate acts, it is clear that a substantial gap exists between some corporate behavior and society's view of appropriate corporate conduct. The causes of this gap are too complex to permit us to recommend precise responsibilities for independent auditors in this area. Narrowing the gap will require action by the political system to define more clearly the responsibilities of all those involved, including corporate management, boards of directors, regulatory agencies, and auditors.

Confusion Over the Auditor's Responsibilities Concerning Illegal Acts by Clients. The auditor has traditionally acknowledged some responsibility for detecting misuse of corporate assets. However, the idea of misuse of corporate assets has been related to acts of fraud, such as misappropriation of assets by untrustworthy employees and managers, applied within the usual framework of quantitative measures of materiality.

The auditor's responsibility for detection and disclosure of illegal acts is less clear. By training and experience, auditors are knowledgeable about certain matters of business law. For example, auditors are familiar with the federal income tax laws and would be expected to recognize tax evasion by a client. Normal audit procedures will detect many types of tax evasion if material amounts are involved.

In specialized industries, violation of some laws might have a direct and material effect on amounts in financial statements. For example, lack of conformity with government contracting regulations could invalidate related receivables. Auditors normally consider such possibilities when planning and conducting their examinations.

Many auditors are familar with the financial reporting and related provisions of the securities acts and, to a lesser extent, with financially oriented laws such as the Robinson-Patman Act and the antitrust statutes. Detection of some violations of the securities laws, such as failure to make required disclosures in financial statements, are an integral part of the auditor's responsibilities. However, other securities laws violations, such as insider trading, often involve acts by management that bear no relation to the accounting records of the entity.

Auditors are neither trained nor necessarily able to detect violations of those laws or of the myriad other laws that govern corporate conduct, and they have not traditionally been considered responsible for detecting such violations. Of course, any act that has economic consequences for the entity will ultimately affect its financial statements. However, such acts cannot be detected in an audit until they result in transactions or events that are ordinarily recorded.

Auditing standards are often not specific on the precise action that an auditor should take if he detects corporate acts that might be illegal. However, inaction is not an acceptable alternative. For example, if an auditor finds a material misstatement of fact in another part of an annual report containing financial statements he has audited, SAS No. 8 advises that

> the action he takes will depend on his judgment in the particular
> circumstances. He should consider steps such as notifying his client in writing
> of his views concerning the information and consulting his legal counsel as to
> further appropriate action in the circumstances.[8]

If the auditor finds that financial statements of prior years reported on by a predecessor auditor may require revision, SAS No. 7 suggests that

> he should request his client to arrange a meeting among the three parties . . .
> and attempt to resolve the matter. If the client refuses or if the successor is
> not satisfied with the result, the successor auditor may be well advised to
> consult with his attorney in determining an appropriate course of further
> action.[9]

Recently, the Auditing Standards Executive Committee issued SAS No. 17 specifically on illegal acts by clients. If an illegal act has a material effect on the financial statements, the act must be disclosed. However, for any illegal act he detects, the auditor is advised that

> when an illegal act, including one that does not have a material effect on the
> financial statements, comes to the auditor's attention, he should consider the

[8]Statement on Auditing Standards No. 8, *Other Information in Documents Containing Audited Financial Statements* (December 1975), paragraph 6 (AICPA, *Professional Standards,* vol. 1, AU section 550.06).

[9]Statement on Auditing Standards No. 7, *Communications Between Predecessor and Successor Auditors* (October 1975), paragraph 10 (AICPA, *Professional Standards,* vol. 1, AU section 315.10).

nature of the act and management's consideration once the matter is brought to their attention. If the client's board of directors, its audit committee, or other appropriate levels within the organization do not give appropriate consideration . . . to the illegal act, the auditor should consider withdrawing from the current engagement or dissociating himself from any future relationship with the client.[10]

The SAS also states that

deciding whether there is a need to notify parties other than personnel within the client's organization of an illegal act is the responsibility of management. Generally, the auditor is under no obligation to notify those parties. . . .[11]

These Statements, particularly SAS No. 17, provide much needed guidance in this very complex area. However, we suggest later in this section a framework for auditor participation in achieving corporate accountability that we believe is a more adequate response to the strong forces suggesting greater auditor action. The approach we suggest for auditor involvement is an extension of responsibilities specified in SAS No. 17.

Limitations on the Auditor's Ability to Deal with Legal Matters

Several fundamental considerations suggest limits on the extent of the auditor's responsibility for detection and disclosure of the illegal acts of clients. Auditors cannot reasonably be expected to assume responsibilities for detection or disclosure of a client's violations of law in general. Auditors are primarily accountants, trained and experienced in activities that are basically financial. They are not lawyers nor are they criminal investigators, and they do not possess the training or skills of either group.

Similarly, in matters involving litigation against the corporation, the abilities of auditors are limited. They can readily ascertain the existence of litigation when provisions for losses are recorded in the accounts, when litigation is mentioned in documents such as the minutes of directors' meetings, or when they know of events that are likely to give rise to future claims. However, the auditor is not trained to recognize all the complex circumstances and processes that give rise to litigation and that suggest its outcome.

Society has developed an elaborate enforcement system to help assure compliance with its laws, including regulatory agencies, police, lawyers, courts, and prisons. Independent auditors—by tradition, training, and experience—have played a minor role in this system. Nevertheless, with the current increased concern with "white collar crime," some parties view

[10]Statement on Auditing Standards No. 17, *Illegal Acts by Clients* (January 1977), paragraph 18 (AICPA, *Professional Standards,* vol. 1, AU section 328.18).
[11]Statement on Auditing Standards No. 17, paragraph 19.

independent auditors as public agents to be used to improve the functioning of the enforcement system as it relates to the conduct of business.

The public accounting profession must be responsive to society's needs for evolution of the scope of the services it provides. Section 6 of this report discusses a framework for such an evolution. However, the Commission believes that it would be inefficient and impractical for auditors to undertake responsibilities that would require the knowledge, skills, and experience of members of another profession, namely, law. Thus, the resolution of the issue should be within the framework of the conventional skills attributed to accountants and auditors.

Expanding the Role of Lawyers.   Society appears to want greater assurance on the compliance of corporations with laws and regulations. Securities lawyers now furnish opinions on the conformity of offerings of securities with the securities acts. Although the scope of these opinions is quite narrow, the concept underlying them could have wider applicability. In addition, lawyers of a corporation, at management's request, furnish auditors with information on litigation and other contingencies for disclosure in financial statements.[12] This indirect arrangement is not the most efficient.

If society needs assurance on matters that are principally legal—the conformity of corporate actions with laws and regulations or information on the status of pending and future litigation—the assurance should be provided by those most capable of doing so—management assisted by its lawyers. Therefore, the Commission believes that a substantial portion of the work and responsibilities in these areas should fall on the corporate or outside legal counsel working in close cooperation with management and the independent auditor.

A Framework for Auditor Participation to Help Achieve Corporate Legal Accountability

The auditor must be able to approach the detection and disclosure of illegal or questionable acts by management within a defined and agreed framework.

Specifying Illegal or Questionable Acts.   The required starting point is a clear specification of illegal or questionable acts. Several sources are available, and others will soon become available. In reporting on its voluntary disclosure program to numerous congressional committees, the SEC ex-

[12]The present arrangement is explained in Statement on Auditing Standards No. 12, *Inquiry of a Client's Lawyer Concerning Litigation, Claims, and Assessments* (January 1976) (AICPA, *Professional Standards,* vol. 1, AC section 337).

plained the types of acts that it believes must be disclosed. Many corporations have adopted statements of policy for employee and management conduct. Various legislative and regulatory proposals would make specified acts illegal or define acts that must be disclosed. Several of these proposals contain provisions concerning maintaining accurate books and records and an adequate system of internal control. They also prohibit falsifying accounting records and making false statements to auditors.

Necessary Corporate Actions. Since the demands of society are for corporate accountability, the first responsibility should fall on corporations. As a precondition to any significant auditor involvement, corporations should be required to take several steps. They must be required to adopt, as many corporations have already done, statements of policy or codes of conduct indicating in detail conduct that will not be tolerated. Such statements or codes should not be drafted in general terms, but rather with particular reference to the operations of the enterprise and the types of situations employees might be expected to encounter.

The code should be made readily available to shareholders and others.[13] The Commission believes that this public exposure of corporate codes will provide an important element of accountability, particularly in areas which might be termed "questionable," rather than illegal. The existence of clear, detailed codes that have shareholder concurrence should provide the auditor with much needed guidance in the often ambiguous areas of improper conduct.

If auditors are to be involved in this area, corporations must also adopt policies and procedures to provide for effective monitoring of compliance, and they should distribute the statement to the appropriate levels of employees. There should be an understanding and identification of the parts of the policy statement and the compliance procedures that can be audited.[14]

Almost all of the corporate activities so far disclosed would not be material by conventional accounting standards. Consequently, if the independent auditor is to become more involved in detecting or disclosing such activities, the corporate accounting system and the controls over it must be revised as necessary to provide a greater possibility of detection. For example, some of the changes that will be required include more extensive controls over the activities of top executives, greater accountability for cash funds and intercorporate transfers, and more extensive documentation for payments to consultants and agents.

[13]The means for incorporating disclosure of the corporate statement of policy in a report by management are explained further in section 7.

[14]Procedures adopted to monitor compliance with such policies and identification of which policies are susceptible to audit can be documented in a separate memorandum prepared and agreed to by management, the board of directors (or its audit committee), and the independent auditor.

If a corporation has an internal audit staff, and most large organizations do, the internal auditor should participate in the design and implementation of the programs for achieving and enforcing corporate policy statements in this area, or the company should specifically arrange for the independent auditor to undertake a separate engagement. Designing a program for enforcing corporate policy is not a part of the audit function.

Until a requirement for adoption of a statement of policy on improper conduct is implemented by an appropriate body, we encourage corporations to begin implementation of this proposal voluntarily, and to request the participation of their independent auditor.

Recommendations on the Independent Auditor's Responsibilities.
When a corporation has adopted a policy on corporate conduct and provided for monitoring compliance with it, the independent auditor can be expected to play a larger role in detecting and disclosing illegal or questionable acts. However, the auditor cannot logically be expected to assume any additional responsibility in this area unless management has adopted a statement of policy on appropriate conduct.

DETECTING ILLEGAL OR QUESTIONABLE ACTS.   As explained in section 4, any acts that management conceals are difficult for the auditor to detect. The auditor will not always be able to detect material fraud, and illegal or questionable payments present even greater problems. They are more difficult to detect because the amounts involved are typically small in relation to financial statement amounts. Outside parties involved are usually anxious to keep the payments concealed, so collusion is common.

It would not be equitable if the auditor's failure to detect an illegal act placed him in the same legal jeopardy as the person who perpetrated the act. In the course of an audit, however, the independent auditor should be expected to detect those illegal or questionable acts that the exercise of professional skill and care would normally uncover.

When a code of conduct has been adopted by the corporation, independent auditors should be willing to provide users with assurance on whether a company is taking effective action to control such conduct. The auditor should review the company's code of conduct and the procedures adopted to monitor compliance with it. The auditor should determine whether there are material weaknesses in the related monitoring procedures, and indicate his conclusion on these matters in his report as illustrated in section 7.

It is doubtful that auditors can detect, with any regularity, willfully concealed illegal or questionable acts involving relatively small amounts. Therefore, any expression of assurance implying that the auditor knows such acts have not occurred, or that none have come to his attention, would be of no real value. However, auditors must continue to be aware of the possibility that illegal acts may have occurred and should evaluate the evidence obtained in the audit which may suggest that such acts have in fact occurred. Auditors should be aware that illegal or questionable acts involving immaterial amounts may raise important questions of disclosure. Widely disseminated policies, improved controls, monitoring by internal auditors, and tests of these procedures by independent auditors will help to deter such conduct and improve the possibility of its detection.

THE AUDITOR'S RESPONSE TO DETECTED ILLEGAL OR QUESTIONABLE ACTS. The auditor's responsibility for detecting illegal or questionable acts must be distinguished from his responsibility for disclosing or taking other action when he has detected or otherwise discovered such acts. That is, problems related to finding illegal or questionable acts are quite different from those regarding the response once an act is detected.

In principle, at least, the problem of the illegal or questionable act that has already been ascertained appears more susceptible of solution. If an auditor has discovered an act that he believes is illegal or questionable, he can follow only one course: He must obtain consideration of that act at the appropriate level of authority within the entity.

This responsibility rests on the premise that conventional concepts of materiality, based principally on quantitative considerations, are inapplicable to known illegal or questionable acts. The auditor should not take it on himself to determine that some violations of the law or propriety are more or less serious than others.

Materiality in accounting is essentially an economic concept designed to reconcile the conflict between the almost limitless detail that confronts accountants and auditors with the needs of users for information in an understandable form. It has been difficult to develop precise guidance on determining materiality; indeed, a major project of the Financial Accounting Standards Board is an attempt to clarify this concept. Nevertheless, materiality is merely a convention designed to effect a workable reconciliation of conflicting economic demands. It is not a concept powerful enough to deal with issues of morality or legality, and it should not be invoked in such circumstances.

However, the inapplicability of the materiality concept to the auditor's decision as to whether to act does not imply that his actions should always be the same. The auditor must obtain consideration appropriate to the circumstances of every illegal or questionable act. This involves at least three factors.

The first concerns the auditor's usual response to discovered irregularities. He must determine the extent to which the item might affect the financial statements. In the conventional audit of financial statements, the auditor must determine whether a possible irregularity could cause a material misstatement. If it could, he must perform enough additional or alternative audit procedures to assure himself of the extent and consequences of the irregularity.

The second factor is a comparison of the act with the standard of corporate conduct against which the auditor is conducting his examination. As previously explained, boards of directors, or other appropriate authorities, must set forth detailed and explicit codes of conduct if the auditor is to have a constructive and useful role in the area of illegal or questionable acts. That statement must stipulate, in reasonable detail, the types and magnitudes of infractions on which the board of directors wishes to take action and those which may be disposed of by corrective action by management.

The ability of the auditor to compare a detected act with the standard established by the corporation or other authority once again raises difficulties related to the auditor's limited legal training and experience. The auditor will invariably be confronted with acts that do not appear to be clearly legal or illegal. These problems can be reduced, if not eliminated, by careful preparation of the corporate policy statement. Corporate lawyers and the auditor must work with management, internal auditors, and the board of directors to explore and stipulate appropriate conduct in as many situations as possible.

Even with a well-drawn policy statement, the auditor will be confronted with acts or items whose conformity with policy is unclear. A procedure for ready consultation, presumably with corporate counsel, should be developed to provide the auditor with additional and comprehensive assistance. Such a procedure should, and will, involve the corporate counsel directly in this aspect of the audit. The auditor should maintain an attitude of readiness to explore questionable items. That is, there should be a deliberate bias toward pursuing any suspicious acts.

Finally, the extent of public disclosure must be considered. Illegal or questionable acts that come to the auditor's attention should be brought to the attention of the appropriate person or persons, as specified in the policy statement. The policy statement may identify management, the board of directors, or a committee of the board to deal with particular matters.

When the auditor discovers a violation of the policy statement, he should obtain an appropriate response at the level of authority stipulated in the code. While individual codes may vary, in general, an appropriate response would involve action to stop an existing violation and provision to attempt to prevent its recurrence. If the auditor does not obtain what he believes to be appropriate disposition of a violation at the stipulated level of authority he should proceed to a higher level. If he cannot obtain an appropriate disposition at the highest level available in the corporation, namely the board of directors, then the auditor should require disclosure of the violation. Failing that, it should be disclosed in the auditor's report.

A PROPOSAL FOR REPORTING ON CORPORATE CODES OF CONDUCT. If the company has adopted a corporate code of conduct, the report by management in the annual report should include a statement that such a code exists and that procedures have been implemented to monitor compliance. The auditor's report should state that he has reviewed the company's code of conduct. It should also describe his review of the company's monitoring procedures and his conclusions on those aspects that can be audited. His report should also disclose any violation of the company's code found during the course of his audit if management and the board of directors failed to make an adequate response when he brought it to their attention. An example of the comments of management and the auditor is included in section 7. If a legislative or regulatory rule is adopted to require corporations to adopt and enforce codes of conduct, and if they fail to do so, that fact should be disclosed in the report by management discussed in section 7. If management does not disclose that fact, the independent auditor's report should include a comment that no policy had been adopted or that the company did not establish a means to enforce the policy.

A Proposal for Increased Involvement of Lawyers.   This section focuses primarily on illegal or questionable acts. However, the same considerations apply to the more general problem of legal claims against the corporation, particularly the limitations on the auditor's ability to deal with matters that are primarily legal.

Traditionally, the presentation of financial statements in conformity with generally accepted accounting principles has included a requirement that significant claims against the corporation or claims against its assets be disclosed. In the less litigious environment of past years, this requirement did not produce substantial problems. Disclosure of pending legal matters was often couched in vague and noncommittal terms to protect the corporation from apparent admissions of guilt or liability or to avoid stimulating additional litigation.

In recent years, a great deal more attention has been given to the need to disclose pending and foreseeable legal claims. The result of present auditing requirements is that the auditor, the client, and the lawyer become involved in an elaborate procedure for determining which legal claims need to be disclosed.

This procedure is explained in Statement on Auditing Standards No. 12 and a related release of the American Bar Association.[15] Under the current approach the auditor obtains assurance from management that it has consulted with counsel on its disclosure obligations under Statement of Financial Accounting Standards No. 5 and has made the disclosures the lawyer has advised are required. The auditor notifies legal counsel that management has given these assurances and relies on counsel's ethical duty to object and if

---

[15]*Statement of Policy Regarding Lawyers' Responses to Auditors' Requests for Information* (American Bar Association, (December 1975), in Statement on Auditing Standards No. 12 (AICPA, *Professional Standards,* vol. 1, AU section 337C)).

necessary to resign if management has materially misrepresented the situation.[16] In essence the procedure results in the auditor's obtaining information from corporate management and its counsel to which he adds little if any substantive assurance and which could be directly disclosed to users of financial information without injecting the auditor into the process.

The Commission does not believe that the present structure and division of responsibilities in this area are efficient or effective. As discussed throughout this section, the auditor has only limited ability to evaluate the quality and completeness of disclosure of legal matters; management and its legal advisors should provide whatever assurances are necessary for such matters.

The Commission believes that the information now provided by management, substantiated by the assurances given by counsel to the auditor, should be presented directly to users of financial information. The approach under SAS No. 12 involves written and implicit representations by management and counsel to the auditor. The only change required would be for these representations to be made directly to users when financial information is issued.

The new reporting format suggested by the Commission in section 7 of this report would accommodate this proposal. The report by management could include the statement that management believes that all material uncertainties have been appropriately accounted for or disclosed, and that it has consulted with legal counsel with respect to the need for, and the nature of, the accounting for or disclosure of legal matters. The auditor's responsibility would be to review the information and the representations of management and counsel to determine that the financial statements properly reflect the information provided.

This proposal would not significantly change the present degree of reliance now placed on lawyers for appropriate disclosure by their clients. However, it would correct some of the present misunderstanding of users about the appropriate source for information on legal matters.

However, the Commission's proposal would not satisfy demands for greater audit assurance on the compliance of corporations with laws and regulations. As noted above, we do not believe that such demands for greater assurance in legal matters can or should be satisfied by auditors. Such demands might be satisfied by attempting to increase the scope and extent of assurances provided by lawyers. Meeting these demands, however, in that fashion may require some fundamental changes in the way lawyers view their relationships to clients and their role in society.

[16]We are informed that both in-house and outside counsel are under the same ethical obligations to object in this situation. Therefore, we have made no distinction between in-house and outside counsel in this discussion.

Index

DATE DUE

DEC 1 2 1985			
OCT 1 3 1988			
MAR 0 3 1996			

DEMCO 38-297